GREEN...
AND BACK

A Hilarious Adventure in South East Asia

Francis Abel

Andrews UK Limited

Copyright © 2012 Francis Abel

The right of Francis Abel to be identified as author of this book has been asserted in accordance with section 77 and 78 of the Copyrights Designs and Patents Act 1988.

All rights reserved

No part of this publication may be reproduced, stored in a retrieval system, or transmitted in any form or by any means, without the prior permission in writing of the publisher, nor be otherwise circulated in any form of binding or cover other than that in which it is published and without a similar condition including this condition being imposed on the subsequent publisher.

First published worldwide by
Andrews UK Limited
The Hat Factory
Bute Street
Luton
LU1 2EY

www.andrewsuk.com

Contents

Chapter One	1
Chapter Two	21
Chapter Three	55
Chapter Four	69
Chapter Five	82
Chapter Six	109
Chapter Seven	138
Chapter Eight	157
Chapter Nine	180
Chapter Ten	199
Chapter Eleven	229
Chapter Twelve	245
Chapter Thirteen	294
Chapter Fourteen	318
Chapter Fifteen	341
Chapter Sixteen	364
Chapter Seventeen	401
Chapter Eighteen	429
Chapter Nineteen	444
Chapter Twenty	465
Chapter Twenty One	491

Dedicated to Sam

Foreword

This book is not intended to be a missive on how to cope and subsequently live and survive after a life threatening illness. It is simply a story of an event that happened in my life and a narrative of the following months and years to date.

Some people who have been unlucky enough to share the same traumatic illness, and there are thousands that have, might find some solace to share my experiences and if my witterings bring some hope to them I am thankful. But the intention of my writing is to describe the incredible journey I have undertaken both in health but also in travel.

The outcome of all this is not a medical journal of dos and don'ts, but more of a story of an adventure as things progressed in my life and subsequent events took their shape, unplanned and definitely off piste, as I wandered about aimlessly in South East Asia. As things tend to happen when no forethought has gone into anything, the results tend to be bizarre and very hilarious.

There are numerous good friends, family members and kind people that have helped me along my long journey, but unfortunately I could not possibly mention all of them in this book. I have not set out to write something purely for the reason of name dropping to make me popular within a select bunch of peers, so if I have omitted your name please forgive me and believe me when I say that I could not have achieved what I did without all your assistance. Albeit, you must have been a boring or inconsequential bastard for me to have left you out of my journal.

As I am finally sitting down putting these initial words to paper, the first thunderstorms of Monsoon Season are drowning out all the other noises outside; but I am glad for the cool air the rain is bringing through my window. After five years I have at last taken my chair at my desk and started to recollect.

In part I have my close friend Richie; for giving me not the inspiration to write, but the incentive to start and complete my memoirs. On my last visit to the UK, Richie and I were dining at The Gate of India restaurant in South Road, Liverpool. I decided to tell him of my plans to write this book to which he responded: "Rubbish, who the Hell wants to read *that*?! Do you think you are the only person who has had a stroke?"

I paused for a moment so that I would not pour my glass of Cobra over his head and waste a perfectly good pint. I started to reply to his outburst but thought the better of the idea, not wanting to start an argument. His non-constructive criticism, however, made me start to doubt the validity of spending so much time in front of a laptop when the sun was shining high in the sky.

But as the months passed and I returned to South East Asia, the urge to tell this story became compelling and felt necessary. As I have said it is not meant to represent a missive of how to cope after suffering a stroke - it is more a guide of what you can achieve if you are sheer bloody minded enough.

Over the past five years I have come to realise that the majesty of life is not guaranteed to any person. In fact I have learned how frail the most wonderful of all gifts is and that every day should be blessed. Because of this I have found it true that you must live your life to its full capacity and not to compromise. Most people live their entire lives compromising; whether it is compromising to live with their selected partner, compromising in their jobs or compromising even what to eat. It is living a lie and that lie cannot be undone at your end.

My sudden realisation of this has come about through accident, an accident that has forced me to subsequently look at every day and decide what is best for me. It is a luxury most do not have the opportunity to live; but it is a luxury that has cost me dearly in health, friends, family, job and country to achieve. Gaining true freedom is not an easy thing, as we are conditioned to think, breathe and live in a conformist manner to be accepted into civilised society.

I read somewhere that there is a book hidden inside all of us waiting to be unlocked and to burst forth like a suppressed spring. But I never knew if I would have the time, craft or even the inclination to burst my own forward. My story came about by accident and relating that story by writing about it has both been somewhat confessional but also therapeutic. Delving into the very darkest parts of my life and retelling it, warts and all, has been almost an exorcism for me and a way to cleanse the lingering demons of my soul.

Perhaps the art of good story telling is a structured plot with a start, middle and end. However, in a way my story follows the chronological order of things as my life progressed. In that respect it has its own structure, but the difficult part has been remembering events as they occurred and documenting them in a correct and descriptive manner. I have always had a tendency to digress and actually thought of it as one of my more endearing traits; although, it has been bloody boring at times for my friends. Ronnie Corbett can get a little grating after a while, especially if you are in a hurry for a more direct response.

This snapshot of almost five years of my life has taken nearly seven months to write as many parts of it were extremely difficult to commit to paper. At several points, I must admit that I thought seriously about throwing my PC over the balcony in despair. I thought better of my rash thoughts for two reasons; firstly, I would probably have hit some poor sod below, secondly, I need my PC for my Premiership Forecasting in Shenanigans Pub Jomtien.

The characters and stories are all real and it has been an incredible heartache having to leave out some of the more mundane day to day stuff, as in a way, that is what my life is all about now. However, suffice to say if I had not edited my narrative, you would have needed a fork lift truck to collect the book from the shop.

I don't think Pritchard's Bookstore would have the room to stock even one copy.

Is it possible to change your own fate? Or is your fate or karma dealt out to you at birth to be played as a pack of pre-ordained cards during the course of your life? I am someone who believes that you can alter bits of your own destiny, but whatever the supreme being or thing has got ultimately planned will come to fruition sooner or later.

By this, I mean you can aid and alter the tangible things that affect you: health, wealth, work, friends, etc. But, after a lifetime of dieting and exercise, who is immune from Cancer? A devoted life working passionately for a cause or job you believe in can end in minutes through a change in management. It is these things that you have no control of and I am convinced are mapped out in front of you the minute your head pops out of your birth mother.

Perhaps you can not affect such events when they happen to you, but you can definitely alter where. Your destiny in this respect is in your own hands - rather than sitting and waiting for the inevitable to happen to you, changes can be made. Not everybody wants or needs to make such drastic amputations to their karma, but at least one should consider it. Living life in a rut is a crime, but living life in a rut and complaining about it is a pure sin. The fact that one is satisfied living in such a manner and the only panacea is just to whinge about the situation belays the true nature of the person.

Do not be concerned that the book addresses such monumental contemplative debate. It definitely does not but offers a view of such amputation that actually happened, sparked off by an event that took me to question my own karma. In other words, I had help to bring me to begin to such introspection that many do not. If I'd had a choice of having my stroke or not to bring me to such deliberation, I definitely would have politely refused the illness offered. However, if such a catastrophic event does happen in your life my point is that an opportunity arises.

One thing is certain in life - that death will happen to us all at some time or other and that cannot be changed. I believe that the time of this event has already been decided, it is what we do before the inevitable happens that we can help control and affect. Fear of the unknown is the overriding decision maker in this respect and for some, decisions are easier to make than for others. Options for change do not have to be acted upon, but they should always be formed to question; otherwise, just sit back and be one of life's many complainers.

Chapter One

ARMAGEDDON

I woke well before the alarm went off as I usually did if I had something important with work that day. Today, it was a Middle Managers meeting of which I was to attend and it was happening in Telford. I looked at the clock and it was a few minutes past five in the morning. Christ, it was cold, too early for the heating to turn itself on. I hated winter at the best of times, but especially at 5 o'clock in the sodding morning. I took the initiative and threw back the warm protection of the duvet and stepped out of bed. The next thing I knew, I was lying prostrate on the floor, my right leg giving way under me and I thought to myself: what had I drunk last night? I consoled myself that it was just one bottle of wine whilst watching a film, so I was definitely not hung-over.

I tried to stand up, but my leg was weak and would not support me. Perhaps I had slept awkwardly and it was numb or something. So, I crawled to the landing and grasped the banister and slowly pulled myself up. I paused to collect myself and wild thoughts crossed my mind that there was something seriously wrong with me. I felt my chest and could feel no pain, so my heart was okay; I had definitely slept awkwardly and things would be fine in a few minutes.

I stumbled into the bathroom and turned on the shower which was inside the bath, my next main hurdle. My bath was one of the old type of Roll Top and very deep. It was an original, made of cast iron and could probably fit five people at a Blue Peter squeeze. I imagined the house was built around it because nobody could ever have carried the bugger up the stairs.

I sat on the edge and lowered myself in. Fuck! The metal was freezing cold on my bum, but I knelt down under the hot water and began to wash. Something else was drastically wrong; my right arm would not reach my head. But that made sense, I had been sleeping awkwardly on my whole right side, so when my leg got better, so would my arm.

The shower was a lot hit and miss, but it would suffice and with some effort I managed to extract myself from the tub and stood in front of the wash basin. I checked myself in the mirror. There was nothing wrong with my face or chest so I breathed a sigh of relief and started to brush my teeth. The toothbrush fell into the sink and I tried to pick it up again, but the fingers on my right hand would not hold on to it. Fuck! There was something wrong but what?

I grabbed a towel and with the aid of leaning against the landing wall I shuffled back into the bedroom. Should I go back to bed and phone in sick, I thought? Perhaps the best thing was to keep moving in case anything improved. Besides, I couldn't have afforded to miss the meeting, it was too important. I worked for a global electrical power manufacturer in a specialist division of Energy Management using new technologies. The company was built on traditional large scale power supply technologies: my stuff was like a dark art and treated suspiciously by old school employees. I had reached my position by company acquisition of my previous firm and was very much the new kid on the block within the team.

I had seven sales guys reporting in to me from all over the country and regularly had to go trawling all over the UK to do joint sales visits and wine and dine clients. Most of the time I hated taking customers out for entertainment: "smooching", we called it. I had nothing in common with these boring people and would have far preferred to go back to the hotel and sit in the bar after work to relax.

I began to dress and it was quite a performance. Eventually I had donned a suit, but I still could not fasten the top button on my shirt. I shrugged as it was something I could attend to later.

Tackling the stairs was a different proposition, but luckily the banister was on my left hand side so I could grip on to it as I sidled downwards, negotiating each step gingerly and with immense concentration.

My laptop bag was packed and ready by the door, so grabbing my car keys I stepped out into the freezing cold of a Liverpool winter morning. My hot breath drew steam as I exhaled and I shuffled to my BMW. I opened the door, threw my bag on the passenger seat and gently lowered myself into the vehicle. It was an automatic so I knew once I was on the move I could drive it with my left foot - it would be a bit weird but a good plan nevertheless.

Now I know the person reading this would probably be thinking "What the fuck is he up to? Phone an ambulance you daft bastard!" but in my mind whatever that was wrong with me would probably have been okay by the time I got to Telford. Anyway, I started the engine and slowly edged the car forward. This was going to be tricky, I thought, as I tried to steer out of my road with only my left hand on the steering wheel. I decided not to take the M6 as people would probably expect me to indicate or something technical like that. It would probably have been all too hectic for me anyway as the M6 at that time of the morning heading south to Birmingham was always a mess.

I headed down Derby Road making my way to the Mersey Tunnel, having set everything to automatic. The lights were on, wipers were set for rain and the sat-nav was all working. This was not as hard as I first thought and any worries about my health were soon forgotten by my total concentration behind the wheel. The only real problem that occurred was trying to throw my change into the basket at the tunnel. After about three attempts and a load of wayward coins on the floor of the booth and rolling around inside the car, the barrier eventually lifted and I headed onto the M53.

How was I going to be able to claim back the lost cash from expenses? £1.65 for miscellaneous bad dart throwing at the Mersey Tunnel? I did not think accounts would wear that one. Besides, I did not know what column that would go in on the form, so I reconciled myself to the fact that the £1.65 was now lost for good from my estate and some lucky booth operator had free butties for lunch that day.

I eventually arrived at the office and drove round to the rear car park so that nobody would see the performance of me getting out of the car. Ejecting myself from the vehicle was a far harder job than getting in as my right leg had to support me as I got out, but levering myself against the steering wheel and pushing the seat as far back as it possibly could go, I managed to swing both legs out and stand.

Yes, I had succeeded in parking where nobody could see my triple salsa with toe loop or whatever those gymnasts called it, but I was miles away from the entrance. Then my condition once again became my first priority. Whilst I was driving I was trying pretty hard to concentrate on not killing any wayward cyclist or postman, but in that moment I was very much conscious that my right leg was dragging behind me as I slowly shuffled forward.

Sweat began to drip down my shirt with the effort I was putting my body through even though there were still patches of frost on the ground. I reached reception and knew I looked rough. I picked up the pen with my left hand and scrawled something illegible in the register and proceeded down the corridor. It was still early so not many staff were yet in so I did not have to cope with speaking with anybody.

I walked in to the office and sat down heavily on a chair. Sylvia, our secretary, walked to the coffee machine then looked around to see if anybody wanted a drink. She saw me sitting hunched over and sweating and immediately came over.

"Are you OK? You look dreadful!" she exclaimed. I tried to speak for the first time that day but only incomprehensible babble came out. She rushed back to the machine, got some cold water and came back to me.

I sipped at the refreshing water and noticed Sylvia was studying me, particularly my movements. I sat back in the chair. Christ, I must have looked a mess... but if I did not get my act together soon, I knew I would end up sitting in Telford General Hospital or somewhere equally as fun!

"Can you move your arms?" she asked. Sure enough, I moved them to about waist height to satisfy her curiosity.

"What do you feel?"

Now, I knew this had to be good so slowly I began to speak and surprisingly it was coherent. "I feel a little sick, that is all," I replied.

She moved closer to me and was looking into my eyes. "Perhaps we should call a doctor," she said. Now, I knew I had better get the Hell out of there as quick as possible before anybody else came in to the office and started agreeing with her. If there was something seriously wrong with me and they took me to a hospital in Telford, how could I get any of my things? How could anybody come to see me?

Now at this point I must explain that I was forty seven, unattached and lived alone. Just a normal chap doing a nine to five job to pay his bills. I had little family left, my mother had progressive Alzheimer's and was being treated in a care home in Oxford near my older brother, and my dad and middle brother had both died unexpectedly when I was fairly young. My wide group of friends had been my family for years and mostly they all lived in Liverpool, so how could any of them get to sodding Telford to see me? It would be bad enough being incarcerated in hospital in the first place, but Telford! Not exactly Paris, is it...

I slowly stood and gingerly shuffled towards the door clutching my bag firmly in my left hand. "Where are you going?" a startled Sylvia called after me.

"Please tell Colin I feel a little ill and am going home," I surprisingly clearly and softly replied.

"I don't think you should be driving," she called after me as I made my arthritic pensioner's getaway down the passage.

I made my way back to the car and decided to collect my thoughts at the services just before the M54, but I knew I had to get the Hell away from the office as soon as possible. I pulled into the Welcome Break and turned the engine off and began to take my situation in. So, if it was not a heart attack then what was it? What were the questions Sylvia had been asking me? Why did she want to know if I could move my arms or smile? An ugly thought crossed my mind... a stroke. This was 2007, before the Government's FACT campaign had really taken effect across the country. I had heard something about the illness but thought it was only for old people.

I looked into the mirror and could not see anything wrong with my face. I thought people who had a stroke had dropped faces on one side like Jack Palance. I definitely did not look like the famous Western baddie, so I consoled myself that whatever it was, it was not a stroke. I decided to get home as soon as possible and then have another think. It was now half past nine, rush hour was nearly over so the M6 would be my best bet to get back. Coming along the A roads had proved too difficult, negotiating roundabouts and traffic lights. At least on the motorway, I could sit on the inside lane and just drive straight.

It was far harder than I had imagined: the speed of traffic around me was making my vision blurred and lorries were making it perfectly obvious to me that a BMW 3 Series did not belong on the inside lane of the M6 doing 30mph. My phone started to ring so I took my hand off the steering wheel for a second and pressed the hands-free control.

"Francis, it is Colin." My boss' thick Scottish accent blasted out of the speakers. "Sylvia has told me about you, where are you?"

I sheepishly muttered, "On the M6." I always answered my boss fairly sheepishly because normally I had cocked up something and was in for a right royal Edinburgh bollocking.

"Now listen, I want you to go on the hard shoulder and phone 999," he ordered. Instead, I switched the phone off and continued my journey. I was definitely in for an extra special bollocking when I turned the bloody thing back on again, but what else could I have done?

My mind started to drift as I progressed slowly down the motorway. What would the other motorists have done if they knew they had a black bomb of a BMW travelling in their midst with an incapable pilot behind the wheel? It reminded me of that old Billy Connolly joke about the partially sighted bloke whose work mates persuaded him that it was no longer necessary to wear glasses or contact lenses whilst driving: you could request for one of those new prescription windshields. The next time he drove, all that the motorist in front of him would see in his rear view mirror was that the car behind him was been driven by a guy with a humungous head.

I wondered if people around me looking into the car saw Jack Palance? Suddenly, red rear brake lights in front of me bought me back to Thursday and the M6 and out of my daydreams. It took over two and a half hours for me to finish my journey and get home. I slowly went up the stairs, step by tortuous step, and stripped in the spare bedroom, laying my clothes out as neatly as possible on the bed as they could be worn again tomorrow.

Limping back into the main bedroom, I got beneath the duvet and laid down, absolutely exhausted. Even though I was shattered, sleep would not come as my mind was racing about my situation and what I should do. I tried to move my arm and leg, and they responded so things were not getting any worse. I could leave any decision for another few hours and check again later. With that comforting thought I drifted off into a heavy sleep.

The orange glow of the street lights awoke me as I had not closed the curtains and I saw it was nearly 8pm. I took stock of my situation and with some difficulty moved my limbs under the duvet. So, the nightmare continued and had not simply gone away as I had hoped. Females reading this book will no doubt be amazed about my stupidity, but I was doing what men always do when it comes to their health: forget about it and it will go away. Females are far more pragmatic; if they feel a lump or something, in a few minutes they are on the phone to a doctor, but men?

I hauled myself out of the bed and lurched into the bathroom. I took a long look in the mirror and studied my face. There was no Wild West Cowboy staring back at me and it was definitely my chubby grid in the reflection. My face had not dropped so I took some consolation in that. I decided to have a good wash and go back to bed to try and get more sleep - after all, sleep was supposed to cure most things. I could not face negotiating the bath again so I simply bent over the side and hosed myself down as best I could.

That night was horrendous and not much more sleep came to comfort me. Had I had a stroke? If so, why did I not look like Jack Palance and why wasn't it getting any worse? I thought of phoning one of my mates, but decided against it as my voice might give the game away. The best thing would be to see how I was in the morning and if I was any worse then I would phone the doctor. Then a thought occurred that I might need an overnight bag if things did not go well at the Quack's.

I got up and stumbled around, putting a few things into a holdall for the morning just in case. Then I laid back down and a lump came to my throat. I had never spent a night in a hospital; I had only had cause to visit one on a couple of rare occasions when

I needed patching up with a plaster or something trivial. I had not actually had the pleasure of being an inmate.

Morning could not come quickly enough for me. I checked myself and things had definitely not got any worse. True, they had not improved any, but now I had got used to manoeuvring about. So, a truly brilliant idea came to me: I would go to work and see how the day progressed. In truth, I had an important day as I was to do one of my sales guy's appraisals in one of the satellite sales offices in Wilmslow. The company had loads of little offices dotted all over the country, normally of companies that they had taken over and not yet managed to sell. After all, if I could get to Telford, then Wilmslow would be a piece of piss.

I managed to get to Wilmslow with some effort, but my leg seemed a lot worse as it dragged behind me. Nevertheless, I was sitting in one of the meeting rooms waiting for my appointment to turn up. I booted up my laptop and stared at the new online appraisal software. I had been on a course about how to navigate through this shit but had not taken most of it in. I felt sorry for the rep as his bonus and salary increase would be based on this - but little did he know, his boss did not even know how to fill the bleeding form in. I looked at my phone but still did not have the courage to switch it on to receive the Flying Haggis' messages.

Then something happened. Everything went black and I started to feel really dizzy. I must have blacked out for a second, the screen on my computer was really blurred and I felt really shit. The whole thing dawned on me and I knew I had to face the music: whatever was wrong with me was not going away and I felt very, very scared.

Getting home was a big problem. My eyesight was really blurred and as I drove, the speed made things even worse. However, something inside me got me through the journey. I don't know what, but whatever it was probably saved my life, not to mention all the lives of the other motorists that day that happened to be unlucky enough to travel on the same route as me.

The doctor's surgery was not open again until five, so I would have to wait nearly three hours. I was feeling progressively weaker and remembered I had not eaten for over a day but I did not feel the least bit hungry. Fear and sheer panic was all that wracked my brain; there were no thoughts of a light supper of smoked salmon accompanied by a chilled glass of something.

I sat and just stared at the clock wishing it forward as I had made my mind up and I just wanted to get things over with. I changed into baggy clothes as I knew I would probably get examined and wanted something easy to take off. As the time finally came, I took my holdall and went to the car. I knew I should not be driving, but my doctor's surgery was a ten minute walk away and there was no way I could have survived that. So, to the disgust of everybody at the DVLA, I took to the highway once more.

Walking, or should I say shuffling, into the waiting room, I thought I could feel everybody's eyes on me.

"Christ, get him to a hospital..."

"He is the sickest person I have ever seen!"

"Somebody put him out of his misery..." I imagined they were whispering towards me.

"Francis Abel?"

I finally heard my name being called and saw a light over one of the doors, indicating that the next chicken for the slaughter should enter. Like going to bleeding confession, I thought, and I always hated that too.

I looked at the elderly man sitting behind the desk. I had never seen this one before and I tried to suss him out the best that I could. Definitely Asian, probably Indian or Bangladeshi. I always found it very amusing when people with darker complexions, either foreign or British, aged and they grew white eyebrows. I found myself transfixed and stared with wonder at the two albino caterpillars moving around as the face contorted.

"Mr Abel," a voice brought me back to my current predicament.

"What can I do for you?" he questioned. Christ, if he couldn't see I was having a stroke what sort of doctor was he? He could just pop his head into the waiting room and ask all the patients outside: they all knew.

"I feel a little dizzy," was my reply. He then asked me to roll my sleeve up and proceeded to take my blood pressure.

"High," he muttered. "We will do that again in a few minutes." He got me to stand on the scales. I must admit that I had trouble lifting my leg just a few inches and had difficulty balancing. Eighteen and a half stone... Christ, I knew I was a little Chubby Checker, but not Fats fucking Domino. I was astonished.

He took my blood pressure again. "Still, too high," he said, and the caterpillars looked more concerned now. He then started to write down on a pad and looked up at me. "I think you should go to hospital just for them to take a look."

My heart sank. The very words I did not wish to hear. Why couldn't he just give me some pills or something? I felt like storming out and asking the bored multitude outside for a second opinion.

"Do you have anyone who can take you?" he asked. I shook my head.

"I would phone an ambulance, but with it being rush hour it could take a long time," he continued. "Perhaps a taxi?"

Now, I knew I could not fault his logic in estimating that an ambulance would take some time getting through the rush hour traffic, but surely if you use the same logic then so would a bleeding taxi. Surely I would be safer with some paramedics in the back of an ambulance than listening to Drive Time with Kev Keatings in the back of a cab. However, I did not want any fuss so I supposed a cab would be more discreet.

"Go to Aintree University Hospital," he instructed. "I will phone ahead and let A&E know you are coming." With that, I got once more into the car and went home. I did not fancy leaving my motor outside the doctors' as I didn't know how long it may be outside. I phoned Delta Taxis and left my details on the recorded answer phone, thinking to myself that there was no option for people with strokes and that perhaps I would let them know in a couple of days or so.

A car horn beeped outside my house within a couple of minutes and signalled that my ambulance awaited. Clutching my holdall, I eased myself into the back of the car and looked at the sheer panic on the driver's face in the rear view mirror as I said: "Fazakerley Hospital Mate, and I think you should hurry as I think I am having a heart attack or something!"

The taxi lurched forward as the cabbie must have been thinking of the quickest route to get me out of his cab before I croaked. *Hmm, Dunningsbridge Road or best through Thornton?* his own inner sat-nav mused. Without delay, the cab pulled up outside Fazakerley Hospital's A&E department, or Aintree University Hospital as it was now known. God knows why - there was not a university anywhere near there. I fumbled about trying to get out of the cab as Kev Keating was playing *The Best Is Yet To Come* on City FM. It was not a very auspicious arrival to start my hospital career as the automatic doors opened for me and the rattling exhaust of one of Delta's finest went off coughing and spluttering into the rush hour traffic with a very relieved skipper at its helm.

The scene that greeted me was nothing short of carnage. I had been to Fazakerley on a few occasions in the early hours of a weekend night. You would expect carnage at that time, but it was tea time on a Thursday! I saw a sign saying *Triage* and shuffled over to join the queue. In a few minutes, I had given my details, got a raffle ticket and had taken a seat. They had no record of my doctor phoning and informing them of my case. So, old Eyebrows had done me no favours at all; I would have been better off getting a taxi straight to hospital in the first place and cut the middle man out. At least I would have been further up the queue.

I wondered if the raffle ticket had any significance and if it was pure bloody luck as to which doctor you would see and what diagnosis you would receive. If so I favoured light yellow tickets; any luck I had ever had with raffles seemed to be with lemon coloured tickets and certainly not this red thing I had been given. I avoid red as a colour as often as I can for reasons which will become blatantly obvious later on. I remember winning a Scalextric Kit once with a yellow ticket; the best bloody prize I had ever won, even though I was only about seven.

Then my attention was drawn towards two kids, about twelve or thirteen, who were busy kicking the Hell out of one of the vending machines trying to elicit either goods or cash from their endeavours.

"Maxy, Dwayne, fucking leave it! You're doing my head in!" came a voice from a rather rotund woman to my left.

The two boys just scowled at the lady and continued damaging their trainers against the metal. The woman resumed eating her burger whilst stopping occasionally to glug some of her full fat Pepsi. I scanned the waiting room of the University's Accident and Emergency Unit and I could not imagine any don being proud of this faculty, not even at half term revelry. A drunk then interrupted the two boys' efforts looking for the Merrydown button, and the two scally-wags started to laugh at the hapless oaf as he lurched backwards and forwards trying to insert his money in the slot.

Oh my God! What was I doing here? This was not my life; I had a nice cosy life back in Crosby away from all this reality. I suddenly felt very vulnerable, alone and very, very tired. I did not know what was happening and it all seemed like some sort of nightmare; which for the first time in my life, I had no control over whatsoever.

278 appeared on the LCD screen and a nurse came out, calling my name. I put my hand in the air to acknowledge that I had noticed and followed the nurse down the corridor. I was led to a cubicle where my blood pressure was taken again.

"205 over 120," the nurse said. She noted down the readings, did a quick examination of my eyes and studied my face. "Go back out and take a seat," she instructed, so I dutifully obliged and went to sit with the rest of the X Factor competitors.

I was now completely puzzled. A doctor and a nurse, not to mention Triage, had all examined me and there was no panic. Had I been right all along? Was there nothing to be worried about? After about another hour, I was summoned and once again, my blood pressure was taken and there was more shaking of heads. This time, a doctor was called and he read my chart. I was then given an ECG and once again was told to return to the waiting room.

More time lapsed and I looked over at Maxy and Dwayne. Even with their energetic capacity, boredom had set in and they were sprawled over a row of plastic seats with their eyes closed. There was no sign of the drunk - perhaps he had gone to The Chaser to try his luck in cadging a drink. The Chaser is a local pub opposite the hospital and is not named after a wee nip to accompany your pint. Instead, it has a picture of a horse jumping a fence to remind you that Aintree Racecourse is just around the corner. The pub was brought to my attention by my mum who used to be a night sister at the hospital; one evening I was dropping her off for work and she told me never to go in the pub as most of her TB patients drank in there.

My number came up again and I was ushered into another cubicle. This time, it was not the same nurse: this one seemed more senior and had a different colour uniform on. I think there had been a staff change because I did not recognise anyone there. She was reading my information before I came in and I saw her notice my gait as I walked into the cubicle. She then shone a torch in my eyes and examined them.

"Get a trolley now! Take this patient to emergency straight away," she barked. With that, I was whisked away down a long corridor on what the Americans call a gurney. It is a far better term for a piece of medical hardware than simply a *trolley*. My grandmother served afternoon tea on a trolley! It was certainly not for delivering chronically ill people around the front lounge. Scones and Lemon Drizzle cake, I would agree, but brain haemorrhages and people with strokes? Certainly not.

My trolley was pushed into a large room with many cubicles, most with curtains closed and a table in the centre with about eight people standing around in white coats. This looked like serious shit, a bit like some sort of battlefield medicamp scene where doctors are deliberating on who to operate on first.

I was wheeled briskly into one of the cubicles and the curtains closed behind me. Within seconds a doctor appeared with two nurses. I looked about the cubicle. It looked like an operating theatre and I thought to myself that there was no getting out of this one. The doctor started to bark orders and the nurses sprang into action; all manner of things were probed and pushed into me. I have never been a big fan of needles: not quite a phobia, but certainly not a love affair and now a thing was attached to my arm leading to a plastic bag. It was uncomfortable, but the only real pain was the initial stab when the needle was inserted into the vein.

The curtains opened again and I was wheeled off further down the corridor until the trolley stopped outside X-Ray. It must have been at least 9pm - surely X-Ray would not be open at this time. Whenever I had gone for an X-Ray before, normally after football or something, you had to make an appointment and the place is only open during office hours and not at weekends.

Everything was happening so fast: it was like I had dropped my Frequent Flyer card and somebody had found it and handed it in because now I had definitely been upgraded. Perhaps I would even get to see the Captain or Senior Bloke, whatever they called him.

After X-Ray, I was taken back to emergency and parked in the same cubicle where I had left my holdall. Fairly soon, the same doctor came back with an older colleague with a beard

"Examine his eyes," the older man said, with a knowledgeable smug grin on his face. The younger doctor shined a torch first into my left and then into my right eye.

"Do you see?"

"Yes, yes...some bleeding..." The light was turned off and the older man spoke to me.

"Well, Francis, you have had a stroke," he told me. The words struck me with such ferocity; it was like somebody had hit me in the chest with a sledgehammer. Only old people get strokes... they normally get carted around in wheelchairs drooling over their clothes or shuffle around like spastics. A lump came to my throat, I could not speak... I think I was in shock.

"We can treat you Francis, we can make you feel a lot better," said the older doctor. There was a caring smile on his face and I saw pity in the eyes of the younger man, the first time in my life I have ever seen somebody look at me like that. However, as I was to come to know, it wouldn't be the last time that I would see that expression.

"We are going to take you to Intensive Care now to keep an eye on you for a while," the doctor continued. I tried to clear my throat as best as I could and rasped, "Does that mean that I will be kept in hospital tonight?" They were probably the most stupid words that I have ever uttered, but I was throwing my last dice hoping for a seven. The older man just smiled at me and nodded.

I was taken to Intensive Care and put into a small ward which to my surprise was mixed. Most people were sleeping, but I could tell these were seriously ill people with respirators, drips and all manners of medical aid attached to them. I was physically and mentally exhausted. I lay on the bed and simply drifted off to sleep. To my mind, only a few hours had passed before I was being loaded onto another trolley and pushed around to a lift. It must have been the dead of night because nobody was about and the hospital had an eerie feeling to it.

"Where are we going?" I asked the porter.

"To the Stroke Unit," he replied and finished our conversation. He did not sound too friendly, but I suppose I had interrupted his supper and it reminded me that I had not eaten in days.

We came to a couple of locked doors, a buzzer was pressed and after a minute a nurse came and gave us entrance to the Stroke Unit. I was pushed down a fairly long corridor into a ward. It was dark and I could not see much. I heard distant screams of a woman somewhere and they were frightening. I was placed on a bed and took stock of my situation. There were groans of pain all around me, the man in the corner bed seemed he was coughing up his guts and the screams from the woman continued to be interrupted occasionally by a voice yelling, "Can't you shut her up?!" I was in pure Hell and had no sleep whatsoever.

Morning came, to my relief, and the unit came to life. I had been thinking during the night that I was a member of BUPA in work and because of my position, I had quite a good policy. I would phone Sylvia, tell her what has happened to me and get her to talk to BUPA and get me the Hell out of there. Then it also dawned on me that nobody knew I was here. I would get around to that issue later, but first I had to get out of this place.

A young nurse came to me and gave me a bed bath. I asked her about my BUPA membership and she just shrugged and told me to see the sister. After my wash, I was helped out of bed and put in a chair adjacent. I looked around the ward. It had eight beds in it, all occupied. Each one had a small locker, a table and a chair. I noticed that the other patients were all wearing pyjamas; I had just a t-shirt and jockey shorts on. I did not even own a pair of pyjamas - for as long as I can remember I have always slept naked. Not a pretty sight, but I can't stand wearing anything whilst I am sleeping: things get tangled up, if you know what I mean.

The breakfast cart came around and for the first time in days, I had something to eat: cereal with a nice mug of tea. I began to feel a little more human; I could still not grip things tightly with my right hand but I could hold light items and it wasn't useless. I gently stood up and tottered to the toilet which was just outside the ward and saw the nurse's desk in front of me. It was time to find the sister and get the fuck out of there as quick as possible.

I saw a busy figure in a dark blue uniform gesticulating and giving orders to younger nurses. It was a good bet that this buxom woman with blond hair was the sister, so I approached. I told her my story about BUPA and the ward being a Hell hole and she faced me with a thunderous expression. I had just insulted her ward and therefore gravely insulted her. I had just made a big, big mistake and gained a powerful foe. I cannot for the life of me remember the battle-axe's name so for continuity purposes I will call her Sister Ratchitt after the similar character in *One Flew Over the Cuckoo's Nest*.

I shuffled back to my bed and powered up my mobile. 11 messages waiting. Well, I would just ignore those straight away. I phoned Sylvia and told her my predicament. My voice was blurred and very shaky, but she told me she would screen all my calls and inform Colin as to where I was. She sounded gravely sincere and would phone BUPA immediately. Sylvia was incredibly efficient: she was Colin's secretary really, but also looked after all his managers. I relaxed knowing that the right person was on the job.

I knew I had to tell my friends where I was. It was Friday morning and normally Friday night was Curry Night. Nick, one of my closest friends, and I had kept up a long tradition that every Friday, we would go out for a few beers, bring a takeaway curry back to my house and watch a movie.

How could I phone him? I could not bear the idea of talking to somebody I was so close to and informing him in my shaky voice about what had happened to me. I knew I would probably break down the second I heard his voice. I decided to SMS the news: not the best way to inform a lifelong friend that you have had stroke, but it was the only way I could face doing it.

Within minutes, two messages appeared on my screen: one from Nick and one from Richie, another close mate. They asked what the fuck was I playing at. The trouble with being somewhat of a prankster is that when something really serious happens, nobody tends to believe you. However, Nick was quite shrewd and had phoned the hospital who confirmed that I was a resident patient admitted the previous night. Another message appeared from Nick: "Be there soon".

I waited in my chair with some trepidation. How would I react when I saw somebody who really cared for me? What did I look like? Was I a dribbling mess? The ward was a hive of morning activity with doctors and nurses attending to various patients - time quickly passed. Suddenly, I saw a rather forlorn figure outside talking to Sister Ratchet.

Nick looked over to where Sister Ratchet was pointing at a crumpled figure hunched in a chair and soon realised that it was me. A look of shock came over his face, quickly replaced by one of pity. I saw moisture in his eyes as he came closer, then a broad smile as he stood in front of me. No words were spoken between us, we just hugged. I struggled to hold back my tears but somehow I managed to cope.

"Well, what you have been up to this time?" Nick jokingly teased me. Nick has a very laconic, but sharp sense of humour; often I have been the subject of a severe barrage of wit from my friend. I just shrugged and managed a smile.

My speech was slow, slightly blurred yet deliberate as I recounted a brief synopsis of what had happened. I asked my old friend to inform everybody back home but that I did not want any visitors yet: I simply wasn't up to it.

"What about Anthony?" Nick said. Anthony was my older brother: we had not seen each other for a couple of years, ever since my mum went into the nursing home. He lived somewhere near Oxford but our paths never really crossed. I gave Nick his phone number and left it for him to tell my brother.

My friends back home in Crosby were a different matter - most of them I had known since school and I had socialised with them ever since. Some were married and had kids, one or two had stayed single like me for various reasons and lived to party at the weekends. I saw most of them every week, normally in my local pub, The Edinburgh Inn, or as we called it, The Bug and had stayed very close to all of them.

Nick wanted to know if I needed anything from home and told me he would call back later with some clothes and toiletries. He had a key to my house: at one time he had lived there when his first marriage broke down. I thought it wise that somebody else should have a key to get in rather than just myself. He also was going to see if there was a BUPA 'hotel' somewhere nearby. With all his tasks allocated, he left and I continued with my first day in Aintree University Hospital.

Chapter Two

THE STROKE UNIT

When my friend had left I took in my surroundings and studied the ward. The first thing that I noticed was that the other fellow inmates were far older than me. There was nobody within twenty years of my age and most of them were in far worse condition. For some reason I took some heart in that fact; perhaps my stroke had not been too bad and soon I would be discharged.

Then a posse of people made a beeline towards me. Two doctors followed by a gaggle of nurses in their wake. The curtains were drawn around my bed and I was asked to lie down.

"Hello Francis, I am Dr Sharma," the head guy spoke to me. He then continued reading the chart at the bottom of the bed and occasionally muttered something to the other white coat who dutifully passed the message on to Sister Ratchet who diligently scribbled a note on a file. Surely if the NHS gave Dr Sharma a dictaphone or something more modern, then all these nice people could be doing something else instead of them all being cramped up inside my tent.

After only a couple of minutes the curtains were pulled back and the entourage left as quickly as they arrived. I felt a bit miffed; I hadn't been able to ask any questions and had no idea what had or what was going to happen to me. A voice from the next bed spoke: "You're lucky, Dr Sharma is one of the top guys in the country." I just nodded.

"He does speeches all over the world," they continued. I thought that it would have been nice of him to have given me one in that case, especially since we both happened to have been in the same tent.

I got out of bed and went over to my new pal. Sitting on his chair, we began the hard job of trying to communicate with each other. Ken had severe stroke and was virtually bed bound; his face had dropped significantly on the left side and speaking was extremely hard for him. Mind you, trying to understand him was just as difficult, but I seemed to have plenty of time on my hands. He had a blockage or clot in the brain and was now waiting for an operation on his neck to clear something.

I had better explain that apparently there are two kinds of stroke, a blockage and a bleed in the brain. Also, you can have either on the right side or left of the brain which affects you differently. I did not have a clue what I had, but was very interested what Ken was saying. Twenty minutes sitting by his bed had given me more information than the whole of the bloody NHS so far.

Conversation stopped suddenly as the dinner lady arrived. One thing about hospital that I was to learn is that whenever food is dished up everything stops. I think that is because hospital in the main is boring and the dinner cart is a big event in the day that everybody looks forward to. Not that everybody behaved like greedy fat bastards who were waiting to stuff food down their grids every five minutes.

"Did you fill your card in, love?" I was asked by the lady in the apron. I shook my head. "Well, you will just have to have what I've got spare," was her reply. She plonked a tray of food on the table over the bed and waddled off with one of her wheels squeaking. I looked at my lunch and it didn't seem to be so bad - there was also a little card which was a menu for dinner later. All you had to do was write your name on the top of the card and tick in the little boxes your selection. But I couldn't understand some of the choices: fish and chips, meat pasty with mash and beans... surely the idea was to try and get people better, not kill them with cholesterol.

After lunch I decided to take a little stroll around the unit to see what was outside my ward. I walked or rather limped heavily into the corridor by the nurse's station which was situated on a corner of two main passageways. From what I could gather, the unit was in the form of an L shape with the nurse's station having the view of both corridors. Nobody seemed concerned about my roaming, so I ventured down the same way I had been wheeled in the night before.

I stayed close to the wall as I walked to help support me and I took things in. I could see the double doors at the top which seemed permanently locked. This was a very secure unit for very sick people and visitors were strictly monitored. On the left side of the passageway was the Rehab Unit which in later days I was to find housed a small gym, a fully fitted kitchen and complete bathroom. You were to be tested on your capabilities as well as your health before they would let you out.

On the right side was a series of small rooms. They seemed to be private rooms with one bed in each. The screaming woman was in one of them as I peeped through the door so I quickly moved on. The screaming did not seem so bad during the day but at night it was horrendous. Ken told me later that these rooms were for critically ill patients, people who had either had a further stroke during the night or people recovering from surgery. I did not really care much for that part of the unit; it was too much like reality.

The other corridor was far more jolly; on the right were the wards. Each had eight beds and were exactly the same. They alternated from a men's ward then women's and so on. I think there were six wards in total and I was in the first men's ward. On the left were a series of meeting rooms with flip charts and other stuff like that in. One was used for a type of common room that patients could take visitors to if there were too many to fit round the bed. The end of this corridor was blocked off so there was only one way in and out of the whole unit.

I was feeling tired after my little excursion so I made my way back to the ward to see an altercation taking place by Ken's bed.

A fairly tall man in his late 60s wearing a red dressing gown was getting a proper dressing down by one of the nurses.

"Peter!" the nurse said in a fairly exasperated shrill voice. "For the last time, have you touched any of Ken's things?" The man in the dressing gown just shrugged and looked back at the nurse like a scolded child. His pockets were searched then he was despatched back to whatever ward he had come from.

"That bastard!" Ken said as I went over to him. "Check your things." I looked in my little cupboard and was relieved to see that my iPod and mobile phone were still there. I checked my jeans pocket and the little money I had brought with me was all still there.

"Nothing is safe while he is around," Ken explained. I was to discover later that Peter was a bit of a kleptomaniac; not a bad one, as he did not seem to keep any of the things that he pinched, but more like a Robin Hood. He would take things from all over the ward and simply deposit them somewhere else. However, I must admit that whenever I saw a flash of a red dressing gown I paid attention to all my belongings.

Just after dinner Nick came back with my things. He had a couple of "Get Well Soon" cards with him and said he had told everybody. He had also found that BUPA had a private nursing home on site in Fazakerly Hospital - the Sefton Suite. I made a mental note to let Sylvia know this as soon as I could. Sadly, it was Friday and so I knew Monday was the first opportunity I would have to do this. I had no news really to tell him apart from the name of the doctor looking after me. He stayed for about an hour. He looked pretty much done in and I realised that it must have been incredibly hard for my friend to take all this in, but when he left, I really missed him.

The ward prepared itself for the night. Patients were busily prepared for bed by nurses and medication was administered to all. I was the only one who could really walk unaided so I was fortunate enough to go to the bathroom in the corridor and wash properly. I had decided not to ask Nick for any pyjamas, I would remain a rebel and continue wearing my boxer shorts and t-shirt. However, putting a clean pair of boxer shorts on was not an easy matter. I had to sit on the toilet and try to straighten my leg enough to take off my old ones. My arm would not stretch out enough to put the new ones on, so I sort of had to sling shot them on with my left hand. I was knackered so couldn't be bothered with my shirt; I simply draped a towel over my shoulders and went back to my bed.

My second night in hospital was another sleepless affair. I noticed every cough, snore, occasional scream and minute noise as the unit breathed. Christ, if I didn't get some sleep soon I would die of exhaustion! I laid there feeling very sorry for myself and wished the night away. My arm and leg were aching and I was shattered. I had never felt so wretched in my whole life.

The dawn finally came to take me from my misery, light drifted in from behind the curtains and I could hear faint noises outside in the corridor. Weekends in hospital are very different to that of days of the week. There are not as many people about and things are far quieter. There are no non surgical staff so no rehab unit, no porters ferrying people around for different tests, no doctors… in all it is a far more relaxed and pleasant place. And there seems to be a more relaxed attitude to visitors; people drift in and out all day and the nurses seem quite happy to let them do it.

A new sister appeared and she was completely different to Sister Ratchet. A broad grin was on her kindly face as she entered the ward. "Good morning everybody," her sing-song lilt sounded. "Let's have a little light," she said, and pulled back the curtains to reveal a bright winter's morning. With that, she wheeled away to wake up the next ward. A breath of fresh air had entered the room.

Two nurses then came in. They were very young, perhaps not even eighteen, and seemed very good pals. They started with bed baths for everybody except me, who wrestled in the bathroom, then breakfast was served. I noticed the bed in the corner and saw that there was a prosthetic leg propped up on a chair beside it. No sign could be seen of its owner, as the bed covers were pulled right up. Everybody else was turfed out of their beds after breakfast but no effort was made to disturb this resident.

I went to ask Ken.

"That's Alf, he's really ill," he told me. A respirator was connected to the bed and I could just see the covers rise and fall as the incumbent breathed. "Does he ever come up for air?" I enquired. I never actually saw Alf - only his prosthetic leg, and wondered if he really existed. The only times when the bed covers were actually pulled down were when the curtains were drawn around and a team of medical staff were attending to him.

Laughing drew my attention away and I saw the two nurses standing at the bed opposite Alf. I noticed a genial looking man with what looked like a Stetson on his head. The two nurses were playing with him and had turned a bed pan upside down and placed it on his head. "Go on Bill, show everybody," the nurses said, as they moved aside to reveal a beaming face sporting his new hat. He gleamed in satisfaction at us all. I must clarify that the NHS no longer uses the old metal type of bed pan, it's now a reconstituted cardboard one and I must admit, it does double as an excellent Stetson. I just hope Bill had not used his new hat in the night for its original purpose.

The person in the bed next to me watched the scene before him with bewilderment on his face. He was a quiet man who only spoke when his wife came to see him. She had a very educated manner about her and I could sense the couple were very middle class. I don't know how he was going to break the news to his wife that Saturday was Wild West day on the ward and that next week it might be his turn to wear a mop and be a Red Indian. Oh! The shame in the avenue if that news ever got out!

My spirits rose as I got to know my fellow patients more and my friendship with Ken was growing. He was an Evertonian, like me, and his son was going to come this afternoon with a laptop that could stream the Everton match. I was very much looking forward to seeing the Blues stuff Wigan and the day seemed far brighter to me.

I no longer looked at these people with disdain because they were sick and should have been avoided. I was one of them now, one of the club, and could wear my Stetson with pride.

Nick came early to see me as he had to go somewhere with his wife and son later that day. He had even more cards with him: I had nowhere that I could put them, but was very glad to read them anyway. He told me many people had been asking about me and wanted to come and visit. I agreed that in one or two more days it would be okay when I was stronger but not now. I was still not ready to face the rest of my friends, not yet; there would be time for that later. He would come back later with his son's portable DVD player and some films. I had decided if I could not sleep I might as well keep myself occupied. But I would have to find a good hiding place for the DVD player away from Peter's grasp.

Then something wonderful happened. The new sister came in and scanned the ward. She lingered at me, seemed to make a decision, and marched over. "Follow me," she instructed. She then spoke to a nurse and pointed to my cupboard and my belongings. I followed the sister at a slow place down the corridor wondering where I was going. We then stopped just before the security doors and went into a private room, one of the critical rooms.

"This is spare for the weekend, you may as well be more comfortable," she told me. I could have kissed her - my own room... I almost burst out in tears, I was so happy. It had its own bathroom, TV and about four chairs scattered about. *Wait until Nick sees this!* I thought to myself with a smug grin on my face. I found out later from the nurse that a rather sick patient had just been admitted and they wanted to keep him on the ward so they could monitor him more closely. Sister had thought I was the most capable so had given him my bed.

I went back to tell Ken the good news and saw that the curtains were drawn around my old bed. I thanked God that it was not me. Ken was disappointed when I told him my news: he had got used to me being around. Because he could not walk, I did a lot of fetching and carrying for him that he appreciated and relied on. I had not thought anything of my little jobs, only keeping myself busy. His son came in later with the laptop and we watched the game together. It seemed to cheer Ken up a little, especially the 2-0 score line to Everton.

That night I had my first real sleep in days. I closed the door and simply crashed out on the bed exhausted. The following morning, the door opened and a face appeared in the doorframe. It was one of the cleaners.

"Going to be doing in here in about five minutes, love," she chirped. I nodded, managed to get out of bed and sat myself down in the big chair facing the TV, wearing my shorts and T-Shirt.

Now something I have not explained is that I had been on holiday with Richie in December and had still retained quite a bit of my tan. Although I am fair and in the past had blond hair, I do tan well and so was quite brown. The door swung open and a bin was propped against it to keep it so. Then the woman reappeared with a Hoover and proceeded to clean. She saw me in the chair and yelled, "God, you look really well love. Nice brown legs. Been away have you?" She didn't stop for a reply, just continued.

"Shirley!" she screamed in a thick Scouse accent. "Shirl, come in here girl." A second face appeared at the door. "Shirl, doesn't he look well?" she exclaimed.

"Oh yeah," the second woman agreed looking at me. "He's the fittest looking stroke victim I have ever seen!" Both women nodded their agreement to each other and continued chatting as they left my room.

I burst out in hysterics at my new diagnosis from the cleaners. They were actually quite jealous of my tan and had seemed to completely forget the fact that I was so ill. What was more important was to have a good tan and not let a little thing like a stroke detract from that. My laughing was quite weird and it did not sound right: sort of a high pitched shriek. I stopped immediately and my short term joy faded.

I sort of missed the action of the ward in my little room, but the benefits far outweighed the company. I wondered if Bill was sporting his Stetson again that morning and took a walk to visit my old pals. I passed an elderly lady in the corridor and saw that the complete side of her face had dropped; she shuffled along on a Zimmer frame and did not even seem to notice me. I gulped at her predicament and a chill went through my body.

Nothing much was happening on the ward so I made my way back and settled into the chair. From where I was sitting I could see the security doors and everybody coming and going from the unit. The outside buzzer would sound, then a nurse at the station would look at the security camera and admit entrance to the caller. Most of the rest of the morning was taken up watching the Dick Emery show. Peter had cottoned on to the security process, so every time the buzzer sounded he would make a dash for the doors in a bid for freedom; closely pursued by a nurse, cleaner, dinner lady, in fact anybody who was near, including the odd visitor. The red dressing gown could be seen billowing in his wake as the posse closed in. I half expected to see Sheriff Bill astride a trolley, burnishing a lasso and joining the chase.

Then things quietened down a little and I presumed Peter had either gained his freedom or more likely a fed up nurse had sedated him. The dinner lady came and I was admonished for "going posh" in my new room and not having the decency to tell her. I pointed out the fact that she must have forgot to give me her mobile number - stupid cow.

After dinner, Nick came again with some fresh laundry. He was quite impressed with my new surroundings and he could see that the change had lifted my spirits. I had put all my cards on display on the window ledge and I recanted the tales about the cleaners and Peter. When he left I was in a much better frame of mind. The door opened and a nurse in a white coat entered.

"Just to tell you love, no food after 9pm. I have to take a lot of blood tomorrow, I will be in first thing," she said. My spirits once more took a kicking as I realised it was Monday tomorrow and things would start to happen.

Sure enough, Dracula was at my bedside before 8am. She took seven files of blood from my arm. Actually she was a very pleasant lady and I liked her very much. "You're much too young to be having a stroke," she shook her head in pity. "Far too young," she told me as another file filled up with blood. When she left, I looked at my arm and there was a large black mark where the needle had been and it was getting darker by the minute. I have not had blood taken for some time, but now it is actually quite painless. If they are taking multiple samples from you they simply insert a sort of plug in your arm and drain off as many samples as they want. There is only really one stab of pain; then an uncomfortable feeling thereafter.

It was sort of beneficial that I had been admitted over the weekend as it had given me time to settle in this alien world. I knew that now Monday had arrived all the attractions of the fair would be open, and I had a golden pass for all of them. So far, all that had really been happening was that my blood pressure was regularly monitored and I had been given one tablet at night time. It had lulled me into a false sense of healthiness which was as far away from the truth as it could have been.

After breakfast I took a little walk to the ward. Alf was in residence as I could see the leg flying at full mast on his chair. Then I turned to see Bill in floods of tears sitting in his chair. I went over to Ken and before I could say anything he rasped: "He has been evicted, his son has just visited and said all his possessions were out in the street!" One of the young nurses hugged poor Bill as the old man wept freely in her arms. I felt so sorry for him... I wondered what had gone wrong. Surely a landlord would not kick out a tenant who was ill in hospital. What the fuck was up with this world!

Then Ratchet barked: "Back to your room, you!" She glared at me. Obviously the news of my room change had been given to her. Had she thought I had complained? I had nothing to do with being moved - surely somebody had told her. Anyway, she was not happy with the fact I had managed to escape her ward. Ken looked at me and raised his eyes upwards. I nodded to him. What a fine start to the week!

By the time I had worked my way back to my room there was a porter waiting outside with a wheelchair. "Francis Abel?" he asked. I nodded in recognition. "We had better hurry, brain scan for you!" I panicked a little. What did that entail? I had no time to muse as I was whisked away in a moment.

I must admit, being an inmate had plenty of benefits. I seemed quite a celebratory as I was wheeled through the hospital; people with trivial ailments moved briskly aside as somebody at death's door was pushed passed them. There is a certain hierarchy amongst patients, the severely ill are top dogs, especially if you had a porter as a chauffeur.

We arrived at the brain scan unit and even at that hour the waiting room was full. I was wheeled straight past them and was parked in front of the nurse's desk. Everybody was wearing outdoor clothes and I wondered how long these bastards had been waiting for a brain scan only to have some tanned twat in a wheelchair jump the queue. I was the next one to enter the surgery and felt very smug about it.

It didn't look that bad. There was a bed and a machine sort of set on a pair of runners. I lay down and the machine whirred and pulsed, then went over my head back and forwards a few times, then went quiet. Was that it? Why, that was a piece of piss!

I left the surgery and my porter was waiting for me. *At this rate I will be back in time for lunch*, I thought. So, more Queen Mum salutations and I was transported back to the unit just in time for a cheese omelette. As I was sipping my tea, another porter arrived and instructed me I was to be taken for a heart scan.

Once again I was wheeled through Fazakerly Hospital in all my pomp. This time more visitors were about, but they too moved reverently aside as the sickest man in Liverpool made his way to the cross. Same scenario, I jumped the queue and laid on the bed. My chest was semi shaved and gel was applied. The operator then moved a sensor over my heart. I looked at the screen the sensor was attached to, but didn't have a clue what any of the data meant. This is what was I expecting: a chart with a needle saying "He's a goner" or "Okey dokey, this one's fine and dandy".

Ken had told me that patients had a right to ask for information if they had tests. "Is everything all right?" I asked, but I was simply told to ask my doctor as a report would be sent to him. I looked at the woman operating the machine and knew she was stalling; she was interpreting the data as soon as it came on the screen. I began to worry.

I know that I pissed around a bit enrolling at Aintree University Hospital, but now I was here, I might as well have tried to graduate, so there was no point in lying to anybody about anything and just told the truth. I pressed the woman again to give me information.

"Do you smoke?" she asked. I shook my head. "Okay, we will just do that again." So, more gel was applied and again the sensor moved across my chest. I looked at the screen again, but everything looked the same to me. Going back to the ward, I was not so chirpy as I thought about what had just happened. I must admit I was more than a trifle concerned.

That evening a few more of my friends came to visit as I had told Nick it was okay; I was more relaxed in my own room. I must admit, I did play to the audience a little to my visitors; it is my way normally to be close to the centre of attention. When visiting was over I was pretty wiped out: my play acting of the normal Francis Abel had taken its toll and I was shattered. I slept like a baby that night and for the first time in days I had a peaceful sleep. I do not know why it was important for me to be my best in front of my peers, it just seemed the right thing to do at the time to aid their discomfort at my plight.

The following morning, all Hell had broken loose. A pile of patient files on the nurses' station ready for the doctor's morning rounds had disappeared. The suspected culprit was already being questioned by Sister Ratchet. Peter was sat bolt upright in a chair being interrogated by the gestapo. He was staring down at the floor like a naughty schoolboy and he was being scolded as one. Ratchet knew as soon as the consultants walked onto the wards they would request their files and if she did not produce them she would be held responsible.

I knew that sooner or later the missing documents would be found. Peter had just picked them up and deposited them somewhere else more fitting in his eyes, God knows where, but definitely somewhere more suitable for buff-coloured files at eight in the morning. I looked at Ratchet's discomfort and thought, *One to me, you old cow,* and went to eat my breakfast with a hearty appetite.

When I had just finished, Dr Sharma walked into the room and luckily for me seemed to already have my file. This was the first opportunity I had had to have a one to one chat with the consultant.

"What has happened to me? How long will I have to stay in hospital?" I questioned?. In simple terms, Sharma then went on to explain to me that I had suffered a stroke, to be precise, a bleed of the left hand side of my brain. They had been monitoring me, but there were more tests to be done before the correct medication could be prescribed. Therefore, he couldn't tell me how much longer I would be there.

I asked him regarding the Sefton Suite. To be honest, I had put the issue on the back burner as being in the private room had alleviated most of my problems. To my amazement he asked me for BUPA's phone number and I gave him my personal reference number Sylvia had passed on. One of the country's top consultant specialist doctors then proceeded to speak to some pen pushing insurance lackey about my case.

The upshot? Pen pushing lackey won. They deemed that my stay at Aintree University Hospital was one of rehabilitation and therefore not covered in my policy. Fucking insurance bastards playing with peoples lives! I was fucking poorly and just wanted to get better. Dr Sharma saw the flash of anger in my eyes and shrugged his shoulders, it was not the first time he had had a conversation like that.

"You know it's probably better that you stay here, everything we need is right here," he said sympathetically. Sylvia later told me that BUPA had agreed to pay one hundred pounds a night whilst I was in hospital. Great, a nice fat cheque when I got home - I needed the care now! Needless to say, I will never subscribe to BUPA ever again in my life.

Sharma left and I was feeling quite down as I did not know how much more of my sentence I had to serve. I was soon to feel even worse as Ratchet blustered in. "What is all that mess?" she exploded, pointing at my cards and magazines on the window sill. "Tidy all that up, this is a hospital not a nursing home!" she scolded. "Make sure you are here waiting for the porter at 2pm, you have a CT scan this afternoon."

I was not certain what a CT scan entailed, but the others had been a piece of cake so no problem worrying about it. I decided to go and ask Ken what he knew about them. Just as I had stepped outside the room, a young man with glasses spoke to me. "Francis Abel? I am Simon the senior physiotherapist. Come with me." We walked towards the rehab unit and we passed the same old lady I had met in the corridor two days earlier. She was now in a wheelchair and I was shocked when I looked at her, the other side of her face had also significantly dropped. She resembled the Churchill dog.

Talking to Ken later that day, I found out that it is very common that once a person has a stroke they have another one or two soon after. Sometimes they are smaller, called TIAs, and sometimes they are a full blown attack. Obviously that poor dear had suffered another bout.

Simon led me to the rehab unit which I found to be very interesting. To the right was a small gym, not the type with bar bells and stuff like that, but floor mats and huge inflatable balls. He sat me down at a table and took some paperwork out whilst I studied the other occupants in the room. There were various other elderly patients from the unit, each with a personal physio going through different routines. I did not recognise any of them; nobody from my old ward anyway.

Simon explained to me that I was going to take certain physical tests and I was going to be marked on how I performed in each. Then later on in a few days I would take the tests again and be re-marked. From today I would spend thirty minutes every day here trying to improve my capabilities.

He looked down at my footwear. I think I was wearing an old comfortable pair of trainers. He nodded his assent and we began. Firstly, I had to do infant-like puzzles with a Fisher Price kit. I was timed in all the tests. I found these puzzles quite hard because it was using what they called my fine motor skills - putting small objects into even smaller holes.

Then we moved on to more physical tasks. Could I climb a set of steps? How long could I stand on one leg and could I walk straight down a line painted on the floor? I felt like Kenneth Moore in *Reach for the Sky* after he had just been fitted with his false legs. Perhaps I would ask Nick to bring in my World War 2 Biggles cap so I could look more of the part.

The whole thing took about an hour as Simon was giving me plenty of time to rest after each task. I didn't score too highly, especially on the fiddly bits, but Simon did not seem daunted. He did not yell "Off with his head!" in desperation. He then introduced me to Clair who would be my daily physio. She seemed very pleasant, sporty looking and a very fit looking body. I suppose that helps being a physio, you can't really have a big fat lump of lard encouraging you to exert more energy. Nobody would take them seriously.

After lunch the porter came and wheeled me down to the CT scanner. We seemed to be going into the very bowels of the hospital. I was unaware of the fact that the unit was being rehoused and a brand new clinic was being built for it. This was its temporary home and it was a shit hole. It was like somewhere you see in the films where illegal abortions take place. Dark, dank and miserable with discoloured walls and bats flying around. Okay, I embellished a little with the bats, but I think you understand what I am trying to describe. A shit hole!

The waiting room was a piece of polythene draped over a wooden beam and the throbbing of the machine drowned out the noise from outside. I was waiting for the patient before me to finish and then it was my turn. The throbbing suddenly ceased and the polythene was pushed back to reveal a shaven headed youth. He had a black eye and cuts and bruises all over his face and arms.

Great, I had been hanging around for some thug to finish when I was a genuine case. It never occurred to me that the youth might have been set upon and not as I had just presumed been involved in a pub brawl.

I was led into the dark room and noticed there were several white coats in what seemed to be a large garden shed looking at me through the window. I lay down on the bench fixed to the machine, and then a metal grill was placed over my face. What the Hell was that for? I looked like the Man in the Iron Mask. The technician then handed me a panic button. "Press this if you feel it is getting too much for you," he comforted me.

Then it all started. I slowly was sucked into the machine until my whole body had been devoured. It was like being eaten by a giant pizza oven with a weird smell. The roof and sides of the machine were literally millimetres from my face and body and I felt very claustrophobic. Loud rhythmic noises started to emanate from the machine and bright lights flashed. The tempo and volume gradually increased until it was almost unbearable, the whole machine seemed to be shaking and the room shook with it. Ten minutes must have passed and I was close to pressing that button on numerous occasions when all of a sudden everything went quiet. There was a slight whirring noise and the bench started to move out of the machine.

I was so glad to once again see the grimy room and the grubby technician. But something was wrong - he had a needle in his hand. "Nearly done, I have to just inject you with some dye and a few minutes more," he reassured. *What?!* I screamed internally, *I have to go back in THERE?!* I was very nearly sick. I did not know if I could take another Gas Mark 7. So, I was posted back into the pizza oven to crisp me up a little more. I loathed the machine and hated the CT Unit.

Back in my room I breathed a sigh of relief and started to relax a little. My room was right by the cleaners' rooms and one of them popped in with a nice mug of tea. She must have seen my ashen face when they bought me back from my scan. I turned my iPod on and comforted myself with some Bobby Womack and waited for dinner. That night more friends came to visit. I had about eight people at one stage and knew Ratchet would blow a fuse if she came in.

The day's activities had worn me out and I was actually quite glad when my last I visitor had left. I settled on the bed and drifted off to sleep quite exhausted. When I woke it was morning but something was very wrong. My arm seemed dead. I tried to push myself up to a sitting position but my arm had no power. I gathered my strength and wriggled up the bed. I sat there for a few minutes taking stock and then tried to get out of the bed. My leg was also not responding. Oh shit!

With some difficulty I finally managed to extract myself from the bed and lurched into the toilet. Propped up against the basin I looked in the mirror. Shit, shit, shit! My face had slightly dropped around the right cheek and the right corner of my mouth was turned downwards. I'd had another attack in the night. I had to check how bad it was. Leaning on the door frame I sat back on the bed, I tried to raise my right arm, but could only move it half way in the air. It felt like it was made of lead. My hand was worse, it almost looked like a claw. Trying to stand I knew my right leg had also suffered; it would not take any weight.

The rest of that morning was a real struggle, firstly to dress and then trying to eat my breakfast. I could not hold a spoon or fork in my hand; I simply could not grip anything. I used my left hand to raise some cereal to my mouth, but my lips felt numb and milk dribbled down my chin.

Clair appeared to take me to physio and saw there had been a change in me. "I couldn't fasten my laces," I slurred. She just smiled, bent down and tied my trainers. I shuffled very slowly down the corridor banging against the wall. "Do you know, I think we might try you with a walking stick, it might help," she said. My face looked a picture... finally I was a cripple. She must have sensed my discomfort. "Mostly to warn other people to be careful around you," she said, trying to cheer me up.

Physio was not fun that morning: I couldn't even climb the steps. Clair tried me on the Fisher Price kit, but the pieces were too fiddly for me to pick up, in exasperation I threw most of them on the floor. Clair did not admonish me - she simply smiled, picked up the pieces and took me back to my room. I texted Nick that afternoon that I was too tired for any visitors that night and could he let people know. Later that evening Nick came, he had been every day without fail. He wanted to know why I had sent the SMS and was quite shocked when he saw my current state, but just having him there gave me encouragement.

I lay awake that night thoughts filling my mind and not giving me peace. The biggest question most stroke victims ask is: "How much of my body am I going to get back?" That is a question no doctor or physio can give you an answer to, the severity of each attack is different and in each case the patient's response to treatment differs. The first and most important factor is that the person has to accept what has happened and that something needs to be done. Self-help is extremely important and the ones who sit in a corner and say "Why me?" are the ones who will spend the rest of their lives in wheelchairs, a dribbling mess. That night I vowed to myself that whatever the medical profession instructed me to do, I would follow those instructions to the letter and more.

The following day, Clair gave me my new walking stick. The problem was that I needed it to support my right leg but I couldn't hold it in my right hand. Although I managed to hold the blasted thing in my left hand, it was not really giving my right leg any aid whatsoever. However, if it was going to be any help at all I would continue using it. We went right back to basics in physio, almost how to walk again. Clair was very patient with me and we painstakingly started to slowly rebuild my battered body.

Clair had informed the speech therapist about my setback so that afternoon I had a new visitor. Nicola was tall, dark and very kindly looking, probably around thirty years old. She had bought with her several text books that I was to digest with speech exercises in and we started on my therapy. She produced a small Janet and John sort of book with mundane pictures of everyday items on each page. We stopped at one page she pointed at the picture.

"Tiger," I responded. "Close, a lion," she encouraged. I knew it was a lion, why had I said tiger? God, this was so demeaning... I was forty seven reading an eight year old's picture book.

It was then, for no apparent reason, and unfortunately for Nicola, that I broke down. Floods of tears poured down my face and I sobbed like a baby, I had reached rock bottom and this poor girl I had just met was getting the full blast of my despair. I hugged her like a child and she held me and let me have my moment. It was the first time I had actually cried since my first attack and the reality of my plight had hit well and truly home. The tears ceased as just as soon as they had come and I composed myself a little. Nicola then went on to tell me the brain is like a filing cabinet, I had pulled out the correct drawer, but all the files were jumbled up and I had pulled out the wrong one. We were to set about and to do some tidying up of the filing cabinet, that was all.

Luckily that evening, I only had a few visitors as my mood was not great. Sandy, another mate had noticed my change, but didn't dwell on my appearance and we just chatted about Everton and soul music and other light topics.

After physio next morning, I was feeling pretty tired so I went back to sit down and try my speech exercises. How lucky I was to keep this room, I thought, I couldn't have coped with all of this if I was still on the ward. I was busy reading out loud from my exercise book when there was a rap on the open door and a young lady stood there.

"Francis?"

I nodded. I think she said her name was Helen, but I am not certain, Dr Sharma had asked to see me. "I am a nutritionist," she told me. She was very modern, a stud through her nose and a short spiky hairdo. I wondered if she might be gay; not that I have any lesbian stereotypes, just that I was inquisitive. Under her right arm she had a set of weighing scales.

"Now, I am not here to comment on the medical effect your food and drink intake has on various parts of your body, I just have to get an accurate picture of what your average weekly intake is for a calorific perspective. Shall we start with your alcohol?"

Oh, bollocks.

"Average, you say."

I then reminded myself of my pledge to tell the truth, Oh, fuck, this was going to be embarrassing.

I recalled my normal week in my mind and recounted it to the nutritionist. Monday was Quiz Night in the Bug, probably seven pints of Stella. Then Tuesday, Wednesday and Thursday I normally battened down the hatches and stayed in, so one bottle of beer with my tea and a bottle of wine a night watching a film or TV. The tapping of her fingers on a calculator was bugging me. Then Friday was curry night with Nick, at least eight pints Stella and a bottle of wine each. Saturday, if I went to the match, probably ten pints in the course of the whole day; maybe a couple of shorts if we won. Then Sunday, well that was my big day. I spent nearly the whole day in the Bug with Richie holding court and then back to mine for something to eat. A conservative twelve pints and a bottle and a half of wine.

I looked up at the nutritionist to gauge her reaction. "Well, Francis, are you aware the Government's recommendation for nits per week is 22?" I nodded.

"What you have just told me is roughly 165 units," she said, looking very severely at me. There was a pregnant pause in proceedings to let this news sink in.

"My concern is the calorie intake of all that alcohol," she showed me the calculator screen and pointed at the number displayed. It meant nothing to me, so I shrugged. "Basically the average male should consume around two thousand calories a day. You consume eighteen thousand a week just drinking."

I must admit I was pretty ashamed of myself, but did not expect anything less - I knew I drank a lot. "In a man's terms, you consume nine days' calories every week just drinking... a downward spiral, Francis."

Then an idea occurred to me with a glimmer of salvation, only to be headed off at pass by Sheriff Bill with his tilted bed pan. She was reading my mind: "And don't think you can replace food with alcohol!" Bugger! This one was cute; I was definitely losing the duel. The nutritionist then went on to explain to me how my metabolism worked. Apparently it was like a fire that needed kindling on a regular basis, not some oaf throwing a fucking big log on it when he got home and suffocating the flames. If I did not eat during the day my metabolism would slow down and think it did not need to consume as many calories from me as it was, therefore I would gain more weight.

We then discussed my diet. I knew that was pretty good as I am a keen amateur chef and knew I ate pretty healthily. Little fried food, plenty of vegetables and fish. I loved spice and hot food so I would always choose some Asian dish over that of fish and chips. We ended my consultation with a weigh-in. I was surprised; just on 17 stone. Helen was not very impressed with my body mass ratio, but I knew that in less than one week I had lost a stone and a half. She left informing me she would advise Dr Sharma of her examination.

Well, that went well! I thought. I would go and see Ken to tell him of my recent activities. Slowly I made my way, trying to get use to the walking stick and went into the ward. No Ken was to be seen - some other bloke was in his bed! A nurse saw my distress and confirmed: "Ken has been transferred to another ward; he has his operation on Monday." I felt gutted; my confidante was gone. I never did see or speak to Ken ever again... a sad fact.

Meanwhile, Bill was sitting on his bed looking very dapper in his outdoor clothes. I sidled up to him and we smiled at each other. The nurse helping him with his coat spoke.

"Bill is going see his new flat," she advised. Bill was being let out of the unit for a couple of hours to vet some new bedsit that social services had dug up for him. A chill went down my spine; I knew that Bill would never get out of here whilst he was homeless.

That was the end of my first week in Aintree University Hospital; one I would not like to repeat in a hurry.

Saturday morning heralded a new day and optimism filled my mind. With a struggle, I washed and managed to dress myself in a sort of fashion. I ate a hearty breakfast and decided I would do my face exercises and some speech therapy. I was content sitting in my chair, articulating vowels out loud, when a familiar red dressing gown appeared. Fuck! I knew I should have closed the door, but the nurses hated that.

Peter waltzed into my room, dressing gown swirling behind him. "Not your room, Peter!" I tried to yell, but the words only came out as a faint Roy Hattersley burble. Peter completely ignored me, as I knew he would, and he studied my rather comfy bed. Oh no, not the bed! "Not your room!" I continued hopelessly. The Scarlet Pimpernel then proceeded to sit on the end of the bed. Oh shit, he is going to lie down and go to sleep.

I was very weak, but managed to stand up from the chair and move towards the bed. "Go! Go! Move!" I slurred, spittle appearing out of my drooling mouth. Peter looked at my expression and stirred. He got up from the bed expecting a tirade, but at the same time his pyjama bottoms fell down. Still moving, he tripped and lay prostrate on the floor with his bare arse facing the ceiling. Fuck fuckidy fuck fuck! What does this look like? An aged kleptomaniac debagged in my room and I was standing over him wearing just boxer shorts.

With all the commotion the cleaners had decided to investigate and the same two ladies that greeted me a week ago entered the room. Hysterical laughter then ensued with no offer of any assistance or help in my plight. Peter was groaning that he had hurt his toe or something, but he was hard to take seriously with his bollocks on display. The whole scene was out of a Brian Rix farce, but it was actually happening, and more importantly, to me.

It took Sister Ratchet and her Storm Troopers to sort the whole thing out. *Another black mark in my portfolio,* I mused. Peter was dutifully despatched back to his ward and I was tasked to clean my mess up. The cleaners were also berated and sent to clean the corridors with toothbrushes. I then resumed my speech exercises and the remainder of Saturday passed without event. That evening, many of my friends visited and I sat in my chair like Cyril Fletcher, albeit with a speech impediment, and retold the day's events.

Sunday was by far a much quieter affair apart from an intriguing event. The porters brought up the food from the kitchen for lunch. The security doors were momentarily wedged open as the trolleys were being prepared to be wheeled in. Peter saw his chance, he made his bolt for freedom and nobody but I was watching. He was on a home run. Then to my astonishment Peter paused at the doors, looked about sheepishly, turned and walked back down the passage. Fake! He had no intention of fleeing the confines of his incarceration, the whole thing had been a bluff. Just like his kleptomania - nothing was ever actually stolen, it all turned up eventually. Peter was a sad individual just looking for attention that nobody had the time to give the poor sod.

I relaxed in my chair listening to the iconic Marvin Gaye classic album *What's Going On*, waiting for visiting hour and looking out of my door for any other interesting incidents when something bought a chill to my spine. Two Porters very quietly were wheeling a trolley past my room with a cardboard coffin on board. The scene bought the reality of my situation crashing back to the forefront of my mind and I knew the person who could help me survive all this was myself.

Monday morning, I had different frame of mind. I decided to put all my efforts wholeheartedly into the rehab of my body and mind. Dracula had already called and taken a few pints of Abel Best Blood and I was looking forward to working with Clair. I wanted to get out of there. The following few days were going to be tiresome and hard, but I knew my body would only repair itself with my help.

That afternoon I once again was busy with my speech exercises when a timid knock on the door distracted me. A young girl of around eighteen stood outside my room.

"Excuse me, Mr Abel?" I bade the newcomer to enter. "Hello I am Jane; Nicola said you might want to help," she explained. The mention of Nicola's name grabbed my attention and I pointed to the chair next to mine. Jane proceeded to inform me she was a student at Liverpool University and Nicola had given her permission to hold a Group Therapy class on the unit. Jane was busy asking for volunteers.

I looked at my dance card and saw it was quite empty that afternoon. I felt that I owed Nicola a favour so I agreed; I would join her class at 2pm. Later on I shuffled down the corridor in good time and found the meeting room opposite my old ward. Entering the room I saw Jane and another student sitting next to her. They had arranged a circle of seats for the participants and about six or seven patients were already seated. I noticed the two young nurses from the ward were at the back obviously shirking their duties.

I took a seat and recognised the posh bloke from my old ward sitting opposite me looking very dapper in striking purple and yellow diagonally striped pyjamas. Jane spoke in a very nervous voice: "Hello everybody, we are still waiting for a couple of people, but perhaps one by one we can all say our names and were we live." With that, she introduced herself as Jane, originally from Leeds but now living in Liverpool. Her mate said her name and she was at Liverpool University too. God, this is going to be like pulling teeth. What the Hell did I agree to this for?

The posh bloke said his name was Roland and he lived in Southport. Poor bastard, he must have had his stroke coming back from shopping in town. Why else was he in Fazakerley? Southport General is a far more refined hospital; he must be gutted to be stuck here.

Introductions were slowly circulating around the room when there was a crash at the door. Expletives were being shouted when the door swung open and a little old lady was pushed into the room in a wheelchair rubbing her knees.

"Sorry," the porter said, "I thought the door was open," The old lady had a typical Scouse face of a mother and grandmother who had been, done and seen everything life could possibly ever had thrown at her on the streets of Liverpool.

"Oh Gladys, Hello and welcome. Roland was just telling everybody his name and where he lived," Jane stuttered.

"Sorry love, what did you say?" the pensioner in the wheelchair loudly responded. I then noticed that Gladys had hearing aids in both ears. *This is going to be priceless!* I thought. Two old dears, one with a speech impediment and one deaf were trying to have a conversation together. Poor Roland was now regressing into a gargle as he tried to repeat himself. "What are you saying love, I can't hear you," Gladys responded. Roland tried harder to be more coherent but now Gladys was losing patience.

"I just said Roland was telling everybody what his name was," the student pressed.

"Yes I know dear, you just told me what his name is!" the pensioner said with perfect logic. "And you have told everybody what my name is."

The two young nurses at the back started to giggle as the student was rapidly losing control over the situation. Gladys then took stock of Roland and noticed his pyjamas. "Oh dear, who made you wear those? Somebody should sort your horizontal hold out love, turn it down a bit!"

That was it; I lost control and started to laugh in my new high pitched warble. I had to get out of the room before my side burst. The two students looked distraught as their Group Session was going tits up but I could not sit there anymore being polite - I had to get out for air and sanity.

I made my escape and left behind in my wake a room of utter confusion. Gladys was shouting about tea; she had only come because she was promised some tea, and poor Roland was muttering about his pyjamas and something about his wife. The other patients were supporting Gladys' requests for refreshment and adding their voices to the fray. I hoped Jane had ordered some Custard Creams with the tea or she was in for a geriatric riot.

Sister Theresa, as I now named her, was on duty. She stopped me and told me I was to go for another heart scan tomorrow at 11am so to be sure I was available. I asked her why. She said that at that morning's meeting, Dr Sharma had asked for it. What I didn't know is that every weekday morning the doctors, nurses, occupation health nurses and physiotherapists met and discussed patient case history. Input was required from each department for further treatment or discharge.

Early that afternoon, four friends called to see me. One was the ex wife of one of my friends, but we had stayed close. She was with three regulars from the Bug that she did not know and had just met. Ray, who is the Quiz Master on Mondays, held out a plastic bag full of Stella. I knew if I was found with that then Ratchet would have my hide. I made a mental note to give them to one of the porters but thanked him anyway. Ray was an interesting character from the Bug bar; intelligent, complex and often very humorous. If for any reason he felt bored whilst having his pint he would regularly rope in unsuspecting regulars to self invented parlour games to keep himself amused.

The games to stay clear of were his disputable sweeps, where punters would part with hard earned cash to subsequently find that amazingly Ray had won again. "I don't understand it; mine was the last horse out!" was a regular excuse heard from Ray. Nobody ever knew where the favourite was hidden, but it definitely did not start off in the ash tray with the other nags.

Conversation was a little staid as the room was quite intimate and these people did not know each other. Ray sensed this discomfort and set about alleviating it. He reached for one of my puzzle books on the shelf.

"Let's have a quiz," he proclaimed. Quickly, he wheeled the table over my bed, put it in a corner and sat the two lads from the Bug behind it. They were team A. Helene and I were placed the other side of the bed and we were team B.

Ray then sat on my bed, and proceeded to go into Monday night mode. Nobody had said a word up to then and we were all a little taken aback with the way the hospital visit was turning out. The two lads from the Bug were stuck on a tricky question: "What was Noddy's profession?" I thought I knew the answer and Ray was just about to hand it over to team B... when there was a knock on the door.

Everybody turned and in stepped a grey haired, quite distinguished gentleman wearing a brown jacket, collar and tie into television studio one. I knew all in the room apart from me thought he was a consultant, but it was actually my brother Anthony. I had not seen him for a couple of years and he had gone very grey. I introduced my brother to the room and everybody made their excuses and left, leaving the two of us alone.

Anthony is a teacher at a private school in Oxfordshire. I think he is Director of Music, whatever that entails. He is seven years older than me and we had grown apart over the years with no occasion to meet. My mother was our last common denominator and now she was in a nursing home our paths seldom crossed. Everything was very civil and he asked about my circumstances.

He did not stay that long as he was due back to Oxford that night but he certainly rattled Ratchet's cage. He has a very officious manner and has an extremely posh voice. He demanded to know exactly what was going on with me, what were the test results of the scans I had taken, prognosis of my condition, everything. Ratchet could not answer all his questions, but my brother was to phone in the morning and expected answers. He left just before dinner and I wondered if upsetting Ratchet was a really good idea.

Clair was early the following morning, but I was glad as I had a scan at 11am. She tied my laces and we went for my morning session. I was gradually improving albeit slowly. I was managing the steps better ascending, but coming down was still a problem. Just before the end of the session a woman in a green uniform introduced herself as Sharon, one of the occupational health nurses, and would I have fifteen minutes to spare. I told her of my scan and was assured she would have me back in time.

I was led into a fully fitted kitchen housed within the rehab unit and was asked to make a cup of coffee and a round of buttered toast. Much spilling of milk and dropping of cutlery later, my breakfast was made. Sharon wanted to know if I lived alone and other pertinent questions. I knew this was a test and if I could not prove that I was self sufficient I would not be allowed home. I thought I had better show off a little so told Sharon I enjoyed cooking and was perfectly good at it. She asked me what my favourite meal was, and I blurted out Thai green curry with chicken. Why on Earth I picked that I have not a clue, I liked it but it was not my favourite.

"Why don't you cook it as tomorrow's lunch?" Sharon suggested. She gave me a piece of paper and pen and told me to write the ingredients down as she would go shopping tonight on her way home. Writing the list was difficult; I was using my left hand now and had only started to learn how to write with it. But eventually I scrawled down something half legible and agreed I would come back tomorrow after my session with Clair.

I looked at the clock and Sharon nodded and bustled me back to my room to find a porter waiting with a wheelchair. I was taken to a different place for my second heart scan and they used slightly different equipment on me. But the whole thing probably only took an hour before I was back on the stroke unit. I walked to my room and saw it was empty, all my things were gone and I gulped.

I looked down the corridor and saw Ratchet beckoning to me, she had a broad smile across her face as she told me that the room was now required for a poorly patient.

"You are now in that ward: bed by the window," she said. It was not my old ward, but one further down the passage and my heart sank. I checked all my stuff and it all seemed to be there, there was nowhere I could display my cards or put my magazines so they were all simply stashed in the bottom of the cupboard. I looked about the ward; I did not recognise any of the faces staring back at me from any of the beds. I then knew that I had to get out of hospital as soon as I could.

That night Nick came to see a very sad individual. I didn't really want to talk much and definitely did not want cheering up. He took my laundry and left pretty soon after.

That night I stayed awake watching films on the DVD player until almost dawn, gutted that Ratchet had finally defeated me.

Wednesday I started my crusade in making my getaway. I badgered Clair to tell me what I had to do to satisfy the physiotherapists so they would not veto my discharge. She told me that it was Simon's final decision, but walking up the steps outside would be a good thing to do. I had occasionally been taken by Clair outside the security doors to a flight of stairs opposite and I had tried scaling them with little success. I pressured her to take me there and then. I struggled and strained with the effort but I was determined to succeed.

Almost shattered, I went to see Sharon and posed the same question. "Cook me a nice dinner and show me you can take care of yourself and I have no problem recommending you for discharge," she said with a smile. I stressed to myself, *This must be the best Thai curry I have ever made.* I then proceeded to peel the garlic, onions, lemongrass, ginger (Asda Aintree apparently does not sell Galangal) chop the chilli and fry off the chicken. A little coconut milk, a teaspoon of Green curry paste a sprinkling of coriander and fish sauce to finish and it was done. It sounds easy but believe me it was not. Trying to grip the food with my right hand and using my left for the delicate knife skills was hard.

Sharon did not seem to be perturbed by the flying bits of food dotting the floor and work surfaces. "We can supply you with an adapted chopping board," she reassured me. She was looking for ways to give me my pass out of here and to help me unlike Ratchet!

Finally, lunch was served and another nurse sat at the table with us to enjoy the fruits of my labour. I must admit it was delicious and all was quiet as the food was polished off with gusto. Just then a familiar head popped around the door. It was Tony, my mate from the Old Boys Football team.

"There you are Frank, bloody typical, a curry!" He then addressed the nurses: "I was told he was sick, but things look okay to me!" They both agreed and said it one of the best meals they had ever eaten. I blushed slightly with the compliments.

Tony later told me when he had come to visit, the whole stroke unit stank of curry as soon as he came through the security doors. He went looking for me and a nurse took him to my ward only to be told by a very irate dinner lady that I had pissed off without informing her and I was having lunch with the nurses in Occupational Health. She didn't know what was wrong with her food; I had eaten it before and I had never complained.

Coming out of the rehab unit I saw a glimpse of Dr Sharma: it was very unusual as the doctors were seldom seen on the wards in the afternoons. I chased him down and collared him.

"When can I be discharged?" I asked eagerly. He told me the decision was not entirely his as the rest of the team had to give their input, but as far he was concerned on the medical side everything had been done for now.

I nearly jumped for joy, in my calculations I just had to persuade Simon that I was capable enough physically and I was home and dry. That night I spoke enthusiastically to Nick that I was hoping to be discharged before the weekend. He tried to dampen down my verve a little knowing I would be devastated if this did not happen.

The Thursday session with Clair was critical and with some effort I managed to scale and descend the stairs outside the unit. I left my walking stick behind as it was a hindrance and with Clair's aid passed the test. I badgered her to influence Simon at Friday's meeting that I had passed all the tests with flying colours. She smiled at me and said she would do her best.

Next I tackled Sister Teresa and lied, telling her that Dr Sharma had told me I was to be discharged on Friday. She looked blank as nobody had told her. I pressed her and asked what obstacles could stop this happening. She went on to tell me that I would have to have preen lights from Occupational Health and physio and then my medication would have to be ready.

Pharmacy would only deliver any medication the same day if they had a prescription before noon. Tomorrow being Friday, they would close for the weekend. The review meeting in the morning ended at 11am so if everybody agreed there would be time. Then she said something that filled my heart with hope.

"I am on the early shift tomorrow and will be sitting in on the meeting, I will do my best!" she said. It all hinged on some chemist if I would get out of this place at least before the weekend.

I could not sleep that night; I was too excited. I was at the nurses' station by about 7am, trying to see Sister Theresa to jolly her up. Ratchet was still on duty and was very suspicious of my activities but knew nothing of my plan. I had arranged with Nick that if all was okay he was to come and collect me. He had very kindly offered the spare room in his house for me to stay for a few days until I was a little stronger, a fact I had let Theresa know.

Time dragged that morning until Theresa walked onto the ward with a piece of paper in her hand and a beaming smile. She told one of the two young nurses to get the prescription to the pharmacy immediately. I texted Nick without delay that everything was okay. He replied: "Let me know what time." I was clock watching and paying no attention to anything but the nurses' activities. The dinner lady came and went and still no news from the pharmacy. It was almost 2pm and Nick had texted me twice to ask what was happening. I was beginning to lose hope when Theresa walked in with a bag in her hand. "Francis, you are to be discharged today!"

I have never heard sweeter words in my life. I immediately contacted my good friend and started getting my belongings together. I looked at the other occupants of the ward who had all heard Theresa; some were looking back at me with the same glare I myself had given to one or two people in the last two weeks. *You lucky bastard!*

Within thirty minutes, Nick had arrived. I already had my coat on and when I saw him and I made a bolt for the exit. "Stop!" Sister Theresa yelled after me. She was holding my medicine, shaking her head. Nick took my arm firmly and whispered, "Slow the fuck down!"

He looked at Theresa. "Are there any instructions?" She said they were all in pharmacy bag. "None that go with him!" pointing at me. She laughed and said I must avoid grapefruit juice as it clashed with one of my tablets, and not to be surprised if I was quite fatigued for the first few days.

I paused, turned around and hugged Theresa. "Thank you, thank you!" I enthused. Then with a flourish of my new walking cane, I made my way to the security doors and departed Aintree University Hospital in a little more dignified manner than I had arrived, in the secure knowledge it was too bloody early for Drive Time!

Chapter Three

REHAB

Walking out into the fresh February air for the first time in a fortnight was magnificent. The chill suddenly hit me and my whole right side started to cramp up with the cold. My hand turned into a ball and my arm fused across my chest as it contracted. I was glad to get into the warmth of the car and the spasm soon faded.

It was strange watching normal life as we drove past, people just going about doing mundane tasks and earning a living. I felt self conscious that people noticed the hunched figure in the car driving past them, saying: "Didn't that used to be Francis Abel?"

As we arrived at Nick's house his wife Helen, or "H" as we all called her, was waiting at the door to greet us. I embraced her and said it was so good of them both to let me stay there. She just laughed and a small voice behind her called for attention as William, their three year old son, wanted to join in the welcoming. To say William was a bit of a livewire is to tarnish the reputation of good upstanding livewires, but what else do you expect, he was a three year old boy!

We moved inside into the warm house and H bought in some hot drinks as I relaxed in an armchair. William was dutifully despatched into the other room to play with his chainsaw as the adults drank their coffee and the chill from outside left my body.

Nick was studying my medicines and I was amazed how much of the stuff there was; Baclofen (A muscle relaxant for my high tone), Simvastatin (cholesterol), Perendipil (blood pressure), Dipyridamole (blood pressure), Clopidogrel (blood pressure), Aspirin (blood thinning) . "If I have to take all that I will rattle around like a pair of Maracas!" I exclaimed. My attention drifted as

Nick was sorting dosages and times and I blankly stared at the TV and I dropped off.

He nudged me awake, and I was led up to the spare bedroom. William thought this was excellent as he was staying up later than one of the adults and jumped about with delight. As soon as my head touched the pillow I crashed out into a deep and peaceful sleep, the first really true rest in a long, long time. Later that evening I was bought a tray with some sandwiches and my medicine, but it did not take me long to resume my well deserved rest. Sleep is in an important factor in recuperation, your body's metabolism and daylight functioning almost turns off and all the energy is diverted into repair work.

The following morning I awoke feeling a little groggy as I had a little too much sleep but felt stronger for it. I could hear CBeebies on TV down stairs and knew William was up and about. I laboriously donned a t-shirt and shorts and went to wash. Coming out of the bathroom for the first time, I noticed Nick's stairs were quite steep and the hand rail was on the right hand side. The only way I could tackle this obstacle was to descend by bum. I carefully sat on the landing and similar to a dog scratching his arse shuffled to the top stair. Then I descended step by step sitting on each stair one at a time. William had come to see what the noise was and thought it a great game, joining me on the last few steps. "Wow! Mum and Dad never do that!" the youngster said with great admiration. I could see in his expectant beaming face that I was going to be a most welcome addition to his range of play things.

It was fortunate that I was discharged on Friday as Nick and H both had the weekend off to help with my resettlement. The peace of Saturday was intermittent due to friends calling. William interpreted these house callers were for his benefit as they were arriving at his house and greeted each one with gusto and unfailing enthusiasm, that fact that he did not have a clue who any of them were did not in the slightest seem to bother him.

Later that day we took a trip to get some air at the shore. North Liverpool has a long coastline the links up with the Fylde Peninsula facing the Irish Sea. And the area in Crosby is called Burbobank, affectionately known as Sunset Strip. Believe it or not I have seen some of the most dramatic skies and colourful sunsets in the world from my very own beach. Over the past few years the authorities have worked hard in cleaning up this part of the coastline and have built a proper promenade and grassy bank area for residents and visitors alike to enjoy. In fact a major art exhibition by Anthony Gorley named *The Iron Men* is based along the shoreline. Dozens of six feet tall naked figures of men buried in the sand are scattered all over the beach staring out to sea.

We parked the car and I took my first tentative steps out in the real world. I do not know why, but I hoped nobody would recognise me looking so fragile and frail. I was also conscious of strangers staring at me tottering along with my walking stick. We came to a small ramp leading from the car park to the walkway. I couldn't manage to negotiate it without Nick's help. I felt so embarrassed, never in my life had I been so handicapped and I felt so vulnerable. The wind coming off the sea was blowing hard and there was moisture in the air. I shivered and H decided that perhaps that was probably enough for the day; she then screamed after her errant child who was busy chasing a plastic bag in the wind.

Sunday, after breakfast, Nick suggested that we all took a trip to Speke Retail Park and see if we could find some trendy shoes that didn't have laces for my benefit. I was not too sure if I wanted to face the public again so soon, but Nick convinced me it would be good for me.

Parking the car at Speke Retail Park I knew this had been a mistake. Hoards of Sunday shoppers were busy milling around looking for the bargains that in truth were available all year round. I was led to a massive sports shop that looked like a Rugby Scrum. I knew I was in for trouble, even with my walking stick as a warning to the stupid I was jostled aside by busy shoppers who stared at me as if to say, "Are you fucking daft, get out of my way!" I was petrified because I knew if I was barged any harder I would just topple over and be trampled on.

Nick saw the pure panic in my face and led me to the safety of a shoe counter as he went to look for a pair in my size. But even with the protection of the counter I was pushed and jostled with eager bargain hunters not wanting to miss out on the deal of the century that might have been had. When he returned I had gone and he found me cowering under the sanctuary of safety behind a pillar. He raised his hand with a pair of white training shoes with Velcro fastenings. "Size 8," he said, I just nodded and pointed to the door. He looked very tired with my behaviour, but I just could not stand one more moment in that shop. When we arrived home I was absolutely shattered and was to put bed. I did not wake until the next morning.

The next few days was the same of any rehab trying to adapt to the environment and compromising with your disabilities. I could not properly wash as Nick's shower was in a corner bath that I simply could not get into, so I bathed by sitting on the edge. Eating was the same; I could not use my right hand so I used my left. I even began to learn how to write with my left hand, some of my friends say my writing is more legible now than before, as I was quite famous for having doctor's scrawl. But my biggest problem was speech, with my daily exercises my face had gone back to almost normal, but I still found speaking very difficult especially on the phone.

The days passed and I was slowly getting stronger, I was obsessed with following my health regime. Eating three times a day, taking my medicine at exactly the correct time, religiously performing my speech therapy and taking plenty of rest. I began thinking about going home and the differences between Nick's house and mine and what problems I would have to overcome. I knew that was the next big challenge, my first night alone at home but I wanted it so much.

After about ten days I persuaded Nick and H that I could cope going back to Chez Regina. He agreed, only if for the first few days I had somebody babysitting me. I then phoned around all of my friends and was to be chaperoned each night by who was ever available. Stepping back into my own house was one of the most wonderful experiences I will ever have. Chez Regina had always been a happy home. I had been there since I was 30 and had enjoyed every day living there.

After a few days I was visited by some Occupational Health workers who slowly moved about the house assessing what equipment might help me. The first was a plastic plank that sat across the roll top bath and allowed me to first sit, swing my legs over, and then stand up in the shower. It was wonderful, being able to fully immerse myself in the water and bathe completely all over. The other additions were less dramatic such as kitchen aids and so forth but they were welcome help. It suddenly occurred to me that I had accepted all the assistance without complaint, it had not hurt my manhood to accept these gifts, it was pure and simple common sense. Shortly after that I politely told my chaperones that I could manage by myself.

The following week, H took me to a physio we had picked out of Yellow Pages. I happened to know Sue from years ago when I had used to DJ. From about fifteen I had been a keen amateur DJ, mostly of soul music, and started as a precocious little fart named King Arthur the Soul DJ with trade mark black trilby hat. Can you imagine a fifteen year old kid wearing a trilby hat around Liverpool? Yes! I deserved every bit of stick that I got and then perhaps a bit more to boot. Since then I have performed at just about every occasion, from diamond wedding celebrations to nightclubs in Norway.

Sue was very taken aback when she saw me, but we began twice weekly intensive physiotherapy sessions. Starting with the massage of my limbs, they were stiff almost plank like and Sue was trying to break down the high tone which was restricting a lot of my movement. I was taking Baclofen to try and remedy this, but the trouble with the muscle relaxant drug is that it does not target a particular part of the body. I was on a fairly low dosage and if you simply took a massive amount then it would be like Pinocchio's wires had been cut.

After a couple of months I slowly started to respond and Sue suggested that it might be a good idea to try something different. The clinic had access to a remedial school's specially adapted swimming pool and I was to take hydrotherapy classes. I loved swimming and heartily agreed to the new plan: Wednesday in the clinic and Friday in the pool.

Friday came around and I packed my water wings and flippers and waited for Delta Taxis to take me to the pool. The reality was that Sefton Council had given a grant for the pool to the school under the edit that they had to take a certain percentage of community cases. I was greeted by one of Sue's assistants and shown to a cubicle to change. The heating was full on very different to the chill day outside. My blood pressure was checked 140 over 88; a little high, but okay, and then I was led to the pool.

It was quite tiny but only around five patients were seen at one time. Sue was already in the water and pointed to some gradual steps descending into the pool with a guide rail for assistance. There was another physiotherapist along with Sue and the assistant up on the apron. I was then fitted with floats supporting my head and waist and underwent my first hydrotherapy class. It was really quite a pleasant experience and I could feel the water giving gentle resistance to my limbs as I moved them around in the water. After approximately twenty minutes the session was over and the floats removed.

I loved swimming especially on holiday and in warm water. I quite forgot where I was and the minute the floats were undone I dived backwards into the water. Of course, my right arm and leg would not give me buoyancy and I quickly submerged. "You stupid twat!" I gurgled to myself as my head hit the bottom. Hands were around me in seconds and hauled me to the surface. "What on Earth do you think you are doing?!" a very irate Sue scolded me. I smiled it was more fun than I had had in weeks.

The pool was then cleared of patients as Andrew had arrived. A wretched figure in a wheelchair flanked by two carers was being lifted from the chair into a seated hammock attached to a winch that could be lowered into the pool. The poor being could not have been more than thirty years old and spittle was burbling out of his mouth as he attempted speech. The assistant saw my quizzical stare.

"Very sad, Andrew had a car accident on his honeymoon five years ago and permanently damaged his spine," she said, sadly.

The whole scene bought my own situation into perspective. Disability is a relative thing. No disability is good, but perhaps with some disabilities you can still get on and have a good quality of life. I had an epiphany; I could work hard at mine and improve, and every improvement made my disabilities less and less. A steely resolve took hold of me, one that still lives with me today thanks to Andrew.

The following weeks and months were tough work. I knew I had to adhere to my plan and follow instructions to the letter. I kept a strict diet and was losing more and more weight. I had a new pal, Linz, who was the wife of Sandy. She began to ferry me around during the week to appointments also my weekly shop at Tesco. Without her I would have been scuppered.

After three months I was called back to Aintree University Hospital to the outpatients department to see Dr Sharma for a review. The Stroke Centre is newly built and quite impressive; very modern and is actually in the same building as the Stroke Unit but on the ground floor. I took the usual tests, Dr Sharma reviewed my medication and told me to make an appointment in three months' time. He also asked me to see the Occupational Health nurse down the passage.

I had a good chat with the nurse and she asked me to write a list of the things I would like to help me and put them in order of priority. We could then tackle the top three this visit.

1) Home Occupational Health aid with my Hand and Arm.
2) A Blue Badge for car parking.
3) Aid in trying to get back to drive.

She was to contact Sexton Health Authority and set up my local Occupational Health Clinic to contact me. She would also contact the department concerned with issuing Blue Badges and inform them of my case. Finally, she gave me a list of companies that specialised in car adaptions for the disabled.

Within two weeks I had another physiotherapist to add to my weekly schedule. Also, the Blue Badge department sent and permitted my application. Finally, after my own self assessment, I deemed the only real addition to the car I needed was a little spinner attached to the steering wheel and applied for one on line.

My new Home Therapist was Julie, a nurse who only lived a few streets away from me. She started each session with some gentle massaging of my arm and hand then we would continue with finer and more delicate exercises such as jigsaws. The first day when she arrived on my doorstep in her uniform I almost dragged her in from the street; I did not want any of the neighbours seeing her. I know it sounds very stupid and indeed somewhat vain but I was embarrassed.

I had also recently gone shopping with H and bought an exercise bike that Nick had dutifully assembled for me; it was in response to a suggestion that Sue had made about increasing my daily exercise on a gentle basis. Each morning there was a short regime of exercises and cycling that I would gradually build up over time.

My week was now completely filled. Morning exercises followed by a walk, one hour of speech therapy then the day's specialist visit depending on what day it was.

About one week later my spinner arrived and my friend from the Bug, Dave, who is a mechanic, fitted it for me. With some trepidation I sat behind the wheel of my car and started the engine. I did not know if it would start after such a long time as the car had just been sat outside my house inactive, but there were no problems with the efficient German technology.

So with some nerves I decided to go for a test drive. Dave had long since gone and I was flying solo for the first time in months. Slowly I edged the automatic into the road, but it was difficult judging how hard to press the accelerator and brake to give exactly the right pressure using my right foot. I stopped in the middle of the road changed my position in the seat and resumed using my left foot.

I must admit I did not feel I had total control of the vehicle. The spinner on the wheel was really weird to get used to and the car was weaving all over the road. Going in a straight line was getting easy, but turning corners and navigating through traffic lights was a nightmare. Finally, I reached Derby Road in Bootle: it is a three lane road with a 50 mph speed limit. I decided to hog the middle lane and keep my speed to 30 mph.

Then everything went tits up. Things were becoming a blur, cars were passing me on the inside and outside and I was losing focus of where I should be. The car started to weave again and I slowed almost a crawl as my brain could not decode this information fast enough for me. The journey home was arduous and slow: I made my decision to leave the driving for the time being.

That night, which was Friday, Nick and Sandy called and took me for a little outing to the beer garden of a local pub for a drink. Since my illness, I had hardly touched alcohol because of my diet, and I had noticed that I could really feel the effects on my body with only a couple of drinks. I did not know if this was because of the medication or that of my new brain. Even today my capacity for alcohol is greatly reduced; I still love a couple of pints, but more that and I get drunk really easily and have little control over my limbs. I told my pals about my morning drive; Nick went ballistic and gave me a moralistic lecture of my reckless and irresponsible behaviour.

Apparently, it was not just my life I had endangered but every motorist in Liverpool. I did not know why he was getting so heated, I told him that I had taken a taxi to the pool the other day and a one arm man was driving. My little anecdote did nothing to calm his ire, in fact he seemed to be getting madder.

"The trouble with you, Frank, is that you don't accept and admit that you have fucked up!" Once again I sat like a scolded schoolboy. *Perhaps he had a point,* I thought, but I didn't let him know.

Life continued with my new regime on a regular and continuous basis. I was called back to see Dr Sharma again. He suggested that for more youthful patients a new experimental treatment was being tested. Willing to try anything, I agreed to see his colleague and undergo Botox treatment.

Two days later I was back at the Stroke Centre waiting for my appointment. A man in his late fifties on a walking stick took the seat next to me. "Have you had a stroke?" the man said. I turned and looked into his eyes and I saw pure, undiluted fear and terror held within them. Poor bastard, a first timer. He had it all to go through, all those days, weeks, months and years of pain and heartache. I simply said, "It does get better," and smiled warmly at him.

I was called into this tiny room smaller than my WC. It was filled with two doctors and two nurses and I was asked to take a seat. The senior doctor was showing his apprentices the procedure he was about to perform on a Flip Chart. He then showed me an array of needles from very large to quite tiny and a few bottles of Botox.

"You are a very lucky man; do you know how much this amount of Botox would cost?" he asked. "Does it look like I use Botox, you numpty?" I scowled at him. He continued his lecture, filling up the largest of the syringes.

"We will make eight or nine injections from the shoulder down to the muscle in between the fingers," he explained. I gulped. My arm would look like a pin cushion by the time this guy had finished with me.

My current muscle relaxant was Baclofen, but as I have mentioned before the drug does not target a particular part of the body, it just relaxes all of the muscles generally. Botox was going to be administered to the exact part of my body the high tone was most prevalent. The first needle went into the top of my arm by my bicep. The pain was excruciating, saliva filled my mouth and I thought I was going to be sick, it progressively got worse and worse as the vicious fluid was being forced into my body. The room became sweltering hot and I was now as white as a sheet.

The people in the room started spinning around me and the face of the consultant became the mask of Sir Laurence Olivier's in Marathon Man, where dressed as a dentist in a white coat he tortured Dustin Hoffman his patient. It all became too much for me and I fainted. Seconds later I came to, nurses were lifting me onto a bed and Sir Larry was continuing with the second injection.

The pain was not diminishing whatsoever as the second dose was administered. To this day I do not know what the problem was as I had grown accustomed to syringes and needles. Had Sir Larry jabbed the first injection straight into a nerve? Had he mistakenly use glue instead of Botox? And more importantly, why did stupid vain people inject this stuff in their faces? After three more doses I simply cried out, "No more!"

Sir Larry ceased, satisfied I had divulged all the secret information he wanted and now he could release me. It took me about ten minutes before I could stand up and I greeted Sully, my mate, who was waiting to give me a lift home; a very different individual than the one he saw disappear into the surgery. My face was still white as I was escorted by the two nurses back to the waiting room. I didn't utter a word on the way back, my arm throbbed and painful ache was growing and growing.

That night it was impossible to get any sleep. I have never known such excruciating pain in my life like it. The only thing I could liken it to was severe toothache down my whole arm. When I finally settled in bed and the pain had died down to a dull ache if I changed positions a millimetre, a shooting spasm would wrack my body and I literally did cry out.

It took six months for the drug to finally work its way out of my system, during that time I was addicted to MS Contin, a powerful morphine based drug to alleviate the pain. But I hate that drug, it makes me physically sick. I was deprived of sleep for six months and could not eat food as I would throw it back up. My rehab was put on the back burner as I felt so wretched, and I lost over a stone and a half in weight. I now weighed just fifteen stone; I had lost three and a half stones from the day I was admitted to hospital.

After that horrendous episode I slowly started to scale up my exercises and effort into my rehab once more. My speech therapy had reached another level; I had progressed from exercise to reading books out loud for about an hour each day. I had decided whilst I was locked away in my conservatory doing this I might start a new project to keep my brain active. From when I was fifteen and my first DJ days I had been an avid music collector. I had assembled a massive, very eclectic and varied collection from Jazz, Classical,

Country to Disco and Dance. But my favourite was Soul Music and out of my collection of around nearly ten thousand CDs, seven and twelve inch singles, also albums on vinyl, about 70% of it was Soul Music.

I decided to transfer all this music on to my PC in digital format. My back room was like a recording studio anyway. I had twin Technics decks, an eight channel mixer and a flight case housing all the amplifiers, active equipment I needed to perform. I purchased a little gizmo that connected directly from one of my turntables to the PC; some software then converted the vinyl to digital format on to iTunes. CDs were easy, I just burned them straight on to iTunes. The whole operation took a year to complete. But now I knew I had all my music portable which unbeknown to me was going to prove very useful in the years to come.

Whilst I was in hospital I had a visit from Colin. The office staff and my colleagues had made a collection and Colin had bought me a huge crate of fresh and exotic fruits, together with a huge array of flowers. There was too much of both gifts and most of residents on the unit benefited from the kind gesture. Whilst he was there, Colin had said I qualified for six months on full pay then a further six months on half pay due to the company's medical insurance.

This was a large weight off my mind as I had a year's breathing space to concentrate on my rehab and not worry about money. I had already made the decision that from now on I would take my life in bite size chunks and never plan more than six months ahead. This policy has certainly worked as I do not worry about the future and how I am going to finance myself; it has given me great clarity and freedom of mind to focus on the present day. Even today the most important thing in my life is my health and this comes before family, friends, work and material things. I have forgotten all about life's essentials: cars, luxury clothes, fancy restaurants, big houses and even collecting music. Believe me; it takes very little time to settle to a life without material shackles.

Most rehabilitation of any kind is extremely boring and it would be wrong of me to let you endure a day to day journal of my arduous exploits over the days, months and years. Suffice to say I kept a strict and rigid regime slowly building from physiotherapy of limbs, to hydrotherapy and subsequently and eventually to a gym regime. I have not driven since that day!

Chapter Four

TENTATIVE STEPS

When I first visited Sue at the physiotherapy, there was a large diagram on the wall of the human brain. It explained the differences that were common in people depending what side of the brain the stroke had occurred.

Obviously whatever side of the brain the stroke happened in, physically the opposite side of your body was affected. But more interesting to me was the physiological differences that occurred.

If the stroke happened on the left hand side of your brain, which was so in my case, then normally the physical effects are greater. But on the reverse side there was a chance of more physiological damage. Bringing with it erratic behaviour, mood swings and forgetfulness. There is also a chance, depending on the severity of the attack, of permanent damage to vision and in extreme cases eventually blindness.

The brain does not repair the damaged cells, they are gone forever. What it does is to rewire itself and teach new cells to operate some of the old functions. That is why rehab is so boring, it has to be. The monotonous repetition of exercises eventually gets through. But it cannot rewire all the functioning if it does not have many healthy replacement cells to work with. That is why the adverts ask you to act quickly; you can save more of the person that way.

Physically I could see my defects and I was taking remedial action to combat my problems in that department. But mentally I still lacked confidence; I continually was mentally exhausted and I would lose concentration easily. That is why now I am far less tolerant of boring people than I used to be. In the past getting stuck with somebody like Tony Hamill in the Bug, I would stay in their company until I could think of a polite excuse like: "The world's running out of oxygen, and I need to go outside and save some in a couple of plastic bags." But now I just tend to walk away and don't give a fuck whose feelings I hurt.

I knew I had to have something to focus and grab my brain's attention other than my day to day routines. Then in June the soul night came around to give me that emphasis. Each year for over a decade now I had promoted an annual soul night, originally for my mates and their other halves, but the event became bigger and bigger as the popularity had grown and word had got around. It had started in a small hall with about a hundred people, and then in 2004 I charted the Royal Daffodil (one of the Mersey ferries) and hosted our first soul night on the waves.

My mates thought I was crazy as just to hire the boat was over three thousand pounds, then PA hire, security, ticket printing and other extras. We would have to make over four thousand pounds on ticket money to break even. That would mean we would have to get around three hundred and fifty punters on the boat and charge them in excess of ten pounds a head for the night. Normally we would have one hundred and fifty people charging a fiver. This was going to be a big step up and all to see four amateur soul DJs play their favourite music.

But I was not deterred and went ahead. The boat had two enclosed decks: upper and lower and a viewing open air deck upstairs. Two PAs were set up, one on each floor and I separated the music policy from northern, modern soul and Tamla Motown upstairs to Philly, 70s and more current soul downstairs. The weather that evening was beautiful and the boat sailed right up the coast past Crosby into a Burbobank special sunset. Coming back it slowed down as the Liverpool City skyline was illuminated against the dark night.

I had done it, sold all the tickets and the night was a huge success. The following two years I had repeated the evening with the same amount of success and now I had been asked if it was going to go ahead this June, obviously because of my illness. The night had a core following and tickets were in demand weeks ahead of the event, people needed to know.

We had a little meeting, my fellow DJs and I. Johnny Hendo, my soul brother, mentor and guru, and Sandy, an old friend. We agreed that the night would go ahead, but I would take a more of a background role. This was primarily for two reasons; firstly I did not know if I physically could cope and secondly I was not ready to face that many people at one time emotionally. I had only just about managed to face my old friends in The Bug a couple of weeks past, but three hundred and fifty people sounded daunting to me.

I was reluctant to face old acquaintances for a number of reasons. My speech had improved dramatically, but I was still not confident speaking in front of large numbers. I still needed my cane to walk and needed to sit down frequently as I fatigued easily. But I suppose the main reason was vanity, I did not resemble my old confident self both physically and in persona. I was a little ashamed that the old Francis Abel had been replace by this more timid, frail version.

The evening arrived and again it was a complete sell out I spent most of the evening sitting behind Hendo as he rocked the upstairs lounge with classic old soul night favourites; Jimmy Radcliffe, Ace Spectrum and Barbara Aklin to name but a few. The punters loved it and the dance floor was packed all night. My seat behind the upstairs equipment was ideal for me to enjoy the party and also to meet old friends on a one to one basis. I was thoroughly enjoying the whole night when Sandy persuaded me to join him on the final set downstairs.

I went into the throng of the downstairs salon about midnight and edged behind the decks. I had been in a similar place hundreds of times over the last forty years but tonight I was crapping myself. I switched the microphone to live and in a weak, faltering voice

I managed to say just two simple words: "Good evening." I was stunned by the reception I received, there seemed to be a pregnant pause before I spoke, people willing me to succeed, then a loud, continuous applause. I was truly humbled by the reception. I could only do one thing in acknowledgement, play my music, so turning up the faders blasted out the Detroit Spinners' *I'll be Around.*

We had never staged the soul night as a profitable enterprise. Any money raised we normally gave back to the Punters in form of free CDs or giveaways. I had decided to give all profits we made now and events in the future to Different Strokes, an organisation set up to help younger people who are fighting to win the battle after having had a stroke. A relatively small organisation, but one that seemed to fit the requirements that were closest to my heart. Hendo, Sandy and Kev F, who was the fourth DJ, were in complete agreement with the donation and it seemed to give the evening an added dimension.

The Soul Boat seemed to break down a mental barrier and I was far more comfortable meeting and greeting people after that. The public in general have no idea, but anybody with a slight abnormality gets the *What's up with him?* glance. It sometimes only lasts for a fraction of a second, but with more ignorant people it is a downright rude stare. However, the person they are checking out receives that look dozens of times a day. It does take time to adapt to, but after the Soul Boat I had more confidence to ignore it. Unwittingly, my mental rehab was also now starting to take shape.

In August, the new football season started. I had a season ticket for Everton in the Park End Stand, but had not used it since I had come out of hospital. Although I had been following my team's performances avidly by radio and TV, I had let my friend Sully take the seat next to my usual companion Kev and I had agreed with Sully that he now took my ticket on a more permanent basis and I would pick my games. I missed going to see my team play; I had followed them since I was about five and the ground was only about ten minutes from my home. My friends were mostly Blue Noses but some of the more misguided ones supported Liverpool.

To be honest, during my lifetime Liverpool have been the more successful team, but once you nail your colours to the mast there is no going back, and as for fashion we have the upper hand. How can you possibly look chic in red? Red goes with ginger hair, buses, freckles and embarrassment - not fashionable at all in my book. So, at least in the pubs after the games we hold the upper hand.

Goodison Park is a very old stadium first built in 1892, and like the old, mostly defunked stadiums is situated amongst a myriad of small streets with houses and shops in abundance. The council in its infinite wisdom, or more likely money making greed, have all but stopped parking anywhere near the ground on match days. My reluctance to visit the Grand Old Lady was not on footballing reasons, although I had felt like that in the past, but on sheer logistics.

But that day, Everton were playing Wigan Athletic, not the most mouth watering fixture in the 2007/2008 calendar, nevertheless one that I wanted to go to dearly. In fact the last time I remembered seeing Wigan I was in hospital. I smiled to myself with the progress I had made. My friend could not park the car anywhere near so decided to drop me off at the bottom of Spellow Lane, and I would walk up to the ground. I had deliberately left home early to miss the crowds, but still I felt very vulnerable tottering up the road on my cane. My walking had improved but the problem was my balance, if I should get a big shove in the back I knew I would simply topple over and getting back up on my feet again would be trouble.

Still, I managed to negotiate my way to the stadium and entered the Park End turnstile. Under the stand the problem was magnified as there was less avoidance space and some of the punters were far from sober. I decided to take my seat early and navigated the stairs to my place in a rather stop, swerve, rest and go manner. Anyway it was all worth the effort, we won 2-1, although typically Everton. Wigan scored a late goal that had all the home fans biting their finger nails till the final whistle.

It was great to be back watching my team. However, after the game I decided that although I had loved going to Goodison Park it was simply too exhausting to endure every other week. I would go whenever I felt strong enough and that way it would be more of a treat. In my mind another milestone had been achieved and another tick could be placed against my "things to conquer" list.

My full pay from my company ran out in September and I then went down to a medical insurance payment of half of my salary for the next six months. I was now receiving incapacity benefit of around eighty pounds per week, but I still knew I would have to dip into my savings to supplement my monthly income. Still, the main focus of my life was my health and to the regime I had now. I was obsessive about continuing on with the tedious, humdrum exercise and diet programme that I religiously adhered to. Even if I could find some part-time job that I could do, it would interfere with my improvements and nothing was going to do that.

I considered what type of job I was even capable of doing. My physical and mental capabilities would hinder most of my endeavours for even the most mundane of tasks. I had taken jobs in the past that I was not really qualified to do, but never physically unable to perform or for that matter even to actually get to.

My first ever position highlighted that: after failing my mathematics O level four (or was it five?) times, my parents deemed that my chosen career should be in banking. It was a ridiculous decision that ended in an unmitigated disaster as National Westminster Bank and I clashed daily over my frivolous and wayward behaviour. Every day I dreamt up new pranks to alleviate my boredom to be constantly berated and thwarted by the poor aggravated and incensed Branch Sub Manager.

It came to a head one cataclysmic day when half the residents of Formby were queuing outside the bank seething with anger and brandishing Court summons aloft as they desperately tried to gain an audience with the Manager. Of course, the whole farce was my fault, some stupid idiot had placed me in charge of setting up the Council Rates Standing Orders and apathetically and bored I had missed out the relevant data for payments from half our accounts.

The complaints went on for weeks as different payment dates were missed. The branch even installed separate complaints booth for irate rates payers that I was permanently ensconced to receive a barrage of daily verbal abuse from apoplectic housewives with nothing better to do.

Subsequent jobs ended in similar fashion as I was forced by my parents to accept any reasonable offer of employment that came my way and the fact that I was not qualified for most seemed to pass their notice. Everything from singeing myself as a short order chef to burning myself with chemicals in a chrome plating factory. No, if I was to try and attempt to do any work whatsoever I would have to choose very carefully what was on offer and consider if I was capable of doing it.

The following few months passed very slowly and as winter started to bite, the cold came with it. Whenever I was not out doing some rehab work I lived like a recluse as I could not stand the cold outside; it still affected my body drastically. Within a few seconds of being exposed to the cold the whole right side of my body spasmed and my high tone kicked in so my muscles contracted with spasticity.

Then in December my company contacted me that Colin, my boss, and a person from Human Resources would be coming to visit me. It was two weeks before Christmas and I had been busy trying to tidy the house up for the festive season as I knew friends would be coming to see me. This time of the year had never been kind to me; both my father and brother had died around Christmas and with it being an emotive time anyway those memories are rekindled every year.

The bell sounded and I opened the door to find Colin and a lady I had never met standing there. She introduced herself as Siobhan and I ushered them both into the house out of the cold. The house was hot, almost like an aquarium, as I now liked it that way. Who would have thought I would have turned into a guppy in another life?

I gave them a brief account of my activities over the past six months as the conversation started with pleasantries. Colin was amazed how much weight I had lost.

Then Siobhan spoke. "Francis, the company is making major restructuring of many parts of the business due to the financial situation." Colin chipped in, "Already one hundred people have taken early retirement or have been made redundant."

I gulped as I knew what they were preparing me for. "In your case the company has decided that redundancy would the appropriate course of action," Siobhan continued. Then Colin went on to explain that my team had been split up and that all of the guys had been placed into other parts of the business. I now longer had a team to manage and therefore did not have a role within the company.

I did not utter a word as I was quite shocked. Siobhan saw my horror and quickly tried to alleviate my distress. "This is only a consultation period Francis; in the next two weeks I will write and let you know your options." I knew what the options would be, take redundancy or apply for a job I could not possibly do, in a place I could not possibly get to. I had hoped by this time I would have recovered enough to resume my duties, but I knew now that I was very far away from that. What did I expect? The company would keep on paying me forever? I should have suspected something when they took my car away a few weeks ago.

The meeting then seemed to close very rapidly as both my visitors had other meetings to attend that day, or nice Christmas lunches to attend. As I closed the door after the departing assassins, I muttered "Merry bloody Christmas to you too," under my breath and decided to ride my exercise bike for twenty minutes or so. I cranked up my sound system in the back room and Aretha Franklin boomed out as I peddled my way to oblivion.

Christmas that year was not my happiest as I had the gnawing doubt wavering over my head and my immediate future was uncertain. I had gone over mathematically my financial situation and tried to work out how much time I could afford to live at home before I would have to sell the house to release what equity there was. I had lived at Chez Regina seventeen years, it had been a very happy home in all those years and something I dearly loved, but I could see no option but to sell. It all depended how much time I could buy with the redundancy money and my savings together with my incapacity benefit. But amazingly I accepted this situation as part of my bite by bite philosophy and to take the appropriate action when it raised its ugly head.

In January, the letter arrived from work stating my redundancy payment would be in the region of eight thousand pounds together with a list of job opportunities within the company. I scanned the list and there was nothing I could realistically apply for. I had ruled myself of any field based work as I could not drive and all the office based jobs were in places I would have to drive to. But in truth I knew I was still far from capable of doing any job and knew returning to employment was not an option. I had to sign and return the documentation within a few days, but not today, I thought.

Then an amazing thing happened. The directors or big wigs must have been horrified to see exactly how much one hundred redundancy packages would cost them and directed their minions to find other options to reduce the cost. In my case, Siobhan did, and looked into the medical insurance policy. She found to my benefit that the policy did not expire after six months as they had thought, it was for three years if the employee fitted certain medical criteria.

Siobhan phoned me to explain the situation. I could still take redundancy or I could receive half pay for another two and a half years. Which would I prefer? It was no contest. I immediately accepted the half pay and would be ready to receive a representative from the insurance company when they wanted to come and examine me. A week later, a questionnaire arrived by post from the insurance people which I dutifully completed and returned to them. I had given them access to all my medical files so they could see my history and waited for their visit.

I returned to my calculations and discovered that if I was more economical at home then half pay together with incapacity benefit would be sufficient to pay the bills and live without touching my meagre savings. I breathed a big sigh of relief, I could return to my rehab one hundred percent without having to worry.

Then a few days later something really eerie happened to me. I returned home from a Hydro session at the pool and must have caught a chill or something because I started to shiver and feel very dizzy. I went up to bed and decided to lie down for a couple of hours under the duvet to warm myself. But the symptoms got steadily worse and I began to worry. I was now getting pains in my leg and felt much disorientated my head was spinning on the pillow and I was feeling nauseous.

I struggled down the stairs, took my evening medicine and also some Co-codamol for the pain. I did not sleep much that night and stirred in the morning feeling just as rotten. I shivered despite the fact I had left the heating on and I had no strength in my limbs to rise. I thought about phoning my GP, but even if she did agree to see me who was going to let her in the sodding house. So I just stayed put hoping it was a twenty four hour bug or something.

Two whole days I lay in bed feeling very ill indeed. The pain in my leg had subsided somewhat, but I was still feeling constantly horribly nauseous, I had tried to be sick several times, but I had had nothing to eat to throw up with. After about three days I was feeling strong enough to get up but could still eat very little. I did not venture out of the house for almost two weeks and in that time I was too weak to do any of my rehab work. When I could finally muster enough strength to visit my doctor she couldn't tell me what had been wrong, but took some blood samples for analysis. She also weighed me and I had lost nearly a stone of weight in a fortnight. I was now under fourteen stone, four and a half stone lighter than when I had my stroke almost exactly one year ago.

After my illness I found a disconcerting side effect it had left me with. I had seemed to have lost my appetite and taste buds. That weekend I wandered to the Bug to meet Richie. Normally Rich and I were like the Tetley Bitter Men, we had our own oversized, engraved tankards (Yes I know, a trifle Albert Tatlock) and quaffed away to our hearts content. Recently, I had cut back on the quantity, but still enjoyed a pint of Bitter. Richie was a philistine when it came to his favourite tipple; he would not thank you for a pint of Real Ale, and instead nurtured his Tetley free flow as if it were ambrosia from the Gods.

I took one sip of my pint and disaster! It tasted disgusting, sweet and very sickly. Richie tasted his and said there was nothing wrong with the beer. Oh my God! I could not drink my favourite beer. Was this permanent? How could I survive life without the crutch of Tetley Bitter? I tried Guinness, Stella, and Carling all to no avail, the only thing my palate seemed to accept was cider. This was going to be a long, hard winter indeed.

Mike, the licensee, thought that this dilemma was most amusing. In fact the last time I had actually seen him laugh was when he had put the prices up. Cliffy, one of the regular patrons of the bar was convinced that Mike used to go down to the cellar not to change barrels but for a secret giggle, as nobody could possibly be that permanently miserable.

I still do not know what that little episode was about, but it was my first proper illness since my stroke. Of course, the first thing that comes to mind is, "Oh shit, another stroke," but it taught me one very important lesson. I will have other illnesses in my life and not all will be linked to my condition; the thing to do is not to panic and take stock of the situation. Easier said than done!

My weight loss had been considerable. When I was in hospital Dr Sharma had asked me to lose three stones but I had decided my goal was to double that. In my first year I had shed well over that and I was pleased with my progress. However, every good action has a flip side and mine was, none of my clothes fitted me. I was on a quite strict budget so fitting out a new wardrobe was going to take time, plus the fact what I buy now hopefully will not fit me in twelve months or so.

My first action was to make wardrobe space. I had decided to jettison nearly all my old clothes, more of a gesture than anything. I was never going to return to my old body and promised myself that whatever happens in the future I would never buy such large clothes ever again. Clearing out my wardrobes and cupboards was a pleasant cleansing project. Firstly, I decided to start on my business clothes. I had never quite bought Hugo Boss, but I had approximately ten very good suits. Next the size eighteen and a half collar shirts, there must have been at least twenty. I bundled these items in numerous large sacks and Linzi and myself delivered them to local charity chops over the next few days.

The following week it was the turn of my leisure clothes, so numerous pairs of jeans, endless amount of t-shirts together with all my XXL underwear, all were despatched in a similar fashion to my suits. Finally, it was the turn of my outdoor jackets and coats, which included three leather and a number of fashionable bomber style jackets that simply did not now go any ware near fitting me.

The whole process took over three weeks and around twenty large refuse sacks. I could not possibly guess the monetary value of all the items but it must have been colossal.

All that I can say is that there are dozens of very sharp dressed, rather rotund hobos roaming the streets of Crosby. If any visitors came to North Liverpool for the first time they would think that the area is very affluent indeed. "Look Doris, even the vagrants here are wearing Marks and Spencer clothing, we could do far worse than relocating here!"

Jettisoning all my old clobber was not just practical, but also therapeutic. It was like a statement saying goodbye to my old life forever. I did not know at the time but this was not the only cleansing I would undertake in my pilgrimage to seek the new Francis Abel, far more drastic surgery was to follow on my chattels.

My attire in the following weeks was to say the least a little Bohemian, but I sort of liked the maverick person I was becoming. Many social behavioural conventions I refused to adhere to and I didn't give a shit any more who considered it a trifle strange. One last thing bugged me, the Velcro shoes Nick had bought me all those months ago remained a glaring statement of my disability every time I wore them. I decided to return to my old shoes and if I could not manage to tie them myself then I simply ask somebody who could.

Chapter Five

WARMER CLIMATES

The weather remained atrocious in March and April of 2008 and the cold still remained one of my worst enemies. I suppose I had less lard on my body to act as an insulating agent, but I knew this climate was a big hindrance to my progression. I was not going to remain a prisoner in my own house and I refused to do so. I had done my sums and had more than enough savings to fund a holiday.

The prospect of undertaking such a venture was daunting to me but I was convinced that it was a hurdle I must conquer. The following weeks I bitterly complained to Nick that I had to seek the refuge of the sun. I had always loved hot weather and can quite easily sunbathe for hours on end soaking up the rays. Eventually he got fed up with me whinging and persuaded Richie to take me on holiday.

Rich could take some time off work in early June so we planned a week vacation somewhere hot. I normally went on holiday with Richie and another pal Kev; as three of the single members of our group, we could realistically both afford and had the time to holiday whenever we wanted. The past few years we had always tended to take long haul trips for a couple of reasons. Firstly, to venture to places that perhaps in later years for whatever reasons were inaccessible to us, but secondly and most importantly to avoid the British.

It was not that we disliked our fellow countrymen; we simply did not see the point of travelling thousand of miles just to sit next to somebody from Huyton on the beach. It might sound a trifle elitist, but whenever trouble breaks out on holiday abroad it is normally the drunken antics of our compatriots to blame.

Whenever I see the Dog & Duck or Rose and Crown on my travels, I give the place a wide birth and normally cross the road; there would be plenty of time for a pint of best bitter when I returned to Blighty.

I also liked to travel far afield as I had been most fortunate in my life to have had jobs where I have travelled extensively at the company's behest and expense. So, I like to take the opportunity of visiting new places and discovering the soft underbelly of somewhere exotic.

Richie contacted his sister-in-law Michele, who was a travel agent with the following brief: find somewhere we had never been to, not too far away, guaranteed sunshine and finally not too expensive. After considering several options we decided that Cyprus was just the place for us.

I rejected the idea for once to go long haul as it would be the first time I had been on a plane since my stroke and I did not know how I was going to cope. Also, the fact that we were only going for seven days meant there was no point travelling somewhere it would take days to get to.

The following couple of weeks I had to prepare. I did not know if the airline would permit me to take my wooden cane on the plane. So, I scanned the internet and found a rather dapper tartan fold up little number that seemed just the job. Then I had to find some suitable clothes. On the next Tesco run that Linzi and I made, we took a detour to an outlet mall and I purchased shorts, t-shirts and the like. I was all set to go until somebody reminded me about travel insurance. My bank account automatically gives me this insurance, but after enquiries I was told that because of my condition I would have to contact the insurance company direct to ensure they would cover me. Several phone calls later, and eventually after disclosing my recent medical history and current medication, the cover was extended for a hefty fee. I have an intrinsic dislike of insurance companies and it took all my self control to be half civilised to the agent on the phone. I thought to myself, *The greedy bastards, they make me sick!* then smiled at the irony.

Liverpool has an airport, the John Lennon International Airport, and I liked to fly from it if possible. But they offer very few long haul destinations, and in this case we had far more options flying from Manchester. Richie picked me up in a taxi as to help me with my suitcase and we set off on an overcast June morning to the airport. I looked out of the window of the cab. *This is summer, missing nothing here then...*

Terminal Two was packed, and the queues for the Thomas Cook desks seemed to take all available floor space. For some reason the numpties had decided to have all their flights checking in at the same few desks. I looked at Richie and said, "I can't stand up in that for very long." But we attempted trying and joined the back of the queue. It was horrific, even with my natty new cane I was being jostled and shoved and my energy levels were rapidly depleting. *Sod this*, I thought, and grabbed a rep's arm and tried to explain my difficulty, but was simply ignored. In the past I would have taken my rejection as final but not these days. I walked straight to the front of the queue and vented my frustration, of course in a very polite manner, and was led to an empty desk that was closed. We checked in and within five minutes had cleared security and were sitting drinking coffee in the departure lounge.

The flight was delayed as unsurprisingly, not all of passengers had checked in on time. We sat drinking our coffee when a thought occurred to me: did I have to board first as an assisted passenger? I would certainly hold everybody up behind me if we went by seat numbers. Richie asked the Thomas Cook representative and he was told I could wait and board last.

The flight was eventually called and the normal bun fight started. All the years I have been travelling by aeroplane this debacle had never ceased to amaze me. Passengers already with allocated seats that nobody was going to steal from them, turn into some sorts of raving monsters. Firstly is the kestrel: they watch every move the rep behind the desk is making and as soon as the microphone is switched on they swoop down on their prey. Next, the pigeon, pretending to hang around the gate as if they have something important to do; then wham, join the queue as soon as the boarding announcement is made. The worst is the shitehawk, who cares nothing for deception; just shits on everybody barging in wherever he can. My favourite is the dithering dodo, who just happens to be passing the gate; hears the announcement, checks their ticket and happily ambles straight to the front, totally unaware of the glares behind. "Didn't he know there was a pecking order?!"

We waited patiently in our seats, finished our coffee then as the last passenger went through the gate into the melee of flying feathers and squawking we took our turn. I had folded up my cane just in case some officious twat made a big scene over it and limped past the rep. There was no gantry, the plane was parked below and all the passengers were negotiating the stairs and walking across the tarmac to board. I saw a lift so thought I would ease my effort a little. There were only two buttons so I pressed the lowest one and exited when the doors opened. There was something wrong; there were no people and a sort of seat belt on two metal poles barricading the doors.

Oh fuck, why hadn't I just taken the stairs like everybody else? With some effort, I limboed under the blockage, pushed the metal Fire Exit bar on the door and stepped out on to a walkway under the terminal. I looked up at the gantry and saw what direction I should be walking. Turning a corner, I saw Richie at the bottom of the plane's steps arguing with a stewardess and gesticulating to the base of the stairs to obviously where I should have been.

"Where the Hell have you been?" my friend greeted me. I did not have the nerve to tell him how I had cocked up, otherwise I would be the butt of his jokes for days, so I simply shrugged and faced the challenge of the steps.

Stepping into the plane as the last passenger I could feel the icy glares of all the other shitehawks. "How dare he delay my holiday by five minutes, we could have been in the air now if he had only just barged in like I did!" Taking our seats I realised now why Richie and I normally travel by scheduled airlines. There was no legroom whatsoever. Thank god it was only a four hour flight, I do not think I could have survived any longer. The flight was tortuous, I could hardly move my legs at all and a dull ache went down my right side. I was so glad when we finally landed and I could stand up again to relieve the pain.

Passing through security we entered another bun fight; this time in the baggage hall. The usual suspects had been on the prowl and secured the only available trolleys so we just waited by the carousel for our luggage. Unbelievably, our bags were the first ones out and as Richie lifted them off the belt I looked around at the shitehawks. Their faces were a picture. "Well, who would have thought that! Last ones on the plane and first to get their luggage, lucky bastards!"

We were staying in Kato Pathos Cyprus at the Alexander the Great Hotel and a tour bus was waiting to take us there. On the way we got the normal sales pitch from the tour rep, but as usual completely ignored everything she said. I felt a little sorry for the reps as they were completely wasting their time with us; they would be better off selling ice to the Eskimos or something. We had never taken an official tour anywhere; the very thought of being cooped up with people who did want to take tours put me off the whole idea.

It was like that famous letter that Groucho Marx wrote to his new exclusive Beverley Hills golf club. The club, hearing that they had a new movie star in their area thought that they would like him as one of their patrons. He wrote a letter back declining the offer stating; "Any club that had people like him as part of their membership, he would certainly not want to join!"

The bus arrived at the hotel and we checked in. Our room was nicely furnished, quite small but would suffice for a week. Deciding unpacking could wait, we headed downstairs to discover the hotel's amenities. First stop, the bar. As I have detailed, my alcohol intake had drastically reduced and I became drunk very quickly now with very little booze. I painstakingly explained this once again to my pal, "I cannot do what I used to do. I will come out, but will take things easy, at my pace." Richie nodded, but a nagging thought kept on reoccurring: *He does not believe me.*

We finished our pints and went to look outside. There are not many good beaches in this part of Cyprus and most sunbathing is done by the poolside. The hotel pool was very large and jam packed with people squeezed into every available sun bed the hotel could cram around it. Alexander the Great had an unusual policy of selecting your preferred sun lounger on first arrival, then retaining it for the whole duration of your stay. There was a hierarchy of sunbathers; the regular patrons and big tippers were given the best choices, then the luxury suites next followed by the eight hundred other mere mortals. Our two loungers were by the indoor pool that only received the sun after 11am.

In most places, the first awake gets the fist pick of where they want to spend the day sitting. I did not know if this was a particularly anti German policy the hotel had, but it was very strictly observed. If your arse so much as touched a sun lounger, other than your allocated one, then you would forfeit your place at breakfast. That fact did not bother Rich and I one iota as breakfast was normally a rare treat on our holidays, unless we were just returning back from the night prior.

The rest of the hotel was quite good. It had a number of restaurants and a couple of bars, the best facility was the Spa Centre. Sauna, steam and massage rooms, health centre and large indoor pool. The pool was excellent, large and all one depth from end to end. It would be ideal for me to exercise in every day and the best thing about it was that it was continuously empty.

Around 7pm we went to explore Kato Pathos. I said I wanted to eat fairly early which Rich grudgingly agreed to. Kato Pathos is a small town on the harbour about one kilometre from Pathos itself. I had heard stories about Pathos being like Stag Party City which I wanted to avoid, so we had booked Kato Pathos. There are two main areas too frequent for nightlife in Kato Pathos: the infamous Bar Street that will rival anything the centre of Pathos has and the more upmarket harbour area where most of the restaurants are situated.

Bar Street was quite acceptable in the early evening and the 2008 Euro Championships were being played in Austria and Switzerland. We decided to wander down and watch a couple of games before dinner. The street was fairly narrow with a one way traffic system in place. In my view it should be totally pedestrianized as later on in the evening the local poseurs in their customised Vauxhall Corsas tended to clog up proceedings. One end of Bar Street led down to the main road and our hotel, the other end was towards the harbour and where most of the nightclubs were to be found.

We found a bar advertising Happy Hour where we could sit outside and watch the match. A very popular drink in Pathos is Brandy Sour; each bar seemed to have its own recipe and took pride that their concoction was the best. I had never sampled Brandy Sour before so the waiter was despatched to knock a couple up while we started with two cold beers. Richie struggled with most foreign beers, or British for that matter, if it was not smooth flow Tetley bitter. But Cyprus had Keo, a local beer that was very acceptable; although a lager, it had a distinct hoppy taste and was very refreshing.

The worst place to visit is the United States if beer is one of your top priorities. Both Richie and I had not visited for some years now, even prior to my stroke, due to beer standards. I cannot fathom why all Americans insist on imbibing Lite Beers, all ice cold even in the middle of winter. They are tasteless, perhaps that is why they are served so cold so at least give your throat gets the sensation of burning. If Americans think that drinking twenty Lite Beers followed by a massive burger is cutting out the calories, then a trip to my nutritionist at Aintree University Hospital is in order.

The weather had been glorious since we had arrived and even in the early evening the temperature was hot. I could feel the warmth penetrating my body almost to my very core and I knew the benefit it was giving me. The waiter had double looked at me when we had walked into the bar - why was I on a stick? I looked fairly fit and healthy, so why the stick?

After the first match we decided to walk back towards the hotel where we had seen a restaurant over the road. I stood up and could already feel the alcohol taking effect. We had had two beers and two Brandy Sours each and I could notice the disorientation starting. To this day I am not certain if the medication I am taking has any major effect on my alcohol threshold or it is purely the legacy of the damage done to my body by the stroke. But I was walking with a slight limp again and I loathed and detested that.

Outside the restaurant, we were both dithering if we were hungry enough to dine yet when I stuck my nose up a little street. There seemed to be a few more local restaurants situated there, a little off the tourist beat. It was there we found Billy's Bar, a shack propped up against a crooked wall. It looked just the sort of place we both loved and was advertising the cheapest booze in Pathos. Inside it was larger than it had originally appeared. There were tables and chairs for about twenty people and a pool table at the rear of the bar. Some Tony Christie song was playing whilst mine host whistled away, cleaning a glass ignoring any potential customer.

That was my very first meeting with Billy. Possibly, with the exception of Mike from the Bug, the most unlikely person ever to run a bar. He was a Cypriot and had a dour expression on his burly tanned face. I estimated he was in his early fifties and possibly had been bequeathed the business from some old relative that had passed away. At any rate, he certainly did not relish his present position and had no hesitation in letting people know that fact. It was because of Billy's rude and off hand treatment of unsuspecting, jovial holiday makers that made his bar our regular haunt.

Billy could easily spoil the enjoyment of a table of merrymakers by claiming there was no ice left or a particular favourite tipple had run out. He would despatch this news with much glee and satisfaction and almost smiled as the disgruntled party left his bar with threats of never returning. He would normally claim insufficient language skills at moments like this but we knew differently. Sitting on the two bar stools each night we learned that he spoke excellent English and had a very dry sense of humour, perhaps too dry to be a bar proprietor.

After our first visit to Billy's Bar we went to dine at a restaurant opposite, but still in the same street. I looked around and the place was packed, full of very brown faces of the expats who now lived in Cyprus. The whole street was the same, restaurants and bars run by local Cypriots and frequented by some locals, but mostly the expat community. It was where the best and most affordable places to eat where situated, not quite with a harbour view, but definitely the best value for money.

By this time we were both famished and so ordered the mezze for two. For diners who have never sampled Greek cuisine, a mezze is a selection of courses that can include just about anything. But if you are watching your diet or simply not starving it is not an advisable choice. In tourist resorts and some less traditional Greek restaurants it is just a mass of meat and fish. A mezze should be a selection of small freshly cooked dishes of what was in season and locally available.

The former was the case here; absolutely value for money, but one can only eat so many chops, sausages, steaks etc. I can see why expats would like it as it was more of a massive mixed grill, but as for authentic Cypriot cuisine?

With our waist lines fit to burst we took a night cap at Billy's. I simply could not fit any more beer in to my poor bloated stomach, so opted for a brandy. Metaxa is the Greek flagship brandy and for those people who have only sampled the cheap firewater of Metaxa One, then they will be glad to know there are two alternatives. Metaxa Five is more like a French Cognac whilst the top of the range Metaxa Seven is almost a honey tasting liqueur. I have often wondered what ever happened to Metaxa Two, Three, Four and Six. Were the Metaxa distillers so pissed when they were developing new beverages to their range they simply forgot what number they were up to? "Ah, this is nice, let's go with this blend, hic... What number are we up to Costas?"

After the brandy I knew I was up to my alcohol limit for the night so informed Richie that it was bedtime for me. We walked, or in my case slightly staggered back to the hotel. "Is that it?" my friend stood on the corner with his hands on his hips and an exasperated expression.

"What do I do now?" I started to begin to explain, but did not have the energy for an argument so I carried on crossing the road to the Alexander. "Well, that's just great!" I turned to see my friend heading off alone in the direction of Bar Street. A pang of guilt hit me. I felt strange. Part of me was sorry for letting my friend down and another part of me was sorry for myself; I wanted to go with him like the old days.

I fell on my bed absolutely exhausted and felt very, very full. It had been a long time since I had eaten a meal as big as the one I had just consumed. I forced myself to undress and take my night medication then after a wash I went to sleep.

I woke with a bright shaft of sunlight shining through a chink in the curtains and looked over to see my friend asleep in his bed. I had not heard him returning to the room last night as I was so tired and in a deep slumber. I noticed something dark on his pillow, like a stain or something. I leaned over slightly to get a better look; the stain was a dark brown like dried blood. Oh shit, the hair on the back of his head was matted with the same stuff. It looked as though he had a bad cut somewhere and it had been bleeding onto his pillow.

I had heard stories of Bar Street being very rough at night and wondered if Rich had been in an argument and had been bottled or something. My friend does get somewhat belligerent when he is drunk and will argue the hind leg off a donkey if he thinks he has just cause. The truth is that he will continue to argue a point, even though he knows he is in the wrong, just to get his poor opponent to submit out of sheer boredom.

"Richie, what has happened?" I yelled. There was no response, so I shouted even louder. "Richie, I think you have been bottled or something!" Finally, my mate stirred and looked at me.

"What the Hell are you going on about?" he said in one of his most cantankerous voices. I explained to him about his head and was wittering on to him about hospital and doctors. Rich touched the back of his head and his hand was covered in blood.

"You stupid twat! Very funny!" he growled as he lay his head back on the pillow. My concern was not diminished one jot as I pressed the matter further. "Look, you are bleeding, wake up and see!"

"I see you have lost none of your sense of humour!" Richie said ironically. I was puzzled, he was covered in blood, it was all over his bed and he was not in the least bit concerned. "Where did you get it?" he asked. I was now standing over his bed and was inspecting my friend closer. It was not, blood but some sticky brown stuff that smelled just like... Chocolate!

I started to laugh; I had roused my friend from his drunken stupor only to inform him he had chocolate in his hair. I remembered when I had returned to the room the previous evening, room service had turned the beds down and placed a complimentary chocolate on the pillow. The stupid dummkopf had not seen it and had been rolling around on a fondant fancy all night.

He was not in the least amused and was convinced I had planted the confectionary as one of my jolly japes. I left him back to his sleep and went to the pool as once again we were both too late for breakfast. Checking that I had my unique numerical identification pool tag I found my allocated chair. How many uninvited guests do they have usurping Alexander the Great's very own sun space? There was not as much security back in the hospital, but I suppose it all boils down to priorities and supply and demand economics. There were plenty of sick people around available to fill your hospitals, but not enough parking places for sun loungers in the Alexander the Great Hotel.

That evening after Billy's miserable hour we ambled down towards the harbour. It was a very pleasant walk and there was a plethora of good restaurants and upmarket bars to choose from. There are even Pink Flamingos wandering around further around the bay owned by some hotel or restaurant; apparently that is the way towards the "Tomb of the Kings" suggested as a worthwhile tourist attraction. We had dinner and consumed too much Retsina wine so I suggested a nightcap for me and cutting up a side street found that we were in the far end of Bar Street.

Two Margaritas later I was struggling to stay vertical. I informed Richie that I could not walk back to the hotel even though it was probably less than five minutes away. He agreed and pointed to a taxi rank over the road. Pathos taxis are a nightmare; do not merrily flag one down or just jump into one, you will get royally ripped off. Always agree a price before you get in one, or at the very least insist on the meter being run. It seems to differ if you ask a restaurant to call one for you; they use more reputable drivers and will fix a fare for you.

Most of the taxi drivers around Bar Street are of the more entrepreneurial type. They have no shortage of drunken revellers to pick from and take advantage of. Our bartering down the rank of cabs was not meeting with any success; we had no option but pay the exorbitant fare. Richie was going to stay in Bar Street, but was so incensed with the driver he got in the cab too and argued back to the hotel. The journey took about three minutes and cost ten Euros. Slamming the taxi door, Rich stormed off muttering something about Billy's Bar and I pottered into the hotel and to bed.

The following morning was as usual; glorious and hot, and we were both squeezed into our parking bay with the rest of the sardines. We were both discussing the Pathos taxi situation when Rich remembered about an authentic mezze restaurant Billy had recommended to him and suggested we try it that night. The day turned into what became a routine, plenty of sunbathing interspersed with exercises in the indoor pool for me and splashing around outside for Rich.

After I finished one of my stints in the pool I decided to explore the Spa centre and saw the massage rooms. I was given the tariffs by a rather exotic sounding young lady and looked at the prices. It was expensive, a normal massage for an hour was nearly fifty quid, but anyway I went ahead and decided to have one.

I have had massages before in Malaysia which were brilliant and cheap apart from one particular one on the beach I care not to remember. In my pre stroke days my feet often used to swell up due to the weight they had to carry and were particularly bad after a long flight. A couple of days after arriving in Penang I was walking down the beach to be accosted by George, a local beach masseur. He was touting for business and was pointing to my rather swollen red feet and assured me he could alleviate my discomfort. After parting with some Ringgits I sat on a wooden stool and George went to work on me. Basically the massage consisted of George whacking my feet with a piece of wood, not dissimilar to a rolling pin, and then trying to push the fluid out of my toes. It was very, very painful, but brought thorough enjoyment to Rich and the small crowd gathered around witnessing the Malayan ritual of torturing newly arrived visitors that have fat feet.

I was called in for the massage and walked into a small room with a raised bed. A young woman wearing a very formal clinical uniform gave me a towel and asked me to change. Minutes later I was lying down on the bed explaining to my masseur about my recent illness and the problems I had. I felt sorry for the girl as she seemed terrified to touch me and occasionally when I winced at a little pain her face was ashen with apology. It was not one of mine, or for that matter probably not one of her, best massages ever.

Later, we were sitting on Billy's two bar stools sampling a couple of his finest Brandy Sours whilst mine host rummaged around in a dirty brown drawer muttering to himself. Eventually he produced a rather grubby card with a bloke's name on. I would not go as far to say that it was a business card, but it was something of that nature. Billy was growing on me, his laconic, shambolic way of running his business was far from text book but it seemed to bring him success; rarely was the little bar less than packed. It reminded me of the Wong Kei restaurant in Wardour Street, London; probably the rudest Chinese waiters in the universe but the place was always packed.

Billy had his phone pressed firmly to his ear and was so busy in conversation he totally ignored the large gentleman asking for his bill. "Okay, 8pm tonight. But you must be on time, the restaurant is very busy." So, we were booked into a special place tonight: I was quite excited. The large man was still attempting to get Billy's attention and seemed to be getting quite agitated. "I will phone a taxi to take you there and back," our host and new friend continued as he turned his back to the now red faced man. Billy, then with his priority task management hat on, proceeded to book the cab for us then went to clean a table of some empty glasses. The large man was stuttering with disbelief.

Our taxi took us out into the countryside about twenty minutes from Kato Pathos. We were in pitch blackness when I could dimly see some lights ahead of us. The car pulled outside a large farmhouse brightly lit from the inside as more cars arrived by the second. I was amazed this place was so popular as it was in the middle of nowhere. Two large wooden doors covered in vines marked the entrance and a rather rotund man with a huge white handlebar moustache stood outside greeting his guests.

We were warmly ushered into the building by the owner and passed on to an aged lady with a shawl who checked our reservation. The vast room was on about three different levels, all packed with large rustic dining furniture. It seemed that a few smaller rooms had all been cobbled together to make one huge space. Most of the other diners had already arrived but more kept pouring in.

Mostly the wooden tables were sizeable, big enough to accommodate eight or ten people. We were shown to one of the few small ones. The atmosphere was electric with the babbling conversation of expectant patrons mixed with the loud orders being issued from management to staff. The delicious aromas permeating the air brought saliva to the mouth with great expectancy of what was to come.

As of yet there was no food or drink on any of the tables and no menus had arrived for any perusal. Outside the owner seemed to be turning people away in droves and after about fifteen minutes, he entered the room, closed the large doors behind him and spoke with a heavy Greek accent. "Tonight we will bring you a selection of our food that is totally organic and home grown from the farm. Even the wine we serve we produce ourselves and is not sold anywhere else on the Island. We ask you one favour; please do not waste any food. We will continue to bring you freshly prepared dishes as long as you are hungry, but if any dish is offered that you do not like, please tell your waiter immediately and we can give it to somebody else. Now I hope you enjoy your evening."

This place was fantastic, it had one sitting for dinner and everybody ate the same food and drank the same wine. It was all one price about twenty five pounds per person for as much food or wine as you could consume, there was no separate bar for extras and if you did not like wine you drank water.

The food was magnificent. I was surprised how delicious a lot of the vegetarian dishes were, perhaps because it was fresh, organic and seasonable fare. Even the meat was raised on the massive farm and was so succulent that the slow cooked dishes only needed a spoon to prise the flesh away from the bone. This was a proper, traditional mezze and something I had never experienced before or since. Billy had certainly come up trumps for us and perhaps we owed him a few drinks.

I estimated that perhaps two hundred people dined that night and everybody was served quickly with piping hot food continually, on the basis of what food was ready was served immediately. Each separate dish was announced by its own waiter and if you did not fancy the sound of something you simply did not take it from the tray. You just waited a few minutes until the next delicacy arrived and dived in.

Leaving the restaurant that night I was surprised that I did not feel stuffed. Yes, I was full, but not fit to burst as I thought I would be. The food that had been served was not stacked out with chips, potatoes and a dozen different sausages. It had been quite unique and I wanted to taste as many of the different dishes as possible; the portions were quite small, but if you requested two or three of the same then that was quite acceptable.

The following night we went to thank Billy who accepted our gratitude with the same indifference as his regular complaints. But something inside me knew that the gruff demeanour of the Cypriot was not his true nature. I think he also knew I was aware of that fact.

Cyprus had been very good for me, I returned physically much stronger and relaxed than I had gone. But just as importantly, a few more barriers had been successfully negotiated, albeit with my good friends help, but nevertheless mentally I had improved too.

Back home it was hard for me to settle. I missed the warm climate dreadfully and the nights of late July were already becoming chilly. My routine once again ruled my life and my days were taken up with my physical improvement. I knew that one day I would reach a plateau where I simply would not improve any more no matter how much exercise and treatment I undertook. But when that day was or how I was to recognise it was a mystery to me. One fact was definite; I now knew that I needed to be in a warm climate to have a better quality of life.

A couple of weeks passed and I was getting more and more restless until I made a decision. I would return to Cyprus as soon as possible for at least a month. The next few days I spent trawling the web and discovered possible cheap villa rentals in Kato Pathos. I knew I had to persuade somebody to accompany me at least whilst I was travelling because I was not confident enough to undergo the mechanics of the journey myself.

That Sunday, armed with prices and facts, I strolled down to meet my friends in the Bug for a lunchtime drink. One by one I tried to persuade friends to join me on my trip, and one by one I was declined due to very valid reasons. I was trying to explain to one mate that little things like handling my luggage I could not do by myself and desperation was creeping into my voice. Then all of a sudden a voice perked up behind the bar: "I'll go!"

It was Paddy, one of the barmen. "Don't mess about Paddy," I almost snarled back. "I'm serious, I will take you." Paddy was quite a new addition to the staff, he was the son of one of the regulars. He was only about twenty, but I knew he had some bottle. I knew this because any obviously gay man working behind the Bug bar had to endure a lot of stick. It is not because the pub is a homophobic breeding ground, it is just the fact that Scouse humour is based on finding weaknesses and exploiting them. It does not sound very endearing to the Liverpool race, but most of the banter is not aimed at hurting people, just highlighting a difference so it becomes humorous.

I immediately shook Paddy's hand and the affable youngster just smiled and said, "Do I need a passport?" The bar shook with laughter and Paddy blushed slightly with embarrassment. "What, do you think gays are exempt from travel regulations?" the banter had started. The rest of the afternoon was spent planning dates and looking at the information I had downloaded from the net. We exchanged mobile numbers and I said I would book everything on Monday.

It was agreed with his parents that Paddy would travel out with me and spend ten days on holiday. How I was going to get back I couldn't care less. I would leave my luggage there if it meant spending a month in Cyprus. I found a really nice apartment on a small complex of only four units near the large Paradise Gardens development and had booked it after negotiating a great discount.

The apartment was on the second floor of a two story building and had its own private roof terrace with a large brick built barbecue. It also had access to a small pool which seemed ideal for my exercises. Once I had organised the apartment, I booked two flights departing from Manchester. I phoned Paddy with the news and he had just been to the Post Office to apply for his passport.

Things seemed to be going swimmingly, until a couple of days later, Paddy had still not received news about his passport. He assured me he had applied for an express service, but what he had actually done is apply for a ten year instead of a simple one year passport. The height of summer had now passed and the passport service would not be too inundated, but I had a gut feeling that things were going to get a lot more complicated.

I did not really know Paddy that much, just conversations we had in the Bug, but he seemed a really nice young man. He was polite, humorous and seemed to like partying a lot with his friends. He was very open about his sexuality and never tried to hide that fact that he was gay to anybody, a fact that carried its own repercussions in the Bug bar.

It was Wednesday and the flight was Friday morning. Things were getting a little tight. I phoned Paddy and suggested we went to the main passport office in Liverpool and tried to press our claim a little more forcibly. We took our place in the queue and waited our turn, it was not long until Paddy's name was called and we both went to the desk. They had a record of Paddy's application and informed us that it was being processed. I explained my situation explained Paddy was my helper and I needed his assistance to travel.

The clerk was very pleasant, but could not exactly say where in the processing system the application was. It could be sent out today for all she knew. Also, it was not possible for Paddy to apply for a one year passport as he could not have two applications at the same time. We were scuppered, so decided to wait for the post to arrive on Thursday before we reconsidered anything.

In the morning Paddy phoned and said his passport had not arrived in the mail. But I had made my decision; I was going anyway. Nothing was going to stop me and I would have to negotiate all my obstacles one by one as I came to them. Paddy was going to follow in a couple of days when he could. It sort of defeated the object of Paddy coming with me, as the journey out to Cyprus was my big problem, not particularly my stay there. But nevertheless, it would be good to have some company when I was out there.

Paddy borrowed his mum's car and gave me a lift to the airport the following morning. He carried my bag to check in and apologised profusely about the situation. Once I had checked in, things were fairly easy and I managed to board the plane with no shenanigans this time. But all the way on the flight I was thinking about what would happen when I landed.

With some difficulty, I managed to disembark and clamber onto the terminal bus, no assistance was offered to me, even though with my cane and limp my condition was pretty obvious. The shitehawks had more important things on their minds, like snatching all the available trolleys. I stood at the carousel being jostled and bumped like everybody else when I saw my bag. There was no way I could grip my bag with my left hand and keep my balance with my weak right leg. I politely asked the big man next to me for help, he stared at me as though I was taking the piss, but something about my demeanour changed his mind. Gruffly he grabbed my case and plonked it unceremoniously in front of me. He did not say a word, and wheeled around to continue staring at the revolving belt in front of him.

I had been lucky and managed to secure a trolley, so loading it up with my case and backpack, I went out in the glorious sunshine to find the taxi I had booked. The apartment was a little difficult to find as it seemed to be in a housing estate, but eventually the driver managed to locate it and pointed at some stairs where there was a white door with 2A on its front.

The driver did not speak any English and when I pointed to my bag and then the stairs he just looked at me and laughed. I rummaged around found a five Euro note and repeated my request. Grumbling, he got out of the taxi and carried my case up the stairs, snatched the money and drove off. Welcome to bloody Cyprus! Christ, taxi drivers are the worst ambassadors for their countries. They are the first native people foreigners meet and possibly the very last ones they should meet.

Locating the key, as per my instructions under the mat, I opened the door to my new home for a month. The living area was quite large and open plan; perhaps two rooms combined, and was very light with wall to floor windows at one end. It had two sofas and TV, DVD player, etc. at the front part, then a large wooden dining table with four chairs separating the lounge area from a fully fitted kitchen. Down a small passageway, the twin bedroom was located to the left before a nice petite and very clean bathroom.

The room was stifling hot as it was around midday. I slid open the windows at the far end and walked out on to a balcony. There was a small swimming pool below and my neighbouring apartments formed a courtyard around the pool. To my left were some more steps so I ascended and there was the jewel in the crown. A roof terrace as big as my whole apartment. There was a massive brick barbecue that looked big enough to roast a whole hog next to a double draining board and small outdoor kitchen.

This place was wonderful it even had a patio table and chairs under a sort of Gazebo and two sun loungers. It would definitely be where I would be sending most of my time. From the roof I had a 360 degree view of Kato Pathos. I could dimly see the sea far over to my left and straight ahead was one of the Paradise Gardens developments. There seemed to be houses and apartments all around me and the area was very residential. Perhaps the best thing was that the terrace was totally private, all the developments around seemed to be a maximum of two stories and nothing overlooked my outdoor space.

After unpacking and changing into some shorts, I decided to explore around a bit and see what the neighbourhood had to offer. The small roads and streets were like a maze, new holiday homes were being built all around, but there seemed very few local amenities. I could not find any shops or bars so I just kept on walking, absorbing the hot sun and breathing the heady aromatic scent of pine in the air. Eventually some local expats gave me directions to a local bar hidden away in the maze, I was glad to take a rest and take on board some water.

Finding my way back was a problem: night was drawing in quickly and I could not recognise anywhere. I trundled around for about an hour until by pure luck I was fortunate to stumble across my apartment. I was shattered; my batteries were on red and definitely needed recharging. I decided to go to bed and take a nap for a couple of hours. As soon as my head touched the pillow, I fell fast asleep. I awoke in pitch blackness and did not have a clue how long I had been asleep or what the time was, but I needed to take a pee.

Rising sharply from the bed my head went all dizzy. I tried to stand, but my legs buckled under me and I crashed to the floor. I tried to break my fall with my left arm, but was falling on my right hand side. My head bounced off the bed and crashed into the floor tiles. I could feel blood oozing out of my face. I entered survival mode and lay on the floor bleeding but not moving. I was in shock of my situation and was trying hard not to panic.

Who could I phone? Where was my phone? Had I had another stroke? Questions filled my mind but no answers would come. I knew I could not stay where I was or I might bleed to death so slowly I began a physical check of myself. Moving the large limbs first I was reassured that my right leg was responding and I could stretch it out under the bed. Also, my right arm seemed to be about the same so I breathed a sigh of relief: it did not seem like another attack.

I felt my head and there seemed to be a deep cut around the back where I must have bumped it on the bed as I fell; blood was pouring out of the wound. There was also some sort of cut above my left eye as blood was emanating from there too. I checked my teeth and they seemed all okay, but blood was seeping out of a cut to my hand. I was in quite a mess, but nothing seemed critical so I grew more confident about my condition.

The floor was slippery with blood and I could not stand, so like a wounded animal I crawled out of the bedroom on all fours. I wanted to get to the bathroom to check myself in the mirror, but I felt dizzy again and lay on the floor of the passageway for a few minute. Memories of lying on my landing at home when I had my first stroke flooded my mind and I fought back tears of desperation and the growing sense of panic.

After what seemed about thirty minutes, I managed to get strength enough to crawl into the bathroom and get some towels. I had decided to wrap the wounds and go back to bed until I was strong enough to stand. Probably a bad decision from a medical point of view because I did not know how much blood I had lost, or was losing, but all I could think of at the time as I my brain was very confused and physically I was very weak.

My sleep was restless, all manner of thoughts entered my mind that night. Eventually dawn broke and cautiously I moved from the bed. I looked down at the sheets but they did not seem too bad and the towels had done their job. I knew I would have to replace the bed linen and the towels. Tentatively, I walked into the bathroom and looked into the mirror. It was hard to inspect the damage as there was so much dried blood so I took a shower.

Christ! The back of my head stung like somebody had poured acid over it as I gently patted the wound clean. The cut seemed about an inch long but already a scab was forming, which was a good sign as I might not need stitches. I took more care with my eye and then took my time getting dry. Standing in front of the mirror once more, I inspected myself for a second time. I had been very lucky; the cut over my eye was more of a long graze and was not deep at all. However, I was going to have one Hell of a shiner.

A dull ache was forming in my head and I went to sit quietly in the front room.

The cause of my collapse the previous night was a simple case of exhaustion but more importantly dehydration. One of the medicines I was taking was a diuretic to prevent fluid retention; this coupled with the fierce heat from the sun had caused my demise. I made a mental note for future exploration forays to take my medication more into account when I glibly went walkabout.

My mobile rang and on answering an excited Paddy informed me his passport had arrived and he had booked his flight. It would arrive in Cyprus tomorrow evening at around 7.30pm. I decided I would not tell him about my accident: he seemed quite a highly strung person and I did not want to spook him, he would find out soon enough.

The previous evening had shaken me quite badly and affected my confidence quite a bit, but I was learning: I was not quite as fragile as an egg. Yes, when I took a tumble it was a hard one as I could not put my right arm out straight to soften the blow. But when I was in hospital they had given my body a full M.O.T. and apart from the obvious I was fit as a fiddle. I have never known why that particular instrument is supposed to be the healthiest in the orchestra, but that is conundrum for another time.

That day I was too sore to sit out in the sun. Instead I watched some DVDs I had bought out with me and took things easy. The room was baking hot, the air conditioning units in the living and sleeping areas did not seem to be functioning and there was little or no breeze coming in from all the open windows. I knew I had to go shopping for some water and food, there was nothing in the apartment and I was hungry and thirsty.

Deciding not to follow the same footsteps of yesterday's disastrous debacle, I discovered a small path that led around the apartment to the rear of the Paradise Gardens development. There I found a side road that led to Spyrou Kyprianos which is the main bypass road of Kato Pathos that leads to Pathos Town. Crossing that I came to civilisation; restaurants, shops and bars started to appear as I followed a small road downhill. Passing a cemetery on the left the road forked, the left hand went to join Bar Street whilst the right hand side eventually led down to the harbour. I had been able to walk down to the harbour at a very sedate pace in under fifteen minutes.

I ate a hearty meal at a very authentic Taverna and sampled some local Shellfish which was delicious, but I thought it prudent to stay away from the alcohol for a few days. One or two diners passed curious glances my way, but I was not in the least surprised. My eye had turned black, there were cuts on my hand and I was using a cane to help me walk. I looked just like the drunken thugs I try hard to avoid at any cost.

The following day I felt much better and my mood was far perkier as I knew Paddy was arriving later. I spent the day on the roof terrace soaking in the sun and listening to music on my iPod, ensuring I took frequent sips of water from my bottle. It was blazing hot, Pathos has a terrific climate for those that like arid heat. There is literally no rain from about May to October with temperatures in the mid 30s. During this period the Government have to import tankers of water to the island. The rest of the year, the temperature hovers between 20 and 25 degrees and is sporadically broken by odd storms. My roof was a sun trap with a low wall encircling the whole terrace, keeping the breeze away and the heat in: the temperature must have been close to 40 degrees.

Later in the afternoon, I wandered down to my little pool and cooled down doing hydro therapy exercises. The little apartment complex was so quiet, nobody else seemed to live there. All the windows were closed and blinds drawn, it was quite fantastic having the whole place to myself. This part of Kato Pathos is very much for the resettlement of British expats who either permanently live in Cyprus or rent out their properties to other British holiday makers. Normally it is the sort of place I would not have been the least interested in visiting, but at this moment of my life it would suffice.

After bathing I was inspecting the collateral damage to my face when a loud knock sounded at the door. I had completely lost track of the time, it must have been after 8pm. Opening it I saw the grinning face of my delinquent new friend Paddy. His expression soon changed when he saw me and panic changed his demeanour. I was quick to settle him down and explained what had happened.

"Just cuts and bruises, nothing serious and nothing to worry about," I reassured him. After five or ten minutes being overly cosseted I managed to persuade Paddy what I said was true and showed him the apartment.

I think it was the first time Paddy had been abroad by himself and he loved everything about the place, but he was already complaining about the heat. I had still not managed to fix the air conditioning so it was stifling hot. We agreed to get some air and find somewhere for dinner. I showed him to the bedroom: he had his own large bed and ample cupboard space and while he unpacked and freshened up I closed all the windows and locked the apartment doors.

That night we had a really good dinner and I after I showed him Kato Pathos. I liked being tourist guide to my young friend and I was learning a lot more about Paddy and his character. We walked down to Bar Street and there were some bars he was not interested in even going in to. Paddy simply looked into the bar, scanned the clientele and evaluated he might have a rough time with the patrons so simply past it by. I hate bigotry in any of its hideous forms: racism, homophobia, ageism, religious beliefs or disabilities. In one slight way Paddy and I had a common bond.

I first realised I was a Charlie Bronson avenger when I was sent home from my junior school for bullying. The truth was I stopped a bully tormenting one of my classmates who suffered from a really bad speech impediment. I walked up to him and smashed him in the face with my fist; he soon stopped his tormenting and started bawling.

Unknown to me at the time was that my classmate had been in a horrendous car crash where both his parents had been killed, ever since that day he spoke with a pronounced stutter. If I had known that fact I would have punched that bully several more times and decidedly harder.

The ten days I spent with Paddy were really great fun and I learned a great deal from him. He surprised me frequently with his maturity and diversity and it was a pleasure to share his company. Some nights we did not even venture out, just hung round the terrace; burning food on the barbecue, listening to music, drinking chilled wine and chatting about our different worlds. After he left and went back to the UK, I coped really well and spent the rest of the time accident free and enjoying every moment. I returned home with minimum hassle and arriving at Manchester Airport a feeling of accomplishment filled my whole body; I now knew I could travel and live perfectly well by myself.

I returned back to Cyprus in late September and spent another three weeks there staying in Paradise Gardens with a close friend Colin. It was good to revisit and see old faces like Billy; who welcomed me with barely a wink. I enjoyed Cyprus, but I had noticed that it was not the cheapest of places to stay for a long period of time, not that many places in Europe are these days.

Chapter Six

KOH SAMUI

After my year of test flights, I was now a much more confident traveller. I must admit, it was not a cake walk for me to travel, but with planning and preparation it was completely possible. I resumed my life back at home and kept to my rigid diet and exercise program. I had put a couple of pounds weight on in Cyprus, but had soon jettisoned that and lost more.

I took stock of my finances and was keeping my head above water with my current income flow. I still had a couple of thousand in savings so financially I was stable whilst the medical insurance still paid me half my salary. When that ended I would have to review things again, but that was a concern I would address when that time came.

Then a major opportunity presented itself, one that was to be a life changing opportunity, but at the time I was totally unaware of that fact. Whilst I was busy sunning myself in Cyprus with some well deserved rest and recuperation, Richie was growing jealous and wanted a holiday. He phoned me and asked if I was capable of travelling long haul again. Questioning him, I discovered he had been given a Kuoni travel brochure from Michele and had seen somewhere he wanted to go to.

There was no point venturing to Europe in November and early December as sun would be hard to find, so long haul was the only option. We had both wanted to travel to Thailand after our trips to Malaysia but my stroke had put a kibosh on that, but now...? I was not really listening to my mate on the phone after the first few words that he had said to me - I had already made my mind up. A week earlier, I had passed a milestone in my recovery: I no longer used my walking cane. It had been more for confidence than anything else; nevertheless, packing away my tartan companion was a life statement and I was definitely feeling stronger and fitter.

That weekend, Rich showed me the brochure and suggested that we have a two week holiday in Koh Samui, then spend three or four days in Bangkok before returning home. Samui looked idyllic and I just told him to go ahead and book it, I needed no persuasion. We both were two nuggets who were not aware of the political unrest brewing in Thailand in November 2008.

The journey was going to be quite difficult for me. First, an Emirates flight from Manchester to Dubai with a couple of hours changeover, then a second Emirates flight to Bangkok Suvarnabhumi airport and another few hours wait there before a Bangkok Airways flight to Koh Samui. The whole trip if everything was on time was going to be in the region of eighteen hours. I knew I would be shattered, but it was going to be worth it to go to Thailand.

The days passed quickly, and I checked with my GP to make sure she thought I was fit enough to undertake such a journey. I had some blood tests done, a check up and was given an all clear in about three days. I had nothing to shop for as I had all my holiday things from Cyprus so all my preparation was done.

Richie phoned and said he was ordering some Thai money from Michele and asked if I'd like some to cover the first couple of days. The currency in Thailand is the Baht and I saw an opportunity to stitch my friend up. Knowing that Richie was not an avid watcher of the Simpsons, I requested two hundred pounds of mixed notes - some Barts, D'ohs and Apus. I thought asking for some Santa's Little Helpers might give the game away. About an hour later I received an SMS saying: "Twat!" Apparently, the big numskull had bumbled into the travel agents and had requested four hundred pounds' worth of the mixed notes I had informed him of. Customers and staff alike burst into hysterics in Crosby Villages

Co-Op as Michele asked him was he sure he did not want some Lisas and Marges too.

Before I knew it, once again Richie and I were in a taxi heading our way to Manchester airport on another adventure. The queues at the Emirates desk were sedate and casual with no sign of the previous charter flight menagerie and we checked in with no hassle whatsoever.

The whole journey went without a hitch, but was extremely long. I found that sitting for more than three hours without moving was very difficult for me and cramps developed in my right leg. It was uncomfortable but not exactly painful and the goal at the end of this endurance test was worth all the discomfort. Finally, excitingly gazing out of the window of the Bangkok Airways Turboprop plane, Koh Samui Airport's landing strip rushed up to greet the plane's wheels and we landed nearly eight thousand miles away in Thailand.

Samui is Thailand's second largest island behind Phuket; it has around sixty thousand residents and caters for one and a half million tourists a year. It is quite a beautiful tropical paradise; varying from lively nightlife to secluded sandy beaches it has everything. All life revolves around the coast as in the centre of the island is the large jungle mountain Khao Pom. Exploring the island is easy as one main road circles the whole island from the capital Nakon, which is basically an old fishing port, to the beach resorts on the east coast of Chaweng and Lamai.

The airport at Koh Samui is probably my favourite in the world. Until fairly recently when Bangkok Airways built the new landing strip and terminal it was little more than a jungle strip of grass and clay. But the new terminal is marvellous, the buildings are all single story with thatched wooden roofs and the sides are open to the elements.

Little tram buses with wooden seats ferry the passengers to and from the planes, it really is a fantasy land of an airport and brilliantly designed. Taking a transit flight from Bangkok straight to Samui is the easiest way to clear Thai immigration, the wait at Samui is minutes, whereas the Bangkok Immigration hall is infamous for very, very long delays. In some cases I have heard passengers quote easily two to three hours to clear through immigration at Suvarnabhumi.

It is possible to go from the mainland and then take a ferry to Samui. You have to travel south down the country from Bangkok by road to either Surat Thani or Donsak and then three operators Seatran, Songserm or Raja will ferry you across to the Nakon. What you save on air fare you will certainly lose in time, but if you have a day to spare and want to see some Thai countryside then it is a valid option.

The hotel we had chosen was in the busy resort of Chaweng beach, the liveliest on the island, but compared to Phuket Town or Pattaya it was tiny in comparison. Rich had booked the Centara Grand Beach Resort which is one of the top hotels on Koh Samui. The Centara Hotel Group is one of Asia's most prestigious hotel chains and I knew from the price we paid it was going to be luxurious.

Walking out from the terminal a representative was there from Kuoni to meet us and show us to our transport. Nok spoke excellent English and was typically Thai; she was petite, extremely pretty and had beautiful, flowing jet black hair. The bus transfer took only twenty minutes and Rich and I expectantly gazed at the passing sights and smiled at each other. It was exactly just what I hoped Thailand to be. We passed old motorbikes carrying whole families, little shacks selling exotic smelling food and many, many smiling faces. Thailand is nicknamed the 'Land of Smiles' for a good reason; the indigenous people are marvellous, fun and are especially happy most of the time.

Chaweng is built up on the beach road parallel to the long, sandy beach that runs on the east shore of the island. From north to south it is about one kilometre long and the Centara is located at the southern end. Most of the noisy nightlife is situated more to the northern end of the beach road; but a plethora of restaurants, shops, bars and massage parlours run all the way along from north to south.

The hotel was magnificent; we were greeted by staff in Thai National dress and ushered into a huge reception area. It was double story high, very airy with plenty of dark wood furniture set about. Through the massive windows I looked out on tropical gardens and beyond that the blue waters of the Gulf of Thailand. I think it was then that my love affair of this wonderful, diverse and captivating country first started.

We were seated, given fresh wet flannels and cool drinks to refresh us after our transit journey. I had almost forgotten my fatigue of the long journey we had just undertaken as my senses were alert taking absolutely everything in around me. An elegant lady with her hands palms together in front of her face, bowed in front of us. This is the Thai way of greeting people, used extensively across the country from Buddhist monks to car mechanics. I was told by a local that it was not just a polite, ceremonial custom but a practical one too. It was a very hygienic way of saying Hello - much cleaner than shaking hands.

She repeated the gesture to Nok who gave her all our documentation before leaving us with an envelope containing the Kuoni welcome bumf. We continued to relax whilst the Centara staff processed our check-in and about five minutes later the same elegant receptionist showed us to our room. From what I could gather, the hotel was four stories high but only two from street level. There is a building regulation that prevents any building over two stories high on the island. Two wings were connected to the central building and our room was on the second floor in the north wing.

I had to almost run to keep up with the receptionist and Richie as they ascended stairways and long open walkways. Finally, we arrived at a door; the receptionist took off her shoes and opened the door for us to enter. Another common custom in all South East Asia is to remove any outdoor footwear before entering any domestic building or services premises such as massage parlours, hairdressers etc. Once again the purpose of this is obvious, the Thai Nation overall is very poor compared to Western affluence, but they persist in taking as much pride as possible in the cleanliness of both themselves and their homes.

Kicking off our shoes we walked, stocking feet, on the bare wooden floorboards into our room. We were shown all the amenities that were available to us and led out on to a marvellous balcony facing the gardens and beach. A porter at the open door stood there with our suitcases whilst Richie fumbled around with his Simpsons money looking for a tip. Both well remunerated, the porter and receptionist both bowed then left us alone.

Rich and I had been on similar journeys before and found that the best way to defeat jet-lag is to immediately accept the time zone you are currently in. To go to bed and rest now at 4pm would be a disaster even though we both felt shattered. The best thing to do would be to unpack, have a good look around before a leisurely meal and a fairly early bed time.

The room was quite large with two queen size beds and everything that you could possibly wish for in terms of comforts. The bathroom was a little strange with saloon type doors as you entered, but had a very modern walk in shower and a bathtub. The Thais have a very different view on many things we straight laced westerners are conditioned to find socially acceptable. Privacy is one of those things, and any overly bashful tourists considering visiting Asia would be well to consider that fact. Sexuality is another but that topic is for later on in the book.

Whilst Richie soaped up in the saloon, I went out on to the balcony. The sound of the rolling waves and surf greeted me as I stepped out; it is a familiar, comforting noise to me as I have always resided by the coast. This was far more exotic than the Irish Sea, it was the Gulf of Thailand washing over that sandy beach ahead with all its magical history and mystical stories riding like stallions on the blue foaming water. A lump came to my throat as I absorbed the wonderful vista before me, a lump formed of pure happiness. I had come so far to be here, not just in miles, but in my own personal journey. I was glad my friend could not see the tears forming in my eyes.

Decked out in suitable tropical attire we explored the hotel. The Centara was massive; it housed four restaurants, three bars, gym and large swimming pool. The gardens in front of the hotel had large grassy lawns for sunbathing and strolling and there was a purpose built wooden sun deck for the serious sun worshipers. The whole hotel sat on Chaweng beach and numerous sets of small steps were dotted about to allow access to the golden sand.

Strolling along the beach numerous vendors were selling their wares and you could purchase just about anything from an ice cream to a fake Gucci handbag. There were little covered wooden platforms where beach masseurs plied their trade and aromatic snacks cooking on little portable clay pots. My favourites were the fresh fruit vendors selling pineapples, mangoes and other non recognisable delicious delicacies. The beach was marvellous, alive with activity but quite sparsely populated by tourists.

Even at just after 5pm the sun was still hot and high in the sky. Thailand's climate is tropical, but it does differ from north to south and east or west of the peninsula. Koh Samui located in the South East of the country and has a fairly equitable temperature never dropping below twenty five degrees all year round, but has a monsoon rainy season in September, October, and November. When it decides to rain, it could last for days; a continuous torrential downpour that makes roads impassable and venturing out nigh impossible.

We worked our way back to the hotel and strolled onto the main road of Chaweng, the beach road. For a main road it was quite narrow and in fact halfway along its length it is one way as two vehicles could not pass. When that happens, the road splits and the other half continues on the other side of the buildings, running along one side of the large man made lake behind.

On either side of the road there was a higgledy-piggledy arrangement of all manner of establishments. From restaurants and bars to artist galleries and places for massages. There were petite convenience stores next to small Seven Elevens to shop for groceries and a plethora of gift shops.

The more unwelcome doorways are the Indian tailor shops. They harass you everywhere and are a royal pain in the arse: the young salesmen outside their shops will grab and claw at you for attention. They are so bad that there are even t-shirts you can buy at the tourist stalls with the slogan: "I don't want a FUCKING suit," completely useless anywhere else in the world but jolly handy in Samui. I am completely baffled why the Samui authorities let these hawkers be so aggressive in their sales techniques; unless, of course, there are some sharp dressed civil servants in Nakon Town Hall.

Negotiating along this busy road was difficult as the pavements were a nightmare. They seem to last for varying, very short distances and are different levels and widths, but mostly they are quite high. There was also an assortment of sandbags piled up against shop fronts, for a reason that was to become quite apparent in the next few days.

One year ago there was no possible way I could have considered Chaweng as a possible holiday destination and even now it was extremely difficult for me to confidently walk along these paths.

Families with pushchairs found it nearly impossible to cope and I sympathised with them.

Barring interference by the pestering tailors and numerous obstacles, it is possible to amble from one end of Chaweng beach road to the other in about thirty minutes. The fastest way is to walk along the beach and cut up one of the many Sois leading to the road. A Soi is a small side street or path and is usually referred to by a number, i.e. Soi 1, Soi 2 etc. or by a landmark. For instance, if a Soi has a small hotel on the corner it might have a name, like Soi Palm Beach.

There is a public transport system which consists of large trucks with a crew bus seating arrangement in the rear called Songthaews, or locally, Tuk-Tuks. They stop just about anywhere; simply jump on and press the buzzer or bang on the roof when you want to get off. Depending on distance, it costs around fifty baht for the fare. If you are flying solo then motorbike taxi is another option, but the metered taxis tend to be very expensive on the island.

Samui is famous for its art, and you will find many galleries with local artists at work selling their paintings at very reasonable prices. Also, there are many barbecue restaurants lined up on the main road. These are great value for money and usually have large frozen cabinets on display showing their choice cuts of meat or freshly caught fish, everything from giant Shellfish to succulent barracuda.

Perhaps the most popular activity Samui has to offer is world class massages. There are massage shops just about everywhere offering authentic Thai massages that are famed throughout the country. Most stay open until midnight and are a great way to relax and unwind after a long day on the beach. A full one hour body massage will cost around three hundred and fifty baht and believe me it is worth every D'oh. Do not expect these establishments to offer a happy ending to your massage; these are reputable businesses offering a professional service with trained employees not a backstreet boudoir. If it is the latter, then perhaps a venture down one of the darkly lit Sois might suit requirements a little better.

Straight across from the Centara is Zico's, a huge Brazilian restaurant with a very acceptable upstairs bar. The place is actually owned by the Centara and it offers two Happy Hours, one in the early evening and one much later on. This became our regular first starting place each evening when we would decide what was on the agenda for the night.

This part of the beach road has few actual bars you can frequent and just have a quiet drink. There are numerous restaurants and Beer Bars but not places you could sit and chat over a cold beer. A Beer Bar is somewhere stacked out with scantily clad ladies selling bottled Singh, Chang or Leo beer and trying their best to prise a drink from their patrons. Actually they can be quite fun; for the price of a drink, a noisy hostess will trash you at Pool or Connect Four and then howl with delight at your demise. Some of the girls will offer more services than just playing board games, a polite but definite "no" will suffice if the mood does not take you.

After a couple of beers in Zico's we wandered down the road, trying our best not to argue with pesky tailors, and perused restaurants for later on. The choice is very varied from the barbeque establishments to typical little Thai canteens, and even for the philistines, McDonalds and Pizza Hut. For the Egon Ronays of the world, there are also fine dining establishments dotted around the island, but normally transport is needed to access them.

My favourite places are the local Food Halls. Here, delicious, freshly cooked Thai food is served piping hot on small plastic plates at ridiculously cheap prices. I love the buzz and atmosphere of these huge places; the aromatic aromas of lemongrass, lime, galangal and sweet basil permeates the very warm air as busy young waitresses hop from table to table. The searing sound of fish or meat cooking in scorching hot woks dominates the noise levels as Thai cooks ball out their orders in an Asiatic Operetta of cuisine.

Greenstreet and Back

By now we were pretty hungry and a little tired, so we decided to eat. Close by on the opposite side of the road, there was a restaurant called Andaman's; it looked very acceptable so we went in. Immediately we were greeted by mine host; Benz was a small bespectacled Thai gentleman with a beaming smile who spoke very good English. He ushered us to a table and beckoned to a line of waiters to immediately come and attend to us.

The place was only a third full so we seemed to have the whole waiting staff at our disposal. There was a knife waiter, a spoon waiter etc. Richie and I started to take the piss and deliberately asking for items of cutlery or condiments that were not present just so we could add another waiter to our list of attendants. We requested the wine list and it was if we had just demanded the Crown Jewels; the butter knife waiter discussed our request with the apprentice crumb spotter and the message was then passed down the line until Benz's manic grinning face appeared at our table.

He held the wine list aloft as though he had just magically plucked it from thin air and wafted it in front of us. I noticed that Benz; although his English was very good, it must have been taught to him by some aged hippy or somebody as he sounded like an extra from some 60s film starring Dennis Hopper. He had one phrase in particular that was his favourite: "You got it! Right on! Yeah!"

This catchphrase became our regular retort to any question asked of us during our whole holiday. In fact we became that used to saying it at the drop of a hat, that the Bug Bar suffered our repetitive slogan for about two weeks after our return. We even perfected the pronunciation to Benz's exact deliverance. He would actually say the words whilst somebody else was talking, highlighting their own accuracy of understanding something he had just said.

For instance, if in conversation with Benz your reply was, "I understand now", his would be "You got it!" If you said "Turn left at the police station", he would reply, "Right on!" "And it is third on your left..." "Yeah!" The "Yeah!" was accompanied with a knowing wink and flash of his manic smile as though you had just understood the Theory of Relativity, not the directions to Starbucks.

I must say, the meal was excellent and washed down with a glass of Regency brandy, one of Thailand's better offerings. There was a very pretty Thai lady who supplied our bill and as we were both shattered we said our goodbyes to our new pals.

"We are both very tired," we said.

"You got it!"

"So, we go back to the hotel now."

"Right on!"

"Thanks for everything, goodnight!"

"Yeah!" I turned and saw Benz waving animatedly as he gave me the final knowing wink of the evening.

Waking in the morning, I could hear the unmistakable sound of rain outside. I looked out of the blinds and saw a curtain of water cascading from the grey sky. Rich was still asleep so I yawned, stretched a little and went back to bed.

A couple of hours later, Richie woke me to give a weather report: "It's raining." I shook my head, he would never make an after dinner speaker. Opening the curtains fully he let the grey light drift in the room and I could see the weather had not abated one jot.

That day was a total washout; confined to our room by the monsoon, we idled the day away taking regular naps and watching films. There was not even any point sitting on the balcony because there was so much torrential rain about an inch of water covered the whole floor. There was a squall far out at sea and the horizon was a dark blue almost mauve colour, a heavy swell was in the leaden water and I was glad that I was not a sailor. I had experienced the monsoon before in Penang, but there it only lasted a couple of hours each day; this had been a constant eight hours at least.

At around 6pm, the rain lessened to just a bad storm, so we decided to try a venture as far as Zico's. The hotel had supplied umbrellas for the guests, so donning just shorts and flip flops, we faced the weather. Peering out of the side entrance of the hotel, we were amazed at the devastation in front of us. The beach road was now a river, perhaps one or two feet deep. There seemed to be a sort of tide as the water was certainly flowing, but perhaps that was the drainage system trying to cope. One or two brave fools were trying to navigate mopeds along the flooded highway; they were locals and knew the higher parts of the road to travel along. A few minutes later after studying the routes the cyclists took we undertook a path that only got our feet wet and arrived at Zico's, a little damp, but we had survived.

Zico's was not surprisingly, completely empty. We sipped our beers and looked out at the horrendous weather that had seemed to have taken a turn for the worse. There was no big problem as we could eat in the restaurant and have an easy night, but we both decided this was as far as we would go tonight.

The following day was exactly the same, nothing but a deluge of water from the sky and once again we were prisoners of the hotel. The Centara has many amenities, but it does not really have a snug bar for settling down for a couple of hours. The best bar it has is on the beach and that was open air so not an option. We attempted to go out for some food and coffee, but the weather was so bad we scurried home and ate in the hotel instead. Another early night in idyllic Koh Samui for room 225.

Finally, we woke to a dry day, somewhat overcast but no rain. So, we spent the day on the beach relaxing by the sea. Rich suggested that we both tried a massage and so we headed out in the early afternoon to pick somewhere from the multitude of choices. I found one called Lotus where an array of ladies clad in spotless orange uniforms were seated to choose from. Selecting my favourite, I was then presented with a menu.

There were foot massages, head massages, aromatherapy massages and many, many more. I opted for a one hour oil massage. It was a far cry from what I had experienced in Cyprus and my first ever proper Thai massage. It was superb and an experience not to be missed travelling to this part of South East Asia.

My whole body felt relaxed yet invigorated by the healing hands of the petite, young masseur. She could not have been more than twenty, but she definitely knew her trade and applied just the right amount of pressure on my aching muscles. She immediately recognised that I had a problem and took extra care on my weak limbs not to hurt me. The cost was amazing three hundred Baht, which in 2008 was around six quid; I tipped generously and went to find Richie to see how his massage had gone.

He too had had a wonderful time and we both agreed that we would go every day before we changed for the evening's activities. It is a really good way of putting some of the moisture back into your skin after a long day of sunbathing and your whole body tingles with the heightened alertness of your nerves.

That evening we decided to walk further down the beach road as we had not really explored that much due to the weather. We passed Andaman's and received a royal wave and manic grin from "Right on!" and continued our stroll. As we moved further up the road, things got much livelier and we discovered Soi Green Mango. It is actually a "U" shaped Soi with both entrances returning to the beach road. It houses a number of Beer Bars, but also two of the island's most popular night venues; The Green Mango and the Sweet Soul Cafe. Soi Green Mango is not what I would call family entertainment: it is loud, brash and normally very busy, but nevertheless somewhere to have fun and part with a few Baht.

Past Soi Green Mango things stay on the more nightclub and lively side, and if that is your cup of tea, then Bar Solo and Bondi

Bar are worth visiting. It is this part of Samui that houses Starbucks, McDonald's and pizza Hut, so you can estimate the clientele they are aiming at.

Samui is also quite renowned for two specialist Ladyboy Cabaret Clubs called Christy's and Starz. Here, ladyboys lip sync through songs whilst parading in very glamorous gowns to the music. Some of the katoeys are breathtakingly beautiful, not to be confused with their prostitute counterparts in other parts, and should be treated respectfully. I admit there are some that are more akin to Barbara Cartland on Prozac, but in the main it is the former.

Katoeys are sometime referred to as the Third Sex and are accepted fully into Thai culture. There are different stages to a katoey's life and some do not take the whole metamorphism, preferring to keep their male genitalia and opting just for hormone treatment. Thailand is a very tolerant, accepting country: I think their Buddhist religion is the main reason for this, which accepts a comprehensive tolerance to differences. For this reason also there are many very open and out gays who are a key part of Thailand's social structure; again, respected and totally enveloped into society.

Over ninety percent of Thailand is Buddhist, but other religions are more than tolerated and practised. It is common to see local Buddhists pray on a Hindu Festival day or simply visit one of the marvellous Hindu temples and offer prayers and flowers. Christian and Muslim religions are also present, the latter normally by immigrants, the former actually by Thai Nationals.

I had enough exploring for one night and suggested a Regency and Coffee at Andaman's. "Right on" had left for the evening, but the attractive woman from the previous night served us our brandies. Her name was Sue; she was around thirty and immaculately dressed. Her raven black hair was swept aside so her attractive face was fully visible and she had a most engaging smile. Her English was quite good and she explained to us that she and her husband owned the business. Richie asked about Benz explaining that we thought he was the boss. Sue laughed and shook her head saying it was a common mistake: Benz actually believed he was the boss, but she tolerated his Walter Mitty behaviour as he was actually a very good worker.

The alcohol had done its business and I knew I had to retire for the evening, my leg was not responding too well to what I was trying to tell it and I had trouble standing still. Sue had noticed my limp before and knew that I had been ill, so called to one of her staff: "Johnny, get motor bike!"

Within seconds, a rather noisy moped was revving up outside the restaurant and I was loaded on the back of the bike. The journey took about one minute and the barrier at the main gate of the Centara was raised to let us enter. I could not swing my leg over the bike to get off, it felt like lead. Whilst Johnny sat on the front stabilising the contraption, two security guards whilst laughing lifted me off the bike and plonked me on my feet. Not a very elegant way to arrive at the Centara Grand Beach Resort's reception and I hoped no new guests were waiting to check in and witnessed my performance.

The weather was the same the following day, overcast but no rain. Rich was still fast asleep when I woke, a normal trait, so I went to sit by the beach. A couple of hours later, my friend arrived and told me of a small bar that he imaginatively nicknamed Pool Bar, located right opposite the main gates of the hotel that had stayed open till four in the morning. He had found some new chums and I was glad; I didn't feel so guilty for being such a lightweight.

Later I was waiting for Richie in Zico's after an afternoon massage. I was sipping my beer when I glanced at a television on the far wall. I could not really make out what was happening, but there were a lot of people wearing yellow shirts sitting on the floor. *Not really good reality television*, I thought, but the staff seemed captivated by it. Richie then appeared and ordered two beers to catch up with me, why he had to catch up baffled me as he would out stay my evening by many hours. He checked his phone and saw there was a message from his brother Kevin asking was he OK. "That's strange, he doesn't normally ask how my holiday is going..." he muttered more to himself, than directing the comment towards me.

Richie and Kevin own a family retail business back home and have a traditional butchers' shop that does a fine business. I had never heard of a butcher before who fainted at the sight of blood, but Richie will faint if he sees other people's blood whilst Kevin will faint if he is bleeding himself. It will be a disaster one day if Kevin cuts himself in front of Richie; first Kevin would keel over, closely followed by his sibling. It would be a scene to rival any from Pulp Fiction, two butchers in blue striped overalls lying in a mess of blood, knives scattered around their prostrate bodies.

We did not get very far that evening as it started to rain again heavily. Richie took me to meet Vaughn the owner of the Pool Bar; it would be easy for us to make a dash home for sanctuary from there if the weather got any worse. Vaughn was a rather buxom, rotund Thai lady that was busy potting a ball when we arrived, I had already surmised why Rich had nicknamed this the Pool Bar. I don't know if it actually has a name, it is just there and that's that. Vaughn welcomed Richie as though he was her long lost brother.

"Where have you been?" she asked. Richie shrugged. "I have missed you darling," she continued. This did not surprise me; Richie is quite a raconteur and has a way of making his presence felt in a place, especially if alcohol is involved. No doubt he had been lording it up the previous night, regaling many of his tales that have no basis of truth in them whatsoever. Vaughn had moved her attention to her Irish partner as he was requesting another drink whilst fondling her behind. A very old ghetto blaster was behind the bar playing some dreadful cover music and we just sat on barstools drinking and occasionally me watching Rich play pool. After about an hour, there was a large flash in the sky and distant thunder could be heard rumbling so we took our leave of Vaughn and scurried back to the hotel.

Returning back to the room, Richie turned the television on and started flicking through the channels. On every Thai channel there were more pictures of the sitting down Thais with yellow shirts on; nothing seemed to be happening apart from one of the older ones occasionally wafting themselves with a hand held paper fan. It certainly was not exciting or riveting stuff. I knew it was some sort of demonstration, but could not fathom out where it was or what they were supposed to be doing. It was most refreshing when Richie finally found the cartoon channel.

It was not until the following morning that we awoke to Richie's mobile phone ringing. Rich answered and his face changed, an unusual solemn expression set in and his voice was barely audible. He turned to me and said that it had been Kev; he was worried about us due to the troubles in Bangkok. I shrugged as I did not have a clue what Kev was going on about.

Rich turned the television on and found BBC World News, some bloke was wittering on about a new Japanese gadget that could cook an egg in a minute. Fuck me! If you can't even wait three minutes for an egg to cook you must be one impatient bastard. I went to the saloon for a wash and I was just brushing my teeth when Rich shouted my name. Sitting on the foot of my bed, I stared at the screen: it was Thailand and the main news item. Apparently, the reality TV show I had seen in Zico's was actually a major political incident.

The People's Alliance for Democracy Party or PAD, also known as the yellow shirts, had taken control of Bangkok's two airports in a political coup. Suvarnabhumi Airport is Thailand's major airport and is fairly new, being built in 2006. It is one of Asia's most vital hubs, an extremely busy destination for both passengers and freight. Don Muang is the old airport and is now used for all domestic flights within the country but even so, a major artery in Thailand's transportation system.

We did not know how exactly the sit in would affect us or even if the situation would get any worse. However, there was nothing we could do about it ourselves and seeing the sun was finally shining, we thought it more prudent to spend the day on the beach and relax. Walking through reception was like a scene from a Vietnam War film where desperate Westerners harangued poor Asian officials for more details of their plight. I could see Nok surrounded by about ten people all gesticulating and demanding information. I wondered if I had remembered my sunscreen.

Later that day, an envelope had been put under our door from Kuoni stating that Nok would be available in reception every day at 10am for one hour due to the political situation to provide information and help. I pitied the poor girl, what the Hell could she do? Go to Bangkok and one by one physically remove all the yellow shirts? She would have a very sore back indeed if Kuoni requested her do that. I did not fancy her chances claiming on her policy with BUPA on that one.

Walking down beach road, we saw a very animated "Right on!" waving frantically at us, he was wearing a yellow shirt and I looked at Richie and smiled. He ushered us into Andaman's and two beers were ordered. Benz had now turned into a self proclaimed agent for the PAD party on Samui and he could give us any inside information on the movement we required.

Thanking our new political activist and ally, we reassuredly carried on with our night out saying we would be in touch if we needed the resistance to aid us. A little further on we saw a tiny Rock Music bar that we had overlooked previously; it had two tables and a couple of bar stools, the music was mixed so it was okay. It was owned by two English guys and one was in conversation with a man called Ken. He was distraught saying his flight home had been cancelled. We did not pay too much attention as our flight to

Bangkok was in over a week and many things could happen before now and then.

The waitress in the Rock Bar had more than a passing resemblance to James Brown. It was not that she was particularly ugly more that she had a very large chin and coiffured, ginger tinted hair. A fact I disclosed to the owner, who had not noticed the resemblance previously, and with every glance in her direction he saw more confirmation that I was correct. However, with each glance his laughter grew louder and we left before a very irate *Sex Machine* put her *Good Foot* right up my arse.

After a fantastic Thai meal of whole steamed fish in lime soup, garlic and chillies we decided to try Soi Green Mango. There was a girl at the entrance of the street with a large pole that old people in yellow coats use to help children cross the road. Written on the "Lollipop" stick was the slogan, "Follow me for a suck!" It sort of summed up Soi Green Mango, close to the bone but also very funny. I lasted about an hour before the professional Connect Four players had finally beaten me into submission and I hailed a motor bike and went home.

Walking through reception in the morning once again poor Nok was receiving a serious barrage from the irate Kuoni holidaymakers. A sort of spokesman had been elected and was speaking on behalf of the group. Who the Hell did they think they where, a bloody Escape Committee? The fat spokesperson reminded me of a Richard Todd character who was lecturing the Camp Commandant on the Geneva Convention whilst Lionel Jefferies and Dickie Attenborough were pulling faces at the guards.

I sauntered past in my flip flops ignoring the whole debacle to enjoy the sun which now finally seemed a permanent fixture. I passed the picture of Charles Hawtrey and remembered it was the King's birthday today and wondered what the celebrations would be like later on that night.

The grounds of the Centara to say the least are vast, with hundreds of available places for you to sit and enjoy your day. Most are on the expanse of lawn with many trees to give shade and comfortable chairs to relax in. There was however, only one real sun trap apart from the beach and that was the wooden sun deck stacked out with only about twenty loungers. Between every two loungers there was a table and a Sun Umbrella! I could not believe my eyes as some stupid twat was raising his umbrella so that his wife and he could sit in the shade.

It had been sodding raining for nearly one week and this was the first real sun that I had a chance to sit in, this pillock was blocking out some of its rays. Why the fuck did he not go and sit under the trees, the numpty? I threw an empty water bottle at the umbrella in disgust, but my aim with my left arm was not good and it clattered into the back of his chair. He turned around with a scowl on his face, I just pointed at his umbrella and then to my shaded leg. He turned and completely ignored me, the bastard.

By the time Rich had come to join me, I had calmed down and moved loungers away from the pillock. I was a little embarrassed at my earlier behaviour and did not disclose my actions to my friend. I knew he would disagree with my sun bathing etiquette especially as he had booked the Centara Grand Beach Resort with his sister in law Michele; Richie was a bit of a snob that way. I told him about the escape committee and he was of the same opinion as me, that they were a bunch of hysterical twats.

That evening was a big surprise to both of us, the anticipated jubilant celebrations we were expecting for the King's birthday did not materialise. In fact every bar was closed with respect to their revered monarch. Andaman's served us drinks in Coconut Husks whilst Benz predicted blood on the streets from his fellow conspirators. Sue came into the restaurant accompanied by a small slight man she introduced as Din her husband, pronounced Tin. He had heard of the money we had spent in his business and joined us for about an hour buying us dinner and drinks, he was an animated man and seemed tuned in to every conversation taking place in his restaurant. He was somebody who took life seriously, and was nobody's fool.

Our expectation of the King's birthday was one borne out of sheer ignorance. I had explained about the painting in the Centara Lobby and tried to describe to him who Charles Hawtrey was. Tin cut me short and did not find my amusing anecdote at all humorous. The king of Thailand is revered amongst his people, described by a Thai poet as: "A caring monarch who loves his people."

Unlike the British Monarchy, King Rama the Ninth is not just a PA puppet of the government. He has devoted his life to worthwhile projects all over the country for his citizens; from building roads, bridges and irrigating farmland to ensuring planning for hospitals and schools was not held back by corrupt Red Tape. Bhumibou Adulyadej is the longest serving monarch in the world and when his time is finally ended Thailand will mourn for weeks, perhaps months. Before every film in the cinemas a brief film of the King is shown and everybody including farangs, stand and bow to show their respect. A vast majority of the Western world could learn valuable lessons from Thailand in respect to their tolerance and morals.

A few more days passed much the same, the weather was glorious and we spent most of our time outdoors. Every morning the escape committee met and Richard Todd had the Centara Lobby alive with activity, a team of forgers, tailors (not the Indian pests) ,linguists and tunnelers were briefed with the days' chores. A bald man was crying because he was informed that as his glasses were not from Specsavers he could not accompany the rest of the team on the escape.

We bumped into Ken numerous times on our evening promenades and things were pretty grim for him. He had run out of cash and had been thrown out of his hotel, the owner of the Rock Bar had fixed him up with some digs, pretty squalid but cheap. His airline was a budget Russian company and they had left him high and dry: they were not even answering their phones, it looked as though they had closed shop on all their refugees. He also had no access to any of his money back in the UK and was at a loss how and when was going to get home.

Nevertheless, things were getting a tad tight for us. In two days we were due to fly to Bangkok and spend some time in the capital, but then we were due to go home. Richie phoned a mutual friend, Sharon who worked for Emirates Airlines. She informed him absolutely no fights whatsoever were arriving or departing from Suvarnabhumi Airport, the whole airline industry in South East Asia was in chaos with the actions of the yellow shirts. However, we were confirmed passengers for our flights and we just had to sit it out and hope the demonstrations ended by the due date.

The situation in the hotel was getting a little eerie. Nok had managed to get the whole escape committee by ferry and road off the island. Where they went from then I haven't got a clue, my guess was a long road trip to either Kuala Lumpur or Phnom Penh and fight alongside every other evacuee for a seat on a plane they were not booked on. People were leaving Samui in their droves by ferry, but no new tourists could arrive. The whole place looked like a ghost town.

The actions by the People's Alliance for Democracy Party had been a well thought out strategy and eventually was to lead to elections and the downfall of the Government. However, it came at a crippling price for Thailand's economy. The tourist industry was to suffer the backlash for years after and many freight company's re-routed their cargoes to avoid Bangkok. A battle won, but at a hefty cost to a country they were now going to govern.

Our final night was a little subdued due to the uncertainty of our situation in the morning. Rich and I had decided we would simply stay put for another three days and take stock of the situation then. Sharon was informing us of all the Emirates advice so there was nothing else we could do. We strolled down beach road past all the empty restaurants and bars and bumped into Ken. He had managed to borrow some money from the owners of the Rock Bar and could pay his rent and eat. He had also e-mailed a friend in the UK to ask him to send some funds via Western Union so hopefully he could try and get back to the UK soon.

We dined in Andaman's and "Right on!" was in jubilant mood until Rich pointed out that there were no diners in his restaurant and the likelihood was there would not be any for a long time. This nugget of information seemed not to register in the zealot's mind, as is often the case with such people. The big picture is often obscured by the fervour of mob rule. Sue was a little more thoughtful; she knew tough times were ahead of her and her business.

The following day, Rich and I awoke early and were relaxing on the deserted sun deck when a frantic Nok came scurrying over to us.

"There you are, I have been looking for you for days!" Rich and I looked at each other as nonchalantly as we possibly could trying not to look phased by events. "You are due to check out today, I booked you three more nights in a similar standard hotel in Rangon on the mainland! Your ferry leaves in two hours." We had already discussed this issue and decided to decline any option such as this and stay on Samui to save all the travel hassle.

We told Nok our decision and she sat on a chair next to us. "I wish all my customers were as easy as you two," she said in a loud sigh. The past week must have been terrible for her and I felt truly sorry for the young girl. Although there were plenty of available rooms at the Centara, Nok was not authorised in her budget to offer us this option. We said we would pay for the three extra nights ourselves and try to claim back the difference on our return to the UK. Nok left us saying she would arrange everything with reception and wished us luck in our efforts to get back home.

After that Rich and I partied the final few days trying to forget our plight, but the uncertainty of our future nagged at my brain. I knew I had only a few days supply of my medication and soon despite all our bravado, this situation was going to get very, very serious. And then, as if by magic, the day before our scheduled departure the yellow shirts won their negotiations with the authorities and left the two airports.

A letter from Nok was delivered to our room stating that we were booked on Bangkok Airways flight in the morning at 10am to Suvarnabhumi Airport. Our first Emirates flight to Dubai was not until around 9pm the same evening, but Nok had decided to give us as plenty as time as possible in case of problems.

The following day we landed at Bangkok International Airport a little excited and nervous of what was going to greet us. We thought it safer to take our baggage with us and not check it all the way through at Samui so we had to wait a short while to reclaim our cases before making our way to Departures.

The scene in the Departure Lounge was nothing short of carnage. Bodies were strewn everywhere, for over a week people had been living and sleeping here as they simply had nowhere else to go. There was actually a trestle table staffed by British officials as a temporary consulate. Apparently, the official British Embassy in Bangkok was so full of temporary residents they had to set up another here at the airport. We made our way to the Emirates desks and passed an airways office with a familiar sign.

"Isn't that the airline Ken is flying with?" I said. The budget airline had done a bunk; whilst every other airways office was brimming with customers here the shutters were firmly closed. No wonder they were not answering their phone... I then thought of Ken and wondered if he had been here yet.

Emirates' check-in desks were mobbed. The queue had disintegrated into a mass brawl and I surveyed the scenes around me at some of the other airlines desks and they were the same if not worse. We joined the back of one throng and set in for a long wait. After about two hours, we finally faced a very tired but irate Emirates member of staff. Rich produced our tickets and were curtly advised we were not on the passenger list. Rich asked her what the date was today and what the next flight number and time to Dubai was. He then pointed out on our tickets the corresponding information. We had arrived the correct day, correct time and had confirmed numbered seats for the next flight to Dubai. The check-in girl then showed us a list with our names on standby; we had been thrown off the flight together with about another fifty people. Rich demanded to see a supervisor, so we were directed to the Emirates Office where another forty eight irate passengers queued.

I knew exactly what had happened, although we were on time for our flight all the first class passengers from days of cancelled flights had pulled rank and Emirates had thrown us off the plane. It was wrong, unfortunately for them their flights had been cancelled, but ours had not and we had valid tickets to fly on that plane. My leg was now aching with the strain of pulling my case and being jostled from pillar to post in the crowds. This was horrid and I knew I would not be able to stand much more of it, my energy levels were getting extremely low.

By the time we got to the front of the next Emirates queue the supervisor had gone to lunch so we had the same argument with a rather irascible lady. She was basically telling a pack of lies saying our flight had been cancelled. I pointed to the departures board and flight number and time of the next Emirates flight to Dubai, then to our tickets with the exact same information on. The best she was prepared to offer us was a flight the following evening; also, she had no accommodation for us as we did not qualify. Sharon had told us of the requirements laid down by Emirates and we knew we did, the truth was they had no rooms left in any of their partners' hotels, they were all full due to the backlog. She knew that we were aware this was a game and we knew she was lying, this made her even more indignant and she brusquely told us to find the supervisor whose name was Jill.

We stood there getting jostled in the crowd trying to decide what our next actions should be. We were getting a little irate with each other and that was not going to get us anywhere. Then I saw a lady in a dark blue uniform different to the fawn ones worn by the rest of the Emirates flight staff. She was standing with some colleagues behind a closed desk, but I could see her name badge: Jill. I knew we had a justified and valid case to demand our original seats on the flight, but decided for the first time to take a different tack and explain my physical condition and ask for pity.

Jill was a very intelligent and capable lady and listened to what I was trying to explain to her, but at the same time was holding three other conversations. I did not know if she was paying any attention to me whatsoever. Half way through the conversation she picked up the phone and started to talk to somebody else. I was getting frustrated because I was unaware she was actually working on my behalf. Eventually she asked Rich and me to follow her.

"I have pulled in a favour from a friend," Jill explained to us as we arrived at the Qantas desk. She shook hands with the Australian man behind the counter and wished us a safe flight. Jill had managed to wangle us seats on the next Qantas flight to London and then a British Airways Shuttle flight to Manchester. Because there was only one hour wait in London we would actually arrive home before we were scheduled to do so by Emirates. I could have hugged Jill; it was not Emirates that had sorted our problem out, it was a gem of a woman who called in a favour. I wondered had she known somebody who had suffered a stroke like me - was this a secret private club I had unwittingly joined? We breathed a sigh of relief and thanked ourselves we were bright enough to have our luggage with us, an unusual spot of forethought on our behalf.

We waited three hours and around 10pm boarded our flight to London. The plane closed its doors and we taxied to the runway. We waited and waited whilst there was several whirring noises as the pilot tested his equipment and then silence. After about ten minutes the pilot advised us there was a problem and we had to wait for an engineer. I looked at Rich and just raised my eyes; he knew we had a very short time for our connecting flight also. An engineer arrived and attempted to fix the plane whilst we sat on the runway apron. More whirring noises and again silence. This time the pilot advised us we were going back to the terminal for more repairs.

Eventually just after midnight the Qantas flight finally left Bangkok and we were on our way home. I did not sleep at all on the journey as I listened to every mechanical sound during the whole flight, expecting the engine to drop off at any minute. The technical problem was probably only small, but any problem in a plane is most unsettling. Perhaps the First Officer's dashboard cigar lighter would not work or something of that nature, but better to be safe than sorry - the last thing the flight needed was a nervous First Officer biting his fingernails.

By the time Rich and I reported at British Airways Terminal 5, our flight had left one hour previous. Because of the ramifications of the yellow shirts' actions there were stranded passengers all over the world: there was not another available flight to Manchester for eight hours. The B.A. representative saw our beleaguered condition; I was very close to tears from sheer exhaustion. She took pity on us and gave us passes for the executive lounge. It was a life saver, we were able to take a hot shower and shave and feel a little more human. We patiently sat and waited the whole day; finally were able to board the 17:35 shuttle to Manchester.

Arriving home in a taxi Richie helped me to my door with my case. He walked down the path saying he would see me tomorrow sometime. I called after him, "You got it!" He turned and replied, "Right on!" and in unison we both said, "Yeah!" I put my key in the lock: it had been exactly thirty six hours since we had left the Centara Grand Beach Resort and I had deducted the time difference.

I dumped my bag in the hall and wearily made my way upstairs, I was physically shattered and my whole body ached. The house was freezing, but after a quick wash I climbed under my duvet and slept deeply from sheer exhaustion. The holiday had been a huge adventure and experience; I had survived another testing and trying ordeal which would stand me in good stead in the years to come. I have never liked the colour yellow to this day.

Chapter Seven

THE CRYPT

My health continued to grow with my rigid regime, although no new dramatic improvements to my movement of my right arm and leg. I assumed that I had reached my plateau and what I had was as good as it was going to get. But it was not a time to slacken my exercises and diet; I needed to stabilise and I set a goal to lose two more stones in one year.

My speech was almost back to normal and there was no legacy of any problems with my face. My ugly mug was the same as before the stroke, much thinner but just as ugly! I still hated the cold English weather and it still affected me dramatically when temperatures dropped. I had this nagging feeling that perhaps I would have to leave old Blighty and my beloved Liverpool one day.

I needed a project to keep my brain active and I decided that I would organise another Soul Night. This time I would leave the boat and put on an even more spectacular event. I had the time to devote my whole attention to this event and would endeavour to make it the best ever. The following weeks I searched for an appropriate venue as this would be the key to success. I had a few ideas; Liverpool Town Hall and Sefton Park's Glasshouse, but they were too small. I wanted somewhere the punters would never have been to, somewhere extraordinary in their city a hidden gem.

Then I stumbled, more out of good fortune than planning, on a potential site for the event. I was walking through the city and I noticed an advertisement for C.A.M.R.A. Liverpool's Beer Festival weekend in the Roman Catholic cathedral. Liverpool has two cathedrals; the giant, elegant Anglican one perched on St James' Mount above the city and the more modern Catholic Christ the King Cathedral, nicknamed Paddy's Wigwam, built in the 1960's.

A single street links the two buildings, aptly called Hope Street. The first blueprint plans for Christ the King Cathedral were of a building far grander than the one actually erected.

The cathedral was going to be the largest in the world and would have dwarfed Mount Pleasant. But the Second World War broke out just as some of the foundations were laid and after hostilities finally ended, the world was a very different place. Finances were now not available to fund this colossal project and so the more modest building that now stands was put it its place. However, some of the original design crypt and associated ecclesiastic chambers were completed and it was here the Beer Festival was to be held.

I solicited the aid of Tony, one of my mates, and after consultation with him, within a few days I had the name and phone number of the person I needed to contact at the cathedral. I phoned and made an appointment to see him in the following week and was pleased at my progress.

The next day I was on one of my weekly Tesco runs with Linzi and animatedly told her of my idea for the Soul Night. Linzi had been to most of the nights, as her husband Paul is one of the DJs. I use the term Disc Jockey very loosely in reference to our activities. She thought it a wonderful idea and wanted to accompany me to the appointment as she had never been to the cathedral. I jumped at the opportunity and with the promise of lunch at The Quarter, I had sealed my lift.

The morning of the meeting arrived and I looked out at the grey skies from my bedroom window. Occasional snow flurries whipped around, playing with the bare branches on the naked trees, and a thin white carpet had begun to form on the road. I shivered in anticipation of how cold the temperature would be outside and remembered how much I hated British weather.

I had not yet purchased a new winter coat, so took an old heavy leather jacket from my wardrobe; it seemed the warmest in the closet. It was one of my pre-stroke winter collection, not that I held a fashion week or anything to declare the season's new ranges from High & Mighty, it was just a phrase to describe my coat. I tried the jacket on and laughed, the garment could have wrapped around me at least twice. Christ! The thing used to fit me. I hadn't realised I was such a tubby twat.

The problem with growing obese over a long period of time is that you are not fully aware of exactly how much weight you have gained because you don't have a starting point to make a comparison. What do you do? Go back until you were ten years old? It is gradual process and over the years the clothes sizes move up one notch to accommodate the new model. It is not until something dramatic occurs, for example my case, that you are able to make a true judgement upon yourself.

Linzi's car pulled up outside and I hurried the best I could down the stairs and out of the door. Linzi had been a loyal and generous friend to me since my stroke; she had two young children and still found the time during the week to ferry me to the gym or take me shopping. To be honest, the shopping trips were more of an excuse for a good gab more than anything else. I am somewhat of a budding practising chef and would impart snippets of culinary advice and suggestions for perking up Wednesday night's tea. She would tell me what mischief her girls had been up to that week often sending me into fits of laughter. The car was warm and Linzi's broad Aberdonian accent greeted me.

"It's as cold here as back at home," she said. I have always loved the way Scottish girls spoke; their singsong lilt is almost melodic and the further from their homeland they were, the more pronounced it seemed to be. I directed Linzi to the cathedral and we managed to park in a 'wee' place right outside the door of the cathedral's offices.

Gingerly stepping out of the car, an icy blast of wind rattled my bones and I pulled my cow hide tight. Linzi laughed at my attire. "Where on Earth did you get that?" She had seen my jacket. I shrugged and grinned back at her. I must admit the coat looked like I had borrowed it from George Melly. A thought suddenly occurred to me. *Does the cathedral have a dress code or something?* I didn't want to upset the priest or whoever before I had a chance to even speak.

I pressed the bell on the wall and we were granted entrance by a buzzing sound. We sat in a small waiting room sparsely decorated with a large cross on one wall. Within minutes, a tall, bald headed man entered and greeted us.

"Hello, I am Barry Norman," the gentleman spoke in a soft but articulate manner. The entrance to the offices were just like any factory, and were it not for the towering structure above, you would have had no idea where on Earth you were.

Barry asked if we'd seen the crypt before and with our negative reply proceeded to take us on a tour. He led us past more offices and modern corridors until we eventually came to a sturdy locked door. Using a key from a bunch he had in his hand, he unlocked the door and a huge staircase of stone steps led downwards. The walls had changed from the laminated wood of the offices to smart red brick and stone. The first thing I noticed was that the acoustics were totally different; I could hear faint echoes of hushed voices and steps on stone. The sounds were almost serene and peaceful.

As we descended the impressive stairs, Barry informed us of the history of the cathedral which I was aware of, but Linzi listened too, captivated. Eventually reaching the bottom, we arrived at a large arched passageway. Here, there were glass cases displaying drawings of the intended original building. They were quite staggering, if in nothing but scale, the cathedral would have been colossal possibly the largest building in the United Kingdom. And here we were in the original foundations of that proposed massive structure.

Terry asked us to lower our voices as we passed a chapel that was open to the public. "They are getting ready to hold mass this morning," he explained. Sometimes on one of the quieter days, mass is held in one of the chapels instead of the main cathedral.

Eventually after passing numerous chambers, we stopped at a quite unassuming doorway. Barry fumbled with his keys and eventually opened the door. What was to greet us was magnificent. It was a large underground church, but instead of an altar, it had a huge stage with a bank of seats perhaps ten rows high behind - I presumed for a choir. At the opposite end was a glorious oval stained glass window that dominated the complete wall. Even on this dull day the light shining through divided into smaller rays that lit up the stone floor with vivid laser coloured shafts. Against the two sides were a series of arches that supported the vaulted roof. "This is the room," Terry whispered in a matter of fact tone.

I had already made my mind up, we had not even discussed terms, but I knew this was going to be our next venue. I would buy a ticket just to be able to visit this majestic place, to use a hackneyed phrase, it was awe-inspiring. As we explored the space it became more magical and ideas of what I could do with it were cramming my mind. I took many photographs to remind me of dimensions etc. and asked about two dozen questions. What about toilet facilities? Where is the bar? Public entrance? Fire escapes? Security? I then asked a question that to my shame I had never asked on previous conversations such as this. "What about disabled access?"

My condition had given me a far better insight into a world that had previously been almost alien to me. Although I had only had one occasion since leaving hospital of having to use a wheelchair, it had been a frightening and harrowing experience.

Before my stroke, every year Nick, H and I would go to Aintree Racecourse for the horse racing of the Grand National Weekend. We would always go on the first day which was Thursday so as to avoid the large crowds of Friday's Ladies Day and the Saturday Grand National. In April 2007, just four months after my stroke,

Nick persuaded me to go to Aintree. We had argued for weeks before hand as I knew there was very little seating to be had at the racecourse and the crowds frightened me. I could not possibly stand all day being jostled and bumped into; I would not have the strength.

Nick came up with the idea of a wheelchair for the day which from the outset I was totally against. I do not know if it was pure vanity or the fact I knew I would meet people there that I had not seen since my illness and I would feel like a fraud being pushed around in a wheelchair. It was a different matter being scooted around hospital corridors; but out in public?

Eventually I acquiesced and it was Nick's job to be my carer. I had made a decision to be a little truculent and tiresome during the day to cement my slight disapproval over events, but inside I was glad that I could go racing. As Nick pushed me through the streets leading to the racecourse we encountered numerous pedestrian crossings and I found that the rumble strips to alert blind people of the location of a crossing rattled the wheelchair immensely. If I started to exhale in a monotone manner as we reverberated over the rumble strip, my voice sounded as though I was being shaken by my ankles.

The noise was infuriating. Nick was getting extremely embarrassed by my behaviour as the throng of other race goers stared at us, examining what my carer was doing to me. Nick constantly chided me and I only stopped my infantile behaviour when he threatened to push me in front of a bus.

Entering the Queen Mother's stand at the racecourse, things got progressively worse. Sitting so low in the chair gave me a different perspective on things and I began to realise some of the problems wheelchair bound people face. The first thing that I noticed was that staring at people's groins all the time was slightly unsettling, if not a trifle uncomfortable. Also, trying to be heard or hearing others was a big problem that had not occurred to me before. My neck was aching just after a couple of minutes looking up at people constantly and I was continuously rubbing it to gain relief.

H had gone to the bar to get us all a drink and Nick was in a hurry to place our first bets, so he looked for a safe place to park me. Just by the side of the tote was a wall that was part of the corridor leading outside to the course. It seemed the quietest place in the packed bar below the stand so he left me there to wait for H.

All was going swimmingly until a row started close by within a group of women. Like all typical Liverpool lasses on an excursion or day out, the ladies were dressed impeccably. But also like typical Liverpool lasses at a grand event, a large amount of alcohol had already been consumed. I had no idea what the argument was about, but a fight broke out between three of the orange tanned young ladies.

At first it was humorous because the whole thing looked so ludicrous. Milliners' finest hats were the first thing to go flying in the air as an assortment of peacock feathers, decorative veils and feather boas littered the floor. A sort of pill box type of hat was thrown in odd job fashion at the head of one of the combatants. The woman ducked and the missile missed its intended target to crash into a tray of drinks being carried from the bar by a well dressed man. The tray erupted like a cork spewing from a shaken bottle of champagne, drenching the man and several others around him.

One of the women fell and as she lay on the floor, stiletto shoes were used as improvised cudgels in an attempt to maim her. The other two women soon ended up rolling around the floor with the first. Dresses were ripped, stockings torn, lipstick smudged and hair was tugged. A large black hair extension was hurled across the room as though the victim had just been scalped by the hairdresser from Norris Green.

The melee was far too close to comfort to where Nick had safely parked me. I gripped the wheels of the chair to try and roll myself away from the danger, but the sodding thing would not budge. Nick had put the brakes on and I had no idea how to get them off. It was all too late anyway as the tussling trio crashed into my wheelchair catapulting me from my position like an ejector seat as it slammed into the wall with a tremendous clatter.

Everything suddenly stopped when the collision happened as the realisation of what they had just done seemed to bring the ferocious femme fatales to their senses. I was helped to my feet by a group of concerned race goers whilst others collected my chair put it upright and I was plonked back down. I was covered in shit from the bar's floor and the wheelchair was showing signs that it also had been into battle. One of the contestants in the brawl burst out into tears when she saw what she had done and drunkenly sat by one of the wheels on my chair petting my leg as a sort of pathetic apology.

The women fighting was a ferocious spectacle; I had seen something like it before when I was DJing in the infamous Wispa Club in Liverpool. A mass brawl between two groups of girls erupted and even the notoriously violent bouncers in the Wispa did not dare step in to break it up. I was shitting myself as the DJ booth was situated in the middle of the dance floor and the fighting took place all around my isle of sanctuary. But that was nothing to the fear I had experienced at Aintree Racecourse; I had felt so vulnerable from my seat in the wheelchair.

Nick and H returned almost simultaneously from their respective chores to be greeted by the carnage of what had just happened. Nick shook his head in disbelief that I could have got in so much trouble in such a short space of time. I began to try and explain that I had nothing remotely to do with anything, just sighed and let the leg petting continue.

Back in the crypt and before we left, Barry led us to a door opposite to the one we entered. It was an exact replica, two plain, wooden curved doors with large metal handles. We stepped into another chamber that Barry suggested we could use for a bar and pointed to some steps that he informed, lead to an outside entrance on Brownlow Hill. Then once again he rattled his keys and opened the door behind us. What greeted Linzi and I was staggering. It was a huge hall, something like a Castle Banqueting Hall in an old Robin Hood movie.

"This is the room they use for the Beer Festival," Barry nonchalantly said and added: "The University Sports Department used to use it for Archery practice!" I was right, it was Robin Hood land. "We had to stop them because some of the missing arrows were damaging the stonework," Barry continued, and had called this vault a room! It was nothing like any room I have set foot in before. My uncle Jimmy was rich, but he never had a room this big and he lived in Elton Avenue. It could have easily sat one thousand people for dinner if you had that many mates. Barry went on to tell us it was originally planned to be the priest's robing room - that indicated how big the cathedral was going to be if this chamber was simply a dressing room!

We left this wonderland and returned to the offices. Although the cathedral had held a Beer Festival and some classical concerts, it had never hired the crypt out before to something like I was proposing. Tony, who had originally found Barry's phone number, had a mate who was Barry's outside caterer and ran the cathedral bistro. Andy had been on the Soul Boat and had already told Barry what kind of professional event we ran and the link with the donation to Different Strokes.

I hoped he had not told him about the time we had to dock at Seacome to throw the two prostitutes off the boat. It was a hilarious mistake I had made but never admitted to. The Soul Boat of 2008: we had almost completed loading all the punters from the Pier Head, Johnny Hendo and I were helping security on the gangway when I saw two ladies in their party frocks standing up on the quayside. I beckoned to them to hurry up and ushered them on board without even checking their tickets. What I had not realised that the two local girls had seen the crowd queuing and went over to see if there was any business to be had.

About twenty minutes into the trip, the girls were causing quite a commotion by one of the gents toilets trying to ply their trade. Security stepped in and informed the captain. They were unceremoniously chucked off at the other bank of the Mersey; they seemed non too happy with the way their evening was panning out, judging by the screams of abuse and gesticulating the two hoes were offering to the boat's wake.

Barry seemed fairly happy to take a gamble on our proposed venture if I was to assure him to abide by the rules and regulations in their hire contract. I convinced him there would be no problems and we shook hands on a deal. I was in a jubilant mood as Linzi and I left the car and walked to the Georgian Quarter to have lunch. She was just as excited as I was as we discussed my plans for the event in between mouthfuls of steaming hot Scouse. My mind was racing with so many things I wanted to try on the evening, and for once I had time to devote to it.

That weekend I met up with Johnny Hendo and Sandy in the Bug to tell them what I had done and discuss our plans. Sandy already knew as Linzi had told him and was a little wary of my decision to take the night away from the boat. But we all knew that we had problems with Mersey Ferries every time the event was held, normally with the franchise caterer and the security but nevertheless major problems. The cost of hiring the boat also had increased dramatically so we all agreed we had to move on.

But the new venue also held its own difficulties; we could only have one room for music. Normally we split the DJs into two separate rooms depending on genre of Soul. Our regular clientele was split into two groups, the Northern and Motown brigade, and the Modern Soul and Weekender Classics mob. This was going to be a tricky obstacle to get right.

The room was massive, although a limit of four hundred punters was set because of fire regulations, I estimated the Crypt could accommodate at least six hundred people. We were going to need a very big PA system. As we voiced our concerns, it seemed obvious that numerous visits to the cathedral were going to have to be made to perfect arrangements.

The following week, Hendo and I went to a couple of Sound and Light companies. Our usual guys did not have anything that could cope with what we needed so we looked at professional PA hire. We found a place in Bootle that had a specialist lighting designer and could offer two sound rigs. One was 20kw and the other 50kw, that one had just been used for a Girls Aloud tour. The lighting guy was really interesting and when I told him about the venue, he described how we could use LED lighting to really highlight the classic features in the crypt.

The Sound Hire was reasonable, so we agreed a hire deal for that then and there. He was going to design a lighting rig once we had taken proper measurements of the dimensions and cost that later. Feeling like proper concert promoters, we chatted in the car about the night. Hendo had been working on a new hobby of creating his own video shows. We had tried using them in the past, but there was nowhere on the boat we could properly display them... in the crypt, however, there was.

Back home at Chez Regina, Hendo showed me on his laptop some examples of what he had done. They were great; old movies and cartoons set to classic Soul Music. He offered to expand his work for the Crypt and try to have a continuous loop of film projected all night. Things were slowly coming together.

This new project bought some new mental vitality to my life, before I was mostly focusing on my bodily improvement, but this venture was testing my brain properly for the first time in years. I had negotiations on the go with all manner of companies from T-Shirt suppliers to ticket printers, then advertising posters and designers. I felt alive again and of some worth, it was only one small, rather insignificant event, but to me it was going to be the best small, insignificant event ever.

Weeks later Hendo and I visited the Crypt and took all the measurements needed. He came up with a great idea, the stage was so big we could have a massive screen behind the D.J's and we could back project his films onto it. I was really taken with his proposal and we added it to our list to discuss with the lighting designer later that day. Hendo loved the Crypt and he said we should market the night as "Taking the Music back to the Church" it is an old saying from the Deep South of America where many of the Soul Superstars started their careers, singing in the Church Choir.

Later that day we had a meeting with the P.A Hire Company, the lighting designer worked around our hastily taken measurements and in about twenty minutes had sketched out a proposal to us. With the giant screen for stage illumination we were only going to have two small lighting gantries above the technical equipment. The really clever lighting would be inside the Crypt highlighting specific architectural pieces such as Arches, etc. The problem was going to be cost; this was really expensive to do properly.

The designer seemed more interested in getting the design right than making a huge profit. I re emphasised any profit would be going to charity and that we all were devoting our time for free, which was the case. Hendo, Sandy and I were all doing it for the music, nowhere in Liverpool played this type of Soul or really never had and it was great to hear how it should sound, Loud! Of course, I had the extra incentive of being able to donate some money to Different Strokes, something very dear to me.

Johnny Hendo was my Soul Guru and mentor and was far the most knowledgeable man I have ever met on Soul Music. He was about eight years older than me which was a crucial period in the development of Soul Music in the U.K. His collection was mostly on seven inch vinyl and must have been worth ten's of thousands of pounds. He had first original pressings of some classic Soul tracks imported from the States and to say I was jealous of his "Aladdin's Cave" of treasures would be the biggest understatement ever.

Hendo however, had built up his private collection for his own pleasure and until around ten years ago when I persuaded him to join our DJ roster he had never really done much DJ work. I thought it was a shame that so much good music was not getting aired and people had not had a chance to hear it; he had to become part of our team and now is the main attraction for many of the punters.

Sandy and I were contemporaries at school, we both had quite wide appreciation of music, but Soul was by far our favourite. It was Sandy, who in the early 80s introduced me to the Caister Soul Weekend. The Soul Weekender was held at Caister on Sea near Great Yarmouth twice a year, and was the founder of today's music festivals and weekenders. Great luminaries of the Soul and Dance music world had cut their teeth at Caister; Chris Hill, Robbie Vincent, Pete Tong and Jeff Young to name but a few. It was with Sandy that I opened the ill fated Spinners Discs record shop in 1983.

Different other friends, passionate on the music, were also drafted in to assist on the decks from time to time as the occasion demanded; notably, the Mangan Brothers and Fordy. As for myself, as previously mentioned, I was the one with the most DJ experience and it was on my equipment that the first Soul Nights were presented. That was the team, gifted amateurs who gave up their time in the hope that their efforts in some small way were helping keep Soul Music alive.

The weeks and months flew past and the evening was rapidly approaching. The event had totally sold out a couple of weeks after the tickets were printed. We had a loyal hardcore of followers who had been with us for years, taking advantage of a rather rare unique evenings entertainment. What staggered me was the influx of younger people attending every year: it proved to me that the music was far from dead and nowhere catered for this demand. In all the years we have promoted this evening, all over Liverpool, not once had I seen a punch up, which was quite amazing considering the very mixed age group and different dialects that attended. We have had visitors from Norway, Germany, and France as well as many regulars from London and elsewhere from around the country; quite remarkable, as the news was passed all by word of mouth.

Preparations had been very thorough; in the adjoining room to the crypt, there was a large permanent bar and Andy had instructions how to stock it, and more importantly, to have sufficient bar staff to serve a thirsty audience. Andy was also providing the catering from the Cathedral Bistro and their menu was far from the normal fare expected at such an event. Down the two sides of the crypt where the arches stood, there were going to be a number of candlelit tables were tired punters could rest their legs - the naked flames of the candles would add to the ambience of the lighting.

I had designed a logo for the evening which I pinched from *Sex and the City*. In the same font using the same vivid pink colouring the logo was *Soul in the City*. This was set on a black background and was printed on banners, for the stage and entrance, T-shirts, tickets and the now-famous giveaway CDs of the evening. I had hired some licensed doormen from the Everyman Bistro and everything seemed under control.

Finally, the day of the event arrived and Hendo and I went up to the cathedral at 10am to oversee the set up. Barry's assistant Joe was there to greet us and already his team of staff were carrying tables, chairs and all manner of other paraphernalia into the crypt. Soon after the PA truck arrived, but with only two engineers. I voiced my disappointment of the lack of bodies, but was curtly answered that a large gig was also happening that day. I didn't give a rat's fart who else was in town; we had spent months planning this night.

The two engineers also seemed to be on a work to rule; miffed that they had no roadies to help them, it was going to be a long, long day. It took until almost midday just to unload the truck and I was getting a little irate and concerned. However, we had other matters to attend to; Andy and his team had almost finished their work. The food counters had all been set up and large vats of pre cooked stews, curries, chillies and various other offerings were resting on hot plates. The bar had been stocked and the cold room was stacked to the rafters of replacement drinks.

The public entrance was up two levels on the street and we fixed our banners at the entrance to enable our punters to locate where the Hell we were. The last thing I wanted was a bus load of Soul Night punters crashing into Evensong at the cathedral requesting some Jackie Wilson.

Everything was set and ready apart from the main event: the sound and lighting. The engineers had made some progress on our return and the giant screen and stage lighting had been erected. Whilst the grumpy pair were wrestling with numerous large flight cases, Hendo and I set our attention to the PC and projector. It took us nearly one hour to perfect the synchronisation and clarity of the films, but we finally got it right and stood under the huge window admiring our handiwork. It looked superb and would be even better when the lighting was correct.

Bill and Ben had finished all the heavy work and were now were taking a late lunch outside. There was nothing we could do but wait until these two numpties decided to return and so we sat in Hendo's car listening to some inspirational tracks to cheer us both up.

The rest of the afternoon was a race against time, but slowly, bit by bit things started to take shape. Most of the LED lighting was in place and looked fantastic. Arches and stone features were just glowing different colours and it was impossible to see where the light was coming from. Once the sound started these colours would change and pulsate to the music in a festival of light. The room would almost come alive in the darkness of night; I doubted the crypt had seen the like of this ever before.

It was now 6pm: the lighting was all completed and the stage had been set up. We had been told by Barry that there was evening mass at 7pm in the chapel next door and under no circumstances could any music play before 8pm, and then only after we had been given the okay, the doors of our night opened at 8pm! We were on a fight against time to get the music up and running and a sound check.

The engineers were still working at a snail's pace and now the technical part of their job was in process, they were treating their work like open heart surgery. At a quarter to seven we had our first sound check. The music was bouncing around all over the place, the high vaulted ceiling together with the numerous arches were playing havoc with the acoustics. We tried changing the angles of some of the speaker cabs which improved the sound quality in the main body of the Crypt, but on the peripheries it was still bad.

An agitated Barry appeared behind the stage and stopped our work, mass was starting in ten minutes and some of the congregation had started to arrive. Oh fuck, we would have to continue trying to sort the sound out during the gig, never a good thing to do: it looks and more importantly sounds so unprofessional. There was nothing else we could do so Hendo and I nipped home for a shower and to change. We said little to one another as we were both so concerned, we just listened to some music.

On our way back we picked up Sandy and returned to the crypt. The room looked marvellous and the smell of the food most inviting. I quickly greeted Andy who was completing his preparations and handed all his staff *Soul in the City* t-shirts as uniforms, keeping some back for the bouncers. Joe and his team were busy polishing glasses and checking tills so they were all sorted, I handed him more of the shirts.

Ten to eight and soon we could finally try to fix the sound. Bill and Ben had tidied the stage up and wired the decks and CD players to the mixer. Hendo immediately noticed that one of the decks did not have a cartridge, so a disgruntled engineer was despatched forthwith to Bootle. I knew at the time I should have returned home and collected my own Technics turntables, but I had other pressing matters to attend to.

Joe whistled at the door and gave us the thumbs up to turn the equipment on. The crypt sprang to life as Bobby Womack boomed out rattling the stage lighting gantries. It is always difficult to do a proper sound check in an empty room for volume as peoples bodies absorb sound. But you can more or less correct reverberation and other sound qualities such as pitch and tone. We tried again moving some of the forward facing cabinets and had the sound quality perfect in the central areas but the sides were still a major problem. We had no other option than to place the stage monitors to the side and hope they would be powerful enough to compensate.

Then bang on 8pm the first punters started to arrive. It has always been a trait of our Soul Nights that the event fills up very quickly early on in the evening. I think people's attitude is that they have waited twelve months to hear this music so there is little point of staying two hours in a pub before hand.

We turned the house lights off and Sandy kicked off 2008's *Soul in the City* playing *What About My Love* by Johnny Taylor. The first hour was hectic, but is always the same as an organiser. I spent most of it with the doorman at the entrance sorting out ticketing problems. I looked out on to Mount Pleasant and it was a filthy night, the rain was coming down in sheets and it was hard to clearly see the street lights on the opposite side of the road. I was glad we had not gone sailing this year after all; people would have been throwing up left, right and centre on the boat.

I was amazed that I could just about hear the dull thud of the music from the massive PA downstairs. I suppose all that stone and brickwork was a very effective sound insulator, you could have walked right passed the entrance and not been aware of what was occurring below. Two double decker buses pulled up outside and I recognised many of the faces aboard. The Bug had chartered the transport for its patrons to attend the gig; I think it was more a case of Mike not wanting any of his regulars finding alternative drinking venues than his pub.

The night was alive and kicking and apart from a few grumbles about the sound from one or two people on the sides the vast majority loved the new venue. Later in the evening I took a beer and stood once more with Hendo at the back of the crypt under the stained glass window. We surveyed the scene before us: the crypt looked unbelievable. The lighting engineer had done his job well and the old gothic interior of this most atmospheric of buildings seemed to effervesce in pale greens and blues. The giant stage was dominated by the big screen which was bordered by the black *Soul in the City* drapes, and the sound where we were standing was simply sublime pumping out classic soul music. But the most important thing was the punters, they loved it. I looked at my soul brother; we smiled, raised our glasses and toasted each other.

About eight years ago we had decided to give away a thank you present at the end of the evening to our loyal punters. It was to be a reminder of the night they had just attended and were some of the tracks compiled from our different playlists.

The playlist on the 2008 *Soul in the City* CD was as follows:

Ron Henderson & Choice Of Colour - Love Is Gone
Billy Joe Royal - Heart's Desire
Al Wilson - Do What You Gotta Do
Ben E. King - Music Trance
Aretha Franklin - I Can't See Myself Leaving You

Benny Johnson - Baby I Love You
Laura Lee - To Win Your Heart
Chukki Booker - Games
Bonnie Herman - Hush Don't Cry
Karin Jones - Here I Go Again
The O'Jays - Family Reunion
The Four Tops - Can't Seem To Get You Out Of My Mind
Kindred And The Family Soul - Stars
Michael Henderson - Take Me I'm Yours
Brian Holland - I'm So Glad
Melvin Davies - You Made Me Over
Maryann Farra & Satin Soul - Stoned Out Of My Mind
Bobby McClure - Was It Something I Said
Jean Plum - Here I Go Again
Ann Peebles - If This Is Heaven

Chapter Eight

A FIRST BANGKOK EXPERIENCE

The Soul Night's success was a big boon to my year: the event had suffered from some technical problems, but overall the effort I had put in to make the night happen was very beneficial to me personally. My confidence took a vast leap forward from that night and my mental agility had been tested and was shown to be above par. Sometimes after my sort of illness you are not aware of any mental damage that has been done and therefore it is hard to correct. I was glad that in my case this didn't seem to be a major problem.

But now things had settled back into a relative norm. The Soul Night had been in June and now winter was fast approaching and I knew I was in for an uncomfortable ride. I pined to once again be in the sun and particularly return to Thailand. My finances would take a battering in about twelve months time as my medical insurance would stop, so if I was to consider another trip it had to be fairly soon. I nagged Richie and he agreed to go on a short holiday in November and to save our money for something more exotic in the New Year.

We went to Egypt; staying at a friend's apartment in Sharm El-Sheikh. The heat was magnificent and was a great place to go to recharge my batteries, constant sun beating down every day. Apparently it had not rained there for five years. It was the first time I had experienced the desert and I was a trifle awed by it. The solitude and desolation of its vastness was humbling to a mere mortal and it somewhat frightened me.

The problem was that it was freezing cold when we returned. I was now dreading coming back to England after every trip and it did not seem to bother me that this was my frame of mind. All my friends were mostly in the UK and I never thought I would ever consider living anywhere else, but now the weather killed me. I was uncomfortable, miserable and fed up being hunched up like a cripple, I had lost some of my quality of life and it was seriously becoming a major problem.

Rich and I decided we would take another long haul trip in late January 2010 and return to Thailand. This time we would ensure a stay in Bangkok and spend a few days there before relaxing in Samui. Once the holiday was booked with Michele I endured the Christmas weather as I knew I had something to look forward to, but I counted every day down on my wall calendar. We were to have three nights at the Holiday Inn Silom Bangkok and then fly for a two week holiday to spend at the Centara Grand Beach Resort Koh Samui. It was a trip that was to lead to a most unexpected turn in my road of life, one that I always will be thankful for.

Leaving Liverpool early on another dark, dank and rainy morning I looked out of the cab window and noticed how grey everything looked outside. I was glad I was leaving it all behind, at least for nearly three weeks. All the flights and connections were as scheduled and the following morning the plane touched down at Suvarnabhumi. Bangkok International Airport was quite a different place to the last time we were here, organised and efficient, a bustling hub of transit.

Clearing immigration seemed to take an eternity, but finally we collected our luggage and found the Kuoni representative. It was not long before we were in an air conditioned mini bus speeding on the Expressway towards the capital. Suvarnabhumi (pronounced "SU WAN NA PUM") Airport is approximately 25 kilometres from Bangkok city centre and takes about thirty minutes by car on the Expressway. Once you have exited, the motorway traffic can be abysmal.

Bangkok skyline was drawing closer and I was impressed by the sheer size of the great city. Skyscrapers loomed in the distance while the urban outskirts were crammed with all manner of factories, apartment blocks and ram shackled housing. I could see the traffic on the minor roads below us jostling for position on the highway all fighting for their own piece of free tarmac.

Bangkok's Thai name is Krung Thep which translates as "City of Angels"; however, it is nicknamed "The Big Mango." It is a city of around twelve million souls and is Thailand's capital and most important city. Thailand has a population of just fewer than seventy million and although the economy is based on rural activities it has several cities with populations over the one million mark. Nakon Ratchasiama, Samut Prakan and Si Racha are a few to mention while the big northern cities of Chaing Mai and Udon Thani are metropolitan centres in their own right.

The mini bus drove up a ramp and halted outside the Holiday Inn Silom Bangkok. I added the suffix Silom to the hotel's name as there are two Holiday Inns in Bangkok, this one being the best. It was not a very glamorous building from the outside, but entering through its main automatic doors, the lobby was most impressive and was bustling with liveried staff. As always with Thailand, the buzzing noise of animated voices trying to make them heard greeted us, all manner of people were wandering about the lobby from all corners of the globe attending to their own pressing business.

The rep led us to the check-in desk and started to natter away in Thai to the receptionist. He turned to us and enquired matter-of-factly if we wanted a double bed. Richie and I looked at each other to see if we looked overtly gay or something and politely declined the offer, but pointed to each other mouthing "It's you" accusingly. I made a mental note to change the colour of my eye shadow the next time I checked in at the Holiday Inn Silom.

Rich nudged me: "Looks like we picked the right hotel to stay in," and moved his eyes towards the clerk. I didn't have a clue what he was wittering on about, until I looked at the extremely attractive Thai girl processing our passports and nodded back to

Rich mouthing, "Yes, very pretty." He pulled an exasperated face at me then moved his eyes towards the receptionist again, but this time fixed his stare at her bosom. I was almost too embarrassed to follow his gaze, but glanced at the receptionist and saw Rich was looking at her name badge; this very attractive, pleasant lady was named Superporn.

Giggling like naughty schoolgirls, Rich and I were given our passports back and taken to our room. Unfortunately, not by Superporn, but a rather aged hall porter who walked a little like Joyce Grenfell. He had long romping strides that his arms seemed to follow as if tied by an invisible thread, a most odd way to walk. Did the Holiday Inn not have a preferred walking gait for their staff? As we both romped behind Joyce Grenfell down the passageway I began to wonder what Superporn's family name might be... or was Superporn her surname and she had another Christian name? Roxanne or perhaps Sadie would be suitable. I grinned knowing I had just thought up a drinking game for later on and was very smug with myself.

The excitement of being in Bangkok washed away any tiredness we had from the journey and the pair of naughty schoolboys were desperate to explore the city. After a quick wash and scrub up we were soon standing on Silom Road debating in which direction we should walk. This was typical of Richie and me, no forethought or planning in our actions. Most new visitors would be scouring over tourist brochures or pestering employees at tourist information booths, but like the numpties that we were, once again we were venturing out half cocked!

It was getting to around 4pm, and at that time in the early evening Silom's rather sober daytime identity starts to transform. Street vendors were appearing from every nook and cranny setting up stalls along the pavement to sell their wares. Noisy, dirty buses were jam packed, vacant faces pushed at the windows as commuters wearily started their journeys home.

We opted to walk right as to our left was the highway intersection that we had just descended from in the mini bus, and there was not much sign of fun there. Unbeknown to us at the time, but by pure fluke we chose the correct option; we were headed towards Lumphini Park and the centre of Silom.

Silom by day is sometimes referred to as Bangkok's Wall Street and the area together with Sathorn is the major finance centre of the city. By night, things start to morph and the area takes on a far different identity, as restaurants, bars, stalls, nightclubs, food vendors and late night shops all stay awake for the night people.

The first thing that really hits you about Bangkok is the smell. Hundreds of street vendors all over the city are busy preparing hot food by the roadside for consumption. The aromas permeate the air even through the foul smell of exhaust fumes from the gridlocked traffic. Some of the best food to be had in Bangkok is the street food; everything from spicy curries to fried fish can be eaten perched on tiny stools precariously tottering on edges of packed pavements. It is a wonderful way to eat and most of the workers have their evening meals in such fashion before making their way home.

We ambled along Silom Road, fascinated by the alien activities taking place all around us. Bangkok is chaotic, loud, brash, fast, dangerous and dirty; everything a great city needs to be. The Big Mango is my favourite city in the world by far, there is no place quite like it, the City of Angels has its own unique identity. Old next to new, McDonalds opposite Buddhist temples, skyscrapers flanked by shanty towns. All in a pulsating melting pot of chaos, but a chaos that seems to work.

Richie was feeling peckish so I saw a small Soi opposite a Hindu temple that seemed to have plenty of street food for sale. We weaved our way down the crowded little road, bustling with different stalls, busy serving steaming hot bowls of food to their clients. It was the sort of place we both loved and found a little table against a wall that was vacant. It was difficult to work out who owned the table we were sitting at, but within seconds a young boy of around twelve appeared with two laminated menus.

He disappeared as soon as he had arrived back into the throng of people trying to navigate their way along the Soi. I looked at the menu and it was all in Thai, but had small pictures of plates and bowls of strange looking dishes to choose from. Most of these stalls specialise in one dish and cook that one dish over and over again fresh every time. It may be noodles, soup, fish or some rice based meal. I have never had a problem after eating at such places ever, all the ingredients are fresh that day and cooked over red hot flames in skillets or usually woks.

One of Richie's favourite Thai meals is Kaeng Keaw Wan or Green Curry and he spotted it on the menu. I tend to like my food extremely spicy and back in England would commonly eat Vindaloo or Phal in an Indian restaurant. The boy came back with a small pad in his hand and we pointed at the dishes on the menu we required. He then turned the laminated card over and a selection of drinks was listed. Rich pointed at two big bottles of Singha and the boy scurried off with our order.

We were only on Superporn's second surname when the boy came back struggling with a tray through the crowd. I had no an idea where the meals were cooked as we were sitting on the side of the road and I could not see a nearby restaurant or cook for that matter. The bowls of food were piping hot and smelled delicious, two ice cold bottles of beer were unceremoniously dumped next to the food and once again our waiter dashed off seeing two potential diners sitting on some boxes at the entrance to a barber's shop.

The food was marvellous, just the correct amount of spices and heat. Richie's aromatic curry was devoured in minutes and he declared and stands by his statement to this day: "That was the best chicken green curry I've ever eaten in my life!" We polished off the two cool beers and hailed our waiter for the bill. The boy came back with a tatty piece of paper with a scrawled figure on it.

In 2010 the exchange rate was roughly £1 to fifty Thai Baht, but neither of us had really got to grips trying to convert the currencies over. The bill or rather the piece of tissue the boy had given us had something that looked like two hundred and eighty written on it. I tried to work the exchange rate out but got it wrong. I worked out two hundred and eighty Baht was just over five quid. Rich tried the calculation on his phone and came up with £5.60. That could not possibly be right; we had eaten two main courses including rice and drank a pint of beer each.

I placed three hundred Baht on the table to see the boy's reaction. He smiled and went to go. It was bloody correct, the whole thing had cost just over a fiver. Rich thrust a red one hundred Baht note into the boy's hand, his small face lit up as though he had just won the Thai lottery. We had given him half the cost of the meal as a tip, an extremely generous two quid! For information, the two names we had come up with for Superporn's new surnames were Superporn Sleazebucket and Superporn Goodgoose. It surprised me but much later on in my sojourn a Thai friend informed me that Superporn was not that an uncommon name in Thailand. I think his name was Khun Lying Git.

Refreshed by our pit stop, we weaved our way out of the Soi and back onto Silom Road to continue our exploration. We came to a major junction with a road three lanes wide across Silom's path. Crossing the road was like the computer game Frogger, where the aim of the game is to get a rather dim witted frog across roads and rivers by dodging traffic and landing on objects for safety.

Crossing Bangkok roads, or for that matter, any Thai roads, is not for the faint hearted. The Thai Nation are notoriously bad drivers, there is no safety on pedestrian crossings or any such highlighted right of way. It is not wise to step out on any road to cross unless it is free from any vehicle whatsoever, regardless what any traffic lights or signs indicate. I grew not to be surprised by this, although the Thai's are supposed to drive on the left hand side of the road it is common that you will see a Tuk-Tuk or motor bike come roaring down the road or pavement the opposite way making a bee line straight towards you.

The best course of action I have found when hindered by such an obstruction is to pick out a local who looks as though he has no bumps and bruises, tightly grab his coat and enjoy the ride. You might upset one civilian, but you will arrive at the other side of the road unscathed to live and cross again another day

The other way to avoid the hazardous traffic is to join it. Metered taxis in Bangkok are very cheap and air conditioned, but they tend to get snarled up in all the traffic jams which the city is famous for. Motorbike taxis are ideal to avoid the delays but usually only take one passenger. Tuk-Tuks are a very expensive tourist option and I find extremely dangerous, but it is worth taking a ride in one just for the experience. They are like motorised Rickshaws, with the front end of a moped welded on to a small covered chariot behind with a bench seat in the back accommodating up to four passengers.

The public transport system is excellent: I avoid buses for the same reason as metered taxis, but the Skytrain (BTS) and the Underground (MRT) are the best way to find your way around Bangkok. Clean, safe, punctual, cheap and easy to navigate, they are by far the best way of getting about.

Eventually we managed somehow to cross Narathinat Ratchanakarin Road and continued our journey down Silom heading to Lumphini Park. Since the road junction things had become three dimensional as the Skytrain rattled loudly above us supported by huge concrete pillars in the centre of the road. We passed Bangkok Christian Hospital on our left and now we were in downtown Silom.

Greenstreet and Back

The pavement had become almost impassable due to the amount of temporary stalls now set up for business. Electric wires hung down from awnings and were strewn across the floor resembling a nest of rubber snakes. The was only room for one person at a time and it was treacherous, I was glad I was not drunk as I probably would have either garrotted myself or tripped on a live wire and blacked out half of Bangkok. Little wonder there was a hospital so close by, they must pay the street vendors a fortune for sending them so much business.

We came to a large Soi on the left with a sign: Patpong Night Market. In the centre of the road was a large array of what seemed to be permanent stalls, all haphazardly lit by light bulbs hanging down from bits of wire. The market ran the whole length of the Soi and was flanked on either side of the road by neon lights advertising sex shows. It was only six thirty and Rich and I were not in the mood for either of the services being offered. We stumbled across O'Reilly's Irish Bar under the BTS and popped in for a drink as we were gasping.

The bar was cool and I was glad to sit on a stool, the walk had been a lot longer than I had thought and I was pretty tired. If we had taken the same walk at 3am then we could probably do it in half the time as there would be no dodging the kamikaze traffic or braving the treacherous pavements. The bar was quite large and was advertising live sport on its big screen. I don't know quite why, but I didn't like it much so we only stayed for one drink and went back out into the sweltering Bangkok heat.

Bangkok is hot all the time, the humid temperatures are added to the heat generated by the city; bus engines, air-con extractor fans, red hot woks, people rushing about and all manner of other activities associated with urban living. The heat added to the continuous cacophony of sound make Bangkok a less than relaxing place to be.

I spotted a busy thoroughfare on the opposite side of the road so we decided to investigate. Crossing the road here was a little easier as the BTS pillars provided a sort of central reservation and so halfway there was some sanctuary. The opening of Soi Convent was a hive of activity, many food stalls were lined up along the kerb and behind them was a vast array of restaurants.

It was a little bizarre as the clientele was split between Thais eating al fresco with their plastic tableware, whilst behind air conditioned glass windows, farangs sipped a glass of chilled Chardonnay. I must say the local residents seemed to be having a more fun time of things and seemed completely oblivious of the rather staid, foreign visitors experiencing true Bangkok cuisine in La Tosca's.

We saw a couple of very attractive ladies wearing cut down denim shorts, cowboy hats and holsters with toy guns outside a bar named Coyote. This seemed a rather good place for a pit stop so we climbed the steps and entered. We were greeted by more attractive Thai girls clad in the same attire who asked did we want to dine or just use the bar. "Just the bar," Richie said in his best Texan Drawl. We were not hungry, but if we were, Rich and I would sit outside with the locals anyway.

I looked about and saw that Coyote's décor was based on a Mexican Cantina and served Tex-Mex type cuisine. We were given a Tequila drinks menu and to say the least it was extensive. It was Happy Hour and Margaritas were two for one, job done, a no brainer. Margarita is one of my favourite tipples and I need no encouragement like Happy Hour for me to start consuming one of the sour little beauties at any time.

Rich was firmly engaged in chatting one of the Coyote girl's up whilst I sipped the delicious cocktail. I saw the hat on the girl Rich was talking to and memories of Sheriff Bill in Fazakerley Hospital came flooding back. I wondered where he was now. Was he healthy? Did he have somewhere to live? My recollections were interrupted by my friend: "This is Apple." I shook the girl's hand and realised just how attractive she was. "Pleased to meet you," she spoke in excellent English with a slight American accent. It was quite mesmerising.

Two more drinks were ordered as we continued our conversation with Apple; I asked if there were any more fruits in the family to which Richie guffawed in his best Kenneth Williams impression. I had meant it as a joke, but Apple looked quite bemused and Richie was insistent that I had made a faux pas. He can be such an arse at times so I let him have his moment and make me out to be a twat in front of Apple. She looked quite relieved that a customer wanted her and made her polite excuses and hurried off.

Happy Hour finished, after one last round and saying our goodbyes to Apple, we left onto noisy Soi Convent. I was feeling a little flushed with the alcohol by now and a little uncertain on my feet, but I could see that my partner was just starting and was raring to go. We crossed Silom Road again and walked to Patpong where we had passed another Mexican looking bar before. The taste for Margaritas was our driving force.

Patti's Fiesta Bar is right on the corner of Silom Road and Soi Patpong. Loud Mexican music was blaring out of the door as we entered. A trio was on a tiny stage to our left and there was about four tables on street level, descending down a flight of four steps was the bar surrounded by stools. We had timed it perfectly, just for Happy Hour! *Great timing for future reference*, I thought. Richie ordered a pitcher of frozen Margarita. "Saves messing about," he explained as if I had any idea what the fuck he was going on about.

It dawned on me. "Happy Hour... then we would get another pitcher!" I looked at the oaf and shook my head in disbelief. "You know my alcohol limit!" The Cheshire Cat just beamed his stupid grin at me. Christ it was only 7pm and I was getting fairly pissed, but looking at Richie, it was though he had not had a sniff of a drink. I have always thought that there is something quite atmospheric about drinking underground and watching peoples feet scurry around above you; it is though you are spying on them or something. But it definitely feels that you are doing some illegal activity, prohibition or the like.

After the second pitcher I was fighting to stay on my stool and my speech was slurred. Drinking alcohol for me now is a hazardous occupation as no warning lights come to notify me. Green; everything is okay, but then suddenly Red; now you're screwed! There is no Amber telling me I'm tiddily. Richie saw the danger signs and suggested we leave; paying the bill was a farce as I could not make out the currency at all. I just give a fist full of Bahts to Rich and let him deal with all the hassle.

He led the way up the steps, I levered my way off the stool and then things became rather blurred. My right leg gave way under me and my head hit against the stool then slammed into the bottom stair, glass smashed around and I felt hands grabbing me pulling me to my feet. Richie was totally oblivious any of this was going on as he was out on the street. The barman and a member of the band ejected me from the bar and a rather battered and bruised Francis Abel appeared on Silom Road with blood gushing from his head.

Richie was at a loss as to what had just happened to me and I was too pissed to tell him. "I leave you alone for two minutes and look at you!" He was actually berating me rather than offering any assistance. "You are going home." Rich hailed the first available transport which happened to be a Tuk-Tuk. The driver did not seem to be the least phased at the state of me and I was unceremoniously bundled into the back of the Tuk-Tuk banging my head again as they did so; I was then sent packing back to the hotel.

Around only five hours previously I had arrived in an air conditioned mini bus up the same ramp of the Holiday Inn Silom. Now a rather forlorn passenger hung on for dear life as a rattling Tuk-Tuk bounced up the same ramp. The driver and one of the hotel staff prised me from the transport and I took stock of my situation.

I knew I was outside my hotel so all I had to do was get to my room and things would be okay, I was very aware to be as discreet as possible and not make a scene. *Oh fuck fuckidy, fuck and the fuckingtons!* The hotel foyer was jam packed with people in dinner jackets attending some formal do. I looked at myself, I had ripped my T-shirt and a huge blood stain covered my shoulder. There were also speckles of blood on my shorts; I suppose I must have cut my leg on some glass.

One of the hotel porters eyed me with suspicion as I wavered about on the same spot. I had decided I had better make my play, lurching through the doors it was like a scene from a ski holiday. Where an inept skier had just been pushed out of a gate at the top of a black run by some prankster, probably the Austrian version of Richie.

I almost ran into the lobby as my brakes did not seem to be working. My body was almost bent backwards as my legs were too fast for the rest of my body, so after adjusting my tilt control I then careered head first into a group of Rotary Club dignitaries. Bouncing off the penguins like a billiard ball I then ricocheted into a waiter with a large gold chain around his neck, carrying a tray laden with a wine bottle and glasses that on impact crashed to the floor. The second collision was fortuitous as it seemed to put me on the correct trajectory for the lift.

I could hear behind me the chaos in my wake and raised voices in anger, but I had made it to the lift. Well, I actually smashed into its doors, but nevertheless I had stopped. Luckily for me the doors opened instantaneously and I fell into the lift. The rest of my return to the room is a little vague, but I must have been successful as I woke up, fully clothed on my bed.

My head ached and blood was everywhere, on the pillow, the duvet, the floor and all over the bathroom. I sat on the toilet recollecting the previous night's activities and began to feel really embarrassed. What a total twat I had been, I knew I could not risk getting that drunk anymore and yet I had gone and done it. I felt the back of my head and there was a large lump forming, but there did not seem to be any large wounds. Most of the blood seemed to come from small cuts on my legs, nothing serious at all. I breathed a sigh of relief; I had been very lucky. From now on I would take things easy and restrict my alcohol intake dramatically.

Going back into the bedroom Rich was still fast asleep so I decided to try and find the pool. The hotel is formed by two towers, the one we were in; a little shabby and worn, and the second is the club tower where the executive suites are. To get to the pool I had to go down one lift to the ground floor, walk down the connecting passageway, then take the other tower's lift to the 8th floor where the leisure centre is. I knew the oaf would struggle to find his way and that cheered me up somewhat. I felt very sheepish walking about the hotel; but was washed, scrubbed and hiding behind a large pair of sunglasses; nobody seemed to recognise me as the careering Eddie the Eagle from the previous night.

The pool was quite large with plenty of loungers and I put my iPod on and relaxed in the hazy morning sun. The enticing aromas from the street were wafting upwards and already making me feel hungry, whilst the buzz of the frenetic Bangkok traffic eight floors below was still audible through my headphones. I did not completely, however, drown out the soft high mesmerising voice of Curtis Mayfield which was playing at the time.

A few hours later a bemused Richie appeared. I took one consolation in that he looked the colour of boiled shite. "God, this place is difficult to find," he said. I smugly grinned, I knew him so well. We recollected the events from the night before and it was not long until the pair of us were in hoots of laughter, especially when I retold my home coming and my collision with the Sommelier. Rich had gone back to Coyote Bar after despatching me then had gone on to a nightclub with Apple till about five in the morning. So, our first night in Bangkok had been quite eventful and as time would tell, would be far from the most lively we were to experience on our many nights in Thailand's capital city.

We decided to have a lazy day and just hang around the pool taking things easy. It had seemed ages that we had been in Bangkok but we had only arrived yesterday. Late afternoon, about half past four, the weather clouded over. We decided to shower, clean up and get ready for an evening out. I announced my desire for an early night and some sobriety on my part which was greeted by raised eyebrows by my erstwhile companion.

Having showered I saw a set of bathroom scales and stepped on; twelve stone dead. I was flabbergasted; since my stroke in January 2007, I had lost six and a half stone. A third of my body, where had it all gone to? There were no pouches of excess skin hanging about idly doing nothing. It was like losing an arm and a leg; I now knew how Rolf Harris felt after changing from his Jake the Peg character. I dressed feeling very pleased with myself, sporting a large satisfied smile of a job well done.

Walking into the lobby, I was a little nervous that some irate man was going to collar me for his cleaning bill. I saw another exit from the hotel and Richie and I descended the escalator to the rear entrance of a Sports Bar named Jameson's and dived in for cover. It was a place for expats and tourists with a couple of pool tables and many TV screens dotted about. The good thing was it had draft beer; most bars for Thais only sell bottled beer and you have to search around for a bar catering for farangs if you prefer your beer on tap. We took our time and had a couple of ice cold Singhas to cool us down. There were English papers which were quite recent so we relaxed and spent a nice leisurely hour catching up on events back home.

I asked Richie what time he wanted to dine. He suggested an aperitif at Coyote's and we could decide where to have dinner there. Taking two motor bikes, as we were both too lazy to walk, we arrived at Coyote's. Apple greeted us warmly with a big smile for Rich. I asked him what he had got up to with the lovely lady, but he just shrugged and said nothing. We stayed for two drinks under my instruction and went to look for something to eat. Crossing the road we found ourselves outside Patti's Fiesta Bar. "Do you think they will remember me?" I asked. "One way to find out," Rich replied and walked in.

We were greeted like long lost family and ushered down to the bar, a waitress held my arm protectively in case I repeated my actions from the previous night. One of the Philippino wags on stage made a very amusing anecdote about me on the microphone to which I grimaced. The waitress who held my arm laughed finding my embarrassment funny. I looked at her and noticed she was a ladyboy, a fact that had completely past me by on my first visit.

As I sat on the same ill fated bar stool, a hatch behind the bar opened and a cook with a grubby white hat just pointed at me in fits of hysterical laughter. The Thais sense of humour tends to be quite slapstick and if the subject of their laughter is hurt in anyway then the whole joke is doubly funny. My rendition of up hill stair climbing using your face would have rated high on the Thai Clapometer. The bartender was no less amused and presented our drinks, offering me the loan of his motor bike helmet while I imbibed in his establishment.

I was starving and noticed that a large menu on the wall was advertising Phad Thai; it is a speciality dish that I had never had so we decided to eat in Patti's. Phad Thai is a dish of fried noodles inside an omelette; it can be with almost anything, chicken, pork... but most commonly with prawn. It is not particularly spicy and I found it tasty, but a little bland for my taste buds. Nevertheless, it was cooked to perfection by the laughing cook and was consumed whilst I stayed perfectly safe in my chair.

Another pitcher of Margarita arrived and I held my hand up. "When we finish that one, I am heading off for an early night." Rich seemed to accept my ultimatum and said he felt shattered too and would also be back before midnight. After the meal we left Patti's to a roll on the congas by one of the trio and an "Ole!" by the band. I jumped on a bike and Rich said he was going to amble back to see what we missed on the other side of the road yesterday. Waving goodnight, I headed off into Bangkok's night traffic. In the distance I heard a faint "Right on!" behind me.

The following morning was overcast and cloudy and I did not see the point of sitting by the pool. Whilst I was watching BBC World News my friend stirred from his slumbers and we discussed our agenda for the day, considering the rather inclement weather. I wanted to buy a decent pair of jeans, not something that would fall apart in five minutes, so we agreed we would go to one of the many shopping malls dotted around the city.

I had heard about MBK Mall which is quite affordable; a bit like an indoor market a friend had told me. There are swankier malls depending on your budget; Siam Paragon and Siam Discovery to name but two. The former also has a sixteen screen cinema built inside. All these malls are on the BTS line and are extremely easy to get to.

We asked at reception for directions to the nearest BTS station and were told to take the train to the National Stadium for MBK Mall. The BTS stations are all elevated for the Skytrain and I had to negotiate a busy flight of stairs to board the train. The first thing I noticed was how modern and clean everything was, the station was immaculate and the very polite ticket lady provided us with change to purchase our tickets from the machine. The platform was crowded with people milling around all taking different journeys for their own different reason. The train ghosted into the station and we boarded in a uniformed sort of rolling maul of a rugby scrum.

The carriage was ultra modern, air conditioned with tinted glass windows to keep the glare of the sun away. It was also wide, much wider than the tube and the passengers were all talking to one another unlike London. There were TV screens showing news events and some advertisements; in all, a very pleasant way to travel.

The biggest thing that struck me on our journey standing by the doors was how tall I seemed. I am only five foot eight whereas Richie is nearly six foot and we both dwarfed the other passengers. I felt elated as it was not a common occurrence for me and I was tempted to ride around on the BTS all day. The activity of the city below was clear to see as the futuristic Skytrain raced along the tracks and I became George Jetson for twenty minutes commuting home to Jane, the kids and Astro the dog.

Playing *The Jetsons* when I was a kid was a great game. Firstly, you had to wait until your plastic Wembley Trophy football burst, then all you had to do was cut it in half and turn it inside out. You then had George Jetson's space helmet; the old football's valve made a really realistic aerial that you could accept intergalactic messages on. The orange Wembley Trophies made the most authentic space helmets, as the white ones were always a little grubbier after being kicked around the street for two weeks prior.

The train pulled into National Football stadium station and we alighted, leaving George to continue his journey home. It was a short walk to MBK and we entered the mall, first impressions were the scale of the place and that really dented our adventurous spirits. Richie seemed bored already and we had just arrived, he really is a crabby twat sometimes! I made my way down a few floors to where there seemed to be many little stalls selling clothes. Browsing through a stall and inspecting a few pairs of jeans I noticed there seemed to be no fitting rooms. We were leaving in the morning and I was not going to get up at the crack of sparrows just to exchange a pair of sodding jeans.

Nodding to my disinterested and bored friend I gestured to the escalator for us to leave and his face lit up his dejection lifted immediately. "Where to now?" I asked. "How about a drink?" came the reply. It was 2pm, we were both hot and a tad sweaty from the humid air, a cold beer sounded just the ticket. We walked around outside the mall, but there did not seem to be anything remotely like a bar for us to gather our thoughts. Our deliberations were interrupted by a Tuk-Tuk driver calling to us from the roadside and waving for us to go over.

We began our negotiations with the driver to take us to a bar. He seemed deep in thought, probably trying to think which was the nearest place one of his friends owned. Richie stressed that we were not interested in glitzy, trendy bars we just wanted to go to a local establishment that Thais frequent. We wanted to explore the dark underbelly of Bangkok; well, at least a Thai version of the Bug.

Instructions digested, the driver nodded his understanding and we climbed aboard the unstable contraption. The engine started to a loud cough then a huge plume of smoke farted from the exhaust. Tuk-Tuks really are dirty, smelly, and very noisy things, but we wanted a bit of a laugh so we quite happy tootling along Bangkok's highways and byways in the two stroke monstrosity. The driver must have taken his driving lessons from Sterling Moss as he was a lunatic; the vehicle sped along the road weaving in and out of the traffic with little concern for any other road users or pedestrians with the decrepit engine blowing blue and grey smoke billowing behind.

There were a set of lights ahead and a large queue of traffic three lanes abreast was stopped ahead of us. I could see the traffic on the other side of the road also halted by the same set of lights on the opposite side of the junction. Our driver saw his opportunity and we careered across the central reservation heading the wrong way up a three lane carriageway. "Whoa, those lights are going to change!" Richie shouted in a strangulated, high pitched shriek. Just as a wall of traffic hurtled towards us we veered onto the pavement dodging petrified pedestrians and turned sharp right sending me crashing down into my friend.

The Soi led into a rabbit warren of smaller Sois and I could see a police motor cycle following us. It was not what you would call a high speed chase as a Tuk-Tuk maximum speed is probably only forty miles per hour. However, in these tiny little streets with all manner of stalls, people, animals, monks and other Tuk-Tuks, it was probably the most precarious journey I have ever undertaken. We continued our evasive action in the maze of Sois until we turned a corner and came screeching to a halt in a haze of smoke; our way was barred by a smiling motor bike Copper.

The driver just laughed, it was a game and part of Bangkok's regular daily motoring activity. He handed the policeman some money and we continued on our way. I could not believe it, he must have committed a hundred road violations and we were let off with a small fine that went straight into the Copper's top pocket.

The Tuk-Tuk eventually pulled up outside what looked like a Casino, it did not look at all what we wanted, but we were both glad to get out of the death trap and went inside the building. Within two minutes, we were both on the street getting back into our transport. He had taken us to a secluded, dingy brothel and neither Rich nor I wished to contract some bizarre sexual disease and so we left. Actually, in retrospect, I should have known it was not a Casino as gambling is banned in Thailand apart from the State Lottery. As with all sorts of prohibition, it has just driven gambling into the hands of the Mafia and big money is to be made illegally.

Scratching his head after Richie slowly reiterated our instructions, the driver set off in the opposite direction to which we arrived. Ten minutes later we stopped outside a large farm-like building next to a small canal. It had a roof, but no walls, and we could see many Thai patrons inside enjoying themselves. This place would suffice: it looked exactly what we wanted. Entering through a wall, there was an old television set on the far table with a man singing into a microphone looking at the screen. Thais love Karaoke and it is a favourite pastime combined with drinking whisky or beer.

We sat at a table together with our driver and he ordered three beers. A rickety wooden trolley was wheeled over to us with three large bottles of Leo, glasses and an ice bucket. The driver then went off in search of the Karaoke menu whilst an extremely young waitress attended to our drinks. Rich and I took a long draught from our glasses as we were parched; it had almost been an hour since we had left MBK and this was our first beer.

After a short time I needed to take a pee and the teenager pointed to a bamboo door in the far corner. I pushed open the creaking piece of Rattan to reveal a toilet I have never seen the like of before or since. There was no back wall to the tiny room; the floor was made up of large Bamboo poles that jutted out over the wall hovering above the canal below. The art was to stand as close to the frayed edge of the Bamboo floor as you dare and aim your stream into the canal. I did not dare to think how women coped or indeed how you took a number two.

Finishing my latrine duties I looked about for a tissue or basin, but to no avail, a tap with a dangling piece of rubber hose was the only cleansing option. Gingerly, I handled the rusty piece of metal trying not to think whose hands had been touching it before. I would not have liked to repeat the same operation had I been pissed; I wonder how many budding Karaoke stars had been lost in the depths of the murky canal water below.

We spent a pleasurable hour and a half in the bar and our driver surprised us with his expertise on the microphone. Several beers had been consumed and the pair of us needed to eat. Paying the ridiculously cheap bill, we tipped heavily again and gave our chauffeur fresh instructions to find a similar establishment but serving food.

I had no idea what part of Bangkok we were in as driving around the maze of Sois earlier had completely disorientated me. It had been like a game of pin the tail on the donkey, where a competitor is blindfolded, whirled around a few times then has to find an ass' ass and stick a tail with pin onto the beast. Our driver came up trumps with his selection of eatery: we drove into a relatively more upmarket area and he found a small Soi empty apart from a large restaurant at the bottom.

Absolutely no other farangs were dining there which we liked immensely, the restaurant was clean busy and very, very noisy. We had both grown quite attached to our guide and asked him to join us for a meal. After helping us choose a selection of dishes from the Thai menu; he politely refused our offer and sat back on the Tuk-Tuk to have a smoke. The food was excellent even though we were not sure what the Hell we were both eating; the main thing was that it tasted delicious and we were both famished.

It was close to 7pm and this was the first sustenance either of us had consumed the whole day. We discussed how much our driver would want for ferrying us around for close to eight hours and decided we would instruct him to take us back to Coyote Bar in Silom and pay him off.

The Tuk-Tuk chugged to a final stop outside Coyote's and we clambered out as the contraption rocked like a small boat with the shifting of the weight. We asked our new friend how much we owed him and he simply replied, "Up to you!" He was trying to persuade us to keep him on for the duration of the evening, but we declined several times before he accepted our money. The whole day cost two thousand Baht which translates into about forty quid. He was exceptionally happy with his fare and suggested he take us to the airport in the morning. Laughing, we shook his hands warmly and then he was gone in a cloud of exhaust smoke and toot of the horn. I would normally not advise Tuk-Tuks as a viable means of transportation in Bangkok, but if you have time free and fancy an adventure then it is not a bad way to spend a day.

The following morning we rose early and packed our bags. Within minutes, we were in the back of a mini bus heading to the airport for our flight to Koh Samui. Checking in at the Bangkok Airways desk, we cleared domestic security and made our way to the lounge. Bangkok Airways advertises itself as Thailand's Boutique Airline and if you fly with them from Suvarnabhumi Airport then all passengers can make use of their very comfortable executive lounge. It is not a cheap airline, but some destinations are only served by them and therefore you have no choice but to pay the fare.

The three days in Bangkok had been very eventful for a number of reasons and

I had enjoyed it immensely and looked forward to returning as soon as I possibly could. But now, from the big city's glamour and hectic pace, I was quite looking forward to some relaxing beach time.

Chapter Nine

A RETURN TO SAMUI

The Centara Hotel welcomed us on our return and we had a room in the same wing as last time. The weather was completely different to our first visit; there were blue skies and bright sunshine. We both changed hurriedly into shorts and donned some sun cream before making our way outside to relax in the hot sun.

That evening after a massage we crossed the road to Zico's. The welcome from the staff was quite unexpected and very genuine on their part. On our previous holiday DJ Patti a tall, black Dutch lady signalled the end of Happy Hour when she started spinning Brazilian tunes at seven thirty. Her job had seemed perfect; she had room and board in the Centara and was also paid for living on this Island Paradise. Her girlfriend was one of the Brazilian dancers in Zico's and the couple seemed to have life sorted. There had been a change of music policy and DJ Patti had been replaced by a Philippino band, Road Block. We consumed our Happy Hour quota of Singha rather rapidly and exited briskly to see our friends at Andaman's.

Passing the Rock Bar on the way I half expected to see a beleaguered Ken still lingering around trying to get home, now looking dishevelled and attired like Robinson Crusoe, collecting bits of driftwood for a raft. Peering into the bar I saw one of the owners who did not seem to recognise us and there was no sign of Ken or James Brown.

Arriving at Andaman's, I could see Johnny outside but no sign of Benz. Johnny hugged us tightly and was delighted that we had returned. He ushered us inside to meet Sue and she immediately phoned Din to come and meet us. She was surprised how much

I had changed and how much weight I had lost and was very complementary towards the new Francis Abel. We enquired about "Right on" and Sue was a little upset when she told us that he had left quite unexpectedly a couple of months ago, leaving the business with a few financial anomalies.

There is a minimum wage in Thailand, but compared to Western standards it is still a pittance. For example, a barman's wage for a month would be between four thousand and eight thousand Baht depending on the establishment. This would equate to one hundred to two hundred pounds for a seven days a week position with probably two days holiday per month. It is because of these low wages that Thais change their jobs regularly and move about frequently in employment. So, expecting to see the same faces in regular haunts on holiday is unusual. I must also point out that a barman is considered a rather decent position to have and there are many occupations paid far lower than that.

Din arrived like a whirlwind and shook our hands vigorously whilst chatting all the time as he did so. He told us to quickly finish our drinks as he had something to show us. We followed him down the beach road and noticed a few new additions to the strip. About four doors down from Andaman's was a new bar called Oasis, and a genial wave and smile was proffered to us from Win, the manager, as we passed. "Remember him?" asked Rich, but by the blank expression on my face he explained, "He used to work in Andaman's!" I must admit that I had forgotten all about Win, as Sue and Tin had many employees.

A little further a black sign, Duke, advertised a big new bar that had a loud Rock band playing on a small stage inside. Then Din pointed up to another sign on the building behind the Duke. Andaman's Restaurant! He had opened a second restaurant and seemed very happy with his achievement.

Andaman's 2 was much larger than the original, possibly three times as big. It had the added bonus of straddling the land between

Beach Road and Lake Road and had entrances facing in both directions. As with all the barbeque restaurants on Beach Road, Andaman's 2 had huge refrigerated cabinets displaying its fare to the street. Din prided himself that his display was the best in Chaweng; a whole suckling pig was roasting over hot coals on a spit while one cabinet displayed juicy steaks and brochettes.

The fish display was magnificent, a huge selection of exotic, freshly caught marine creatures lying on a bed of cascading ice. Barracuda, shark, tuna and all manner of giant shellfish including lobster, prawns and various types of mussels and clams. Tourists were stopping and taking photos of the display and an army of staff clad in chefs' white tunics and hats attended to the diners, helping them pick their selection before sending it to be cooked.

Din led us past satisfied diners tucking in to large platters laden with obscene quantities of food and showed us the rear part of the restaurant. Here things were a little quieter and we took seats around a spare table.

"Eddie!" Din called out and waved to a farang with long black hair, standing by a table. The man came over and shook our hands, then rather brusquely excused himself in a thick Australian accent and walked off to talk to a waiter. Eddie was Andaman's front of house greeter and was responsible for attracting tourists off the street into the restaurant and part with some of their money.

This part of the establishment was open air which I found to be quite a unique asset to the restaurant. However, Din disclosed his plans for extending the roof over the front part to cover this area also. Whilst we were chatting, Din called a waiter over and started to give him some instructions. After a very short time a team of waiters were bringing tray after tray of food to our table. Din explained it was his pleasure to offer a selection of his food for us to sample.

There was everything from succulent Australian fillet steaks to gargantuan sized lobster tails and exotically spicy Thai accompanying dishes. It was a feast of delicious tasting and large proportioned high class fare that a five star restaurant would be proud to have presented.

As we all were having a glass of Regency Brandy as a digestive, Din started musing out loud to us in between heavy inhalations of his Marlborough Light.

"I have been thinking what to do with this place to bring some extra revenue to the business." One thing Richie and I had noticed about Chaweng is that it very successfully caters for the Backpackers Club Scene and also for the family orientated restaurant crowd, but there is nowhere for the twenty five old plus punter to really go for a little excitement. Yes, there were the beer bars and the sex options, but sometimes people just want a really good, clean fun night out.

We explained this to Din and he nodded in agreement blowing out a large plume of smoke. We had been thinking on the same lines as him and had just confirmed his thoughts. Richie, totally unexpectedly, then piped up with an after dinner speech extolling my virtues as the best DJ he had ever heard. Din sat up at this news and quizzically stared at me.

"Could this person sitting opposite be the answer?" I was a little flushed with embarrassment and very surprised; Richie rarely compliments me and certainly not in company.

"The problem is when my customers finish their meals, they then go to Duke's next door for the remainder of their evening," Din was airing his thoughts out loud again. "I need to find a way to keep them here." The second statement was more of a question and was directed at us. Eddie came back to the table and briefly spoke to Din about some problem occurring. "Okay, I will be right there," he dismissed Eddie. "Why don't you both think about it and we will talk later in the week."

With that last ambiguous comment Din shook our hands and left the table smiling as if he had just solved his problem. We didn't have to pay a single Baht for our dinner and were both rather full walking to the Pool bar to say Hello to Vaughn. I was pressing Richie about what he though Din was trying to suggest to us.

"That's easy; he wants you to be his DJ," I stopped in my tracks. "Really?" "Yep, that's what he meant," he replied.

I could not sleep with excitement; is that what Din really meant? Or had we lost something in translation? Did he just want us to come up with an idea? I tossed and turned, my mind racing twenty to the dozen. I was thankful Rich was absent most of the night being involved in Thailand's Open Pool Championship, that coincidently, luckily enough, was being hosted by Vaughn over the road.

If Richie was right and Din did want me to come and work for him, was I ready to make the step? I began to doubt myself; was I good enough? If I was physically up to it, what would happen if I was sick again over in Thailand? This self questioning and doubting kept me awake the whole night.

The following morning I was lying in the sun, occasionally dozing from lack of sleep. I still had multiple doubts running around my mind. I had come up with a solution for Din even if I was not going to be a part of it myself. The big problem I could see that Din had was that he had an established business that was successful; he did not want, or need to risk that business in any way he wanted to augment it. My plan was to turn the restaurant into another venue at midnight; the dining patrons could stay if they desired, but new punters would also be attracted to come to also. I had not thought exactly the form of what the transformation would be, but had one or two ideas on it.

The next few days Rich and I spent on a fact finding exploration of Samui's night life, it was a tough job but somebody had to do it! I had already told Din I was working on the problem and he said he wanted to meet me again next Tuesday, so we had five days' research time. The week almost had a routine; sunbathing followed by a massage, then Happy Hour attendance at Zico's for thirst quenching Singha Beer, and Oasis for pre dinner Margaritas. Then after eating, normally at a Thai Food hall, we would explore the strip's entertainment; purely on a work related basis!

During the week, Samui filled with a younger, backpacking crowd that came for the Full Moon party on the nearby island of Koh Phangan. The Full Moon party is not surprisingly held once a month and it is an all night rave on one of Thailand's remote islands. Koh Phangan is a small fishing island barren of hotels, bars and entertainment, but every month it is the venue for a debauched all night party that thousands of ravers from all over the world attend. There really is nothing to do or places to stay on Koh Phangan; so there tends to be a monthly influx of Full Moon Party goers spending a few days on Samui before jumping on small boats for their rave.

When this happens, Soi Green Mango and the nightclubs come alive with the extra night people. The trendy bars like Ark, Solo, Bondi and Tropical Murphy's all benefit from the extra revenue, but the now crowded venues drive away the other holiday makers from the area, and the established older venues, the Reggae Pub and Camp Beer, take their custom.

It proved to me that there was a large hole in Samui's nightlife not being catered for by anybody: the wealthy older crowd that still have life in their legs after midnight and want to spend their cash having fun, not being drowned out by house music. I had my idea; what was missing was a type of seventies club, a Flares or Car Wash, I told Richie. Surprisingly, he totally agreed with me, a fact that I noted in my diary later.

In a couple of days I had come up with a name: Boogie Nights. It was the title of an old song by Heatwave and described the type of venue I was proposing to a tee. Whilst I was busy filling my brain with logical solutions to Din's problem, I had deliberately pushed to the back of my mind a huge doubt; did I want to be a part of it all?

I voiced to Rich my doubts while we were in Oasis one night. It had become a regular haunt of ours; James the bartender was a character and enjoyed making our Margarita's as strong as possible to see the effects his handiwork had on our behaviour. Pu was one of the waitresses who would regularly bring us our drinks and was one of the most beautiful girls on Samui, Rich often used to embarrass me with his corny chat up lines towards the young woman, but they seemed to make him happy.

Richie turned to me in between turns of Connect Four with Pu. "I don't know what you are worried about, if it does not work out you can always come home." I could feel I did not have his full attention as he returned his gaze to the game. "What?" I responded; just to try and get a little of his time, as this was an important issue and decision for me. I was still not one hundred percent certain if Din was offering me a job but he seemed to be. A loud triumphant scream went up followed by clapping as Pu pulled tongues at Rich having beaten him for the umpteenth time that evening.

My grumpy friend continued our conversation. "What's the problem, are you getting windy again?"

"It's not that, I just don't know if Din wants to employ me?" I replied. Rich was trying to goad me into a decision, but I was not ready for that yet until I had clarified things with Din in the morning. I left Rich at the Pool Bar and went to bed early that night: I wanted to rest and consider my options.

I had arranged to meet Din at lunchtime and was lying on the sun lounger feeling very nervous. Rich, for once, had surfaced before midday and was sunning himself next to me reading a book. He was not speaking, but I knew his presence was his way of giving me his support. I looked at the time on my phone: it was quarter to twelve, fifteen minutes before my meeting. I had the time on my phone because I did not own a watch. Well, that is I lie, I actually own several watches, what I meant was I was not wearing a watch. Since my stroke I have never worn one, initially because I couldn't fasten the strap, but subsequently as a symbol that time means little to me. I had to get a move on not to be late!

Arriving at Andaman's, there was no sign of Din, nobody knew where he was. I saw Johnny and he offered me a Coke Zero which I accepted, and I sat in the shade waiting. I had waited all week for this meeting and Din had not bothered to even turn up, perhaps I was right, there was no job for me. I had not given him my plan for the future of Andaman's; surely he wanted to at least hear that.

After thirty minutes, very confused, I walked back to the Centara. Rich was just as puzzled as me as I sat back down on my lounger rather pissed off. But my bitter disappointment at my rebuttal came as a surprise to me and then my mood dawned on me: I wanted this job, I wanted to stay in Thailand. Subconsciously I had made my decision.

That evening, we saw Sue at Andaman's 1, who was not aware Din had arranged to see me earlier that day: she had been with him at the wholesalers and he had not mentioned anything. A dull pang of disappointment filled my body, Din had not mentioned anything to his wife about his thoughts for the business. It did not bode well for the future of Boogie Nights.

We went on our usual evening stroll and I forgot about Boogie Nights to some relief, as I did not have to make the life changing decision I had been wavering on. A holiday pipe dream, that is all it had been all along. That night we discovered a fabulous area to dine, a collection of around ten Thai food stalls surrounded by six or seven open air restaurants: Chaweng Food Market. It was a short five minute ride in a bus near the far end of the lake. The Tom Yum Talay, a mixed seafood spicy soup was fiery hot and I have become almost addicted to it ever since. In fact all the food was exceptional and all at a budget price for the local Chaweng residents.

Returning from our gastronomic experience, we pottered around the north end of the beach road and messed about in Soi Green Mango for a couple of hours. Walking back we passed

Andaman's 2 and Din rushed out to greet us. He apologised about the meeting saying he had mixed the days up and could I see him tomorrow. I clarified that he had told Sue of his plans and he confirmed to me he had.

The following day I repeated my previous morning actions and at ten to twelve on my Nokia phone, I strolled to my appointment. This time, Din was there, and seated with a rather serious looking other man I had not seen before. They both stood at my entrance and we all shook hands. The stranger was introduced simply as Khun: "a very important member of Andaman's staff." During the whole meeting; Khun did not utter one single word; he just sat slightly behind Din looking around suspiciously.

I poured out my plans to Din. I had to describe to him what a 70s club was and described the type of music policy Boogie Nights would have and what sort of clientele would be attracted. He loved the idea that his premises would become dual purpose and the outlay for the new venture would be fairly minimal. We inspected the building and located likely spots for a stage and PA equipment. Din was caught up in the whole idea and was busy talking out loud about logistics.

We returned to the table for some drinks and as we sat down I noticed the butt of a revolver in Khun's trouser belt. What the fuck was Din doing with a body guard? I did not like this new turn of events, it worried me greatly. I returned to the Centara about two hours later.

"Well? It must have gone well if it took so long!" my friend looked up from his book. I nodded with a huge grin on my face. "He liked the whole thing," I responded. "But he has still not actually offered me anything."

That night, we saw Sue on our way for a game of Connect Four with Pu and James. She simply said to me that Din wanted to talk to me before I went back home to the England. The final few days Rich and I chatted constantly about my plans for Boogie Nights. I was like an excited teenager bubbling with enthusiasm, but slightly tempered with apprehension especially about Khun and the gun.

But I never did see or speak to Din again that holiday. On our final night, we both had dinner at Andaman's 1, and Sue reiterated Din was still interested in the project but was busy. I gave her my mobile number and asked her to pass it on to her husband when she saw him again.

About one week later sitting in Chez Regina, after just braving the weather for a gym visit, my mobile phone rang. I picked it up and looked at the number +66; that was Thailand.

I phoned Richie at work. Bingo! I told him that I had just spoken to Din and he wanted to know when was the soonest I could return to Samui to start my new job. He asked me what I had said and I told him I had informed Din in one month. Richie wanted to know why I wanted to wait for so long, why did I not just jump on a plane next week? Funny; that is exactly what Din had said, but I knew I had to get my music prepared. In the past I was actually quite a good and popular DJ, but that was mostly down to preparation.

I made a 'Things to Do' list. Music, visa, clothes, money, house, medicine; it was getting quite extensive and I knew it would take at least a month to get it all together. I arranged to see Rich in the Bug that night, I was so excited with my news and since he was the only one who knew my future intentions he was the only person I could speak to about all this without sounding like I was bragging.

Nick had been on holiday when I returned from Thailand and hadn't a clue what I had been planning over there. He always joined us for a drink on Monday for Ray's Quiz Night in the Bug. For some reason I was a little apprehensive in telling my good friend my news and was waiting until after the quiz.

Actually, Ray had retired from his Quiz Master duties and according to Richie it was to take up residence in a retirement home for Cross Dressers. Now a rather irascible chap named Mick

Lanham stood on the lectern. An odd choice, as Mick had the quietest voice in the pub and had to be home for his tea at 8.30pm on the dot or his wife would come and interrupt proceedings to drag him out of the bar. He did however, a wonderful impression of Julie Andrews: not dressed in a Nun's Frock running on Crosby Beach singing "The dunes are alive to the sound of music," but impersonating Mary Poppins saying "Spit spot" as the quiz clock ran down in a 'Countdown' fashion.

After a tough tie break question in the quiz of 'how many of Snow White's dwarves wore glasses?' The Lemon Drizzle Cakes were victorious, and enjoying our free pint when suddenly, Richie blurted out; "Have you told him your news?" nodding towards Nick. I told Nick my story; the news seemed to go down like a lead balloon. I do not know if it was shock or the fact he was worried how I would cope by myself, but he did not seem too pleased. He had the look on his face to say; "Can't I leave you two idiots alone for just two weeks without you both causing chaos?"

The following morning I set about tackling my list of chores, booting up my PC, I punched in Thai visa requirements. I was directed to the official site and started to read what my options were. If you hold a full ten year British passport then you are allowed to stay for one month. There were longer visas available: a three month one and a twelve month one. The twelve month 'Retirement' visa looked a bit complicated to me, so I chose the three month option. I looked down the list of consulates and noticed there was one in Liverpool so I phoned and made an appointment later in the week.

I then started the job of on line shopping for 70s compilation CDs. I have a vast collection of music, but it would be too much hassle to search through all the tracks picking out individual songs and then burning them to playlists. Luckily I had gone through the exercise of converting all my vinyls and CDs to my iTunes library so I would take my laptop and burn any discs I needed while I was over there.

It pained me to part with my dwindling reserves of cash on some of the pieces of shite that I had to, but I had to be prepared for any requests that came my way. 100 Classic 70s Country Songs would not be an album I would normally purchase, but needs must. Marvin Gaye would be turning in his grave if he could have seen me and I hoped that his attention was turned elsewhere.

Linzi came to take me to the gym the following morning, and she was most enthusiastic about my decision to live in Thailand. However, she posed one question I had not even thought about, what about the invalidity benefit, does it still get paid if you are abroad? I did not have a clue if it did or it didn't, I knew I had better find out before I went.

I knew my rehab and fitness regime would take a knock moving abroad, but perhaps once I was settled I could investigate ways of resuming my work. I told my GP of my intending action and I was called in to take a raft of blood samples and general prodding about. After a few days the results came back, my iron was low, whatever that means, and I might have to have an endoscopy in the near future.

Later I phoned Rich on a bit of a rant. "If that is the camera they put down your throat I would say no! I hate anything lodged in my windpipe, I have a fear of choking. I would simply drop my trousers and ask them to shove it up my bum instead as I hear they can do that too. At any rate, they gave me a supply of medicine for three months and that is all I needed."

The house was a bit of a problem as I would be still paying the mortgage and utility bills whilst I was away. I decided to wait to see how things worked out, but I would have return sometime to either sort out a more permanent solution to my property or to settle back home with my tail between my legs. With that decision finalised, I went on the Emirates web site and bought a return ticket from March 17th to June 10th. The ticket was flexible so I could change my return date.

My good friend Sully said he would call to the house once a week and sift through my mail, and if anything important cropped up he would either phone me or scan it and email it to me. Rich was a bit of a Arthur Mullard when it came to technology, he did not even own a PC. Emails were something he thought ravers took before they went clubbing.

Friday morning arrived and I set off for my visa appointment. I decided to take the Northern Line as Waterloo Station was close by and I could get off at Liverpool Central. I could not quite work out where the Thai Consulate was; on the phone I was given directions that it was on Lord Street and part of the Boodle and Dunthorne building. Lord Street is one of the main shopping thoroughfares in the centre of Liverpool and Boodle and Dunthorne was one of the most famous jewellery shops. What possible connection could the Thai Immigration Authority have with an earring supplier? It did dawn on me it would be a pretty handy place to sort your travel arrangements once buying an engagement ring for your intended. A one stop wedding and honeymoon service, the Thai ingenuity astounded me.

Walking up Lord Street with my coat tightly fastened and hat pulled firmly down, I struggled against the blustery wind coming straight off the Mersey. The wind carried with it squalls of rain on a very dark, dank day in the city. I could see the Boodle and Dunthorne's shop, but was at a loss to see the official Thailand Consulate building. Peering down North John Street, rain lashing in my face I saw a small doorway with a plaque with the Garuda. The Garuda is the National Emblem of Thailand; it is a mixture of Buddhist and Hindu mythology and is a sort of a ferocious winged creature.

Taking shelter in the doorway, I pressed the button in front of me. An electronic buzzing sounded and I pushed the door and entered a small reception room with a blond haired lady sitting behind the only desk. "Hello, I am looking for the Thai Consulate," I declared before the lady had a chance to show me the new range of White Gold jewellery from Africa.

"Do you have an appointment?" she queried. I nodded as confirmation. The pleasant receptionist picked up the phone and spoke: "Sue, it is your eleven o'clock."

She pointed to a small two seater sofa, the only furniture in the room. "Have you filled in the form?" Again, I nodded. I had downloaded the application form and brought with me the required passport photos, cash and passport. She smiled genially at me and we discussed the atrocious weather, we could both hear the wind howling outside battering against the door and grimaced to each other.

Whilst we chatted I enquired what were the requirements for a one year visa. The retirement or white haired visa as it is sometimes known is available once the applicant is fifty and can prove evidence of having eight hundred thousand Baht in savings. I was a little excited as it was my fiftieth birthday in April and I would be able to apply for one of those in a couple of months.

A door suddenly opened that I had not noticed before and a rather official lady carrying a bundle of files came in to the waiting room. She introduced herself in a soft Liverpudlian accent as Sue: she was the Consulate. I don't know what I had expected, to be ushered into a plush suite of offices staffed by attractive Thai ladies in National Dress. The visa was processed then and there, I parted with seventy five quid for a triple entry three month visa and my passport was duly stamped.

Five minutes later, I was back out on the street braving the weather walking towards Liverpool One Mall. Over the past five years Liverpool has reinvented itself as a city. Its transformation came about when it was the European Capital of Culture in 2008 and millions of pounds of investment has revamped the city. Now it has become a favourite tourist destination, the world over; not just for its infamous nightlife, but also for its stupendous architecture and museums.

The shackles of a terrible militant past have been thrown aside and now Liverpool has once again regained its title as a truly cosmopolitan city. Liverpool One is one of the largest shopping malls in Europe and was constructed during 2008, housing retail outlets together with restaurants and cinema. Liverpool Football Club opened a Megastore there named "Liverpool 1" and a few months later, Everton F.C a couple of doors away opened their second shop and named it "Everton 2".

Browsing through the HMV store I asked directions to the Shite CD Compilations section. I was exceptionally embarrassed paying for my selections at the counter: I had never bought so much crap all at one time in my life, but I knew Bachman Turner Overdrive and the like would be just the ticket for Boogie Nights. I also managed to procure a large CD storage carrying case that had capacity for one hundred CDs. I then purchased a couple of Chelsea Football shirts for Din, as requested, from a nearby sports shop and my morning business was completed.

Returning home on the train I looked at my passport and studied the new visa feeling quite like Alan Wicker, a true globetrotter. One thing concerned my greatly about the visa, written in large letters across the bottom was "Tourist Visa, No Employment." I had to discuss with Din a way to resolve this.

The next week I began organising my 70s music collection into a workable and easy to use compilation. I also collated and burned several playlist CDs with defined classic tracks by genres. There were specialist 70s Soul, Rock, Reggae, Country, Pop, Fast, Slow, Start of Night, End of Night etc. I covered every permutation that I could think of; it was this sort of preparation that made me quite a successful DJ. There would be no uncomfortable pregnant pauses in my sets, a killer of an occurrence for any dance floor and DJ. I could put my finger on any request in a matter of seconds and I was satisfied with the music library I was taking with me.

My work was constantly interrupted by exercise breaks and visits to the gym together with constant visitors calling to see if I needed any help or assistance. My close group of friends were rallying around giving their support; it almost made me question what I was doing. The days passed quickly and weekends were crammed with last get-togethers as my departure date was looming quickly. I still had bits and pieces to attend to and was rushing around like a madman to finish everything.

Trawling through the web, I had designed a logo for Boogie Nights; cobbling together some images and adding text. I was quite pleased with the end result; it pictured two dancers male and female with authentic 70s clothes and hairdos. The man had a massive afro and was wearing ridiculously large flared trousers, the lady had huge pieces of jewellery adorned over an extremely figure hugging cat suit. And in red letters blazoned across the top of the animated dancers was the slogan: "Boogie Nights." The logo could be used on anything and really depicted what the whole venture was all about.

About three or four days before I was due to fly out to Thailand, the unthinkable happened. On the 12th of March 2010 the "United Front for Democracy v Dictatorship" party a.k.a "Red Shirts" demonstrated on the streets of Bangkok. Once more there was political unrest in the country and it looked very serious and more menacing than before. The Red Shirts are supporters of Thaksin Shinawatra, the deposed ruler who was ousted in the September 2006 Coup. Since then Thaksin was in exile on alleged charges of corruption. This was not going to be a peaceful sit in, there was going to be blood on the streets in the coming weeks.

Two days later there was held the Million People March; actually only about one hundred thousand protesters marched, ominously it was by people outside Bangkok. Most of the activity was peaceful and seemed centred around Phan Fah Bridge. The protesters were demanding new elections and a change of government. Rich phoned me to see if I had been following the news. I said I had but it all seemed quite peaceful and under control. I was not going to put my trip back for anything.

Unlike the Yellow Shirts who wore the King's colours and were known to be the party of the elite, the Red Shirts were the party for the masses, representing manual and rural workers and the poorer population in general. Thaksin's previous stint in government was claimed to have been a corrupt and highly dubious rule by criminal methods. He is however, loved by a vast swathe of loyal followers who he provided education and medical care free for the common man.

Later in my sojourn, a close friend; Ton, said to me that he had three influences that ruled his life; first were his parents, second the teachings of Buddha and lastly Thaksin Shinawatra. Before Thaksin, he had not been able to go to school as his family were too poor, but after his election he was able to study and even attend university. Thaksin had changed his life forever, and nobody could ever take his education away from him.

Many people will remember Thaksin as the wealthy Thai business man that purchased Manchester City a few years back, but had to sell due to financial irregularities. That more or less sums Thaksin up, an enigma; loved or loathed depending on where your allegiances lie. But definitely somebody that has changed the shape of Thailand's future for good or bad.

My final weekend was rather a boozy affair as I said goodbye to my friends. On Saturday night I went on a pub crawl with four mates in town. My favourite drinking part of Liverpool is away from Matthew Street and the stag party areas. Round the cathedral part of the city is far more relaxed and has old genuine, traditional boozers.

We took the train and then a taxi to Egerton Street and had our first drink in Peter Kavanagh's, then tootled down to the Blackburn Arms followed by the Belvedere. Crossing Hope Street and turning down Rice Street, next was Ye Old Cracke with a brief pit stop at the Pilgrim, before working our way to The Grapes on Roscoe Street reputed to be the most haunted pub in Liverpool. By then, I had reached my alcohol limit so we all piled into Sultan's Palace for the obligatory curry to end proceedings.

The flight was on Tuesday at 2pm and on Monday I went to the gym as I did not know when the next time I would have an opportunity. Donna; a very old friend, had offered to give me a lift to the airport and I cordially accepted as I knew she was a very organised person and would not let me forget anything. I was aware I needed checking every now and then.

Packing was fairly easy as I had decided to travel light. T-shirts, shorts and other clothing could be bought cheaply enough over there, apart from tailored suits! Most of my case was filled with the technical things I would need for my job. I knew this was a risk, but I couldn't possibly take them all on as hand baggage. I had a Technics shoulder bag for my laptop and personal items and that was heavy enough for me to struggle with on a long journey of this kind.

That night I had agreed to have a quiet farewell drink with Richie and Nick at the Bug's quiz night. The trouble with goodbyes in a pub is that there is alcohol involved and when drink is added to an emotive occasion feelings tend to be amplified. Richie called round to walk to the Edinburgh Inn with me and I collared him in to bring my case downstairs to the hall, a trick I had not quite mastered yet.

The evening was most jovial and I took it really easy on the Stella so I would not get too sentimental, also I had to wake fairly early the next morning. One or two other mates popped in during the proceedings to give me their best wishes and to say farewell which I freely admit gave me a problem keeping steely eyed. I have always been a very emotional person and worn my heart on my sleeve and was finding it most difficult not to shed a tear or two. Finally, it was time to go and I embraced my two friends warmly; Nick was still quiet as he had been since my announcement, but Richie had a stupid Tetley Smooth Flow grin all over his face which made it easier for me to depart.

Donna was prompt, as expected; she lifted my case into her car and we sped to Manchester Airport. On the way she was reading from a mental check list and asking me all the relevant holiday questions. Satisfied I passed her test; she dropped me at Departures and drove off to work. Manchester Airport is a pretty quiet place on a March weekday, so I cleared all the official obstacles rapidly and made my way to the bar as I had an hour and a half to kill.

To say I was apprehensive is the biggest understatement in the history of apprehension. Butterflies were fluttering in my stomach; self doubt and questioning almost made me queasy. I walked to the bar and requested a Stella to calm my nerves, the barman asked me if I was going anywhere nice on holiday and an alien voice responded: "I am going to Thailand to live." I turned around to see if somebody else had uttered the words; it all seemed so bizarre and unreal that this was happening to me. SMS messages of goodwill flooded my phone which bought sentimental thoughts as I replied so I decided one beer would be enough and made my way to the gate for the flight to Dubai.

Chapter Ten

BOOGIE NIGHTS

The Emirates 380 touched down on schedule at Suvarnabhumi Airport in Bangkok the following day. Everything had gone smoothly and the connections had been on time. I had the obligatory long delay at Thai immigration and by the time I had reached baggage control, my case had been off loaded from the carousel and was waiting for me amongst hundreds of others in a pile.

I had booked three nights in the Holiday Inn for a short break before I flew to Samui to start my new working life, a fact that I had reserved from telling Din. After the long journey and having my suitcase with me I opted to take a taxi to Bangkok rather than struggle with the train with my luggage.

Suvarnabhumi Airport has a wonderful system for hiring taxis that more international airports could do with adopting. Once locating the official airport taxi rank outside of the terminal, there are six or seven desks lined up with staff in uniform attending. Once informing the officials of the desired address, they will then call the next cabbie in line and issue him with a price for the journey and instructions in Thai if he does not know the destination. You are issued with a copy of the agreed price stamped by the airport and thus no haggling needs to take place.

This is a simple and very fair system to operate, there are no shitehawks making the taxi rank a free for all brawl and it stops any rogue operators from ripping you off. I could think of many supposedly civilised western airports that are not as considerate to their patrons. The fare was three hundred and fifty Baht, around seven pounds including tolls, but it depended where in the city you were going to.

Arriving up the same ramp as a few months ago; I made the familiar way across the lobby to the front desk of the hotel hoping I might see Superporn. Memories came flooding back of the less than conspicuous entrance I had made after my Margarita Night with Rich. I told them my name and was immediately informed this was not where executive residents checked in. As a treat I had decided to upgrade and have some luxury for three days as I did not have a clue what my accommodation would be like in Samui. To be honest, due to political situation it was not really that expensive, all hotels in Bangkok were fairly empty and rates had been slashed across the city.

The Yellow Shirts' actions in 2008 had bought devastation to Thailand's tourist industry and the ramifications were still affecting tourism including the hotel trade quite drastically. The new outbreak of political unrest was adding more fuel to an already smouldering situation; visitors simply did not trust precarious Thailand and considered it a highly dangerous country to visit. Florida was a much safer bet to risk hard earned holiday savings.

A porter took my luggage to the twenty third floor of the executive tower where the lounge was situated. I was directed to take a comfortable seat whilst the glamorous assistant processed my check in. I looked around at the plush surroundings of the room; the thick carpets and soft furnishings and smiled to myself in satisfaction that I had chosen to upgrade. Only a couple of minutes passed and the same porter who had been waiting showed me to my room.

The room was magnificent, large and well appointed with the same shag pile, deep carpets. There was a King sized bed with a choice of pillows, depending what filling you preferred and a large desk equipped with everything a business man might require. There was even a tray with complimentary fresh fruit and Belgian chocolates together with a vase of flowers.

I opened the blinds and looked at the city far below me, it was a stunning view. I could just see the Chao Phraya River and small crafts navigating their way on the water. The Bangkok skyscrapers loomed up out from the ground below like metal and glass talons scratching at the clouds. I was in awe of the Big Mango and I could just imagine the hustle and bustle of daily life taking place at this very moment down on the tiny streets. My impatience to be a part of it all was overwhelming, but I knew I had a few chores to do first, and one was to bathe. It was over twenty hours since I last showered or had a change of clothes and I was beginning to smell a little ripe!

The bathroom was almost as big as the bedroom and was spotlessly clean with large fawn tiles from floor to ceiling. There was a separate, glass surrounded shower and a huge shallow bath that I was now filling with steaming water. Robes hung on the back of the door and a selection of soft white towels to choose from were piled in orderly fashion on heated stainless steel rungs.

Immersing myself in the water, I relaxed for about thirty minutes, letting the aches and cramps of the journey ebb away into the warm soap suds. I did not want to ever come out from this blissful experience, but it was nearing six o'clock and I had been told complimentary food and drink was served in the executive lounge from six to eight o'clock. Not wanting to miss out on anything, I towelled myself and changed for the evening.

The lounge was fairly quiet. I had been expecting quite a bun fight with free booze on offer, but it seemed executives in South East Asia can afford their own refreshments. I was staggered at what was on offer, there was a fully stocked free bar with everything from bottles of spirits, a choice of wines and a selection of beers. There were large tureens with sumptuous selections of hot food, trays of cold snacks and sandwiches all presented in five star elegance. You could either help yourself to whatever you desired or take a seat and ask an attendant for service.

I took it easy; especially on the hooch. But there must be some greedy bastards that take full advantage of all that is on offer. I remembered how easy it was to gain weight when staying at hotels away on business, when things are free such as now or when your employers are paying it is hard to keep self control and decline what is presented to you.

Later that evening I took a short stroll down Silom just to get reacquainted and orientated with the surroundings. I ate dinner sitting in the street down a small Soi and discovered Laab, which has become a firm favourite of mine. It is a Thai salad which consists of minced pork or chicken with raw green beans and a sort of raw crispy cabbage or lettuce. It is not for the faint hearted as it is fiery hot and very spicy, nevertheless is delicious and even better washed down with a cold beer.

Returning to the hotel before nine o'clock, I retired to my comfortable bed as I was quite shattered by the trip. I took my medicine and fell into a very deep and untroubled sleep; I did not wake up for eleven hours. Feeling refreshed from a good night's rest, I went to the lounge for breakfast. Being a member of the executive club gives you the privilege of not having to fight your way through throngs of hungry tourists just to get a plate of scrambled eggs. It was just after 9am and I was served a leisurely breakfast in a deserted lounge, I presumed all the business men would have already dined and gone to their appointments. Looking out of the window I saw it was a glorious morning, just right for a spot of relaxation by the pool.

That night I went to Coyote and had a chat to Best, the assistant manager; the place was empty and he said Apple had taken the opportunity of going to Switzerland to see her boyfriend, a fact that I think Richie was unaware of. I had one drink and wandered over to Patti's Fiesta bar, the atmosphere was flat there also, in fact the whole of Silom was very subdued; no tourists and not many people on the streets. It was like being in the eye of the storm waiting for the impending chaos to be unleashed.

Saturday came and I was very relaxed having a rather quiet time in Bangkok; I was a little apprehensive in the taxi to the airport as my brief halt in proceeding had ended and now I was to start my new life. As I waited in the Bangkok Airways departure lounge I received a phone call from Din asking what time my plane landed. Reality had raised its head and I began thinking of my job ahead and the preparations needed before Boogie Nights could be open for business.

Rather relieved that my case had turned up, I grabbed it off the carousel myself; turning it upright I wheeled it out into the bright Samui sunshine. Din was already in the covered walkway waiting for me, he rushed up to greet me with a huge grin on his face from one ear to the other. He shook my hand vigorously and chatted away about the alterations he had already made to Andaman's. He led me to a big swanky, silver pick up truck and I could see Sue in the rear cabin animatedly waving at me. Any lingering doubts I had for my future instantly disappeared at this warmest of welcomes, I felt secure with these genuine people.

I do not know why, but I was surprised by the leisurely and sedate pace Din drove the vehicle. He chose a different route from the airport that I had never been on before; in fact I had never been out of Chaweng to my shame. I saw parts of Samui away from the tourist tracks and I promised myself to explore more of the Island.

Soon we were at the restaurant and Din parked at the lakeside entrance where three or four of his staff came out to greet us. I had not noticed before, but the back of the truck was full of provisions. Under Sue's supervision, the staff began unloading the vehicle as Din showed me his handiwork.

The restaurant was being prepared for lunch, but amid cooks, waiters and cleaners all going about their daily duties, there was a team of workmen in the front of the restaurant constructing a stage. The noise was unbelievable; nail guns exploded sporadically whilst electric saws buzzed away in accompanying discord. Pieces of timber fell onto white linen tables and waiters and joiners shouted at each other angrily. I felt sorry for any hungry tourist popping in for a quiet dinner with his wife as Din was on a mission; to finish the improvements as soon as possible.

I could not help wondering why Din was constructing such a large stage; all I required was a small booth for the CD equipment. I did not air my thoughts as Din looked so happy with the progress the workmen were making. We sat at a table in the rear part of the restaurant where it was a little quieter and Sue soon joined us. I took out my laptop and showed Din what I had done so far. I had compiled a list of my requirements; CD decks, PA equipment, lighting, signage, DJ booth, and more. It was comprehensive, but Din only seemed interested in bits of my plan.

Over the coming days I was to learn that Din only shows part of his hand in negotiations and planning. He keeps a lot of information to himself and is likely to change his mind at the drop of a hat. He did not like my logo and chose another from my reserve art work that I had prepared just in case. It was of three silhouetted figures dancing with an orange/red sunrise glow behind them, quite striking and very effective.

Sue ordered some lunch for us as we continued to natter on excitedly about the plans. Din's English is good, until he does not want to be understood. This can occur when a problem arises that he does not want to face and then he falls into an act of misunderstanding and vagueness.

During lunch we listened to some sample music over the restaurant house PA system. Din liked it, especially our theme tune, Boogie Nights by Heatwave, he loved that. The few diners that had braved the noise and mess to eat also tapped their feet and bobbed their heads to Gloria Gaynor, Rose Royce and The Real Thing. Din saw an opportunity and went around each table informing the tourists of the upcoming new addition to the Chaweng nightlife scene, his very own Boogie Nights. I couldn't help but admire the young entrepreneur; he did not miss a trick.

The meeting went on for hours, interrupted by Din's occasional berating of the workmen for corrections to their work. Around three o'clock, Sue left us to prepare her own restaurant for evening dinner service. Din ordered two beers, lit a cigarette and smiled at me.

"How are we going to work this?" he said, referring to my personal reimbursement. Before I had a chance to speak, Din pre-empted my response to soften the blow. "You have full run of both restaurants to drink and eat what you like whenever you like." I decided to keep my mouth shut and hear his full proposal. "And I will also pay for your accommodation." That was the deal, Din was to fund my total expenditure, there was no salary at the start, and in return I was to DJ six nights a week for him.

This is what I had been expecting; we were both taking a risk on each other. My investment had been the cost of a flight and was going to be my expertise in DJing. Din's was his monetary outlay which was mounting up to a considerable sum. We were to discuss a percentage of the profits of the business as a salary later if Boogie Nights became a success. This was fair, so we shook hands on the deal and clinked glasses together, both of us smiling in satisfaction and happy with their own side of the deal. The bonus to this scheme was that I did not need a work permit; I was not actually being paid by Din.

Quite suddenly Din stood up and started talking to a couple of his staff who both burst into action. "Come, we will go to your hotel," and gestured for me to follow him. Lin, a close aid to Din, held a key in his hand whilst another guy had my case. Johnny was outside and greeted me cordially then tagged on to join the hotel entourage. We walked diagonally across the road and opposite the Duke pub was a sign: "Kings Gardens".

Walking through a gate was a small car park and an office that was locked; looking through the window I saw it was nothing but a storeroom and full of cases of beer and soft drinks. On the left there was a small wooden bungalow painted white with a mini balcony a sort of porch at the front. Lin was on the porch and unlocking the door with the key he had earlier. One by one, we kicked our shoes off and entered my new abode. I was pleasantly surprised, the room was light and airy with a double bed. It had large double windows on the side of the building and a glass door covered by a net curtain on the far wall next to the bed.

Johnny was checking the air con unit whilst Din was ensuring the TV was functional. Lin disappeared through a door that I presumed led to the bathroom and the other guy placed my suitcase on the bed for me. I had never quite had a check in like this before; it was my own personal move in squad. There was no sign of any staff of the Kings Gardens Hotel, typically, Din had taken control and this was now Andaman's territory. I never did actually check in to Kings Gardens, they never had a copy of my passport or even knew my name, and in retrospect it should have been quite disconcerting in a way.

Satisfied everything was in order, Din was the last to leave the room. Handing me the key, he told me to take it easy and he would see me later at the restaurant. Closing the door behind him, I surveyed my new home. The large room was a little sparse and the furnishings somewhat basic. The floor was covered in a rather faded Lino that had been mended in patches. A large wooden wardrobe was opposite the bed with a small television set fixed to the wall in the corner. I went into the bathroom; it had an electric shower so I had warm water and a separate basin near the toilet.

My new home was not five star luxury but I liked it; it had a rustic charm to it and everything I needed. Coming out of the bathroom, there was another door: it led to a small store room that was empty apart from a fridge. I noticed it had a lock and it would be ideal to stash my case and valuables.

Once I had unpacked and showered, I took a stroll around Kings Gardens to get my bearings. It was aptly named, as the hotel was set amid luscious greenery and colourful flowers. The accommodation was a series of around thirty bungalows similar to mine, all located discreetly in the tropical gardens. They were situated so no bungalow overlooked another for privacy, almost hidden amongst the trees and flora. There were two main paths weaving their way through the trees until a clearing appeared with a large lawn and beyond that was the beach and the clear blue sea.

It was idyllic, one or two bungalows were actually situated so that stepping out of the front door your feet were greeted by golden sand. Next to the lawn area was the actual Kings Gardens Reception and a small restaurant that only opened during the day. On the verge betwixt the lawn and the beech were two raised, wooden structures that acted as Masseur huts, open on four sides but with a roof. Four ladies attired in striking yellow blouses were plying their trade to prostrate bodies lying on mattresses.

Taking off my flip flops, I walked onto the hot sand and looked either way up and down the beach. Kings Gardens was located almost in the middle of Chaweng beach a very central place to be. In the far distance to the right I could just make out the Centara Hotel and happy memories flooded my mind. It was good to be back on Samui, I knew so many people and the fact I was nearly eight thousand miles away from home was tempered by this knowledge.

I walked in the direction of the Centara and breathed in the clean salty air deep into my lungs. I thought of the days ahead and was pleased with the deal Din and I had struck up; once the initial set up was finished and Boogie Nights was up and running, I could settle into a routine. I would not have to go to work till late in the evening, so everyday I could relax in the sun and take things easy; I knew I was going to like my job, but I was going to love my lifestyle.

Later on when I had returned from my walk, I was sitting in my room when I heard a brash Australian voice outside the door calling my name. Through the mosquito door I saw the silhouette of a man, so I went out onto my little porch and greeted my first visitor. Eddie was sitting on my bench smoking a cigarette; he nodded to me as a way of a greeting.

"Hello, I'm Eddie," the Australian said in a harsh accent. I explained that we had already met a couple of months ago, a fact that he had completely forgotten about. I studied my new acquaintance: he was over fifty, tall and thin. His long straight hair was parted in the middle and framed a craggy, scarred face. To use the expression he had a lived-in face would be vastly inaccurate, it was a more lived-out-of face. He was like a burnt out hippy, but someone that would become a good friend to me.

He was interested in seeing my room so I ushered him in. His face did not register if he was impressed or he disliked it, but he sat on the bed and asked was Din paying for it. There is something quite disconcerting about a relative stranger being so familiar in such a confined personal space. I walked towards the door to put some distance between us as we continued the conversation.

"How much does this cost?" I shrugged as I had no idea. I had not even checked in, never mind about asking what the tariff was! After a couple of minutes, Eddie stood up and said he had better head off to work and left my room, lighting another cigarette. This was to be the first of numerous house calls I would receive from Eddie, all at very unpredictable times and differing occasions.

Before going to meet Din and dine at Andaman's, I strolled down to Oasis to see my friends. Dodging several suit salesmen I saw Win outside the bar. He was delighted to see me and put his arm around my shoulder and led me inside. James let out a loud shout in greeting as Pu rushed up to kiss me on the cheek. Within seconds I had an iced Margarita in front of me as I explained what I was doing back in Samui so quickly. A customer who was waiting to be served scowled in my direction as the staff completely ignored him wrapped up in my news. It was a nice feeling being a local celebrity: one that I could get used to. A few months ago I was jealous of DJ Patti and her lifestyle, and now it was my turn to live the life.

Andaman's was fairly quiet when I finally reached it: I could hear Eddie's voice long before I could see him. He was touting for custom and harassing any potential passers by for possible trade. He was quite good at his job though, very personal with the punters; pushy, but not overly so, confident that the magnificent food displays would be enough attraction for the restaurant. He saw me and shouted: "It's those bastards in Bangkok, scared all the tourists away." He was referring to the Red Shirts' continued demonstrations, and he was completely right.

I explained to him that I was now a member off staff, a fact I knew that Din would have omitted to tell anybody. I asked him what did I do if I wanted anything. He led me to the back part of the restaurant and got one of the young girls to bring me a menu. I was relieved that the building work had relented for the evening and looked about for Din. He was nowhere to be seen. I sat and ate my meal; a spicy bowl of Tom Yum Talay soup with steamed rice. Eddie sat with me for part of the time and we chatted about Eddie's role at Andaman's.

Eddie had known Din for some years and they had first met each other when they were both working at another restaurant close to Zico's. Din was then a chef and Eddie was the front of house manager. Eddie was very candid that the pair had little qualifications between them for the jobs they were doing, but had blagged their way into their positions. Eventually, Din had saved, cadged, borrowed and cajoled enough cash to open Andaman's 1, whilst Eddie had gone back to Australia for a brief period. When

Eddie returned, Din had opened the new restaurant and since then, Eddie had been working for him.

At around 11 o'clock, Sue suddenly appeared and said that Din wanted to see me. Eddie could come also as the restaurant was now empty. I didn't have a clue where we were going, but walking outside, Sue went straight next door to the Duke Pub. A loud Rock band were playing and the pub was quite busy. We pushed our way to the bar and Sue ordered some drinks, then she led us to a table where Din was ensconced.

Three other men were also seated at the table, one I already knew: it was the sinister Khun, who as usual was sat slightly apart from proceedings and was not holding a drink. The other two men were strangers, but together with Din were talking very loudly. I noticed a bottle of whisky on the table and several bottles of Singha Soda water. The whisky was almost finished and I wondered if it was the first bottle the men had consumed, as everybody apart from Khun seemed rather drunk. A pall of smoke hung down over the table like a city fog, and underneath the conspirators plotted.

One of the other men had a uniform on and it seemed to me of a high ranking police officer judging by the amount of gold braid on his tunic. Also, his hat which hung on the chair next to him. The second man was a large, fat, pock marked faced man who was sweating profusely. There was a thin, dirty moustache under his pudgy nose whilst his face was flushed bright red with the alcohol. He seemed to be acting very obsequiously to the policeman by pouring him drinks and lighting his cigarette. His shirt was white silk with gold cufflinks and he had a thick gold rope chain around his thick neck. He obviously had money by his expensive tailored shirt and the amount he must spend on his food bill.

I had no idea what the men were saying as it was all in Thai, but every time the policeman spoke it was greeted with nods of approval or polite laughter. Din looked up when we approached the table and with pride in his voice introduced me as his new DJ.

The policeman genially shook my hand whilst the fat man stayed seated and just waved in acknowledgement, Khun did not even recognise I was there. Did the policeman know there was a man with a loaded gun sitting opposite him? Before I could sit down, Din whispered in my ear: "Go get the Chelsea shirts." I nipped across the road to retrieve the merchandise and was back in a couple of minutes.

When Din had asked me to buy him a Chelsea shirt I had bought two: the home strip of all blue, and a new away hooped one. Din laid the two garments on the table in front of the policemen, picked the all blue shirt up and put it next to his hat on the chair. He then stood up, shook my hand and in rather slurred, halting English, thanked me for the gift. I had not bought the sodding shirt for him, it was for Din, but he seemed quite content to give away one of his presents.

We were not invited to join the table and so the three of us returned to some seats at the bar to listen to the band. It was not quite as though we were dismissed; clearly our presence was not required. I studied the table and the etiquette being displayed; the policeman was certainly the guest of honour and seemed highly respected by the Thai patrons of the Duke. A tall, well dressed man approached holding a box of Johnnie Walker Black Label Whisky, and presented it to the policeman, bowing. He turned and returned to his table with a smile of satisfaction of a job done well. There was no hint or intimation that the policeman was going to share his Malt Whisky as it disappeared to join his new shirt.

I had seen Din drunk before when I was on holiday with Richie and he definitely was not tonight. His behaviour might have suggested otherwise, but I could tell by his actions that this was a front. The whisky was flowing, but not in large measures in Din's glass; he was continuously topping his drink up with soda when the other two men were not paying attention. I realised that there was far more to Din than met the eye and he was a person to be respected. The whole time Khun surveyed the room with his beady eyes, especially checking out every new arrival to the pub with great interest.

Two policemen entered, walked to the table and saluted the senior officer. The fat man stared at them with distain while Khun warily observed their movements. The policeman then stood up rather unsteadily and placed his cap on his head. He passed his gifts to one of the attending constables to carry and shook hands with Din and the Fat man but curiously not Khun. As he left, many Thai men stood as he passed and bowed slightly in respect. Once the policeman had left, the little gathering soon dispersed and we all went back to Andaman's: Din wanted to get drunk.

Later, I asked Eddie who the people were. The policeman was none other than the chief of police and the big fat man was one of the high ranking Thai Mafia bosses on the island. I enquired about Khun; Eddie said he had not been introduced, but warned me not to ask Din. Samui's nightlife and dubious money making ventures are apparently controlled by two families that have carved the island up between them for their own benefit.

Back at Andaman's, Din was in serious conversation with Sue and Eddie had gone to see his girlfriend, so I decided to retire and go to bed. I found it hard to sleep that night firstly because the noise from the Duke across the road was very loud, and secondly because there were constant scratching sounds on my tin roof followed by the occasional dull thud. When it first happened I thought somebody was trying to break in, but as the noises persisted through the night I presumed it was some sort of local wildlife; rats, geckos or the like.

The following morning, I woke to my first day in Kings Gardens. Already the birds were chirping merrily and bright beams of sunshine pierced through my curtains, lighting up the room in a healthy glow. I could see little tracks of dust in the suns rays dancing in the air, normally invisible to the naked eye. It looked a glorious day in Samui so I leapt out of bed to experience some of it for myself.

On holiday I rarely rose early like this, it was not yet 8am. But when I do, I love the beach that time of the morning. After quickly brushing my teeth, I pulled on a pair of shorts and stepped into my flip flops on the porch. I had become not as ashamed of my body now and did not see the need for a shirt at that time. Strolling along the path down to the beach, I felt contented and happy: this was to be my new lifestyle, an idyllic island existence. I said Hello to a couple of workers already busy with the daily tending of the tropical gardens of the hotel, and they responded with large smiles as they resumed their jobs. Thailand is known as the Land of Smiles, and to a large extent the marketing slogan is spot on.

The beach was magical; almost deserted. The sea had a gentle swell that bought small waves tumbling onto the sand leaving hissing white surf behind. I stepped into the already warm water and stared out at the horizon. Far out in the distance I saw small black specks as ships traversed the Gulf of Thailand on their voyages and wondered where they were bound.

Paddling in the noisy surf, I took an early morning promenade along the beach. Life could not get much better than this; I thought back to the bad, dark days of my recent past, this was payback time. A small black dog was jumping about in the water trying to catch and eat the breaking waves. Its mother, head tilted to one side, was looking bemused at the youngster's behaviour. The puppy dejected by the lack of success catching waves had turned its attention to the little silver fish swimming in the shallows. I mused that even a dog's life in Samui is a pretty good one.

Passing the furry bundle of activity, totally oblivious of my presence; I continued my amble along the sand, the sun was becoming stronger and the heat was beginning to intensify. My back began to itch as it was catching the rays and I knew I had no sun block on yet. I had reached as far as I could go and turned to survey the whole expanse of golden sand which is Chaweng Beach that was spread out in front of me. It is a fairly long and wide beach probably one of the best on the island which accounts for its popularity.

Returning in my own footsteps, I passed the Centara and it was already a hive of activity. Teams of liveried employees were combing the sand for any litter or debris whilst their colleagues straightened up sun loungers to their correct positions in line. It was nice being cosseted every now and then, but I much preferred the freedom I had now. I reached Kings Gardens who catered more for the casual beachgoer: it had rickety sun beds for hire for fifty Baht a day and a large chest filled with ice where passersby could purchase cold beers or water.

Darting back to my room, I collected some things to be more comfortable sitting in the sun. I was not due to meet Din for hours yet so I had plenty of time. There were one or two loungers on the lawn so I picked one out and sat down. If you were a resident then the fifty Baht fee was waived, although nobody even seemed to notice I was even there. There were not many staff at Kings Gardens, if you wanted something you had to go looking for it. It was handy on the occasions that discretion was called for.

I settled down listening to some Teddy Pendergrass and watched beach life, fascinated. As the days and weeks would pass, I was to become a familiar figure to the locals going about in their day to day life. Tourists would come and go, but the masseurs, gardeners, beach vendors and DJs all remained constant attendees of Chaweng Beach.

Andaman's was almost ready for lunch service when I arrived. The joiners were doing their utmost to scare punters away with their circus trapeze acts on bamboo ladders creating chaos below. I smiled thinking of the crazy strict health and safety laws we have back home. Where was the clip board man with his hard hat obstructing all the progress?

Din's car pulled up outside and the usual swarm of bodies unloaded its cargo. I had no idea of exactly how many people Din employed. He had two restaurants of which this one, Andaman's 2, was the largest. Here; he had two chefs in the main kitchen with about three assistant cooks and a full kitchen team. Front of house, he had cooks tending the barbeque, griddles and rotisserie. The waitresses were all young girls, teenagers mostly, and then a gaggle of more mature ladies who were the cleaners.

He then had his management team, in the very loose meaning of the phrase, they all seemed to be blood related and did not seem to have specific jobs. There was Lin, Lionel Ritchie; that was my nickname as he had a very large chin and somewhat resembled the Soul crooner, Charlie, Baz and lastly Eddie. Din's treatment of Eddie varied from one of an old friend to one of a dogsbody, depending on what mood the entrepreneur was in.

Din was sitting at a table with Sue and I sat down to join them. They were having lunch and Din asked me what I would like: he knew I had a penchant for hot food so before I could answer he had already requested my meal. We were to go shopping after lunch for audio equipment and I was a little surprised that we could purchase such stuff on the Island, thinking we would have to make a trip to Bangkok.

The conversation was interrupted by my meal arriving: I had never had anything like it before, it did not seem Thai to me. "From my home," my employer proudly boasted of the fare in front of me. It was a steak on the bone of some sort of large fish such as tuna or shark, sitting on a thick, almost dark brown sauce. Accompanying the fish was a bowl full of garlic, unpeeled yet separated into individual cloves and some fresh green stalks of some plant.

Din showed me how the dish should be eaten; firstly, separate some flesh from the bone and dip it in the sauce, once that is consumed, take a couple of cloves of garlic and some of the greenery and munch that to follow the fish. It was pungent, spicy, extremely hot and quite a taste sensation for my palate. The chef came to the table to see if the farang had enjoyed the authentic Burmese food: Sue introduced him as her brother. He was quite surprised and impressed I had scoffed the lot, he beamed a toothless smile at me and nodded in deference to my ability to consume such extraordinary hot food. He had probably never seen a farang eat something like that before.

My employer laughed out loud and said something to the chef who looked at me and nodded, accepting what Din was saying. Apparently, when the meal was ordered the chef had asked if it was for me and was going to tone it down a touch for my western palate, but Din had insisted that it was prepared authentically as he knew my tolerances for heat and spice in food.

After the meal my mouth felt like a furnace but I was not going to show anybody my slight discomfort. We seemed to be waiting for somebody before we could go, and soon a young man turned up. Bets was very quietly spoken and quite shy, he was a personal friend of Sue and was a guitarist. He had long hair that was tied back in a pony tail and I noticed a long nail on his little finger. On his arrival, Din leapt up and the full Andaman's management contingent, including Bets and me, crammed into Din's truck.

Eddie, late as usual, raced up on his moped and parked. Din barked some orders to the very tired looking Australian and we drove off as Eddie sat on the step for his first job of the day, a cigarette.

"Fucking Eddie," Din muttered under his breath, and the speed of the car suddenly picked up pace. We headed out past Tesco junction to the main road that becomes part of the ring road.

I had never been down this road before and there were all manner of shops for the residents of Samui. There were builders' merchants, paint shops, garden furniture showrooms, electrical wholesalers; every type of trade was catered for. We passed a few music shops, but carried on to a car showroom and pulled in to the forecourt. The doors of the truck all opened and everybody got out. I presumed Din was thinking of buying a new car and was impressed that it was a management decision.

Bets sidled up to me and he spoke very good English: he requested a playlist for Boogie Nights so that his band could practise some songs. I did not have a clue what he was going on about, but could see no harm in burning him a CD or two. He surprised me when he fished a dongle out of his pocket and said: "Just load it all on there!"

The car showroom actually turned out to be a PA equipment shop: it was large and had a vast array of speakers, amplifiers and other necessary sound equipment for a band or club. The Andaman's team descended on the store like a plague of locusts, heads rammed in speaker vents, fingers pushed into CD trays, ears pressed to mixers, all thoroughly enjoying their days' excursion away from work. I made my way to some CD decks over in the corner and the assistant, seeing a farang interested in one of his products, made a bee line towards me. The problem was he didn't speak a word of English, but it did not really matter: I knew what I wanted.

There were only three sets of CD decks; one seemed to be second hand whilst the second was very limited in its technology. The best was a brand spanking new Denon mixer, coupled with two integral CD players sitting in its own flight case. I knew the Denon was by far the best piece of kit, but I knew it would be far too expensive and probably overkill for what we needed. Din came wandering over when he saw my interest, I asked him if there were any more places that we could visit and explained why. The Denon was too expensive, but I did not like either of the other two.

Din asked the sales assistant the price and then for a full demonstration of the Denon equipment. The shop was turned into a complete abortion as different amps were plugged into varying mixers and then wired to different speakers to try every permutation possible. Lionel Richie turned out to be very technically aware of what he was doing, while the rest of the Andaman's team just partied to the music during the sound check. After possibly one hour I was really impressed what the Denon kit could do and Din asked me if it was okay.

After my confirmation that I would like the Denon equipment, Din and Sue then spent a further hour locked in the manager's office haggling over the price. I was confused as we had not selected amplifiers, mixers or speakers yet but negotiations were already taking place. I presumed Din must know of somewhere else for the other stuff. Finally, I saw Sue take a cheque book out of her purse; it surprised me that she was in charge of the purse strings as it seemed that Din made all the decisions.

We loaded up our new purchase in the car and headed back the same way we had come, but stopped at an electrical shop. From the road it had seemed just a general electricians' store, but entering it was huge. At the front of the shop were reels of wires and drums of cables but as you went further into the premises the merchandise became more varied and expensive. Flat screen TVs, DVD players and more domestic consumables. Finally, we came to an open area that had larger goods and I could see big speakers and other PA stuff.

The Andaman's team were working their way through this labyrinth of electrically related produce like Fagin's army. Not that they were stealing anything, but items were picked up at random, held up; then switched on, turned off, shaken, prodded, tapped, turned upside down, sniffed, licked and listened to. They were the perfect mobile consumer testing panel as every item was scrutinised and inspected thoroughly, regardless if they were for purchase or not.

Apparently, I was not required for advice on anything being purchased so I retired to the cool A/C of the truck along with

Bets. After another long wait, the Andaman's team exited the store carrying various boxes of goods. I didn't have a clue what they had just bought, but noticed no speakers or the like were part of the shopping trip.

On the way back we took a detour and drove down a dirt road, it was a residential area and some of the houses were quite large. We turned down a little lane and stopped outside a brick bungalow, Din's and Sue's house. I was not what I was expecting; the house seemed very nice, but the outside was a shambles, reminding me of Steptoe and Sons' yard. All types of articles were lying around either in the front garden or down the side path. I saw a full PA speaker system lined up, the wall covered by a tarpaulin roof. Next to it was a rowing boat and then a child's climbing frame. I half expected to see Harold and Hercules appear around the corner at any moment. Nobody got out of the car, the front door of the house opened and two children rushed out, clambered into the back of the truck and Din then took us all back to Andaman's.

When we arrived back the restaurant had been cleared for evening service; the workmen had left, completed the stage and had now started panelling the roof with wooden tiles. To my amazement there was a ram shackled assortment of speakers and other sound equipment plied on the new platform, where it had come from or who had deposited it there was a mystery. I was despatched to get my music whilst Din and Lionel Richie oversaw the unpacking from the shopping trip.

On my return the restaurant once again looked like a bomb site, tables set for dinner were now covered in polythene bags and cardboard boxes. The CD equipment had been plugged into amplifiers and speakers on the stage and Din had set up his new toy on the bar - he had bought a laser! I was staggered; all his attention was consumed trying to work out the technical light source worked... how much had it cost him?

The Denon equipment was rather complicated; it had multiple functions and was far more than just a CD player. Trying to get it to work was difficult, especially as I had the hindrance of the many helping hands of waiters and various other staff. Lin had decided the instructions were far too valuable to lose and before I had a chance to study them had locked them away in the office. At last I managed to work things out and *Boogie Nights* boomed out over the sound system. Din looked up from the laser like a demented Peter Sellers in Dr Strangelove as soon as the music started.

He had a demonic smile on his face as if to acknowledge his master plan for the World's destruction had finally come to fruition. "Louder," he instructed Lionel Richie, who had now nominated himself as the sound engineer. An early diner almost cut his finger off with a steak knife as Lionel Richie turned the amplifiers on maximum wattage output. Din did not seem to care that there was a cacophony of noise blaring out from his restaurant, the band from the Duke next door had stopped playing and had come to investigate their noisy neighbours.

Sue came running out of the office with the two children in tow, her arms waving in the air to get everybody's attention. She demanded that everything stopped immediately, and rushed to help the man with the bleeding finger. As she did so she started ranting at Din at the top of her voice. The man whose finger she was holding looked terrified and wanted to escape from the mad house as soon as he could reclaim his damaged digit from Sue's vice like grip.

Din did exactly as he was told and it was the second time today that I had my confirmation who was the true dominant partner in their relationship. The management team dispersed rapidly, not to catch Sue's attention, whilst Din sloped off into the kitchens. Sue, whilst placating the diner, was restoring order back to the restaurant, barking orders to the waiters and cleaners to tidy the mess her husband had reeked and return Andaman's back to normality. I admired the petite, softly spoken lady; she was quite happy to follow Din's mad cap ideas, but she was always behind the scenes ensuring there was some order and sense to it all.

As everybody had scarpered there was no point in hanging around, so I went for a therapeutic massage as all in all it had been a pretty hectic day. After an hour of soothing and pampering, I showered and changed and went for a visit to Zico's and Oasis. By the time I returned there was still no sign of anybody. I had enjoyed a few drinks on my stroll so I returned home to Kings Gardens to have an early night. The noise from the Duke or my roof did not disturb me and I quickly nodded off.

I was awoken by a familiar Australian voice shouting through my window. "Hey Frank, Din wants to have a rehearsal!" It was past midnight. I groaned as I was tired and sleepy, but I knew I had to get up. When I arrived, I was surprised to see Bets on the stage playing guitar and singing into a microphone. Din was sitting at a large table with about ten tourists playing mine host. The table was littered with wine bottles and various other alcoholic beverages and it looked like it had been a good night.

Lionel Richie had set my equipment up on stage balanced between two tables. I waited for Bets to finish his song then launched into some classic 70s disco tracks. The ladies in the dinner party stood up immediately and started to dance around the table as Din had not cleared the dance floor of dining tables. Then as Lionel Richie perfected the sound on the mixer, Din led the dinner party to the bar area to have more room. The kitchen staff and young waitresses soon joined the action as Barry White was followed by Candi Staton's *Young Hearts Run Free.*

A group of six British girls, all about eighteen, walking past heard the music and walked in off the street to join the fray. The party was in full swing and one or two more couples returning from their night out popped into to see what this new place was all about. Din was in his element and kept on sending beers over to me, keeping the wheels of industry well and truly oiled. It all finished around 3am when alcohol took its effect and the stamina of the guests had waned. I was happy how our impromptu soirée had gone and it proved that our plan would work: there was nobody playing party music like this on the island.

The following morning was a bit hazy; I woke late and just lay on the lounger dehydrated. I pottered to the restaurant around 2pm and Din was outside talking to an American. He was pleased to see me and wanted the graphics of Boogie Nights to give to the gentleman who was the sign maker. Din stressed the signs had to be ready in three days as we had a grand opening on Saturday the 27th. That was news to me as we had not discussed it, but I was now getting used to being surprised five times a day.

We went inside and I took a bottle of water from the fridge behind the bar. Din had instructed me to just take whatever I wanted, but the barman resented me for this freedom. In retrospect I suppose he was accountable for his stock. It was far easier when one of the young barmaids were on duty; they just gave me whatever I requested and I did not have to serve myself.

Sitting down beside Din, we chatted about the previous night and he was excited about the prospects of our venture. He wanted me to go with Eddie and Lin to the printers and produce a flyer and poster advertising the Grand Opening Night of Boogie Nights. He was going out for the day with the children and Sue and would see me later.

We took the truck and Lin drove. On the way, Eddie explained to me that the two kids were from Din's first marriage and lived with their Mum back home in Burma. I stared at Eddie; I had presumed Din was Thai.

"No mate, they are all Burmese," gesturing towards Lin. *The whole fucking lot of them?* This gob smacked me, how was Din able to operate his business? Thailand has strict employment rules: if a foreigner opens a business it has to employ a certain percentage ratio of Thai nationals to foreigners in its workforce, and it is a high percentage. I just hoped Din had the correct number.

Over the next couple of days, my services were not really required, so I took things easy before the big night. One night, I walked up towards Soi Green Mango and was sitting outside Coyote Bar, a sister restaurant to the one in Bangkok. Sipping my two for one happy hour Margaritas, I then saw one of Andaman's little gophers handing out handbills on Chaweng Beach Road, and gestured for the boy to come and join me. We knew each other from the restaurant and he was always a jovial little chap interested in whatever I was doing.

One of the Coyote Girls held her hand out as if to stop him, but then retracted it when she saw me waving towards him. He saw my drink and looked in wonder; it occurred to me that he may have never tasted a Margarita or in fact sat in such posh surroundings. He was in Thailand to simply work and send all his savings back home to his parents. I pointed at the vacant armchair for him to sit on and ordered another cocktail. I looked at the flyer and was pleased at the result from the printer, it was good work. The Margarita was served and placed in front of me, I pushed it towards my young companion whose face lit up in delight when he realised it was for him.

I then sensed my guest was a little uneasy about something so I reassured him that I would not tell anybody about his tea break. He settled back into his comfortable chair relishing every sip of the exotic drink and enjoying every minute of this unexpected luxury. I could not understand when he tried to tell me his name as he spoke no English and my Burmese is a tad rusty! Eddie just called him "Monkey Head Boy", not in a racist way, but to describe him as he had a thick head of jet black hair that reached his forehead in a furry peak. It was however, not a term I ever used. My companion finished his drink, stood and bowed to me, then with a large satisfied grin he turned and left. I never broke the confidence, but I had a feeling that perhaps he might have.

Walking back to Andaman's, I was reflective of how much I take for granted as part of my lifestyle in general. Popping in to a Wine Bar for a quick drink is something I did not think twice about, but for somebody like my little friend it was a rare treat and an event. In some ways I was not certain who had things right, him or me.

I could hear music emanating from the restaurant and then noticed an orange glow above Andaman's, the Boogie Nights sign had been erected and was illuminated against the dark of the evening. I was so proud that I had achieved what I had set out to do; now the hard part would start as I had to make a success of it. I looked at the stage and Bets was accompanied by four other musicians two I recognised from the Duke. Din had done it again; he had pinched the band from his next door neighbour an act I knew would not be warmly accepted.

After service, we had a staff meeting as the Grand Opening was the following night and Din was marshalling his troops. He surprised me as his rhetoric was very business like and was similar in many respects to a trained western business manager. Satisfied everybody knew their own individual roles for the evening, he took the whole entourage, me included, to the Reggae Pub for a staff party. Bottles of whisky were ordered and everybody had a ball.

The following day, Andaman's woke late as various members of staff were still being located dotted all around the island. There was to be no lunch service as the day was dedicated for preparations. I oversaw the new position for the DJ equipment behind the bar as the stage was being utilised for the band. Places were being laid at tables for confirmed bookings; two large settings of over twenty were positioned in the rear part of the restaurant whilst there were others of fours and eights mingled around. Almost three quarters of the dining part of the restaurant had been already reserved, leaving the dance floor and bar seating area free for walk-ins. It was going to be a sell out; perhaps two hundred people.

If everything went to plan, I was to play background music until service had finished, then whilst tables were being cleared, the band would do their set. After that, Andaman's transformed into Boogie Nights and I was at the helm. Time flew and guests started to arrive to take their seats for a night of food and music. The two large tables filled up fast and they were Din's personal guests. One was the Samui immigration office and the other party was the local police. Typical, those on a freebee are always the first to arrive.

The rest of the restaurant soon became full and the ensuing chaos of service began. Din had chosen a set menu for the evening: a choice of fish or meat platters for the entrée. It was quite clever as the front of house cooks could take some of the pressure off the kitchen staff by barbequing the different meats and fishes and also cooking all the baked potatoes and sweetcorn. The waiting on staff were busy seating guests and taking orders, but the strange thing was Din was nowhere to be seen.

From there on, things started to go tits up. I asked Eddie where the Hell Din was and was told he was at the Airport collecting some Dancers from Bangkok. I stared at Eddie quizzically.

"You know, fucking Strippers!" my erudite antipodean responded. I shook my head in disbelief. Then as soon as I had recovered from that shock, Eddie introduced me to a new face. "This is Simon, Din thought you might need some help," The young, black Londoner was carrying an Apple MacBook and was a fellow DJ. I was livid and was close to walking out there and then, but Eddie intervened and took me outside.

"Look, go with the flow and talk to Din later," was the sensible advice the pragmatic Australian gave me. The plan of simply turning the restaurant into a 70s disco had just changed into a Berkeley Busby production of epic proportions under Din's directorship. Instead of one DJ, namely me, there was now a band, a troop of erotic dancers and a back up DJ. I had not been a party to any discussions on this and was as miffed as miffed could possibly be.

I went back inside to continue playing background tracks fuming at the way Din was handling things. If I could have got my hands on my little Arthur Daley Asian friend I would have strangled him. About half an hour later, Din turned up with the suspicious Khun and a gaggle of very noisy women. The whole troop went straight inside the office.

Time was pressing on and nearly all the diners had finished their meals and were ready for some entertainment. One or two guests actually left fed up of waiting for something to happen. I do not know what discussions were being held in the office but nobody knew what to do. Eventually Lin came out and instructed the band to start playing. This changed the dynamics of the atmosphere a little and a few punters left their dining seats and stood at the bar to get a better view of the group and to be able to socialise better. The staff cleared the couple of emergency dining tables off the dance floor and things took an upturn, for about two minutes.

Din finally emerged from the office and gave me a bunch of CDs to play for the girls to dance to. I did not have a chance to collar him in order to tell me what the fuck was going on and looked at the CDs. They were all Thai bands and no tracks had been earmarked for play, they were still in their original cellophane wrapping and I presumed Din had just bought the sodding things from the Family Mart.

The dancers appeared and stood in line waiting for some music to dance to. What was I supposed to do? I hadn't a clue what to play. I just unwrapped the first CD on the pile and played track one. Some garbage music started to pound out of the speakers and the dancers did not move as they too had never heard the track before. One of them stomped up to me and grabbed the CD cover from my hand; she looked blankly at me as she did not recognise the artist. Din actually had bought the CDs himself, it was unbelievable. Whilst we were trying to organise some music Din thought the addition of the laser show might break up the pregnant pause a little. The ambience of an evening of fine dining and fun entertainment had now changed into a sleazy Patpong sex club. It was not a case of Gilding the Lilly, more of Crapping on the Petunias.

The music changed and the girls started to perform. It was not a synchronised dance routine, it was individual performances of gyrating eroticism. One or two or the performers then started to turn their attention to male members of the audience rubbing their behinds against groins and legs like lecherous canines. I surveyed the room and noticed that quite a few of the diners had returned to their tables, especially the couples. As the music pulsated and grew in intensity, various items of clothing started to get shed which seemed to please the few men that were left standing, but was definitely offending many of the patrons who were leaving.

As the first track and dance ended, Din appeared and started to round the girls up ushering them to retrieve their discarded bras, stockings and thongs from the dance floor. The dancers were herded away never to be seen again whilst I was instructed to play some music. How could I possibly follow that? The room was in turmoil, waiters rushed around attending to certain irate customers who wished to pay their bills and leave. Other members of staff had turned the main lights on and were cleaning the dance floor of various foam and oil used by the girls.

It had been a debacle: there were certain times and places for entertainment such as that and the opening night of Boogie Nights certainly was not one of them. Disheartened that the evening had turned so flat, I tried to work the room and played some blinding tracks but mostly to no avail. Punters had either left or had returned to their tables to chat about what had just happened.

Din had again disappeared into the office, keeping his head down from the tirade. I knew Sue was delivering. So, I handed control of the music to Simon, who plugged his laptop into the mixer and started to play House Music. I collected my things together and went back to Kings Gardens to go to bed; I was totally and utterly pissed off.

Chapter Eleven

AN UNEXPECTED TURN OF EVENTS

About two hours later, I was lying on my bed and Eddie knocked on my door. I was not sleeping as my mind was still trying to understand the recent events and I was trying to decide if I wanted to be part of this venture anymore.

I stepped out of my room and sat next to my friend on the balcony. I offered him one of the beers that I had taken from my fridge. "Din wants to see you, he wants a meeting." I shrugged and told Eddie my feelings and my anger at what Din had just done. "Aw that's just Din, listen to what he has to say," he consoled. I took a long drink of my beer and nodded. As we walked over to Andaman's, Eddie surprised me when he ushered a very rare platitude: "This is Thailand, always expect the unexpected."

Din and his team were already sitting around a table by the bar: there was nobody left and the place was closed. He looked like a child and somebody had just burst his balloon, so I decided to hold my anger back.

"We have had our license pulled," Din sheepishly said. "No more dancing, no more DJ." He looked at me and I stared back allowing him to continue.

He went on to explain how events had panned out earlier on. When the girls were halfway through their first dance, one of the policemen from the big table had stopped the performance. He informed Din that his license did not cover dancing and therefore was in violation of the terms of his entertainment agreement. He could no longer have music in the restaurant from that moment on. Din had tried to phone his friend the Chief of Police for help but unsurprisingly he was unavailable.

Din had oiled the correct palms for a smooth passage for Boogie Nights by getting the permission of his friend the policeman and the okay from the gangster that they would not oppose his application for the license. But somebody else had gone higher up the chain with more powerful allies, and had the license pulled. By parading the erotic dancers, Din had played into their hands and had given them right what they wanted, an excuse to close Boogie Nights down.

It was pure greed as our small venture did not encroach upon any of the more lucrative ventures further up the beach road. The clientele we were trying to attract would not be going to the nightclubs or the trendy bars, in fact at the moment there was nowhere for them to go. The situation changing did, however, defuse the argument that I had brewing with Din. He was angry that his so called friends had deserted him and said he would go to Bangkok later that day and try to sort something out. I did not have a clue what he meant, but I was told to relax and take things easy.

For the next few days, that is exactly what I did, during the day I lay by the beach and at night I ate in the restaurant and strolled down the strip. I was getting fond of the chef's spicy Burmese food; it was more akin to Indian than Thai cuisine and very tasty. I did not actually order any dishes, I just let the chef give me what the kitchen staff were eating, most of the time I did not have a clue what was on the plate.

The noise from my roof and the Duke pub was making it hard for me to sleep at night and so I had requested a move further away from the road. The problem with the roof was not the local wildlife as I had earlier thought, it was because a tree overhung my bungalow and was dropping its fruit on the tin roof sounding like a snare drum. I moved to number thirteen; it was slightly smaller than my old one, but had recently been refurbished and also had

Wi-Fi. I could finally get in touch with the outside world via email as my T-Mobile mobile phone package was only for UK.

The new bungalow was excellent, still quite basic, but further into the gardens of the hotel so was much quieter. But there was a problem with the lock and I had to mess around with the key to open the door. One afternoon after a spot of shopping for some essentials I could not open the door at all. Kings Gardens is not a place you simply call reception for assistance, you have to go out seeking somebody who suspiciously looks like they work there. I collared a cleaner; I deduced this by the fact the lady was carrying some towels. I showed her my key and then the lock, I think she thought I was a lazy bastard at first and couldn't be arsed to open my own door. But after several attempts by her and her friend to gain entry to no avail they both disappeared.

Not knowing if they were coming back or even if they would pass the message on that there was a stranded farang on his balcony, I took a seat and waited. About fifteen minutes later, a man with a tool bag arrived and started to drill the lock. There was a mechanical sound that did not sound too good, but the door opened. Without a word being said the man packed his drill away and walked off. I looked at his handiwork and the lock did not seem too secure, nevertheless I was in my room.

That night I went to Zico's and Oasis and to be honest had a tad too much beer. On returning home I had to mess around with the lock again for about half an hour before there was a loud snapping noise and the lock opened. I awoke a little late and showered, grabbed my bag and went to go to the beach. The door would not open, I rattled the handle but it would not turn. Christ! Yesterday I locked myself out of my room today I had managed to lock myself inside my room. Messrs. Chub and Yale would be disgusted at my behaviour.

The windows had decorative security rails outside and I could not escape through them even if I physically was able to do so.

I could not phone reception as there was no house phone in my room and I could not get my mobile to work so what could I do? I thought about sending an email to Kings Gardens on my laptop, but it could be days before somebody bothered to read it. Yelling was always a good option for any emergency, but something told me a muffled cry from inside a closed bungalow might be misconstrued in Thailand.

I looked out of my window and saw a young teenage gardener in the shrubbery below the bungalow opposite. I opened my window and shouted at him, he waved back at me with a beaming smile thinking I was just saying good morning. Christ! This was going to be harder than I first thought. I called out again pointing in the direction of my door which was hidden around the corner. He looked to where my finger pointed and saw it was a tree, his expression changed to one of utter bewilderment. "What was that crazy farang doing in the window over there? I don't like this situation one bit."

More shouting and gesturing was not getting me anywhere, in fact it seemed to be having the opposite effect on the youth. He was getting nervous of my intentions and was edging away deeper into the shrubbery. I was most fortunate just at that moment one of his colleagues, an older man, happened to appear from under a bush with some branches in his arms. The two gardeners were deep in conversation about me both looking at the tree I had earlier pointed to and shaking their heads. A thought suddenly struck me; I reached for my key and threw it out of the window on to the path. The younger gardener thought that I was quite mad, but the older one seemed to understand a little.

A couple of minutes later I heard a rattle at the door, the handle turned but completely round and round. I presumed the barrel of the lock had snapped and now was completely useless. The two gardeners outside my door chatted away and I hoped it was discussing my plight and to decide the next course of action.

Greenstreet and Back

I looked out of my window, but could not see anything, but a cleaner walking on the path, then the younger gardener appeared and led her towards my bungalow. The lock rattled again as the cleaner tried her pass key, again the handle just turned and the lock did not engage.

The talking grew louder as another voice added to the conversation outside. Ten minutes passed and I heard the familiar sound of a drill, metal on metal as somebody was drilling the lock. Then in only a few moments the handle fell onto the floor with a thud and my door flew open. Outside on my little balcony was quite a welcome committee; the two gardeners, a cleaner, three children who had wandered over to investigate the fuss and two handymen.

I wondered was there as many people to greet Nelson Mandela when he was eventually freed from his incarceration from Robben Island prison. I was quite embarrassed when the handyman proceeded to dispose of the door handle completely and fitted a large padlock to the outside of the door. He obviously couldn't be bothered with any more of my shenanigans and handed me a key attached to a large round fob, designed for farang numpties.

Later that afternoon, I was in search of somewhere I could take my laundry as I was rapidly running out of clean clothes. Just across the road, an old lady sat on a small stool behind a wobbly looking table on the pavement. There was no shop front, only the chair and desk with a phone on it. Behind her on the wall was a greasy sign saying; "Laundry, Excursions, Overseas Calls". I could not see where on Earth the phone could be possibly be connected, but presumed she had hacked into some line somewhere.

Toting my laundry bag around in the heat was no fun, so I decided to try the old lady's minimalistic laundry. I have since learnt that Thailand's Street Laundrettes are really cheap and normally offer a good service, but it is advisable to make a list of all the items you leave for washing. On this occasion I collected my laundry the following day minus one shirt, but with the added addition of a blue bra. I never did retrieve my shirt and the bra tended to chafe a little under the armpits.

Life in the ensuing days was settling into a pattern: relaxing in the sun during the day and a walk to Zico's, Oasis or Vaughn's bar before an evening meal at Andaman's to try and catch up on news about Din. I had found a place where I could get DVDs from and was retiring home early each night to watch movies on my laptop. I had decided to cut back on my alcohol intake, primarily for my health and also to save money.

Din had gone for almost a week and was still in Bangkok. It was very pleasant doing nothing on Samui on an expensed paid holiday, but the future was looking ominous and I could not expect Din and Sue to keep funding my existence whilst I was not playing my part of the bargain. Suspiciously, Andaman's had live music every night in the form of Bets playing guitar, the band Din had pinched from Duke's had returned to their previous employer under somewhat of a cloud. I had no contact from Din, but disturbingly he had cleared the path for Bets to play live and was in constant communication with Sue, Lin and the others.

Much to my chagrin I was embarrassed by living free at Andaman's whilst all the other members of staff looked on as I ate and drank for free. One night having consumed one or two Margaritas with James at the Oasis bar, I decided to do something about my discomfort.

Joining Eddie at the front of the restaurant I nominated myself as his "Front of House" assistant, helping him to entice people into the restaurant. The affable Aussie did not give two hoots if I was a complete amateur as it gave him the opportunity to skive off for a smoke every couple of minutes.

I was positioned at the large fresh fish display and I must admit, although I enjoy eating the subterranean delicacies, I found it difficult to recognise what type of fish they were with their clothes on. I did not know the arse end from a Barracuda to a Goldfish and there was a myriad of exotic choices to describe to potential diners. There was nothing else for it, I just invented names that I thought described the alien creatures. From the oval "Thai Round Sleeping Fish" to the flat "Flying Siamese Suckling Fish", they were all my own inventions.

One particular smart arse picked up on one of my lies as I was describing a sort of baby Shark as a "Fighting Seabee Fish" to a group of Russian tourists. "Ahem, I think you will find that is a Barracuda my friend." I looked at the smug know it all expression on the twat's face, knowing that I had been rumbled. "Why don't you just fuck off, Jacques Cousteau!" came a warning Australian growl as Eddie blew a long plume of smoke in the tourists face. Exasperated, the chap blustered off coughing down Beach Road swearing he would never dine in our establishment. "Fair dos mate, but you can still fuck off," came the learned reply from Andaman's as Eddie stoically lit another smoke.

Then after seven days, Din returned with the news I had been dreading: there could be no DJ or dancing at Andaman's. The authorities had relented on some live music with restrictions on type and hours. His friends had deserted him bowing down to pressure from above, be it from the authorities or the Mafia. I learnt that the fat man I had met on my first night was now in prison having been arrested by the same policeman he had been drinking with. It seemed that alliances were short lived in Koh Samui and I began to worry about the situation.

Din and Sue were leaving in a couple of days to have a short holiday back in Burma and for Din to renew his visa. I was told to hang on until their return as the situation might have calmed down by then. Kings Gardens reservation was for a month and in the meantime I could still eat and drink at the restaurants as normal. It all seemed too good to be true and I went in search of Eddie for his thoughts of the arrangement.

As usual Eddie was late and had not turned up at work yet so I walked over to lie in the sun for a while. I was quite surprised when I saw Eddie sitting on the lawn by the masseurs having a cigarette.

"Thought I would have a quick smoke before work," the Aussie explained his actions. I remembered it was he that had told me to always expect the unexpected in Thailand. Then it dawned on me: Eddie never knew what he was doing from one minute to the next, so everything was unexpected for him, it was the way he lived his life.

He lay back on the grass telling me of his previous night's problems. Eddie's girlfriend worked as a prostitute in a Beer Bar and had no customers all evening, when she returned home Eddie had no money to give her so she trashed his room and left. Eddie did not seem phased at all by the turn of events, simply saying "I managed to get the old fella away before she found out I was skint," and a broad smile came to his weather beaten face as he remembered the previous night's sexual encounter. I considered; did Eddie have to pay his girlfriend and if so, did he get discount?

I told Eddie my problem and the arrangement Din was still holding firm on for me. "What! Din has paid for your digs for a month," he said incredulously. He rose, and beckoned for me to follow him. We entered Kings Gardens office, the first time I had actually been inside, and Eddie struck up a conversation with the receptionist. After a garbled conference, Eddie turned.

"She is worried that no money has been paid whatsoever for your room." I gulped: was I going to have to pay for my accommodation? The normal room rate was two thousand two hundred Baht a night - about forty five quid!

We both quickly went over to Andaman's and I collared Din straight away. He was pretty laid back over the situation and said his agreement was with the owner and the receptionist would probably know nothing about it. Din assured me he would definitely pay for my accommodation at least until he came back from Burma and then we could talk again. I was less than happy with the situation as I knew how quickly Din could change his mind and I could not see the authorities back peddling over the license in such a short space of time.

Over the next few days, I began to form a plan B in the very good chance it would be needed. I had worked out my finances and I still had a couple of grand in savings behind me so there was no immediate panic: if I had to pay for Kings Gardens myself it would put quite a dent in that, so I would have to act fairly swiftly on Din's return.

Songkran, Thailand's New Year, was in a few days time and my fiftieth birthday was on the 21st April, so I would stay on Samui until at least then to celebrate with my friends. After that I had decided I would go walk about, as Eddie had described it, and go travelling around South East Asia. I spent the next few nights trawling through endless web sites of maps, airlines, country visa requirements, accommodation and began to formulate a plausible trip before my return flight home on the 10th June.

The Water Festival, or Songkran as it is called in Thailand, is to celebrate New Year and occurs from the 13th to 16th of April in all Buddhist countries. The Buddhist calendar is 543 years, different to the Gregorian one used in the Western world, so in 2010 it was actually 2553 in Thailand, Laos, Cambodia and Myanmar. The dates are a little vague, as different places in Thailand celebrate Songkran on different days and for varying amount of days. But in Samui, it is restricted to a one day celebration due to water conservation.

The actual symbolism of anointing one's head with water has altered over the years to become the biggest water fight in the world. Chaing Mai, Bangkok and Pattaya are renowned for being the most raucous with the celebrations in Pattaya lasting almost a week.

The day of the festival arrived, and I had actually forgotten it was Songkran as I lay on my lounger soaking in another beautiful morning's sun. The two gardeners walked past me grinning at the farang idiot they had rescued a few days earlier. They were covered in white paint and I thought they must have a new decorating job. The noise from the beach road was exceptionally loud with music blaring and many voices shouting so naively I went to investigate.

Within two feet of stepping onto Chaweng Beach Road I was covered in white dye and soaking wet. The scene in front of me was reminiscent of the classic Custard Pie fight in The Great Race and I was Tony Curtis the Great Leslie, about to take another one in the mush from a twelve year old boy toting a water pistol, squealing with delight managing to corner a farang.

The road was awash almost as though a sudden cloud burst had just occurred and various vehicles made their ponderous way in a slow procession of disorderliness. It was a public holiday and the locals were out in force to celebrate New Year. Pick Up trucks were loaded with barrels of ice cold water that was unceremoniously collected in buckets and thrown over pedestrian heads; large water guns were being shot by passengers standing up leaning on the railings protecting the bucket throwers.

Passersby with small pail like receptacles dipped their hands in chalky dye and smeared it on anything that moved on the street. It seemed to me that the Thai partygoers took more delight in drenching and daubing a farang than one of their own and I was a prime target as some of my clothing was still dry. I learned that once you were sodden and covered in dye you became almost too dishevelled to be hit and assailants held back their ammunition for worthier victims.

Most of the bars and businesses had closed as their staff were out on the street enjoying themselves and in truth if they had been open it would take weeks to clean the mess up. The convenience stores were doing a great trade in alcohol sales as revellers let their hair down and everyone was getting very drunk, but not at all in any menacing way. I could not imagine this event happening in the UK; it would probably start okay for the first hour and then would rapidly deteriorate into something much more violent and dark.

Around 8pm it all started to calm down and places began to open for business for the evening. I had walked down to see Vaughan and was sitting outside her bar trying to get a little drier in the warm air. Opposite me was the main entrance to the Centara Hotel and I saw a pair of their residents walking down towards the barrier. They were a middle aged couple and were formally dressed for dinner. She wore a long glamorous blue dress and her partner had a jacket and tie. Whether they did not know it was Songkran or thought it was all over they were about to receive a nasty shock.

I heard the pick up truck coming before I could see the vehicle, music was blaring from a sound system on the back and it was crammed with people intent of carrying the party on into the night. It made a bee line towards the best target of the day, the two diners. After it passed it looked like a freak tidal wave had just hit exactly were the couple had been standing. They were both drenched from head to toe and the elegant blue gown was now splattered with white blotches; the ladies' hair previously coiffured in a bun was now hanging down in straggly strands. An argument ensued immediately as the couple turned heel and made their squelching way back to the hotel and safety.

Later that evening Eddie came to visit, he was taking it easy as things were far more relaxed at Andaman's with the absence of Sue and Din. We chatted in my room over a few beers and Eddie opened up some of his past to me. He had not been back to Australia for about ten years and intended never to go back if he could help it; the rough exterior of the person was reflected in a colourful and chequered past. He had spent time in jail for drugs offences and showed me a scar on his chest where he had been stabbed in a fight through the lung. He also had a small scar on his chin a legacy from another altercation over drugs. Even though he was no angel I could feel no malice from the affable Aussie who had shown me much kindness and I couldn't help but to like him. As I had not been out of Chaweng he offered to take me sightseeing the following day on his scooter then left to try and find his errant girlfriend.

Koh Samui island is ringed by single a 51km road that links everything together and it is easy to navigate. All the main tourist attractions are situated off the ring road on smaller tributary link roads and are simple to find. A must see is the fifteen metre high Big Buddha and the adjacent Wat Phra Yai and Wat Plai Laem, the latter being a Buddhist temple that features a huge eighteen arm statue of Guanyin the Goddess of Mercy.

Eddie driving was very fast and pretty aggressive; we occasionally stopped on the roadside for a cool beer or something to eat. The road is in an atrocious condition in places and I was glad we were undertaking the trip in daylight or we certainly would have come a cropper on the bike. We drove to Eddie's favourite place on the island which are some unique rocks near Lamai which is the second most popular town for tourists.

Hin Ta and Hin Yai are two rock formations in the ocean and I could see why they were Eddie's favourites. Hin Ta is a giant rock pushed out of the water in the shape of a giant penis whilst Hin Yai is a circular formation very alike to a woman's vagina. They both have a spiritual meaning to the Buddhists; it is a very revered place for fertility something that was lost on Eddie to many of his "Carry On" film asides. After we drove to a hotel in Lamai where a mate of Eddie was the Assistant Manager, only to be informed that his friend had left their employment twelve months ago. Eddie looked bemused for a second by this news then said, "Ah, I suppose that's right. I haven't spoken to him for a year or so!"

My birthday arrived and I celebrated it in Oasis where Johnny and Win had arranged a cake for me. I could not think of a better place to be on my fiftieth, I was surrounded by my new friends and I was truly happy. I knew back at home it would be a far bigger affair, but this was a genuine gesture of comradeship and I was honoured that I had met these people and could call them my friends. A couple of years back I would never have dreamt that this is where I would be for such an auspicious occasion, in fact I nearly did not make it at all and I was so fortunate to be there.

The day after my birthday the Red Shirts hit the news again, this time they stepped up their protests and entered Chulalonkorn Hospital in Bangkok. It was mostly a publicity stunt to gain global awareness of their cause; in fact the action backfired and was generally condemned by most of the worlds press. The same day there was a grenade attack with one fatality and over eighty people injured, I was growing increasingly concerned with the situation especially as the British Consulate was advising caution and only necessity journeys to Bangkok. The Red Shirts had now moved their base to the Ratchaprasong area of the city and had built a fortress there to sit and wait; the action seemed very sinister in its intent. I knew that area of the city and was sad to see the footage reporting on events on the television, basically it was a no go zone and many small businesses were forced to close and flee.

Things at Andaman's had returned to normal, Din had returned and was as slippery as an Eel to try and pin down for a conversation. My plan was coming together and I had decided I would leave Samui in five days on the 28th. I still wanted to relax by the beach before returning home when my Thai Visa expired so my plan was fly Phnom Penh Cambodia for three days then somehow travel down to Sihanoukville and spend three weeks down on the beach on the Gulf of Thailand. After that I would return to Phnom Penh and fly to Ho Chi Minh City for a couple of days and travel to Vung Tau on the South China Sea before returning to Bangkok then home for the World Cup.

It all sounded simple, but I knew how my trip had panned out so far and I faced the following six weeks with some trepidation. Visas are required for any UK citizen travelling to Cambodia or Vietnam, however these can be partially processed and paid for on line and upon arrival in both countries can be finally completed as VOA "Visa On Arrival". However, Visa's will only be issued in major airports or border crossings in both countries.

I would have to travel as light as possible as I did not have a clue what sort of transport I would be travelling on in the near future and I knew my capabilities concerning handling luggage. The next few days I spent jettisoning my possessions to my friends. Although I had lost nearly seven stone in weight my clothes were still on the large side for most of my Thai buddies so Eddie was very lucky in that respect. I posted all my genuine CD's back home and gave my self compilations in my binder to Din as a goodbye present; he could at least play them as background music. So, apart from my laptop and iPod stuff in my hand luggage there was very little left in my suitcase.

The last couple of nights I let my hair down a little and had a few goodbye party drinks with all my Koh Samui friends; surprisingly Eddie was the only farang amongst them, but in a way that is how I settled so easily in Samui by embracing the local community and customs. In retrospect, had I been with another friend from the UK, I do not think I would have coped so well in terms of having to go out and actively meet other people. I think students taking gap years should bear this fact in mind, it sounds mad, but you do meet more people if you travel by yourself and the added fact that you yourself make the decisions so there is no one else to blame and consequently no arguments.

My final night was a farce as I spent most of it trying to track down Din who still had not paid any money to Kings Gardens. He had gone to ground and was trying to avoid me and therefore the bill. The bill had come to one thousand two hundred pounds and it would have to be settled before I left in the morning. At around 8pm I managed to talk to Din on the phone, but for some reason his English was not too good that day. He said that the accommodation charge was not the agreement he had with the owner, as that was nearly forty pounds per night. He had agreed twenty pounds and would not pay the extortionate fee they were asking. Furthermore, he only would agree to pay twenty one days accommodation, the other seven days I would have to fund myself as I had been on holiday! The fact that he had told me to do so himself did not enter into his reckoning.

Din had screwed me, but I had no other option but to pay. I took Lin to Kings Gardens office with me and he assured them Andaman's restaurant would pay for three quarters of the bill and I would pay two hundred and eighty pounds for my part. They surprisingly accepted this compromise and wanted mine in cash: I emptied my wallet of sterling, dollars and what Thai money I had and managed to scramble the cash together. I breathed a sigh of relief that I had bought the matter to the fore as had I stayed any longer God knows what the bill would have been.

The following morning I left early for my flight to Bangkok so did not have a chance to say my final goodbyes to anybody: although there was a slight bad taste in my mouth how things had ended up with Din, I was excited at the prospect of my trip and new adventures to come.

Changing planes in Bangkok, I looked at a TV in the Transit lounge, Police had clashed with protesters in North Bangkok, one soldier had died and another sixteen injured. Things were coming to a climax in the dispute and it looked as though it would be very messy indeed.

I boarded the Air Asia flight to Phnom Penh the same day and was on route to Cambodia. I reflected on my time in Samui and a smile crossed my face of an experience that I was glad I had undertaken. My confidence of being and coping by myself was now complete, I knew with the correct planning I was capable of doing almost anything and no obstacle was insurmountable. As Diana Ross once sang, "Ain't no mountain high enough."

Chapter Twelve

CAMBODIA

Immigration was quite painless at Pochentong International Airport in Phnom Penh; I had my pre printed, completed E-Visa and two passport photos, plus more importantly, forty pounds which I handed over to the authorities on arrival. My documentation was passed down a line of five smiling officers who each added their own comment and by the time I had walked down the line I was issued with a thirty day Cambodian visa.

Being my first time in Phnom Penh and having booked a small Boutique Hotel, I thought it wise to book a car. I saw a cheerful looking man with a placard on which my name was advertised and was greeted by a warm handshake. My driver spoke excellent English and during my thirty minute trip to the hotel he imparted valuable tourist tips to me, but some of the attractions he detailed sounded a little gory for my tastes, his top two being; Tuol Sleng, the genocide museum and Choeung Elk, the Killing Fields.

The Cambodian Riel is the official currency, but US Dollars are more widely taken as Cambodians prefer the foreign currency. I found that you normally spent Dollars and received Riels in change; if you were to use an ATM then US Dollars would be dispensed. Driving to the hotel I was surprised by the amount of motorbikes on the roads: Thai's use them widely but not to this extent; also, the types and ages of the vehicles were older and more decrepit.

I warmed to Phnom Penh immediately as we passed through the bustling streets, it was like a retro Thailand gone back in time fifty years. All manner of vehicles crammed the highways with the noise and excitement only found in South East Asia. There were some high level buildings, but these were few and the skyline was mostly four stories high of old French Colonial architecture. Two million people reside in the capital so it is thriving metropolis, I sensed that Phnom Penh lived and breathed at its own pace taking things as they came.

The city is actually on the site where three great rivers converge; the Mekong, Tonle Sap and Bassac meet to form almost a perfect X. These rivers bring fresh water to the city and are a valuable thoroughfare for navigating Cambodia and the countries surrounding it. My schedule did not permit it, but I would have loved to have taken a two day boat ride to Siem Reap the capital of the old Angkor region. It is famous for its ancient temples and was the setting for the Laura Croft Tomb Raider film; it has long been a disputed territory with centuries old conflicts between the Siamese and Khmer peoples. Siem Reap actually translates as "Flat defeat of Siam", a name given to it after a famous Khmer victory.

My taxi weaved its way through the chaotic traffic and turned down a quiet narrow street straddled by large colonial private houses surrounded by tall whitewashed walls. It stopped outside a large closed wooden door with a sign on the wall "No. 227 Pavilion Hotel". I was glad that I had taken the taxi as I would never have found the place otherwise, from the outside it did not look at all like a hotel, closer to a private mansion. A thought struck me that I may have difficulty finding it again especially if alcohol was involved.

The door opened, I presumed by somebody being alerted by the security camera of my arrival and I was ushered into a courtyard. There was a small communal swimming pool almost completely shaded by tropical overhanging trees and a few guests dotted around reading books or pursuing other gentle activities and relaxing in comfort. Ascending a couple of wooden steps I entered a large airy room that acted as a foyer and checked in to the hotel. According to the web site the villa had twenty rooms and was described as "An intimate Urban Oasis." It certainly was very quiet and had a relaxed, peaceful atmosphere, a thinking man's retreat.

Once again I had decided to push the boat out and had three nights booked in a private pool room. For sixty five pounds per night the room boasted a four poster bed and its own private terrace with a plunge pool. It also had a day bed for lying down and relaxing during the heat of the day. I had built the price into my budget and knew I would be staying in far less glamorous surroundings on most of my trip and so had decided to start with a little luxury.

Dumping my things in the room I was desperate to explore the city and to have my first glimpse of Phnom Penh and Cambodia. I took a map I had purloined at Reception and walked out onto Street 19. Studying the map it seemed quite logical to find your way around the city. Most of the roads were numbered; even numbers going left to right across the city and odd numbers top to bottom down the city forming a grid pattern. The only problem was that the city was not square and the numbers suddenly changed into names that were sometimes in Cambodian and other times in French. It was not going to be as easy as I first thought and I was to soon find that fact out.

There were one or two Tuk-Tuks on the street waiting for fares, but I wanted to walk as I found that is the best way to really understand the geography of a place. Studying the map I saw the Royal Palace and the Silver Pagoda were quite nearby and decided to take a leisurely stroll to sample some sightseeing, a rare occurrence for me.

In this area of Phnom Penh the pavements were fairly quiet and the roads were wide and shaded by trees, more akin to French Boulevards than Metropolitan Streets. I headed towards the river, guided by my map, and turned left to see a long red brick wall that formed part of the perimeter of the Royal Palace. I walked around the whole length of one side of the Palace and although I encountered gates none seemed open to the public. I turned another corner and saw the main entrance, but again was foiled by sturdy locked gates blocking my entry. I estimated it was around 3pm and wondered why the Palace should be closed at this time of day, perhaps it was a special Cambodian holiday that I did not know about, but one thing was for certain I was not getting in. I glimpsed the top of the Silver Pagoda inside the grounds, but that was about as near as I was going to get to it.

I rambled around back towards the river and passed many squares and large open areas giving the city a sense of space and openness. This was certainly an affluent area and the buildings were reflecting this in their grand opulence, I was quite surprised how pretty the city actually was and was glad that I had decided to visit. I felt safe pottering about Phnom Penh, it is a sense that I immediately felt driving from the airport and it is a sense that has never changed.

By now I was lost; I tried to work out my location on the map using the river as a constant, but it was hopeless there was not enough detail on my tourist map. I looked around in vain for some sort of public transport; I was either off the major commuter routes or had strayed into a no Tuk-Tuk zone, if such a thing existed. I must have looked a typical bewildered helpless tourist as a man driving a rather antiquated motorbike laden with an assortment of bulging plastic bags stopped to assist me.

I presumed the gentleman had been out for a spot of shopping at the behest of his wife and was on his way home. Unfortunately, he did not speak one word of English and I was not familiar with Cambodian either so his Don Quixote gesture of gallantry fell quite flat. I produced my map which I had previously placed an X on the location of the hotel for occasions such as this. The man took the map from me and proceeded to rotate it through 360 degrees trying to decipher its code. I pointed to the river on the map and then to the direction of the river from our position trying to assist my rescuer. I considered that if there was any fresh produce amongst his shopping it would be starting to rot by now the time all this was taking.

Suddenly the man smiled and nodded in contented satisfaction, I was happy as he now seemed to know were we where and where my hotel was. He untied a strap securing some of the bags to the pillion seat and patted the plastic cushion as a gesture for me to sit on his motorbike. I straddled the seat and he gave me his shopping to hold as we set off in the opposite direction he had come from. I wondered what people thought of the two strange characters passing them on an aged moped laden with shopping. It was Felix and Oscar, the odd couple returning from Sainsbury's with the weekly shopping.

I was concerned at the direction we were travelling as I have a pretty good sense of direction and by my estimation we were going totally the wrong way. I did not recognise any of the streets or the landmarks we were passing for the simple fact that I had never passed them before, this worried me greatly. Don Quixote seemed quite perturbed also as he slowed at every junction looking at the street names, then we turned onto a main bypass with three lanes of traffic. This I knew was very wrong and so did my chauffeur as his little moped struggled to cope in the fast moving traffic.

The man exited the bypass at the next junction and stopped the bike on the side of a busy road to multiple beeps and shouts from passing cars and motor bikes. He looked at the map and once again disconcertingly rotated it through 360 degrees, his previous assured look of awareness had changed into a more blank expression of "Where the fuck am I?" I hoped the shopping I was carrying was not for his family's evening meal that night as I could not see him arriving home any time soon.

There was a Tuk-Tuk stand over the road and whilst I guarded the shopping Don Quixote went to ask for directions. A Buddhist Monk joined the group of Automobile Association enthusiasts as they busily tugged, rotated, prodded and shouted at my map trying to discover the lost land of the Pavilion Hotel. After about five minutes of cogitation Don Quixote ran over to me, took one of the bags and proceeded to donate it to the monk bowing in reverence as he did so. *There goes the chicken, sorry kids, only salad for tea,* I thought. Then a Tuk-Tuk with the monk on board lurched into the road and waited for Don Quixote to rev up the moped and follow.

The small cavalcade worked its way through the now crowded streets and within minutes I started to recognise certain sights and finally we turned right into street 19. I estimated I had been on the back of the moped for at least forty minutes and I betted that Don Quixote would never come to the aid of a distressed tourist ever again.

The Tuk-Tuk stopped outside the Pavilion and the monk disembarked, bowed once and disappeared through a large gate opposite the Hotel, then the vehicle took off in a cloud of smoke rattling down the street. I climbed off the bike and gave Don Quixote his shopping back, he did not seem the least bit perturbed about his recent adventure and was smiling broadly at me. I took some money from my pocket and asked him how much I owed him; his reply astonished me as he requested one US Dollar. I could not believe what little pittance he was asking for, we had used up more than a dollar's worth of petrol alone. I handed my gallant rescuer $5 at least as recompense for the shopping he had lost. Don Quixote shook my hand profusely and handed me back a rather crumpled map, then pottered off on the rickety moped in what I thought was totally the wrong direction.

Returning to my room I lay on the day bed to relax from my ordeal, I re-ran the recent events of my walk and was full of admiration for Don Quixote and the other Cambodian's for their earnest and honest attempts to try and help me. The Cambodians are genuinely a sincere and generous nation a fact that would be cemented time and time again during my visit. The vast majority of the fourteen million of the population are very poor indeed, but that fact does not deter the people from having a cheerful and expectant disposition.

Cambodia is still a country trying to rebuild itself from the horrors of Pol Pot's regime when the deranged despot ravaged through centuries of tradition and culture and ripped it all apart like some bizarre science fiction plot. The Khmer Rouge seized control of Cambodia in 1975 and renamed it Democratic Kampuchea, Pol Pot declared himself as Brother Number One: the aim of the regime was to create an Agrarian Communist Utopia and completely evacuate Phnom Penh to destroy old habits of trade and business. It was to be Year Zero.

The Khmer Rouge estimated it only needed two million people to create and sustain this new Utopia and founded a new proverb: "To keep you is no benefit, to destroy you is no loss." An estimated twenty one percent of Cambodians were murdered during the five years of cleansing. All links with the past were eradicated, libraries and museums were ransacked and precious, irreplaceable artefacts were destroyed. The Khmer cultures of music and art were wiped clean of any record and even documentation of traditional Khmer cuisine was burnt. Today, it is really difficult to try and obtain old Khmer cookbooks or find restaurants and chefs familiar with the old Cambodian dishes and methods of preparation.

It was the actions of a fanatical sect led by an even more despicable leader, Pol Pot. To think that humankind is capable of committing such atrocities on its fellow man is unthinkable and gravely disturbing. The world would be a far more balanced place to live without religion and politics trying their best to screw things up for everybody. It was not till 1979 that the horrors of the regime came to an end with the emancipation coming at the hands of the invading Vietnamese Army.

That night I decided to go to Sisonath Quay or known locally as the Riverside. It had been recommended to me by the Taxi driver from the airport and was on the other side of the Tonle Sap

River across the road bridge. The area is famous for its restaurants and bars along the river bank on Tonley Sap Road. To be honest I found it to be a little disappointing with many Beer Bars and average eateries; down the side streets leading off Tonley Sap Road, several Red Light establishments advertised their services and the general area had a seedy feel to it. Many beggars and street people were on hand to rid you of any disposable cash, some genuine cases and others not so.

Having dined on very average tourist Khmer cuisine, I decided the Riverside was not for me and took a motor bike taxi to the hotel. On route I remembered a road recommended by the tourist book as a lively part of Phnom Penh for nightlife. Street 240 is a long road weaving its way across the city, many shops, bars and restaurants can be found along its length catering more for the tourist and wealthy Cambodian clientele. It was there I found "Freebird American Bar." It was a lively noisy place that I took to immediately with many expats and regulars frequenting, it also has an upstairs restaurant for more formal dining, but the best thing, it was only two minutes' walk or stagger back to my hotel.

The following morning I woke refreshed having a peaceful night's sleep. I made myself a cup of coffee and sat by the outdoor plunge pool to plan my day. I knew I had to arrange transport to take me to Sihanoukville on Saturday, the town does have an airport, but from what I could gather it did not service any commercial flights. I studied my map of Cambodia and estimated it was about one hundred and fifty miles to the Gulf of Thailand, south west of Phnom Penh, but had no idea how I was going to get there.

Asking at reception I was informed that the hotel could arrange a private car to take me all the way to Sihanoukville for around $50. There were buses that I could take, but the journey would take around ten hours by that option, I was not too keen on that solution and so booked a car for my trip. Having concluded my business for the day I thought that I would do a spot more sightseeing and wanted to see the Russian Market also in order to buy some new clothes as I was rapidly running out of clean ones from my sparse wardrobe.

Armed with my trusty, yet not so accurate map I procured a Tuk-Tuk from outside the hotel and gave the cheerful cabbie my directions. The vehicle was a traditional type Tuk-Tuk with a rear two wheeled cab being pulled along by half a moped. I negotiated a five dollar return fare for the trip; my logic being that if my trusty cabbie started off from the same place as he was to return to I might stand a good chance of returning home before next week. As we sped along the roads in typical Tuk-Tuk fashion I had the distinct feeling that I had glimpsed Don Quixote; still astride his moped, gripping his sullied shopping and still trying to find his way home.

After about twenty minutes of hair raising Tuk-Tuk driving the cabbie came to a halt outside a far from auspicious building. He took his shirt off and lit a cigarette and I took my cue that we had reached the destination and crossed over the road towards a few tatty looking stalls. If this was the Russian Market then it would only take minutes to explore and I was rather disappointed.

The Russian Market is not really one building; it is a collection of very eclectic bazaars all in one large hotchpotch of a site. There is no real entrance or exit to the labyrinth of retail outlets and I made my way in by way of two small jewellery stalls. The first impression I had was it was like walking into a dark forest, no sunlight penetrated the midnight world of the market and everything was illuminated by dim electric light bulbs hanging down from each stall.

I never had been in such a place, the floor was treacherous as the market is a series of different small shops and stalls all cobbled together under one roof. I made slow progress as I had one eye permanently fixed downwards so as not to trip, and the other looking at the wares on offer. The Russian Market is divided up into unregistered zones, but designated by what produce was on display. Everything was for sale from clothes, jewellery, food, electrical goods, motor bikes, tourist gifts, books it went on for ever. I stumbled across a dining area that would have immediately been closed down by our food standards body, but had some wonderful freshly cooked delicacies on offer.

Sitting on a large wooden bench with some other tired shoppers I ordered some Khmer Sour Soup. It is a traditional vegetable stew that survived Pol Pot's regime and although not as fragrant or as spicy as Thai food was still very nourishing and delicious. Other stalls were serving dried fish salads and chicken broths to hungry bargain hunters pausing in their retail therapy for sustenance and rest. My soup was washed down with local coffee which was not to my liking as it was a sweet, milky concoction made with condensed milk. It is a favourite way of drinking either tea or coffee in South East Asia one of the customs that I have not embraced.

Finishing my lunch I retraced my steps back to where the clothes were; passing an oily, slippery area that seemed to consist of every imaginable engine part available for purchase. Shoppers were passing me, some with Spark Plugs and Engine Oil in their arms others with Freshly Cut Flowers; the wares were that diverse on offer in the market. I secured my bargains and attempted to find my way out of the maze of shops, it was really difficult trying to find the exact spot where I had entered the market, eventually I found my way back out into the sunlight and saw I was not too far away from where my Tuk-Tuk was waiting.

The drive back was no less as hectic and dangerous, my driver seeming to enjoy the thrill of pedestrian targeting as much as his chain smoking of rough Cambodian tobacco. He spoke little English, but kept on repeating that night he would take me to "Heart of Darkness" which is Phnom Penh's premier night spot, an offer I was not to take him up on.

I opened my shopping bags and was pleased at what I had bought; T-shirts costing less than one pound fifty each were well stitched and of good quality cotton as were the shorts and underwear. Hanging some items in the wardrobe I packed the remainder in my case for the rest of my trip and then showered for the evening. I had passed an Indian restaurant on my way back from Freebird the previous night and had made a mental note to return for a meal as I had not eaten Indian food in such a long time and had withdrawal symptoms.

Opening the large wooden door to the street I saw my Tuk-Tuk driver over the road who greeted me as I was his long lost brother immediately embracing me and offering me a cigarette. I declined the smoke and his offer of a ride and noticed the gateway the monk had disappeared through the other afternoon; as there did not seem to be any barrier blocking entry I went to explore.

Wat Botum or the Temple of Lotus Blossoms was right opposite my hotel; its rear entrance faced the wooden door to the Pavilion. The main Pagoda is over one hundred years old and wandering through its grounds I could see many of the monks going about their daily chores and life in their ochre coloured robes. Although the general area around Wat Botun is fairly quiet the tranquillity and stillness to be found there was an oasis in the bustling city. A sense of wonder and enlightenment entered my soul and I felt somewhat fulfilled as I sat under a Lotus tree breathing in its exotic scent.

It is quite amazing that the monks allow you to roam around their home quite freely and without restriction, it is a feeling that I get from anything that is connected with Buddhism. A feeling of simplicity, freedom and of tranquillity without the trappings of ostentatious grandeur that is to be found in Christian cathedrals and churches.

I spent nearly an hour leisurely roaming around the Wat and discovering its hidden treasures. The balance between the ancient artefacts and the modern day activities of the monks washing clothes and praying somehow made the experience more real and tangible. I made my way to the main entrance on the opposite side of the temple grounds to which I had entered, it faced a massive open public space that was like a colossal cemented park with concrete fountains and plenty of places to sit and rest. It was now early evening and the residents of Phnom Penh were undertaking one of their favourite leisure pastimes, dancing.

The monumental area was illuminated by tall street lighting and in the park numerous sound systems had been erected and were competing in volume against one another to blast out fast Cambodian pop music. Every age was represented from toddlers to octogenarians each with one thing in common; they were all shaking a leg. Groups of regimented dancers some as big as fifty were all in line, moving as one and strutting their stuff together in unison. I could barely believe what I was witnessing; a daily work out by hundreds of city workers dancing their socks off in public provided free by the local government. I had never seen or heard anything before quite like it, but it sort of summed up Phnom Penh, a city unified and fun loving. It was the total antithesis of Wat Botum and yet was no less out of place in the city.

Freebird was busy, but I managed to get a bar stool and had a beer as an aperitif to my curry. The bar staff were loud and amusing and remembered me from the other day. The girls were all petite with jet black hair and dark complexions, they wore matching Freebird T-shirts and it was difficult to distinguish one from the other. I suspected many a potential, slightly inebriated, male suitor had come a cropper in that department.

Was it a pre requisite to be a dwarf to be employed as a waitress in Freebird? Or was the staff entrance only a five foot door? Anyway they were quite surprised with my request for the check so soon and I informed the inquisitive elves that I was going for an Indian meal. The girls were really interested what Indian food was like as they had never eaten it before, presumably because of cost so for some reason I announced I would bring them some back as a present.

The meal was very enjoyable although it seemed wrong somehow to be eating Indian food whilst being in Cambodia, but I knew I had plenty more time to redress the balance. Indian was always my favourite choice of cuisine, but was rapidly being overtaken by Thai as afterwards that feeling of being bloated and fit to bursting is not quite there with Thai food. There is the absence of the rich sauces and dairy that is abundant in Indian food and it is far easier to digest. After my dinner I ordered a mixed Tandoori platter and a fiery Fish Phal Curry to test the girl's pain threshold, together with an assortment of stuffed naan, chapatti and roti breads. It was quite a takeaway feast for the lucky Freebird staff.

My gift did not backfire on me as I was treated like royalty on my return. The girls instantly stopped work and for ten minutes nobody was served whatsoever as the meal was instantly sampled to differing responses. As expected, the Phal was considered too hot for my small sampling sirens although the Tandoori Platter was widely accepted as a roaring success together with its pickles and relishes. I did not have to order or pay for another drink all night long and was royally pissing the rest of Freebird's clientele right off for the remainder of the evening, having continually at least two waitresses as constant attendants by my side. I left the bar that night well and truly oiled and staggered home with my gift of three Freebird T-shirts tucked under my armpit.

The following morning I woke with my mouth feeling dry and parched. I never really suffered with a headache after consuming excess alcohol the night previous, I just suffered badly with dehydration and the general feeling of numbness. To say I felt shit was an understatement and it was not until midday that I finally began to feel a little more human. That evening I took it easy back at Freebird, although the waitresses tried their best to repeat Thursday's hospitality. I knew that I had a long trip ahead of me the following morning and there was no possible way I could undertake it if I was in a similar condition.

Saturday morning arrived and whilst checking out of the hotel my taxi driver arrived very prompt at 9am to take me to Sihanoukville. I was introduced to Mr Seng who unfortunately did not speak one word of English and I knew it was going to be a long journey. He seemed to know the receptionist very well, perhaps a relative I thought, but it was of no concern of mine as the nepotism was indeed for my benefit also by the price he was charging me. He led me to an old Toyota Camry that was spotlessly clean on the inside and pushed back the passenger seat so I would have more leg room, he checked the details of the destination with me the Orchidee Guest House, Tala Street, Sihanoukville. After my confirmation that all was okay we set off to the next part of my adventure.

Exiting Phnom Penh was slow due to some sort of parade going on that day; the city was filled with different groups in various costumes making their way to the rally point. I had no idea what the event was for or what occasion it was, but festivals are a regular part of life in South East Asia and at a guess it was probably a Buddhist Religious day. The car headed out towards the airport and Mr Seng drove to an industrial park where he loaded the rear of the vehicle up with an assortment of boxes and after a short break we set off on our way again. I admired the industry of Mr Seng as I was obviously paying for the delivery of the packages; it was no skin off my nose so I didn't care one bit.

We finally weaved our way out of the urban conurbation and joined Highway Number Four the main road route from the capital to Sihanoukville. There are no trains or planes and travelling by road is the only way to access that part of the country. I noticed Mr Seng's hand on the steering wheel and noticed he had a long finger nail on the little finger of his right hand. He saw my inquisitive glance and mimicked playing a guitar; he then rooted around under his seat and produced a tatty box full of CDs. Oh my God, he was going to play his music for me! I was concentrating more on the road as Mr Seng was giving no concentration in that department and the car was swerving all over the road. I was much relieved when he produced a CD he had been ferreting for and placed the disc in the car's audio system.

For the next ninety minutes I was subjected to Cambodian renditions of old hits from the sixties. I had no idea if Mr Seng was playing on any of them, if he was he should have been shot. The music was quite simply terrible and I had nowhere that I could go to escape song after sodding song. I must have heard at least three versions of *The Night They Drove Old Dixie Down* interspersed with dodgy Elvis hits. It all reminded me of my youth when a series of LPs were released called *Top of the Pops*. In the sixties and early seventies it was against copyright law to release compilations albums by original artists and so a very astute producer got around the situation by having second rate bands perform hits of the day. The result was absolute shite of the first degree. Mr Seng's CD reminded me greatly of the *Top of the Pops* series of records and I sincerely wished I had taken the bus.

Time passed agonisingly slowly as Mr Seng's Hitmobile headed deeper into the Cambodian countryside. The road at best was a three lane highway with the middle lane for overtaking, but in parts turned into a single lane, red clay, thoroughfare. It was impossible to travel at speeds over fifty miles per hour due partly to the condition of the road, but mostly because of the others users on the highway. There were herdsmen with Water Buffalo, heavily laden old trucks with every manner of freight imaginable, carts with whole families going for a day out and old buses chugging along so crammed some passengers were travelling on the roof.

It was a shambles and I wondered what the transport minister for Cambodia had as a budget for road improvements that year. Working our way south we passed through numerous small towns that seemed to spring up out of nowhere. They were all built around Highway 4 in a strip of commerce and reminded me of Wild West towns that I had seen in films, popping up out of nowhere in the desert and then nothing but wilderness for miles.

Either side of the road it was mostly tropical jungle with Paddy fields as the main crop activity, small hamlets built on stilts housed the farmers living without electricity, running water or proper drainage. It was a simple, peasant subsistence, but many were going about their business with a smile and enjoying their lives without the essential consumer trappings of the commercial world and oblivious to it's so called luxury. They had nature, family and happiness; not a bad life and one not to be easily dismissed as poor, yes, financially desperately poor, but satisfaction and happiness of life is not just measured in monetary wealth.

After about three hours Mr Seng pulled off the road into a sort of small village where there was a garage. He parked his car under the shade and a man came out and tinkered under the bonnet. Mr Seng did not seem overly concerned and signalled me to follow him to an open air restaurant. I presumed we had stopped for lunch and general maintenance of the car so breathed a sigh of relief we were not stuck there in the middle of nowhere.

The restaurant was more of a home made café with a miss matching collection of tables and chairs, but busy with local farm workers taking a break. Many stared up at me with curiosity and I looked about and noticed I was the only foreigner there. This was not a Welcome Break services and I believed Mr Seng had chose it because of the price and convenience. There was no menu, you simply had the restaurant's dish of the day which was a bowl of vegetable broth similar to the Sour Soup I had in Phnom Penh. It was piping hot and full of flavour with vegetables I had never seen the like of before; nevertheless I devoured the lot to Mr Seng's admiration.

After lunch whilst Mr Seng smoked the obligatory cigarette, I took the opportunity of trying to explain what date I wanted to be collected from Sihanoukville. I took out my mobile phone and brought up the calendar, pointing to the 1st May 2010, "Today," I stressed to Mr Seng. He looked at his watch and the date confirmed what my calendar informed him. I then pointed to 22nd May and tried to explain that was the day I wanted him to come back for me. He took out a scrap of paper and wrote the number 22 down, then 10am and looked at me. I nodded in agreement and that was it, the paper was shoved back into his pocket and that was all that was documented between us, no phone numbers or names were exchanged, just a number and a time on a scrap of paper.

The rest of the journey took over another three hours, another three hours of Mr Seng's *Top of the Pops* music to be endured. The scenery and weather changed quite dramatically as we climbed up over a small mountain range where the wind and rain hampered our progress. The temperature dropped significantly as we ascended and Mr Seng actually turned the heating on in the old Camry as I was shivering sitting in my shorts and sunglasses.

As we came down the other side of the mountains the car swung around a bend and through the drizzle I saw the 4x4 in front of us suddenly swerve across the road, but too late to avoid hitting the animal. A water buffalo had suddenly decided to charge across the road and the Toyota Landcruiser had smashed into the beast head on. There was a loud bang followed by terrible howling from the injured animal that lay prostrate in the road with blood pouring from its head. We lurched to an abrupt halt only feet away from the carnage and Mr Seng got out of the car, I for some unknown reason followed him but god knows why.

The occupants of the Landcruiser were all out of their vehicle and seemed none the worse for wear after their accident. The front bull horns of the car had taken the full impact and the vehicle was perfectly drivable with only mostly cosmetic damage to the headlights and bonnet being the major repair jobs. What if we had hit that animal? The Camry had no protective bull bars and was much lower than the 4x4; I gulped to think of our chances of escaping such a collision. Imagine the shame going to finally meet the creator; arriving in a beat up old Toyota Camry with a Water Buffalo's head swinging from the rear view mirror. Along with being serenaded by *Sugar Baby Love,* not even the real Rubettes, but a crappy dodgy version by the Cambodian Lubettes, it was not as imagined that I would ever enter the kingdom of heaven.

The noise of the tortured water buffalo brought me back to the current situation, the poor animal was lying in a deep purplish pool of blood and was thrashing around hopelessly trying to get on its feet, its front legs were mangled and broken. Everybody just stood around not knowing what to do and one or two more vehicles were joining the small traffic jam. Suddenly a farmer appeared driving a small rustic tractor and took charge of the situation; he and his son took a rope from the contraption and tied it around the water buffalo's hind legs then unceremoniously dragged the poor creature off the road into a ditch to the sound of horrific squeals of pain from the injured beast.

The cars started to drive off and as there was nothing more we could do, Mr Seng and I got back into the Camry and resumed our journey. Mr Seng looked over to me, made a sort of kids revolver with his forefinger and thumb and made a 'boom' sound indicating the animal would be shot. I was glad that the animal would be put out of its misery, but I never did hear the gunshot.

Another hour and I could finally see glimpses of the pale blue sea of the Gulf of Thailand ahead of us. I was excited and the rigours of my long journey instantly faded as we passed signs directing us to Sihanoukville. Sihanoukville is a fairly new town or city as the Cambodians refer to it. It sprung up with the development of a port in the 1950's and was named after a famous Khmer King; King Father Norodom Sihanouk.

Greenstreet and Back

Mr Seng seemed to know his way around Sihanoukville and took a turn that led us down a steep hill signposted Seredndipity & Ochheutal Beaches. The road arrived at a busy roundabout with a large statue of a lion perched in its centre; the roundabout is called Golden Lion Circle and is a famous land mark in the town for direction finding. We drove down a sandy road that was signposted Tala Street and stopped outside a large Villa with a sign: "Orchidee".

Nobody came out to greet me and I retrieved my bag from Mr Seng, handed him the fifty dollars with an extra five dollar tip and he bowed in thanks. Standing on no ceremony he drove straight off down the sandy road again. Was he going home straight away? It was quite incredulous to think so; perhaps he was just late delivering his boxes. I made my way to a small desk inside the house which I presumed was the reception. When I had booked the Orchidee on the internet I had chosen one of their largest rooms as it had Wi-Fi and it was still under fifteen quid per night, the budget rooms were only eight quid.

Two Cambodian ladies were busy talking behind the desk when I entered reception and they were in no hurry to finish their conversation. I waited patiently for the Tate-a-Tate to conclude then handed over my passport. One of the ladies brusquely grabbed my document and looked down a printed guest list; I could read my name upside down and pointed it out to the lady. She looked up at me with a small scowl as if to suggest I should mind my own business that was her job. She pointed to the list and my name and I nodded; then she took a pen and turned the sheet of paper around to face me. I saw there were signatures next to some of the corresponding names and added mine to the list. She seemed quite satisfied with this and spoke for the first time: "Fifty dollars deposit."

Handing the cash over I received my passport back and was given a key attached to a large red disc with a number seven painted on it. It was reminiscent of the one I was given at Kings Gardens when they fitted the padlock; Had they phoned ahead and said there would be a numpty arriving? The lady then tapped a bell on the desk and a girl of about fourteen appeared bouncing her way through reception. She had a broad grin on her face and was humming some tune; I hoped it was not the Lubettes! She took my case and we ascended two flights up a wide wooden staircase with carved wooden balustrades. There was something atmospheric about the Orchidee, something quite unique I couldn't put my finger on.

We arrived at the top floor where two doors faced each other across a large square landing. Outside the room opposite mine there was a large ornamental wooden sofa on which an elderly lady seemed fast asleep under the slowly turning ceiling fan. We entered room number seven and I was shocked. Immediately facing the door was a king sized bed with a large window adjacent, letting floods of natural light into the room and I could see a balcony outside. At the foot of the bed against the wall was a gigantic, black double wardrobe that seemed made out of Ebony or some other exotic wood? It had a carved helmet of wooden flowers and trees and was the most ornate wardrobe I had ever seen in my life.

Then turning right there was a lounge area with two armchairs and a double sofa, this furniture did not quite seem to suit the rest of the room, it looked comfortable, dated in a seventies sort of way, not antique. There was also a flat screen TV and a refrigerator with assorted small wooden tables scattered around. My guide showed me the bathroom which was massive, tiled in an outrageous lime green colour, but had hot water and a shower in the corner.

I was impressed with the room especially for the price I was paying; it was a contradiction and seemed to have been designed by two completely different people. One a throw back from the seventies and the other with a more classical taste in design. But everything was spotlessly clean from the duvet and linen on the bed to the scrubbed tiles in the bathroom and I was content I could live for three weeks there. I needed a long shower to clean after the journey and I took my time unpacking whilst my body dried in the warm air.

Afterwards I explored the Orchidee which did not take me too long. There was a small swimming pool surrounded by about 10 tiny petite bungalows which I presumed were the "back packers" accommodation, but still were very acceptable, the courtyard around the pool was a suntrap and had a few loungers dotted about for guests. Outside near the gateway was a separate building that acted as the restaurant and bar and it was completely open to the elements down one side. A couple of residents were sitting there having drinks in the shade and I was tempted, but decided to keep my powder dry as it was only about 4pm.

The Orchidee was an intriguing place; the original house where my room was situated was a classic Khmer building, mostly wooden interior with large rooms and spaces. The rest of the Guesthouse was a miss match of added on annexes that formed a functional if most unusual hotel. It was owned by a Dutch gentleman whom I had yet to meet.

Sihanoukville as previously mentioned was built around the construction of the port in the early sixties when Cambodia struggled under the waning power of the French and the influence of the Vietnamese growth in the North along the Mekong Delta. Downtown Sihanoukville is based around one main road where banks and supermarkets can be found, but the main reason for visitors is the beach areas. Victory Beach is in the North with Serendipity and Ochheuteal in the centre and Otres in the South, smaller and more secluded beaches are dotted around and various islands are close by for exploration.

I was fortunate that I was staying a stone's throw from Ochheutal Beach as it is the largest and most active with the most life in the town. During the day bathers relax on the sand, renting loungers from the beach bars. Later the bars change more for the nightlife with loud music playing and serving drinks late into the night. It is here a few nightclubs can also be found tending to the very late patronage.

Sihanoukville has two types of tourists, the weekend Cambodians from Phnom Penh and the foreign backpackers. You do not just pass through Sihanoukville it is a place you purposely have to go to visit and that is not particularly easy either. Although there were some rumours that there may be some expansion of the airport in the future, but I think if that ever happened it would be a completely different place indeed. It also has one other attraction; casinos, there were four, and considering gambling is banned in Thailand, a large attraction indeed.

Stepping out onto the dusty, sandy road outside the Orchidee I looked at the direction we had previously travelled. Tola Road was quite a desolate place with hardly any traffic of any description using it. There was a series of six or seven shacks lining the right hand side of the street; they were long, narrow affairs with tables and chairs situated in the open air at the front with a low brick building with corrugated metal roof at the rear. The Restaurant's were separated only by mesh wire or nothing at all and they all seemed to blend into each other.

Apparently, Tola Road was famous in Sihanoukville for its Barbeque Restaurants and food, but the only sign's I could see were; Happy Herb pizza, Mystic pizza and Happy Sihanoukville pizza which I thought rather odd. Did this part of Cambodia have some sort of pizza fetish? Where the residents of Sihanoukville actually descendants from settlers from Napoli? It did not really make any sense, I had not seen one pizza place in Phnom Penh and yet in sleepy Sihanoukville there was about seven in one street.

Ambling down Tola Road the shacks were preparing for the evening trade and I noticed outside each one there was a small display of meat and fish. The displays were in sharp contrast to those lavish presentations in Samui and only had a small selection but nevertheless a choice could be made and the restaurant would cook it on a small kettle drum fire. Why they called themselves pizza restaurants I had no idea, and I suppose Trading Standards Bodies in the UK would have the businesses closed down for misrepresentation.

Actually; later on in my trip, I found out that some of the places did serve a type of pizza. On the menu next to the pizza selections were small, smiley pizza faces and you could choose how "Happy" you wanted your pizza to be. It was not the children's menu, but a way of indicating to the chef how much Hashish you wished him to put on the pizza. One thing that I greatly admire about the Cambodians is their ability to adapt, if Oregano was unobtainable then why not season the food with what was freely available and in this case it happened to be Cannabis. I often saw many happy patrons enjoying their evening meal with contented large grins on their faces and not a drink in sight!

Halfway down Tola Road was an intersection and a small road crossed; left was Ochheuteal Beach and to the right was a small group of bars called Golden Lion Plaza. There was no fancy plaza about it, it was just a collection of very raunchy Beer Bars and just before them was one particular one called Paradise Pub that became a frequent haunt of mine during my stay.

That day I turned left and went to have my first look at Ochheuteal Beach. Running along the beach was a road than ran parallel to Tola Road and in effect it was the beach road called Mithona Street. I crossed that and encountered a sandy path about four hundred yards long that led down to the sea. It was wide enough for one car to travel and on either side was flanked by small wooden huts selling gifts, food or beer. Many people where there, mostly Cambodians either heading to or from the beach in different varieties of undress depending which way they were heading.

As in all of Sihanoukville there was a very laid back atmosphere with nobody seeming to be in a hurry to go or do anything. The few farangs I encountered were either backpackers or throw backs from the sixties resembling aged hippies or remnants from the Vietnam War.

The path ended between two large beach bars onto golden sand and the rather choppy looking sea. The water was a strange colour; it was a far cry from the absolutely clear blue of something like the Caribbean, but more of a murky dark green. There were many small boats anchored just off the beach; they were uniquely Cambodian, brightly painted and resembling a sort of ocean going large Gondola. They were capable of carrying around ten passengers and were powered by a small outboard motor attached to the propeller by a long metal pole. Each was available for hire to go fishing or a day trip to one of the nearby islands, but by the way they were pitching about in the unrestful sea I did not envisage taking such an excursion.

Along the beach were a number of large wooden beach bars all hiring loungers to their own allocated section of sand, some had rather fancy double cushioned seats available and would be ideal for relaxing watching the day go by. The fronts of the establishments were all open to the sea and most had a small wooden bar at the back with a few bar stools and chairs for later in the evening. An ice cold beer cost fifty cents, about thirty five pence and would be served to you in a frosted glass whilst you were sitting in the sun. The two local Cambodian beers were called Angkor and Anchor the former actually brewed in Sihanoukville, both were very acceptable indeed.

I took advantage of the hospitality of the nearest bar and whilst sipping my refreshing Angkor observed everything around me. The unmistakable sound of shrill laughter and yells of delight resonated as the little Cambodian children played in the surf whilst attentive parents looked on. There was a hunger-making aroma of Khmer food permeating the air along with the unique salty smell of the sea all contributing to a typical idyllic beach scene. I sat back in my chair and sighed contently pleased that I had made the effort to come to this part of Cambodia and in the knowledge I had the chance to spend another three weeks there.

The following day I managed to access my email and there was a disturbing message from Sully back home who had recently collected my mail. He informed me that I had been sent an appointment from the DWP in Crosby to review my invalidity benefit. He had scanned the letter and I saw that my appointment was in ten days time at the job centre. What was I to do? I had to contact this Mrs Moffat and get the appointment put back. But would they accept a delay of seven weeks? And was I supposed to be receiving benefit whilst I was in South East Asia? It was something that I had not managed to sort out before I left and now had come back to haunt me.

A plan had to be formulated that was plausible, I knew I had to come clean that I was not in the UK so I decided I would say I was in France holidaying at my brother's. Surely even people who were on invalidity benefit were entitled to summer holidays? What was the difference where the holiday was? My phone did not work and I could not very well email Mrs Moffat so I had to get access to an overseas line. The Orchidee did not have one so I decided to take a stroll down the road to explore some of the little shops I had passed the day before.

Unbelievably, I found a little Internet shop on the corner of Tola Road. There was only a dozen shops in the whole of the beach area and I was spawny enough one happened to offer overseas calls. To call the establishment an Internet Café would be stretching the description wildly; it was a small shop with six tables, on top of each was an ancient TV screen and what seemed to be Amstrad PCs. Four of the PCs were being used by very noisy local kids playing games and describing to their friends in loud Cambodian their progress in killing the computer generated aliens on their screens.

At the rear of the shop were two odd looking booths, they were home made and seemed to be constructed from some sort of recycled Perspex that did not even reach the ceiling for sound insulation. A flimsy door made out of the same material was leant against the frame for access to the booth. In each was a similar PC to those outside and a solitary stool in front of a rustic wooden table.

The guy that owned the shop was only in his early twenties and I presumed this was his first ever business. He was energetic and very eager to please but spoke very little English. I pointed to the Overseas Calls sign in the window and he nodded enthusiastically and led me towards the booths at the back. All the noise in the room ceased instantly at my entrance as the locals stared at the strange farang walking around in their shop, they were most curious of my intentions.

I had timed the call to be at 8am UK time in order to try and talk to Mrs Moffat before she started her daily interviews. The Perspex door was pulled back as the owner and I squeezed into the tiny booth. He booted up the antiquated machine and I fully expected DOS commands to hit the screen, but an old version of Windows appeared and the young Cambodian started tapping on the keypad. Then some software I have never seen the like of before lit up requiring data, it must have been an old predecessor of Skype as there was a plastic phone handset attached to the computer.

The software was simple to use, I just had to punch in the full dialling code for the DWP office and hit enter once the call had been connected. I would know this by listening to the operation on the handset. I thanked my tutor as he wedged the door closed behind him aided by most of the curious patrons of the Internet Café. I tapped in the required numbers and waited, absolutely nothing happened I could not hear anything on the headset. A tapping noise on the Perspex behind me drew my attention away from the screen and I turned to see several youngsters pointing at a red button on the monitor. It was the timing button to start the transmission, so I pointed the curser at the appropriate icon and pressed enter. A murmur of agreement came from the gallery behind me.

A series of most peculiar noises similar to underwater echoes came out of the handset and I was bemused at the progress of the call. Then I could vaguely hear an English voice at the other end of the line, rapidly I pressed enter and I could just make out the words Job Centre. "I wish to speak to Mrs Moffat!" I shouted down the phone, a muffled reply came back after a two second delay, but I could only decipher one word from three. This was hopeless, I was trying to have a conversation with somebody seven thousand miles away using nothing but tin cans attached by a string stretched out under water. I terminated the call and tried a second time to connect to the Department of Works and Pensions in Liverpool.

The second attempt was a total washout and although I could faintly hear a voice on the other end of the line it was blatantly obvious they could not hear me. On my third attempt it was somewhat of a success, I was connected to the Job Centre's switchboard who informed me they could barely hear my voice, but I gleaned from the very short conversation Mrs Moffat was not due into work for another hour. Finishing my call, the door was pulled open by very obliging hands of my audience and I explained to the owner I would return in an hour.

After a long coffee break I returned to the shop to retry my telephone call. The word must have got around locally about the strange farang and the shop's patrons had tripled in number. There was nobody playing games as they were more interested in my activities; the locals were all lounging about, chatting loudly together interested in this welcome break from normal routine. I made my way to the same booth and was followed by the expectant gamers.

This time I was successful on my first attempt to connect, but again Mrs Moffat's direct line did not pick up and once again I was redirected to the switchboard. The sound of the line must have alerted the rather annoyed sounding switchboard operator that it was me again. "I would like to speak to Mrs Moffat please," I shouted as a small cheer went up behind me for my success. After a short delay the Dalek voice informed me Mrs Moffat was busy.

Was I really talking to Davros, the arch rival of the Time Lord? If not, it certainly sounded like I was. I imagined the bored woman back in the UK trying to make sense of what the nuisance telephone caller was pestering her about, after all it was Mrs Moffat's problem, not hers. "I can't hear you, where are you calling from?" Davros questioned me. I shouted even louder "I am calling from the South of France" I lied, as a noisy hubbub erupted behind me. "South of Flance? South of Flance?" My disbelieving Cambodian chorus banged on the Perspex behind me. Obviously the farang did not know this was Cambodia and it was their duty to inform me.

"Where?" Davros reiterated, "The South of France," I lied again. "No, No, No, Cambodia, Cambodia!" my annoyed audience shouted at my mistake. I had to do something as surely Davros could hear my Asian assistants. I turned and put my finger to my lips in a hope that they would understand it as a gesture to shut the fuck up. The puzzlement of my obvious confusion had turned into a major debating point between the shop's youthful patrons and the row was actually getting louder not diminishing.

Davros was getting more annoyed back in the UK as the call was taking far too much of her time and her voice was now raised. The situation was turning farcical and I would have lapsed into a chortling mess had the call not had been so important. I finally made Davros understand who I was and that I would be away until mid June, I could tell by her judgemental sounding voice that she did not approve of claimants taking such a long vacation, but she would inform Mrs Moffat.

Leaving the shop I thanked my helpers profusely for their assistance and assured them I now knew what country I was residing in. I was glad that I had managed to sort the problem out and I made a mental note to come clean when I finally got home and saw Mrs Moffat. I laughed to myself at the total fuck up that had just occurred and it proved that even the most simple of tasks was a major logistical endeavour in this part of the world, nothing is easy.

That evening after surfing the Net about things to do in Sihanoukville I decided to take a trip to a nearby beach called Otres, its claim to fame was that it was meant to have some decent fish restaurants. I went to Paradise bar for a drink and to ask for directions and struck up a conversation with the Irish owner Declan. He had been in Cambodia for years and was in a long term relationship with his Bar Manageress and was a fountain of local knowledge. He informed me Otres Beach was too far to try and walk and I was better off getting a motorbike taxi.

His bar was fairly small, there was two pool tables and a couple of TV screens. Four or five scantily clad hostesses were busy trying to attract passing custom into Paradise and every now and then they would turn their attention to me to see if they would have better luck. I stayed for a couple of beers chatting to Declan and occasionally declined the offers of company from his girls.

Stepping out of the bar a bike pulled up immediately and par for the course a toothy grin was the first thing to greet me. I looked at the wreck of a machine and wondered how the Hell it actually worked. Its rider seemed unconcerned with its condition and seemed quite proud that he actually could afford to have a motor vehicle. The man wore no helmet and had a weather beaten face with a few small scars on his right cheek and chin, but had a beaming smile that spread from ear to ear. He spoke very little

English, but seemed to understand my request to be taken to Otres Beach.

Declan had told me which direction Otres was located and for the second time in Cambodia I was on the back of a scooter going in totally the wrong direction. I shouted at the man as the wind whistled past my ears: "Otres, Otres," but he shook his head and we continued in the same direction. We travelled past Lion Circle and took the main road to Downtown Sihanoukville which only took a couple of minutes to pass through and then started to ascend up with a signpost directing us to Victory Hill. Two or three minutes later we arrived at a small cluster of bars and restaurants and the motor bike stopped.

I got off the bike and questioned the man. *Otres?* It was more of a rhetorical question as there was no sign of any sand, water or anything that remotely resembled a beach. The man just grinned at me and pointed around to the motley collection of shacks and wooden buildings and simply said: "Better here." He had dismissed my request to visit Otres and taken me to somewhere that he considered was a far more interesting place. My initial response was one of anger, but when I looked at the proud expression on the man's face of having done a job well my ire faded instantly. I gave him a dollar which he was delighted with and the old Honda fired up again as my chauffeur waved goodbye to me.

With no idea of where I exactly was or how I was to try and find my way back home I decided the best course of action was to find somewhere to sit and have a beer. The wooden shack opposite me looked like it was a sort of bar so I walked over the road and took a seat. Chickens and dogs roamed around inside and there were various stacks of provisions such as sacks of rice, trays of eggs and bundles of vegetables propped up against the walls. Behind a makeshift bar a rather fat, sweating man with no shirt greeted my entrance with a curt nod.

"Do you sell beer?" I enquired, the fat man nodded again so I sat at one of the two small tables hoping the sweaty man would bring me a drink over. After a short while the fat man waddled over to me with a bottle of Angkor and unceremoniously dumped it in front of me. As I sipped the beer from the bottle I contemplated what had just happened and I had a sort of epiphany.

The man on the motorcycle had acted in what he thought were my best interests; why bother trying to plan each evening where to go to, I could simply jump on the back of his scooter and be taken somewhere. It would take all the hassle out of decision making after a hard days sunbathing and after all I did not have a clue where to go anyway. I was content with my decision and decided to give my pet chauffeur a name; Paul, that is what I would call him, not very Khmer but something I could easily remember.

My stomach rumbled and I was suddenly aware that I had not eaten that day and realised I was famished. I paid for my beer and went looking for some sustenance nearby. Bizarrely next door to the bar there was a small restaurant called Chennai Rottys that I presumed was Indian, it had a large sign in the window advertising "Genuine Brand Liquor". I was not aware that counterfeit hooch was a major problem in Sihanoukville, but was comforted that the restaurant was proud enough to boast the real McCoy!

The place was empty of either patrons or staff, but I sat at one of the few tables and waited patiently for somebody to appear. It was something that I had noticed about Sihanoukville nobody seemed to be in a hurry to do anything; it was all laid back, relaxed and very, very rustic. After studying the décor for some time eventually a young girl with a kitten in her arms entered the room. The girl was quite surprised to see a farang sitting there, but rushed over to show me the tiny ball of fur wriggling in her slipping grasp. I stroked the emaciated animal behind its ears and the creature started to purr loudly to the delight of the girl.

With the noise of the girl's laughter a lady in a beautiful Sari appeared behind a multi coloured plastic curtain and seemed distraught that she had not known I was in her restaurant. The girl was despatched away from my table to play with her pet elsewhere and I was promptly given a menu to peruse whilst the lady set my table. Within seconds cutlery was laid and condiments placed; I have never understood why on Earth Indian restaurants have salt and pepper on their dining tables. Who the Hell puts salt or pepper on a curry?

The attentive lady stood at my table with a small pad in her hand waiting for my order, the menu was not extensive so I just ordered a Mutton Curry, but with extra chillies and steamed rice. The lady disappeared and I heard pans being rattled in the kitchen, she was actually the cook as well. I half expected her to serenade me also whilst my curry was cooking as she seemed to do everything else in the restaurant.

Waiting patiently for my food I had nothing else to do, but to peruse the menu again perhaps for future reference. I came to the drinks pages and remembered that is what Chennai Rottys boasted was their jewel in the crown; "Genuine Brand Liquor" As I read down the list of spirits I came to a very unusual item. I don't know if the Norwegian Translator from Monty Python had been holidaying in Sihanoukville and did a little freelance work, but this cocktail seemed to be the antipathy of what Chennai Rottys advertised; "Chivas Ligal with Cock"! I nearly dropped the menu I was laughing so hard, the cook peered around the curtain staring at the madman in her restaurant but I couldn't help myself. I roared with laughter and took a photo of the page as I knew no one would believe my tale back home.

The food was served by the same woman and she placed it in front of me with a bemused look on her face. I was still checking the menu for more misprints, but did not have the heart to tell her why I was still chuckling, it would be too much of a hassle to try and explain myself and I would probably end up in a worse tangle than her original translator. The curry was delicious and very spicy, the flavours were quite different to Indian food back in the UK, perhaps it was the different fresh herbs used I could not be certain. All in all, my experience of Chennai Rottys was one to remember and it goes to say dining alone is not always a lonely sad affair, without Paul I would have missed the fun and I was glad to have found my transport companion.

Over the following days as usual I began to pick up a routine, not strictly adhered to either by time or repetition, but my days followed a similar routine. I would wake around late morning and potter down to the pool area for some sunbathing and to read the local newspaper, perhaps a break for lunch if I felt peckish then mid afternoon I would relax for a couple of hours in my room catching up with email or having a nap. Then I would normally go and have a chat and a beer with Declan in Paradise Bar before my steadfast guide Paul whisked me off to some new, undiscovered local treasure. Paul would never wait for me which was half the fun of the excursion; he would simply deposit me somewhere to his liking and then tootle off. I was then left to explore and eventually find my own way home in my own time.

Paul was not a licensed motor bike taxi driver and I doubt very much his scooter would have passed any legal checks, but he had eyes like a shitehawk. I could just make one step out of the Orchidee Guesthouse and he would appear from nowhere on the horizon and in a cloud of Two Stroke smoke swoop down arriving noisily to take me away for the evening. Barely a word was ever spoken between us, but over the days and weeks a bond slowly started to form and I began to respect the genial man. I estimated his age to be similar to my own, around fifty, and considered for no particular reason him to be a family man.

The dilapidated scooter seemed his only source of income and I pitied him for that as the machine did not seem long for this world, but his weather beaten face always had a genuine smile that lit up even more when he saw me. I ensured that I always tipped him, not extravagantly as that would have been demeaning to our friendship; I had decided that on my last night I would redress any shortfall in form of a large gratuity. The fact that Paul was not licensed was not unusual as very few riders seemed official in Sihanoukville; Cambodia is a country free of many rules and regulations or that they simply are not adhered to, it allows and encourages free enterprise and the economy seems to work because of it.

However, the downside of such freedom is a general lawlessness within the country especially in rural areas. It is not a place for irresponsible behaviour as the consequences can be brutal and very grave. Drugs and firearms are rife in Cambodia and there is little policing to be found anywhere. The authorities seem to concentrate their efforts on known criminals not on policing the streets and it is widely accepted that corruption is rife within the police force. The real power seems to still lie with the Generals and the Armed Forces and in some areas it is to them the police really answer to and not the government.

During my stay there were two incidents of tourists dying in drug related episodes in Sihanoukville, disturbingly one of which was in the guesthouse next to mine. The poor backpacker died of an overdose in her room by injecting a hundred percent Heroin; she was not accustomed to such pure narcotics and had not cut the lethal powder with anything else. A tragic end to a holiday of a lifetime with a stupid mistake, finishing a life and depriving loved ones of a daughter, friend or sister.

In one incident I myself was lucky; I had spent the day on the beach and stayed late walking from beach bar to beach bar, it was a little daunting as everything was pitch black outside apart from the dim illumination from the bars. One of the larger bars called Insomnia turned into a nightclub later on in the evening and I happened to stay as I was enjoying myself. About 10pm I realised I was getting rather drunk so I decided to get closer to home before I was stumbling about in the sand and the dark night outside. Within minutes of leaving Insomnia I heard a series of loud pops which I totally ignored, concentrating more on my footing.

The following day I was told by Declan there had been an incident down at the beach the previous night. There had been a shooting at Insomnia; a local man who had been barred from the establishment had returned and randomly fired an automatic handgun into the bar. He had killed one man and serious injured several others, farangs included. I had missed the shootings by minutes and the popping noises I had heard were the actual gunshots. Insomnia had been closed, but I decided not to linger at the beach too late in future, the event had been too close for comfort and I thanked God that for some reason I had decided to leave when I did.

I was getting very fond of the Orchidee and was becoming rather a fixture and part of daily life there. I discovered the old woman I saw prostrate on the landing on my first day was the owner's wife; she spent most of her time there as it was the coolest part of the building and the sofa was outside their room. I just passed general short conversation with her as she was Cambodian and my Khmer did not stretch to full sentences but seemed an amiable enough lady. At the pool where two regulars I was on nodding terms with, one was a very strange French man who had very peculiar habits and the other was a very quiet petite Dutch lady that I presumed was connected in some way to the owner.

The French gentleman always had a newspaper that he borrowed from reception; he would examine it thoroughly then would walk over and pass it to me on a promise that I would return it to reception. The Phnom Penh Post was essential daily reading and I looked forward immensely to get my morning fix of Cambodian news. I was surprised that the French man spent so long perusing it as it was totally in English apart from some advertisements. It was not the general Cambodian politics or world news I was particularly interested in; it was the local news items that fascinated me and often were most unintentionally very humorous.

One of my favourite, more bizarre headline read; "Authorities Ban On Mobile Phone Use By Farmworkers," the article then went on to explain the Government's action. Due to the increase of electrical storms over Southern rural areas some peasants and farm workers had actually been struck by lightning and tragically a couple had died. These unlucky individuals had all one thing in common, they had been using mobile phones in the fields; I hoped they were not phoning for weather reports that would have been highly ironic.

Owning and using a mobile phone in South East Asia is a fraction of the cost of that in the Western World. My current Thai charge for phoning the UK using the Thai True network is less than a fifth of the robbing bastards at T-Mobile, and my brand new Nokia phone cost eight hundred baht around sixteen quid. I would like mobile phone manufacturers and operators to explain the vast differential between charges in the different world regions. Do the rich get shafted? Or do the poorer nations get subsidised? I rather think the former is the case as the true corporation seem to file very healthy annual profits. So, my surprise that the peasants of rural Cambodia all having cellular technology was tempered when I learned of the cost they were paying.

The Phnom Penh Post was becoming an enlightening inside guide of true Cambodian life and was written in a rather brusque manner just detailing facts, sometimes seemingly with no apparent consideration of the human element involved. One such report was; "Woman gets mouth blown off by Land Mine". The tragic incident was again based around a poor farm worker who when ploughing her field found her tilling obstructed by a metal object. It was a Land Mine and the unfortunate woman had no idea what the alien object was, apparently after several unsuccessful attempts of trying to destroy the offending object with a scythe and then an axe for some inexplicable reason she bit it. The bomb having enough ill treatment for one day decided to explode taking the poor woman's lower jaw with it. The article was written almost as though the incident was the fault of the ignorant peasant and I assumed this was because it was a far from rare occurrence.

It was an everyday part of life in Cambodia of old war, Ordnance being culpable for many tragic incidents and accidents. Cambodia has suffered greatly over the recent decades of turmoil and armed conflict. The Americans during the Vietnam War carpet bombed vast areas of Cambodia under the excuse that the country was harbouring Viet Kong rebels despite the fact that Cambodia was not actually at war with anybody. After that the Khmer Rouge during their cleansing used despicable methods for their extermination of life, Land Mines and Grenades being a favourite terror method. There have been attempts to clean up unexploded mines, but still vast swathes of land are affected and the simple fact is that there is not enough money to eradicate the problem.

The legacy of the American and Khmer Rouge former policies is left for all to see and is a damming example of politics gone mad led by the fanatical few. Just a quick stroll down Ochheutal Beach will highlight the ongoing and pitiful situation; many amputees are forced to beg for their very existence as the lack of hands, arms and legs prohibits their ability to manually work.

It was actually in Cambodia that the last official battle of the Vietnam War took place. In May 1975 the Americans were ousted by the Khmer Rouge and the last evacuation of South East Asia by the USA Army took place at Sihanoukville, hence the naming of Victory Hill. Ironically I was told to pronounce Sihanoukville as "See-A-Nuke- Ville" which has ominous connotations for the future of the country. It begs belief that an aggressor could attack a country in such an unrestrained way without public damnation, but in the Seventies America did so to Cambodia while the rest of the world looked on. Their world's silence is just as shameful as the physical action taken by the USA and it is a period of history that the so called great politicians of the time should be massively embarrassed about.

Throughout my stay at the Orchidee I was keeping abreast of events in Bangkok on TV and the situation seemed to be growing worse and worse. Bangkok had become almost a no go area and the British Consulate was advising all British citizens not to travel to the Thai Capital unless essential. On the 15th of May the Red Shirts had a prominent member assassinated by the authorities at the demonstration fortress in the city. He was a leader of the Ronin Black Shirts a military division of the Red Shirt movement and it led to a state of emergency being called in seventeen provinces throughout the country by the Government.

The same evening I decided to cheer myself up from the sinister goings on in Bangkok and instructed Paul to take me back to Victory Hill, this time I was successful and he actually took me somewhere that I wanted to go to. Victory Hill is even more rustic than the rest of Sihanoukville and has one particular small street or more akin to a path where most of the bars are situated. In total there could not have been more than a dozen places and most were very raunchy to say the least, Beer Bars abounded and most had girls that would escort you home for a small fine to the establishment.

I stopped at the first bar I encountered which was little more than a one room wooden shack. The owner was a burnt out ex Cockney who looked as though over the years had consumed more of his produce than any of his clientele. There were four tables, two of which were half out in the street and I took a seat at one of them. Within seconds I was joined by two American guys that seemed to know the bar very well, they politely asked if they could join me and I welcomed them to take the vacant seats.

My cold beer arrived and to my astonishment the two regulars requested two reefers, one of the men noticed my surprise and smiled at my astonishment. The Cockney proprietor did not blink or look a bit surprised by the request and went off to skin up the joints. A couple of minutes later the Cockney returned with the order together with a lighter and ashtray. I looked at the chit he placed in their Bin and a simple record was written in pencil on the bill; "J's x 2".

The two Americans just sat and smoked their Dope watching the world go past the bar whilst the Cockney later joined them with a Reefer he had rolled for himself. I had not smoked Cannabis for years, but politely took a couple of tokes to be sociable. I was fully aware of the effect alcohol now had on my body and in retrospect was stupid to join the party, but in a way wanted to test my new tolerance levels. It was an irresponsible act and one that I am not particularly proud of especially with all the hard work I had endured to actually be sitting there.

I do not know if it was my new greatly reduced threshold to such substances, but I immediately felt dizzy and knew not to try and stand. I simply sat in my chair and stared outwards not saying a word. I was unaware if the rest of the table's patrons knew of my near catatonic state but nobody seemed to care. Victory Hill was a place where you could just drop out and nobody would be the wiser or judgemental in any way whatsoever. I waited for at least half an hour for the effects to reduce and didn't touch a drop of my beer, then feeling a little more stable I went back to Chennai Rotty's for something to eat.

Whilst sitting eating my dinner a sharp gust of wind rattled the windows and I knew a storm was on its way. Outside people were closing shutters and battening down possessions, children were being ushered inside for protection against the oncoming onslaught. I took my leave instantly from the restaurant and dashed over to where some men sat astride their motorbikes in attempt to get home and beat the storm.

Only one rider was prepared to take me and soon we were speeding down the hill in the direction of Golden Lion Circle. The sky ahead of us was jet black and looking very, very ominous. I had tried to gamble against the oncoming storm as I did not want to be stuck up on Victory Hill all night, but that decision was going to prove to be one of my worst. Flashes of lightening lit up the gloom ahead of us and I realised that instead of outrunning the storm we were heading straight for it. My driver realised this also and he started to slow down.

Another cackle of brilliant white light fractured the sky followed by deafening peal of thunder right overhead. The noise was so loud that it obliterated any other sound on the road and I knew we were in the eye of the storm. Then one hundred yards in front of us a silver wall of torrential rain appeared, the motor bike's headlights illuminated huge water droplets bouncing off the tarmac forming a sort of surf of running water on the road's surface.

There was nowhere else for us to go, but straight ahead and within seconds we entered the maelstrom. The temperature dropped drastically and the cold rain lashed against my bare legs and arms stinging my flesh red. Still, the thunder boomed all around, it was like being in a bass drum during some rock concert. Disconcertingly a bolt of lightning fizzed only yards away then arced up and struck a nearby tree. My driver slowed the bike to almost walking pace as it was impossible to see through the torrent of rain, although I was getting more drenched I was glad of his prudence as the vehicle was starting to skid on the sodden road.

As we tentatively edged forward the route ahead became a little brighter as street lights started to appear out of the gloom. We had reached the outskirts of Downtown Sihanoukville and the chance of shelter. On the opposite side of the road I could just about make out some form of building and pointed it out to my driver, he turned the bike and headed across the road cautiously towards the hut. The small building was completely boarded up, but had a small awning at the front and we finally found some respite from the weather.

The storms ferocity was not abating whatsoever and the torrential rain bounced off the Tin roof above imitating a rapid machine gun as it did so. Sporadically the dark was pushed aside by silver white claws stretching out in the sky accompanied by the sound of Thor's heavy hammer blows. I looked at my driver and he was smiling back at me glad to have found this small piece of refuge. I was completely sodden and shivering from the cold, damp air. Water droplets bounced off my cheeks from my eyebrows and I do not think I have been wetter in my life, even when taking a bath. I hoped that there were not any peasants out in the fields using their phones during the tempest.

We waited patiently for about twenty minutes until the thunder and lightening had passed. There was still heavy rain and although we had shelter it was not very comfortable where we were. The problem was that although the storm had gone the rain might stay all night and this was no place to spend much longer. The driver produced a rain poncho from the scooters seat and generously offered it to me, then handed me his helmet that had a visor and took my open faced one. I was still shivering and bitterly cold so I gladly accepted the items in an attempt to get a little warmer. I was amazed at the gallantry offered to me by my taxi driver and my admiration of the Cambodian people and their hospitality was further extended.

Once again we braved the inclement weather and it took nearly thirty minutes to get to Golden Lion Circle, by then the rain had slowed to almost a drizzle and coming down from the hill the temperature had risen a little. I thanked my driver and tipped him generously as I wanted him to finish work and go home to rest. He patted my shoulder in a gesture of comradeship and waved to me as he made his way back in the same direction as we had just come.

From the Circle to my guesthouse was only a five minute walk down Tola Road past the barbecue restaurants. I was hailed by a young Cambodian standing outside Mystic pizza, I had been there a couple of times for lunch and he recognised me. By now the rain had stopped and it was still fairly early so I decided to go for a drink. The outdoor tables were all covered so I made my way to the shack at the back and saw that they made cocktails. I was astounded such a rustic place had any ingredients for such libations but soon was to be proved wrong when my Margarita arrived.

Over the next few days I became firm friends with the young Cambodian, his name was Worn and he spoke pretty good English. He had been at University in Phnom Penh, but had to return home to look after his family, his dream was to finish his education and perhaps practise medicine. His uncle owned Mystic Pizza and Worn was working there to bring much needed funds into the family home.

Mystic Pizza was added to my daily routine, normally at the end of the night when I would have a couple of Margaritas before retiring to bed. It was a strange place, one of the barbecue restaurants that were like domestic drives leading to a small garage. There was no separating fence or wall between Mystic and the restaurant adjoining and patrons, dogs, cats and rats were free to roam between the two at will. Unusually it also played background music which was ideal together with a late night cocktail, it was never loud as three quarters of the restaurant was outdoors but still it was music.

I normally frequented Mystic when most of the dining customers had left and Worn had time to sit and chat with me. I burnt some new CDs for him and in return he furnished me with complementary Margaritas, it was an amicable arrangement that both parties agreed wholeheartedly with. I felt sorry for the situation Worn was in, but is often the case in South East Asia. Children are expected to reward the parents in later life with money and assistance, the family bindings stay for a lifetime and do not disappear when the chicken has hatched and flown the coop. The situation arises primarily due to the parents ageing and no longer being capable of manual work, there are no pensions or state benefits and so the household income just ceases.

Our conversations varied from life outside Cambodia to internal family conflicts, occasionally interspersed with debates on a particular track or piece of music. It was enlightening, but humbling listening to the young Cambodian's dreams and aspirations for his future and the sincere doubts that he may never achieve any of them. Many times I would return home and realise how lucky I had been in my life. Yes I had nearly died and I had a miserable rehabilitation, but my life before and after Armageddon had been so fortunate.

Time passed so quick in my rustic haven: I was not ready to leave, but I knew there was only about a week left. Then on the 18th of May, I woke and turned the TV on to see carnage in Bangkok. The Government's patience had run out and troops were sent to clear the Red Shirts enclave and to forcibly evict the demonstrators from their barricades, statistics later showed that forty five people died during two days of armed conflict. It was fascinating news, but also sickening and a further blow to the economy of Thailand, I considered tourism would once again be rocked by the political unrest in the country and pitied the people whose lives had been devastated by the events.

Sad, but also very annoyed, I decided to cheer myself up by sitting by the pool and getting my daily fix of the Phnom Penh Post. I was not to be disappointed as a headline immediately grabbed my attention. "Women and Oxen Struck by Lightning". The article further expanded upon the headline that indeed a woman and her two oxen had been hit by a lightning bolt whilst ploughing a field.

The woman actually died, but unbelievably the article continued to celebrate the fact that luckily the two beasts of burden had survived and barely mentioned the death of the poor farmer. It highlighted the value of human life in a rural, poor economy that the two oxen were more valuable than their owner. Mind you, I did have some sympathy for the two animals that the daft bat had taken them ploughing in a storm in the first place.

That evening I was strolling down Tola Road to visit Declan at Paradise Bar when I bumped into Worn. He explained to me that he had the night off and wanted to take me sightseeing on his scooter. I readily agreed to meet him an hour later outside Mystic pizza and pottered off for a cold beer with Declan. A motor bike screeching to a halt behind me nearly made me soil my shorts and I turned to see which idiot was riding the bike. A beaming smile and then laughter greeted me from the grimy driver; it was Paul, who was in raptures of hysterics at his little prank. I pretended to punch my attendant chauffeur which drove him into a further state of giggles. I then went on to try and explain I did not need his services that evening; he was most apologetic thinking that it was because of his joke, but I assured him that was not the case. He drove off tooting the scooters horn and laughing as he did so. *Really!* That was not the behaviour expected of an adult man!

My guided tour by Worn was extensive as the young man was proud to show me his home town and I was taken to places well off the beaten track. As the evening progressed I suggested we stop for food as I wanted to reward Worn's generosity with a meal. We drove to the Night Market close to the Golden Lion Circle; an area that is packed with small stalls and open air restaurants offering Khmer cuisine. I was contemplating something grander as a treat for my guide, but Worn seemed more comfortable in these surroundings and I did not want to embarrass him in any way.

Strolling around the market the familiar, but unique sounds and aromas of South East Asian street dining attacked my senses.

Worn seemed very familiar with the place and we weaved our way through crammed eateries and eventually stopped at a small restaurant that had a couple of tables. There was a high counter with a cook behind who was slaving over a hot Wok, stirring the pan's ingredients with long chop sticks and occasionally tossing the mixture into the air. Behind him was a large White Board advertising the restaurant's fare: there were no menus to choose from, only what was scribbled on the sign.

According to Worn the little restaurant was famous for its rice and noodle dishes and was one of his favourite places to eat. He seemed to know the cook well and had a short conversation with him whilst we sat at our table. Worn informed me that he had taken the liberty of ordering a selection of dishes for us both and hoped I did not object to his presumption. He had ordered several local specialities for my titillation and young girl brought it immediately to our table.

Dining in Asia does not have the same formal etiquette as in western restaurants; it does not have the same structure of a starter being followed by a main dish and then a pudding. Dishes will arrive at your table in order of when they are cooked, so Soup may arrive alongside or after a fish or meat dish. There are no particular courses and several bowls of food will be placed on the table at the same time for all participants of the meal to share. Because of the ambient temperature the food does not get cold and so the system works perfectly.

I adored some of the strange exotic food I consumed, I recognised some of the ingredients, but some items especially fish and vegetables I had never eaten before in my life. I looked up at the board trying to match up the advertised dishes with the bowls on the table. Then I spotted another example of the Norwegian translator's handiwork: "Fried Squirt with Steamed Rile". I started to giggle again, but I could not explain the humorous phrase to Worn who was a little startled by my apparent short bout of madness.

The cost of the food was almost shameful as it was so pitifully cheap and I almost felt embarrassed paying the bill. Worn on the other hand was delighted with the extravagant banquet and I considered that he probably did not often have the opportunity to dine like that. We strolled around the market after dinner just to let the food settle a little and I selected one or two T-shirts to add to my collection. I pointed to the small road running parallel to the market, I had noticed it before and Worn told me it was locally known as Karaoke Street. Declan had told me about it before with a knowing wink, but I had never been down it as it did not seem to go anywhere.

Worn suggested that we could go and have a look on his motorbike. I readily agreed and we went back to the scooter and headed up Karaoke Street. It was a narrow road unlit by street lighting, illuminated only by the bars and shacks that lined it; most of the road was covered in a red hue emanating from the doorways of the establishments. The surface changed from concrete to red clay and between each building was jungle, it was a lawless place and the Karaoke bars were little more than brothels.

As we progressed up the street we were going further into unchartered territory and the bars became more sporadic, little more that wooden huts surrounded by thick vegetation. Scantily clad women sat outside the huts calling loudly at the motor bike and the two potential clients. I did not want to imagine what sexual diseases could be contracted within those dimly lit doorways; it did not seem a place familiar with sexual health practises. Not wanting to explore any further that night we returned to Mystic Pizza for a night cap and to listen to a little music.

My last day in Sihanoukville was tempered with sadness; I was excited about the trip to Vietnam, but sad to leave, Sihanoukville was a place lost in time and went about its business in a leisurely and unashamed manner. Its residents were poor, but that did not stop them having a smile on their face and facing each day with humour and courage.

I spent the day as normal, but in the evening made a point of saying farewell to all the people who had become friends in my time there. Worn had instructed his uncle to prepare a special Khmer meal for me so before hand I went out to seek Paul and Declan. Paul for some reason was nowhere to be seen, he knew this was my last night so I presumed he had work to do but I was sad I was not able to say goodbye to him and give him his present of the money.

Declan on the other hand was at residence in Paradise Bar and as usual was holding court at the bar. He could not believe that I was trusting Mr Seng to return in the morning after such a long time, but something inside me knew it would be okay. Two of his bar girls pestered me to take them back to the Guest House as it would be the last opportunity for them to try and get some money off me. I laughed and as always declined their offer; something never seemed quite right about the proposed contract.

After a few aperitifs, I walked down to the beach and had a couple more drinks with some friends there and then made my way to Mystic Pizza. Worn was at the restaurants entrance with his uncle and I was ushered to take my place at my regular table. I had brought some more CDs for Worn as a present, but decided to keep them in by bag for later. The Khmer meal prepared for me was superb the highlight being a sort of sweet, creamy fish curry that was quite difficult to eat as the fish was on the bone but the flavour was sublime.

Worn, his uncle and the other three members of the staff joined me after work for drinks and photographs and the Angkor Beer flowed quite freely. His uncle was adamant that we shared the bill for all the drinks and would not take no from me whatsoever. The evening concluded with an exchange of presents; I handed over some music I knew Worn was fond of whilst his uncle presented me with an official Mystic pizza shirt worn by the staff. I exchanged email addresses with Worn and as I left the young Cambodian embraced me tightly for some moments. I could see tears welling up in his dark brown eyes and knew it was time for me to depart so as no embarrassment would come to the young man. Walking back to the Orchidee, I felt moisture in my own eyes and wondered had I broken the embrace for my benefit.

The following morning I checked out and sat in the restaurant of the Orchidee, it was half past nine and I wondered if Mr Seng would actually arrive in thirty minutes. I ordered some coffee and I spotted a familiar figure astride a scooter driving through the gates of the Guesthouse. It was Paul with his trademark grin lighting up his rugged face. I dashed over and briefly hugged my friend as he just laughed and patted my back. I handed him thirty dollars and the smile left his face and perturbed expression replaced it. Had I fucked up? Was I embarrassing my friend with such a gesture?

I pressed the money firmly into his palm saying, "Thanks for everything, I want you to please accept this present." I do not think he understood me, but he eventually put the money in his pocket and the smile returned. I never did know if Paul understood me or not, but if that was the case how did he know the day and time of my departure? We hugged again then revving up the old scooter my friend departed through the gates and down Tola Road and I knew that would be the last time I ever saw him.

Exactly at 10am a White Toyota Camry arrived. Mr Seng had remembered our appointment and had validated my trust in him. There was something about the man that I just knew I could rely upon him and to be honest I had not been let down often in Cambodia. Politely refusing my offer of a coffee and without delay my luggage was placed in the boot of the car and I left the Orchidee with Mr Seng. There were no boxes in the back of the vehicle and just as I was considering Mr Seng had missed out on an opportunity he surprised me by driving to an area of downtown Sihanoukville I was not familiar with and stopped outside a small Guesthouse.

Waiting outside was quite an attractive Cambodian lady in her mid thirties with a small case on the floor by her feet. Mr Seng got out of the car and put the ladies luggage in the boot whilst the lady climbed into the back seat. Was this Mr Seng's mistress? She was too young to be his wife, or perhaps she was his daughter? Had he stayed the night also? It would have explained his arrival at the Orchidee at exactly 10am.

I was introduced to our new travelling companion, but she did not speak any English so the return journey to Phnom Penh was mostly in silence apart from Mr Seng's bloody music. We did not stop for lunch and Mr Seng drove fairly fast the whole journey which was good in respect that I would be in the capital early, but not on account of the hair raising incidents we encountered.

Just as we arrived on the outskirts of Phnom Penh near the airport Mr Seng stopped the car and the mystery passenger alighted. There was no embrace; in fact, Mr Seng did not get out of the vehicle so my supposition of a clandestine tryst had been totally wrong. Mr Seng had just been doing what he did on our first journey, that was getting the most income he could from his exertions.

I spent my last night in Phnom Penh fairly quietly returning to the same Indian restaurant and visiting my friends in Freebird for a couple of goodbye drinks. I went to bed early as I had a 6.30am taxi booked to take me to the airport for my flight to Vietnam the following morning; although I found it difficult to sleep that night due to the excitement of expectation of what was to come.

Chapter Thirteen

VIETNAM

Queuing at the Vietnam Airways check-in desk for my flight to Ho Chi Minh was a bizarre occurrence as I was surrounded by ochre coloured robed monks. It must have been the Red Eye Buddha Express flight as I was only one of a handful of lay people standing aside whilst what seemed to be a whole monastery was processed first. I presumed there was a religious festival taking place in Ho Chi Minh City otherwise the spiritual brothers even enjoyed their vacations together.

Receiving my boarding card I was then invited to step over to purchase my exit stamp at another booth. Without the stamp I could not clear Cambodian immigration and would not be allowed to travel to Vietnam; luckily I still had American Dollars and paid the leaving fine.

A certain feeling of heavenly security filled me as I took my seat on the plane, surely this must have been the safest flight I had ever been on with so many prayers being offered up to celestial bodies by so many of the passengers. I have never heard of a Buddhist terrorist so I did not have to do my normal passenger check as I boarded the plane and sat down contentedly.

As the plane rose into the air upon takeoff and flew east over Phnom Penh I reflected upon my time spent in Cambodia and the friends I had met there. I had not known what to expect from the country and its inhabitants and was totally overwhelmed by what I had experienced. Cambodia is a poor country and facilities and amenities reflect upon that, but it is because of that fact that it had been so alluring and addictive.

The Cambodian people are the heroes, living their lives as best they can with the cards they had been dealt. The country was sometimes dirty, sometimes dangerous and sometimes very, very confusing, but above all that it was welcoming, generous and often highly amusing. I would remember my stay for all my life with great affection and I promised myself I would return one day.

The plane followed an easterly course as Vietnam is the most easterly point of South East Asia and beyond that was the South China Sea. I was more aware of the turbulent recent history of the country as opposed to Cambodia and I think I had more of an idea of what to expect. I had processed my Visa on Arrival on line, paid my fee and had printed off a letter of approval so I did not envisage a lengthy delay at Long Thanh Airport.

The Arrivals Hall seemed fairly quiet as I stood in line at the Immigration clearance queue. After about ten minutes I handed over my Passport, the completed immigration form and the letter of approval. The official stared blankly at me and off handily waved me away from his counter and out of the queue. I had no idea what I should do next, but stood and gathered my thoughts, obviously something was wrong with my documentation but I did not know what.

I looked around the Arrivals Hall and noticed a small queue of non Asian's in the left hand corner at a large glass window. Above the window was a sign: "Visa on Arrival". There had been no instructions when I had processed my documents on line that I would have to undertake further administration but it was obvious I did. I made my way over and joined the back of the queue to wait. The line was moving fast and I presumed it was because everybody had submitted their applications previously.

Around twenty minutes later, I faced my second Vietnamese Immigration Officer and handed over all my documentation. It was blatantly obvious I was not attempting to try and enter another Thailand or Cambodia. These officers were far more sterile, officious and ominously gone was any hint of welcome. My papers were taken from me and the next applicant was curtly beckoned,

I turned and recognised faces previously in the same queue were sitting down patiently waiting.

I just sat and waited whilst Vietnamese bureaucracy took an eternity to process my documents. It was close to one hour until my name was barked out by a uniformed figure who then demanded a further payment for my completed visa. Once again I was glad that I had enough US Dollars for payment, as I don't think Pounds Sterling would have been accepted.

Finally, I cleared immigration and then had the task of trying to retrieve my luggage as the baggage carousel had long since stopped revolving. I eventually found my bag in the Lost Luggage area and attempted to find the car I had booked from the hotel. After such a long delay I did not expect the driver to be still waiting, but unexpectedly a man was wearily holding a sign with my name printed on the card.

The gentleman spoke no English, but simply said, "Lan Lan Hotel?" I nodded and he turned and walked away. I took it as a gesture as one that I should follow and wheeled my bag through the crowd closely behind the man. We left the terminal building and I sarcastically muttered "Good morning, Vietnam," sounding nothing remotely like Adrian Cronauer from the film of the same name. I must have been quite audible though, as another visiting farang tourist looked at me and smiled with a sympathetic look on his face.

Saigon or Ho Chi Minh City Airport had not endeared itself to me one iota and I hoped it did not have portents of things to come. The taxi sped out of the airport's car park and within fifteen or twenty minutes we hit the outskirts of Saigon. The city was renamed Ho Chi Minh in 1976 after the war and the unification of the country, I continue to use the name Saigon purely as it is easier to pronounce. Saigon is the largest city in Vietnam and is the home of nearly nine million people of a huge country of over ninety million inhabitants.

Greenstreet and Back

I had booked a small hotel in District One, the most diverse and multicultural area of Saigon. According to my surfing it was the place to be and was ideal for tourists with many attractions and amenities close by. As the car penetrated the suburbs and started to enter the city the roads became nothing short of chaotic. The streets were thronged with thousands of people all attempting to navigate around the city in their chosen method of transport.

For most that was either by motorbike or bicycle, I have never seen so many two wheeled modes of transport in one place in my entire life. I read somewhere that there are over three and a half million motor bikes in Saigon and I suppose you could double that number for the pedal power version. It was incredible, the noise alone of the high pitched two stroke engines was deafening and I wondered what it would be like outside of the confines of the Taxi.

The types of motorbikes varied from the rather rare, posh Japanese Scooters to the more common Chinese and Russian ancient rust buckets. They made Paul's bike in Sihanoukville look like a veritable racing Ducati and I considered all the exotic places my old companion could travel to if he really did have a big touring bike like a Ducati, he would scare the shit out of some of his fares depositing them two hundred miles from their requested destinations.

The wider roads of the outskirts narrowed as we closed in to my hotel, the streets were now becoming almost impassable as the car slowed to a walking pace hindered by tourist Rickshaw's and street traders hand pulled carts. If I had of known where I was going I would have got out and walked, but I also felt very tired and a little sick, I just put that down to the very early morning departure.

We eventually pulled up at the very inauspicious looking Lan Lan 1 Hotel, the pavement was bustling with activity as I struggled through with my luggage to the entrance of the hotel. Ascending four or five steps I entered a very small foyer with a tiny reception desk. It took seconds to check in and soon I was sitting on the edge of my bed in my hotel room. The room was clean and functional and would suffice for my three days stay in Saigon before I moved on again. But even up on the eighth floor the noise from the street below was loud and penetrating and I hoped it would subside somewhat later in the evening when I retired.

I still was not feeling well and seemed to be weak and tired. I had taken my medicine that morning as usual and did not have a hangover so I was puzzled at my health. Still, the alluring temptation of exploration was too strong for me to take a rest, so I freshened up a little, changed into shorts and decided to take a little walk. I had not realised in the taxi how warm the temperature was and considered walking through the packed crowds was not a good idea. There was a man across the road sitting on a Rickshaw waving to me to gain my attention.

The impulse took me and I agreed a fare of fifteen dollars for a one hour tourist excursion. The official currency of Vietnam is the Dong, but as in Cambodia the US Dollar is widely accepted and in many places preferred. I felt there was something rather immoral engaging what seemed to me was an octogenarian grandfather to pedal me around in the midday sun for an hour, but he seemed more than content with the arrangement.

My driver could speak passable tourist English and he insisted that I placed my shoulder bag and camera on the floor of the Rickshaw as he warned me of the danger of theft which was apparently a common occurrence. My God, did he not realise I was from Liverpool? A place some southerners, my brother included, considered to be more dangerous than 1920's Chicago. The vehicle weaved its way out from the narrow street onto a wide road where a car drew alongside the Rickshaw.

The back window of the car wound down and a rather chubby faced Vietnamese man wearing sunglasses called out to me. My driver shouted something in his native tongue at the man and then fixed his stare directly at the road ahead. The man in the car was now shouting at my driver as the car ominously crawled abreast of us, still my driver looked straight ahead totally ignoring the man. The man in the car was getting more irate and was now shouting and gesticulating very animatedly at the Rickshaw driver.

Suddenly we came to a halt at some traffic lights and the car pulled up beside us, the rear door of the car opened and the leg of the man in the back appeared. My driver did not wait a second and we beetled through the red light into a melee of traffic crossing our path. Horns and shouts were directed at our reckless display, but somehow my driver avoided the obstacles and hazards and at a snail's pace we made our getaway.

The first street we encountered on our left we turned and then subsequently turned left and left again into a tiny cobbled alley flanked by squat wooden buildings. There my exhausted driver stopped and rested while we waited for any signs of pursuit. A couple of minutes passed and there was no sign of the car or the chubby faced man, we both breathed a sigh of relief; my driver's was far heavier than mine. The aged driver explained that the other man in the car was mafia and in some way my driver had disrespected him by defending me, who was the intended target of some sort of scam. I thanked my driver profusely for protecting me; he shook his head and then muttered something derogatory about Hanoi.

Hanoi was the former capital of North Vietnam and is about one thousand miles away. When the Communists took control of the whole country in 1975 they renamed Saigon as Ho Chi Minh City and Hanoi became the capital of the new unified country. But it was obvious there were still some old cultural and political disputes lingering between former foes. The North / South divide in the UK has economic and regional differences in a country that has not been at war with itself for centuries, so I could imagine the problems Vietnam must still face.

After resting we continued our sightseeing trip and we pedalled our way to the War Remnants Museum. It is a place that celebrates the victory of the North Vietnamese over their brothers in the South, but more so over the United States. It is interesting on so many levels the first being the complete different political slant the epic story is told and secondly listening to another side's propaganda is refreshing. It is quite cleverly achieved, as it is not just anti capitalist rhetoric about the invading superpower's eventual rout and defeat by a small, simple peasant country. It is achieved by laying out indisputable facts, figures and dates of events that actually happened.

The first part of the museum is in an open air courtyard and houses the captured or discarded American hardware taken by the National Liberation Front aka North Vietnamese Army. Here planes, helicopters, tanks, artillery, Jeeps, jets and all other manner of military paraphernalia is displayed. Perhaps it is the helicopter that brings back the most striking memories of the American part in the Vietnam War. Often depicted as the seventh cavalry in movies, swooping into action valiantly strafing Viet Cong soldiers whilst heroic Wagnerian music applauds the destruction.

Whilst the display of huge American war machines is impressive and you can admire the actual ordnance on a pure mechanical basis it is inside the museum that the story of the Vietnam War becomes harrowing in the extreme. Here the account of war in all its ugliness unfolds, relayed primarily by photographs and statistics for the visitor to digest. Yes, there is a slight slant of Communist Propaganda, but this is tempered by also highlighting the American losses and casualties alongside Viet Cong.

For me the most harrowing part of the museum was the room dedicated to the chemical warfare weapons the Americans used in the conflict. Agent Orange was one such chemical, sounding suspiciously like a character from a *Get Smart* spoof, the toxic substance was deadly. Its use was sanctioned in 1961 by the Kennedy administration and was totally contrary to the International Rules of Warfare at the time. The rationale behind carpet bombing vast areas of cropland was to deprive the Viet Cong of food and shelter.

The reality of the policy was that thousands of innocent non combatants were killed, maimed or worse; hideously deformed. The photographs of infants and children are the most distressing and these pictures are the most damming condemnation of war I have ever experienced. The gallery is definitely not for the faint hearted, but it is somewhere that gung-ho warmongers should be forced to sit for hours each day to reflect on their violent convictions.

I did not know if it was the affect the museum was having upon me, but I was feeling a lot worse now. I was perspiring and struggling to walk, I knew I had to get back to the hotel and fast. My Rickshaw driver was sympathetic to my plight and he pedalled furiously to get me back as fast as he could. Arriving at the hotel I struggled to get down from the Rickshaw and almost collapsed in the hotel lobby. I was helped to my room by a porter and flopped onto the bed. My God, what the Hell was wrong with me?

My temperature was alternating from sweating hot to bone-chilling cold that I shivered. I knew I had some sort of virus, but I did not know what and was very concerned. I struggled to get under the duvet as I seemed to have no strength whatsoever, but I knew I needed rest. I was booked to stay two nights at the hotel before I was to move on but if the illness got worse I would have to go to hospital. My attitude to doctors and hospitals had completely reversed now, if I suspected anything wrong I would immediately seek attention. With my medical history I knew now I could not afford to fuck about with any delays.

The fever did not abate that evening, but I did manage some much needed sleep during the night. In the morning my bed was sodden with sweat and I hoped the room maid did not think I had an accident during the night. It was still early in the morning, but I could not stay and lie in the damp confines of the sheets, so I decided to try and find a pharmacy to get something to bring my temperature down.

When I returned my room had been cleaned and the linen changed so I took my medicine and returned to bed. I was still exhausted and frail and immediately as my head hit the pillow I crashed out. Waking around four hours later I suddenly found the immediate urge to go to the bathroom. I almost ran to the toilet and not to be too graphic my bottom exploded. I was glad that I sleep naked as I don't think I would have had time to get any pyjama bottoms or underwear off in time. Although my experience in the lavatory was not particularly pleasant I was relieved that I now knew what was wrong with me; I had a chronic case of diarrhoea. I thought back to when and what I had last eaten and I was surprised that I had my last meal in Phnom Penh and it had been at the little Indian restaurant near Freebird Bar. It was ironic really, of all the dodgy places I had eaten in Thailand and Cambodia with no ill effects I now had a dose of Delhi Belly from a pucker Indian Restaurant.

The remainder of the day I spent to and from the bathroom until there was nothing left inside me literally to come out. To quote Del, a friend of mine from Liverpool, my bum felt like "The start of Bonanza". This graphic description is based upon the opening credits of the hit TV show of the 60s. A map of the Ponderosa suddenly bursts into flames from behind starting right into the centre; Del had translated this devastation as arse cheeks singed by the fire between.

By the time evening arrived I was feeling weary and sore but a little stronger. I had drunk litres of water to try and dilute the bug and was still running to the toilet, this time to pee. I figured that a little air and something light to eat would be appropriate, but I would not wander too far as I might have to seek a bathroom in a hurry.

The area around the hotel was busy, a bustling hive of activity with many tourists and locals sampling Saigon's nightlife in the city centre. I still felt dehydrated from all the fluid I had deposited so sat outside a corner bar and ordered a beer. An argument erupted on the street nearby with a huge black American man confronting a Vietnamese motorbike taxi driver over a disputed fare. The American was adamant that he had been ripped off but soon found himself surrounded by a crowd of local drivers. The situation seemed to be explosive until the American backed down and paid the inflated price.

My beer arrived and the waiter seemed to take no notice of the disturbance and I presumed that the scene must have been a common occurrence in Saigon. There seemed to be an edge to the city that I had previously not experienced in South East Asia. I had been to places that were very dangerous and serious confrontations had taken place but here in Vietnam there seemed to be more people on the make and ready to rip people off, especially tourists.

I sipped at my beer slowly digesting life around; still fascinated by the number of two wheeled vehicles cramming the streets. The noise of the city was getting louder as the night time establishments were cranking up their volume in an attempt to lure passing trade. Parties of revellers were sitting at street bars and cafes starting their evening's entertainment or having just finished work. The bars and cafés were exactly as I had imagined them from the old war films; it could have been Paris I was in apart from the noise and the bicycles.

My hunger got the better of me and I strolled around the streets in search of something I could eat that I would be able to keep inside me for more than a fleeting moment. I saw in many small Vietnamese eateries signs for "Pho" which I had heard is almost the National dish of Vietnam. It is a nourishing Noodle Soup that rare slivers of beef are dropped into to cook. I decided to try my luck and entered a tiny restaurant / shop with no more than four tables.

The restaurant only served Pho, pronounced "Fir", so I estimated the chef must be pretty good at cooking the dish if it was the only thing he had to perfect. There were some variations of the soup you could order mostly on the type of meat or even fish you desired. When the stock arrived at the table it was boiling hot in order to cook the raw ingredients and it came with a DIY plate of accompaniments. You could add as much or as little of the proffered chillies, bean sprouts, lime, fresh herbs or meat as you wanted and therefore create and personalise your own recipe.

It was perfect for my needs, but it seemed a trifle odd eating a steaming hot bowl of soup in such tropical temperatures. The shop was not air conditioned and the only cool air was by way of the opened front of the building and the ceiling fan. However, the meal was so cheap the owner probably could not afford to run expensive air conditioning units and after living for so long in this part of the world I was accustomed to the climate.

I scoffed every last bit of the delicious meal and was seriously considering another bowl when I developed stomach cramps and had ominous rumblings in my tummy. I just about made it back to the hotel when I experienced another body explosion emanating from my nether region. I almost passed out on the toilet with the relief of depositing my just consumed dinner and knew I had to be more cautious for the following few days. Sleep would not come at all that night as I had already rested so much, but also because of the racket from the rooftop nightclub over the road. I watched some TV and attended to my email and decided to check out early so I could start the next leg of my journey early.

Whilst I had been in Cambodia I had decided that my trip to Vietnam should include Saigon, as I was nearing the end of my Asian Extravaganza I should also get some sun by way of a beach resort. I had studied the map for the nearest place to Saigon I could achieve this without too much travel and according to the Web it seemed the closest place was Vung Tao. It did not seem to receive many rave reports on my Web searches, only that it was a town that people from Saigon would spend the weekend. I could get there by way of a ferry that only took an hour and a half.

At reception I was told to be cautious about hailing a taxi in Saigon and that they would arrange one to take me to the ferry terminal at Bang Dang Pier at the harbour front. Apparently, many of the taxis, especially the white, ones commonly con tourists over fares. They refuse to use the meter offering an agreed mutual price for their service. However, when finally trying to settle after the ride the previously agreed price is then vehemently disputed. If the passenger does not pay the new inflated price then he is taken away and dumped in a less than salubrious part of the city or worse. Such taxis are famous around tourist locations such as the War Remnants Museum, The Reunification Palace and the Ben Thanh Market.

My taxi was fine and I paid the very reasonable fare for my journey to the harbour and ferry terminal. Two ferry companies offer a service to Vung Tau; Greenlines and Vina Express. Confusingly they both operate from the same terminal and use identical crafts with similar fares. The journey takes you away from Saigon down the Mekong River into the Delta then out into the South China Sea where the boat hugs the coastline eventually arriving at Vung Tao. I walked to the first counter I came to and paid Greenlines for a return ticket which cost about twenty dollars.

The ferry terminal was quite clean and even at that time in the morning was bustling with people. Some were passengers patiently waiting, but there seemed to be many other people milling around looking for some sort of job or task to perform for payment. I looked at the water out in front of the terminal and was surprised how choppy and unsettled the Mekong was. My attention was then drawn to the two crafts moored at the water's edge. They were bobbing up and down with the current and I perceived a rough passage ahead. The boats both companies use are Old Russian

Hydrofoils and are rusty, tatty and aged crafts that looked just about ready for the Breakers' yard. I was not looking forward to this trip whatsoever and I nervously sat waiting for my boat to arrive.

A Greenlines boat then appeared on the horizon and sped towards the terminal with its bow high up out of the water resting on two giant skis. It was quite a small, narrow craft disturbing the water at its fast passage. White foamy water encircled the Skis as they pushed through the waves and the boat bounced around seemingly above the undulating Mekong.

As the boat neared the terminal it slowed and came down off its skis to rest in the water. The noise of the turbines drowned out everything else in the terminal building as the Hydroplane manoeuvred into its berth. I got out of my seat and went to see how and where the passengers disembarked from the bobbing vessel. Standing on the quayside staring at the murky water below I saw there was a series of steep stone steps descending to small floating wooden platforms. One of which was attached to the newly arrived ferry by a treacherous moving gangway. There was no possible way I would be capable of carrying my own luggage down all those obstacles on to the boat, I would have to find some sort of assistance.

The alighting passengers skirted the outside of the building whilst an announcement was made stating the imminent departure of the next sailing. The terminal became alive with people jostling for position at the barrier, I remained where I was, I had paid for first class and had a seat allocated so there was no rush to join the horde.

The chain was moved aside and the passengers raced down the pier to the steps leading down to the gangway. A group of men were hovering around the barrier and I accosted one and took the chance he was looking for a quick buck and not a visiting dignitary or somebody important. I took two dollars out of my pocket pointed to my suitcase and then the boat; the man understood my meaning immediately and nodded his acceptance of the proposed deal.

I was glad I had purloined his assistance as I had great difficulty managing just to get down the steep shallow steps and across the undulating wooden gangway myself, it would have been impossible with my bags. My assistant plonked my case on the deck of the boat as he was not allowed any further, but thankfully a deck hand took it aboard for me after evaluating my unsteady gait. First class was at the prow of the vessel and I was quite surprised how narrow it actually was, it probably had seating for around twenty people in dated airline type seats. The cabin was surrounded by small portholes with rusty metal frames and grubby, stained curtains hung down from plastic washing line cable. If this was first class then I was glad I was not travelling cattle class at the rear of the boat.

Loading of the ferry only took a matter of minutes and then the diesel engines started and the ferry inched away from its berth. The boat shook and vibrated violently as the turbines kicked into life and slowly the craft moved into the Mekong to join the rest of the river traffic. About ten minutes of gingerly navigating through the local harbour boats the engines roared and the boat rose up in the water on its skis. We were now in the centre of the river travelling at maximum speed heading towards open sea.

The river was busy as we departed Saigon and as the boat got further away from the harbour larger cargo ships were anchored in deeper water, either waiting to be unloaded or to begin their long voyages. As we progressed down the Mekong further into the Delta the scenery took on a familiar "War Film" look to it, on either bank was thick green jungle with occasional small tributaries flowing into the main river. I imagined Martin Sheen in his Gunboat heading off with his misfit crew in search of the deranged Marlon Brando right down one of the tributaries.

After a while the scenery was unchanging so I settled back into my seat and rummaged around my bag for my iPod. I knew what the perfect accompanying music was for my epic Mekong Boat trip; it had to be "The Poet" by Bobby Womack. Possibly my favourite LP of all time and the gritty, soulful and slightly dated raw voice of Womack seemed somehow to match the tropical wilderness passing me by either side.

As we headed out of the Delta into the South China Sea the water became rougher and the boat started to pitch more in its passage. The constant drone of the engines almost drowned out Mr Womack, but like the great Soul Survivor that he is not even Greenlines' clapped out old Russian hydrofoil boat could achieve that. Then on cue almost exactly to the time table I saw the intended destination ahead; Vung Tao. I must admit from where I was sitting it did not particularly look anything special, but sometimes looks can deceive and in some of Bangkok's bars that is truly the case.

As the craft neared the harbour it slowed and came down from the lofty position sitting high up on its skis. I could clearly see the terminal and the mooring positions outside and was shocked to see that the water was even more turbulent than Saigon; disembarkation was going to be a challenge to say the least. Because the swell was so severe the Captain had quite a problem parking the boat, but after a couple of attempts by way of gently nudging other moored crafts the ferry was finally secured at its berth.

Waiting until every passenger had alighted I managed to drag my case to the outside of the boat and was lucky to enlist assistance from one of the crew to carry my case to the level ground of the quayside. All I had to do then was to find a taxi to take me to the hotel.

I had chosen the Cap Saint Jacques Hotel from the Agoda Website, partly because of cost, but also for the amenities it offered. It had a swimming pool, internet access, restaurant and even a nightclub. The taxi journey was quite uneventful with not much to see apart from a few tacky bars opposite the ferry terminal; the journey took around a quarter of an hour mostly uphill and soon I was checking into yet another hotel. I had booked two weeks at the Cap Saint Jacques for my final relaxing fortnight that would leave me two days in Bangkok before I went home.

My passport was retained by reception, it is something I hate. Some hotels insist on holding a guest's identification during the length of their stay, but I could never see the reasoning behind doing so. If the receptionist was good at the job then all personal details would be double checked, ratified and recorded and if necessary photo copies taken. Without my passport for identification I was a nobody and the security and protection of being a British citizen are taken away. To be honest it is normally smaller and cheaper hotels that do this, but I had already paid in full for my room so apart from me setting fire to the bloody place what were they worried about?

The hotel was big and reception was quite large with a couple of small shops in the foyer. My room was on one of the upper floors, it was spacious with a double bed and a couple of chairs to relax in, it also had TV, Wi-Fi, Mini Bar and AC which was essential especially at night. I was more than happy with the accommodation and as it was just 11am I was eager to find the pool and enjoy the sun.

Donning my shorts and filling my shoulder bag with sunbathing paraphernalia I went in search of the swimming pool. I had noticed a sign when I arrived and knew it was on the ground floor somewhere. Stepping out of the lift I was greeted by a group of residents who rudely stopped and gaped at me, I did not know what their problem was as my flies were not down and I was not slavering from the mouth so I ignored the rude fuckers and pushed through them.

I spotted the same sign and followed the direction it pointed to; I went down a corridor and turned left when I saw another sign.

Eventually I came to two opaque doors with a larger sign above them depicting a cartoon man diving into three, blue wavy lines. The international acceptance of such a pathetic graphic to describe the existence of a swimming pool always bugs me, it is almost as if some bloke in Luton had scribbled down a drawing to hand to his printers when it blew out of his hand and landed on some oaf's desk at Saatchi & Saatchi; it is that pathetic!

The doors were locked, I could not budge them at all, even when I pushed and pulled at both of them. I looked at some notice on the wall that was in Vietnamese and French and deduced it was the opening times for the pool. 8am - 7pm, well being that it was only 11.30 the fucking thing should be bloody open. Not a soul was around either staff or guest so I had to trudge back to reception to enquire if there was another entrance. None of the reception staff spoke English so I had to do my interpretation of the man diving into the three wavy lines; after all it was an international symbol so they must understand that.

My impression of the little man in the Mouse Trap board game diving off his perch into the red bowl did not achieved the desired affect, blank faces stared back at me. I thought to myself, *This lot must be crap at Christmas when the after dinner charades games start,* so I pointed to the sign and shouted "Kaput!" Now I knew that was the international word for fucked so hopefully my verbal description as opposed to my physical one would work. But I still had no joy; it was going to be a difficult two weeks if my first morning gave any indications of future things to come.

One of the receptionists came from behind the desk and ushered me to a chair by the main entrance. I dutifully sat down and waited for the outcome; did she think I had gone mad? Or was she worried that my antics had tired me out? I sat patiently as guests, staff and visitors trooped in and out of the hotel all staring at me as they did so. I was getting royally pissed off on two counts;

firstly I was missing the sunshine and secondly I still could not figure out why everybody was staring at me.

After a considerable time posing as the hotel's new Alien Guest Reclined statue, a man dressed in white shorts, white shirt, long white socks and wearing tennis shoes made his way over to me. He looked as though he was fresh from filming a Persil advert but the signs were encouraging. Amazingly he actually spoke one or two words of English so I did not have to repeat my Mouse Trap impression as he understood I wished to go to the swimming pool.

We made our way back down the corridor and to the opaque doors. The man then fished around in his pockets and produced a key that unlocked the doors. Opening them for me I went through into bright sunlight to find the elusive swimming pool. It was quite satisfactory, fairly large with twenty or so loungers encircling the kidney shaped pool, all the loungers were in the sun so I sat down on the first one I came to and took my shirt off.

Then unbelievably the man in white sat down on the floor not five feet from me, nobody else was present at the time. It was quite unnerving lying back on the lounger sunbathing in my trunks whilst the pool attendant, fully dressed, sat watching me. After about an hour I tried to explain to him that if he was a lifeguard he need not worry as I was not going to go into the water. From what I could gather from his reply he was not a lifeguard, but was responsible for the key, and had to stay whilst the doors were open. Did the hotel only have one key? If so, what sort of hotel was it? Could I go and get another key cut to help out?

Another hour passed and the man finally moved and spoke to me, it was time for his lunch break could I leave and return in an hour. Grumbling I gathered my things and dressed knowing that I could not put up with this crap for two weeks, although it was quite nice having my own personal sunbathing chaperone I wanted to come and go as I pleased. Did none of the other patrons of the hotel ever take exercise? Did nobody else use the pool? I found it quite incredulous that this was the case but it seemed to be so.

I now had a bit of a strop on and decided to find an alternative place to spend my daytimes. I left the hotel and crossed the wide deserted road to the beach, a couple of local kids stopped their game to watch me make my way and again I checked myself to see the attraction. The beach was deserted with rows and rows of deck chairs neatly placed side by side in the sand waiting for somebody to come and sit. I did not fancy a repeat of a personal escort so opted against the beach and strolled along the promenade seeking something else.

There was an odd assortment of buildings dotted around the pavement alongside the beach, most were closed down or very tatty old restaurants, public lavatories or shops. The whole beach area had a very dated feel to it as though it had past its former glory as a resort and now was sadly in decline. There is nothing more soul destroying and desolate than a beach resort in winter or one that has lost its attraction and custom. Back Beach as this was called seemed to be heading for the latter as few patrons seemed to be around.

I eventually stumbled upon an old outdoor lido, there were signs of life there with children playing in the pool and parents sitting and watching their offspring enjoy innocent fun. The Lido was free to use, but the dilapidated condition of the old wooden loungers reflected this; many of them had slats missing and nails sticking out of broken pieces of timber, but they would suffice. There were no cushions available so sunbathing would be a rather uncomfortable pastime, but I would not be deterred by that. Also there was a little kiosk where bottles of water or beer could be purchased so I decided I would decamp and spend my daylight hours in the future at the Lido.

Selecting one of the better loungers I placed my towel over the dirty chair and lay back listening to some music. The warm sun caressed my rather tired body and Al Green sent me to a contented heaven as I stretched out and deeply relaxed. After some time I stirred from my cocooned solitude and opened my eyes only to find three little faces inches away from me.

They were three Vietnamese children investigating the strange foreign man prostrate in their Lido. I was a little startled at first and looked around to see that once again I was the only farang present, on reflection I had not seen another farang since arriving in Vung Tao and that is why perhaps everybody had been staring at me. I pulled tongues at the children to which they replied in kind one actually going one step further and blowing a raspberry at me. An adult called over from the other side of the Lido and the three youngsters scampered off to their parent.

I was surprised at their curiosity of me as I knew many farangs had been in this part of Vietnam in the past. During the war Vung Tao had been the home of the Australian Army and after that many Russian workers had visited when they had been drilling for oil. Perhaps as time had gone by less and less foreigners visit Vung Tao preferring to travel further up the coast to the newer and more luxurious resorts in the North.

I must admit Vung Tao was not a pretty place and it was only because of convenience that I had visited. Possibly the most notable farang to recently visit was Garry Glitter, it was in Vung Tao that the old rocker was arrested for committing obscene acts with minors. It was the final nail in Mr Gadd's celebratory coffin following his earlier convictions of child pornography in the UK. And it was because of that gentleman that I had not packed my Stack Heeled boots for the trip.

It also had dawned upon me that I had been following in the old Perv's footsteps. Firstly, visiting Cambodia where he was thrown out and permanently deported from in 2002 for suspected child sexual abuse and then to Vung Tao where he was actually nabbed. Perhaps that was the reason people were looking at me and

I could not remember if I had sung "Hello, Hello, I'm back again" anywhere in public. On a serious note it probably did make parents nervous of single farang strangers in Public Lidos.

After a busy day recollecting on the infamous Mr Gadd I crossed the road to the hotel and freshened up for the evening. I had taken a tourist map from reception and thought I would go into the centre of Vung Tau for a little exploration. Walking out of reception I noticed a couple of Xeoms or motorbike taxis; Xeom translates as "Hug Vehicle" which I considered to be an excellent description of the often dangerous mode of transport.

Showing my map to a driver and agreeing a one dollar fare we headed off in the direction of the ferry, only a matter of seconds had passed and my crash helmet flew off in a gust of wind. The driver screeched to an abrupt halt turned the bike around and retrieved the missing headwear. He held the damaged helmet up for me to see and there was a large crack in the tired article. Then the driver started to get really irate and was accusing me of the damage and demanding compensation. I was having none of it as it was he who had secured the strap under my chin, once again in Vietnam I was the subject of a scam. I threw the dollar bill at the gesticulating taxi driver and walked away disgusted at his behaviour.

Almost immediately I managed to secure another ride and went to the town centre. I do not know if it was just because of my excellent recent experiences elsewhere, but I was initially bitterly disappointed with Vung Tao. I tried in vain to find somewhere decent to drink or to dine and walked around aimlessly for about an hour. I stumbled upon a large restaurant that actually brewed its own beer. It was the liveliest place I had encountered and even though the service was curt and surly the beer was good and the food was quite tasty.

After dinner I took another Xeom back to see what the hotel's bar was like. The Cap Saint Jacques Hotel is almost attached to its neighbour the Dic Star Hotel and there is a little al fresco restaurant between the two. I peered in and it was shut so passing the doorway of the hotel's noisy nightclub I decided to take a look. I showed my key card and was let in past security to a rather dated and deserted club playing atrocious music at a deafening level. Turning on my heels I walked straight out and into the hotel's reception.

The resident's bar was on the ground floor and part of the hotel's one and only restaurant. I entered a cavernous room with a large stage at one end and a bar against the wall opposite the entrance. There were a couple of stools at the bar, apart from that no other seating other than that of the dining tables. Not one customer was in the room only an army of staff busy cleaning and other associated tasks. The room was as welcoming as my recent bout of Delhi Belly and I passed on the idea of a nightcap and went straight to bed. Unfortunately, although I was knackered I did not get to sleep until the nightclub below finished its racket. I think the last song that blared out was the Boney M classic, *Brown Girl In The Ring*, but I would have much preferred to have listened to it in Mr Seng's car than where I was.

The following few days dragged on relentlessly and I struggled to settle or find somewhere decent to hang out where I could relax. Barely a day went past without some argument over something trivial and it would normally be sparked off by somebody attempting to rip me off. I made a decision that I would leave Vung Tau early, although I had pre paid for the hotel I could not take anymore. I would return to Bangkok and extend my stay at the Holiday Inn to eight days and somehow try and claim my money back from Agoda when I got home.

My last evening in Vung Tao I didn't even try to explore the town any further, I had decided to eat early in the hotel restaurant and try to make an early start in the morning. I changed for dinner at 6pm and went down to the restaurant, entering what I could only compare as an Asian version of one of the main rooms in

Butlins or Pontins and I was pleasantly surprised to see it a hive of activity.

There was some sort of band on stage and an enthusiastic throng of about fifty children gathered in front jiggling around to the music. I walked to the back of the room away from all of the din and took a seat at a dining table. Surveying the room I estimated there must have been room for at least a thousand diners in the massive restaurant, but at present I was the only person seated. I had not bothered to consider what all the children were doing there it had not crossed my mind that it was a trifle unusual.

The band stopped playing and I thought Children's Hour must have finished and that was what the rest of the diners had been waiting for. Then to my amazement a man appeared on stage to yells of delight from the young audience. A waiter came to my table and with a rather puzzled look handed me a menu and asked if I wanted a drink. Leaving with my order of a large beer he walked to a colleague and they turned, looked at me and then shrugged.

Waiting for my drink my attention was once again drawn to the man on the stage, he had a most peculiar lurid suit on and a hat made out of balloons. Then suddenly he produced a small monkey from out of his pocket to a roll of the drums from the band to more screams of encouragement from the animated throng. It was then that the situation dawned on me, there were no adults present. I had seen a hand written note on the restaurant doors, but it had been in Vietnamese and I had chosen to ignore it. I had just gate crashed a Vietnamese children's birthday party and I was in a quandary of what to do.

I couldn't really just get up and go as that would be admitting my mistake and I would look a twat. Anyway there was nowhere to go but to accept to sit in my room until the party finished. So, I decided to do a Mr Bean and brave things out nonchalantly as though I was fully aware of the whole situation. For all the staff knew adult farangs might enjoy such parties in their own countries, so when the waiter returned with my rather warm beer I ordered some food and sat back to watch the man on the stage.

A plate of rather greasy Spring Rolls arrived almost immediately and I wondered had they been nicked from the kid's buffet. I started to eat as I was famished and one by one a group of curious and rather bored older kids started to appear around my table. Another dish arrived, this time of fried Won Tons and the temptation was too much for two hungry partygoers. The intrepid interlopers clambered up onto the vacant chairs at my table and started to tuck in greedily. That was the signal for a rush of black haired thieves to join the fray. The poor entertainer was up staged by some Won Tons and Spring Rolls proving a good buffet is probably all that the kids wanted in the first place.

I gave my meal up as a lost cause and left what food was remaining on the table to the foraging little hands and gaping mouths of the swarm. I made my way to the bar to pay the bill whilst a young boy grabbed my leg and took a ride on my foot. The conjurer had given up and the band had returned to play music when I finally exited the Cap Saint Jacques prestigious restaurant vowing never to return again.

Chapter Fourteen

AN EVENTFUL RETURN HOME

It was a welcome return to Bangkok and the Holiday Inn and it was going to be a longer stay than I previously anticipated due to the fiasco of Vung Tao. I had checked the rates of the hotel whilst I was in Vung Tao and was surprised how low the Holiday Inn had dropped their prices. Every hotel and tourist business in the city was suffering from the Red Shirt actions and the holiday industry had flopped. I was tempted to stay longer, but knew I had to return to the UK for two reasons. Firstly, my visa was about to expire, and secondly, I was rapidly running out of my medication.

My first evening I visited Coyote Bar and chatted to the manager as there was no sign of Apple. He graphically described the last days of the conflict and said it had been terrifying. As the tension had escalated many businesses around the Silom and Sathorn areas had decided it was prudent to close and barricade the doors. On the final night when the Red Shirts were routed from their enclave there was serious damage and violence. Apparently, according to the manager, a faction of the Red Shirts' 'Hard Liners' had gone crazy.

Shots were indiscriminately fired at people and property; many shops, restaurants and offices were ransacked. A major mall was set on fire with no regard to the safety of innocent people; residents or tourists. The manager's own apartment had been fired upon twice for no reason whatsoever and many of his friends had lost their jobs or businesses. It had been much worse than I had originally thought and I pitied the poor people who had to struggle through such wanton destruction and indeed had lost their lives.

The next few days walking about the capital was a mixed affair, I was so glad to be back in Bangkok, but it was so sad seeing places

I knew so well either boarded up or destroyed. There were few farangs walking around, only the expats, and the street traders had very little custom. I stopped at one to buy some T-shirts and the owner almost kissed me for my patronage. When I paid for the presents she asked me why was I not afraid to be there like all the other tourists, I felt so sorry for her and everybody else like her in Bangkok; just simple people trying to live their lives and exist.

My hotel also showed the signs of the Red Shirts' legacy; it was barely a third full. The bars and restaurants of the Holiday Inn were empty and when I was sunbathing I was the only person sitting by the pool, it was so eerie. However, one morning I was relaxing sunbathing by the pool when I saw a figure on the roof of the building below. The building had a glass pyramid shaped room and it was about two floors below the hotel's outdoor swimming pool complex.

Studying the figure I was disturbed he was wearing a red shirt and a black balaclava type hat. Why was he on the roof? Was it one of the Red Shirts? I looked around the pool to see if anybody else had noticed the same furtive activity. As usual nobody else was there and I was the only witness. Was he going to blow up the glass roof? Or start shooting from upon high?

I jumped off the lounger and felt quite helpless standing there in my Speedos. What was I going to do, try and negotiate with him? I thought better of that idea and went over to the hut that acted as the Pool Bar. Because trade was so bad nobody was there, the bartender seemed to be alternating with another duty, but I knew he would be back soon judging by his normal activities. I cowered down so the man on the roof could not see me and continued to spy on him. His activity was getting more and more bizarre and I was now convinced something was afoot. I studied his dress and saw he had proper climbing plimsolls and a bag strung over his shoulder; this man was a villain!

The white tunic of the barman appeared and he was surprised to see me crouching where I was, I was normally lying flat out in the sun. I ushered him to hurry by waving like some demented lunatic. He seemed very concerned that I was in some way distressed and ran over to where I was hiding; the bartender crouched down beside me to see what was the cause of my distress and we both peeped around the corner of the hut. If any new sun seekers had come up to the pool at that moment then it would have been highly embarrassing for the pair of us.

I pointed to the Red Shirt activist on the roof below, but the bartender did not see the terrorist. I pointed again towards the figure, but again the bartender did not see anything untoward. "Look man on roof, Red Shirt!" I cautiously whispered. The bartender then frowned, stood up and dusted off his black pants. Still crouching I looked at him quizzically; to answer my enquiring look he simply said two words: "Window cleaner."

Slowly I stood, because I did not have any trousers to dust off and I had nothing else to nervously fiddle with; embarrassingly I pulled my swimming trunks out from the cheeks of my bum. I did not have the gall to look the bartender in the eye, no words passed between us; I simply walked back to my lounger and he to his hut and we both continued our day.

Going back home after three months was going to be a little weird, but luckily I was returning to the summer and the start of the World Cup. During the final few days my mood changed and progressively got darker and more morose. I did not know the cause of my malaise, but I did not seem to be able to remain happy for more that one minute. Then with two days to go it dawned on me, I was sad that I was leaving. You would think after three months I would have been glad to see my home and friends again, but I simply did not want to leave. I had fallen in love with South East Asia and in particular my beloved Thailand.

Greenstreet and Back

With two days left I gathered all my clothes into two big sacks and went in search of a laundry on Silom Road. Walking about four hundred yards from the hotel I spotted a 'Laundry' sign down a little Soi on the left. The place was quite confusing as the shop had travel posters in the window but knowing how ambiguous things could be in Thailand I entered the small shop.

There was a counter directly opposite the door with another sign listing charges for different articles of clothing and to the right was a desk that acted as the Travel Agency. Sitting behind the desk was a young Thai man, neatly groomed and talking on the telephone. I waited by the laundry counter and eventually a girl of around fourteen appeared and smiled at me. Opening one of the bags to show my dirty clothes the girl understood and took both sacks from me. I tried to explain my hurry for the return of my laundry but the girl did not seem to understand. Then the man behind the desk said something in Thai to her and she nodded indicating her understanding.

The following day I returned to the shop to retrieve my laundry, but the girl seemed to be in somewhat of a fluster. The same young man as the previous day came to my aid and in perfect English said: "She is not quite finished yet, a couple more minutes." I looked at him and thanked him for the assistance. I was not sure if the two businesses were connected or that they just shared the same premises but it seemed to work nevertheless.

Whilst I was waiting I looked at some of the posters on the wall. Many were offering flights and hotel accommodation on exotic islands, but some were listing apartments and condos for sale or to rent. A sudden erratic and impulsive idea came into my head and I blurted out to the man, "Are there any apartments to rent in Bangkok?" A smile lit up his handsome face at the prospect of some business.

He stood up, came around to pull a chair away from the desk and asked me to sit down. The man was tall for an Asian perhaps two inches taller than me and had the obligatory thin body most Thais have. He then continued very professionally to quiz me about my requirements; time scales, budget, types of accommodation. I just could not stop myself; I invented a scenario of returning to Bangkok in the near future and the requirement for an apartment in the city.

My laundry was finished and neatly packed waiting on the counter but my discussions with the travel assistant / estate agent / laundry man were continuing in a serious manner. He had produced pictures and details of nearby rental opportunities that seemed fantastic value and very tempting. Compared to even the reduced prices in my hotel I could have my very own Bangkok apartment for half the cost.

I was tempted to sign up for something then and there, but knew I had temporarily gone insane, I had not thought any of this through. I made an excuse that I was returning to England to finalise a few business affairs and so I could not commit to anything at that moment. Not deterred the man exchanged email addresses and gave me his business card, I shook his hand and thanked him for his time, collected my laundry and left.

Within twenty four hours I was flying over India feeling down in the dumps, very dejected and truthfully close to tears. I had never returned from a holiday before feeling so low, but it had been more than a vacation. I had initially intended to go and live, work and settle in Koh Samui. Only circumstances had changed that and my original decision that I had agonised over was still valid, nothing had changed in that department.

Sully was meeting me at Manchester Airport from work and as I waited outside the terminal on the pavement I was shivering violently against the cold. Christ, it was the middle of June, the English sodding summer; the shock of the cold brought the whole thing crashing down upon me, that was the reason why I had left Britain in the first place.

Greenstreet and Back

It was good to see Sully again, he had been a rock keeping me informed of all my mail and looking after the house. I was lucky to have such a friend and although I had turned my back on my country I could never do that to my friends. Driving back to Liverpool did not cheer me up one iota and if anything I was feeling more depressed the closer I got to home. I felt as though I had failed in some way, it was a ridiculous emotion as events had progressed out of my control; but I had a nagging doubt, could I have done more to stay?

Even though I was fairly shattered by the journey we drove straight to the Bug and a few of my mates were there to share a welcome home drink. As I relayed some of my stories it was obvious that some of my experiences did not translate well into Liverpool life. It almost sounded as though I was bragging and my enthusiasm waned of the narration of my trip.

Being back was not all a disaster, the World Cup had started and I could resume my gym work. I had not done any real exercise in three months and I had put a little weight on. However, the weather was foul and I felt cold day and night. I decided to spring clean the house and I had an idea for another project to keep me occupied.

The DJ that had appeared on the opening night of Boogie Nights had intrigued me with the software on his laptop and I phoned Hendo to investigate the technology. If I could get hold of such virtual decks and have the software on my laptop then there would be no need for me to cart around CDs. I could travel anywhere in the world with my PC, plug into an amplifier and start DJing straight away.

Hendo came around to Chez Regina one evening with a few choices he had found. The problem was the best software is for Apple Mac and mine was a Dell using Microsoft. We played around for days until one piece of software seemed to work pretty well called Ultramixer. But, as always there was one major flaw, all my music was now on iTunes and Ultramixer only used MP3 files. I could not afford a new Apple Mac, but one thing I could afford was time. Hendo found another piece of software that converted iTunes to MP3 so I could construct a separate DJ library by converting the tracks. It was not an easy solution but one that would eventually work and would give me what I wanted.

I also took stock of my financial situation; my sick pay was still propping up my existence together with my reinstated invalidity pay. I had sorted out my problems with Mrs Moffat and forfeited some of my entitlement for some weeks. Also, I still had a couple of thousand in savings so I was in no way destitute. However, I decided to go on a crackdown and try to save as much as I could in the coming weeks, it would boost my savings and also help trim my stomach.

The summer finally did turn out to be an actual disaster. The weather was foul; cold, wet and generally miserable. England's performance was woeful in a generally poor World Cup in South Africa and my pining to return to Thailand would not diminish no matter what I did. I settled back into a general boring regime that seemed to pull me back almost to Rehab and my state of mind at that time.

Then one day something happened to bring a chink of light flooding back into my world. I received an email from Thailand; it was from the man from the laundry in Bangkok. He was enquiring had I finished my business in the UK and what dates would I be returning to Thailand: he had plenty of potential property to show me and it was a really good time to rent as it was so quiet in Bangkok.

That little spark was all that I needed to ignite a flame that had been burning in my heart since I had returned home. I missed Thailand so much I knew I had to return, but unsuccessfully had been trying to suppress my ardent desires. Not a day had gone by that I had not thought of the oriental jewel, but my yearning was always tinged with sadness as I was so far away from my dream land.

The email kick started me into activity and I started to formulate a plan of action. Firstly, I would have to ensure finances were in place to fund a return trip and those finances would determine the length of time I could afford to stay. I would need a visa, medication, music software completed, various other travel necessities and probably a medical check up.

Later that morning in the gym I ran through dates in my head and considered that I could realistically attend to all my chores in three or four weeks, that would mean I could go back to Thailand some time around the end of October or the start of November. My peddling on the exercise bike increased in velocity as a renewed vigour filled my whole body, I felt alive again and for the first time in weeks truly happy again.

Returning home I ate a light lunch and then retired to my lounge to delve into my finances. They were still in quite a healthy shape as it had not cost me any more to exist in Asia than in the UK, the extra cost was paying for the flights and the accommodation. I had enough in my savings to easily cover both and I worked out I could afford a trip of around six to seven weeks. If I managed to pick up any DJ work whilst I was there then that would be icing on the cake.

I was almost shaking with excitement as I emailed my contact back later that afternoon. I informed him of an approximate arrival date and that I would require an apartment in the Silom area of Bangkok for one month minimum. That would leave me a couple of extra weeks to sort out whilst I was there.

My day to day living expenses whilst I had been away on my travels were actually less than I spent back home, coupled with the savings on heat and light it was actually cheaper to live there than in Liverpool. The only big extra expense was paying a second monthly sum for accommodation. I had considered renting my house out in Liverpool and then I would be self sufficient as long as my sickness pay continued.

I mused over this course of action and decided that if things worked out whilst I was away then on my return at Christmas I would look into that possibility. What I did not realise at the time was I was actually planning to emigrate; my new philosophy of taking bite size chunks out of life was now instilled in my very core and I subconsciously lived my life that way.

The following morning as soon as I woke up I booted up my laptop whilst I was in bed to check if I had any mail. I was like an excited child eagerly opening a birthday present and hoping it was going to be something I liked. I was not disappointed as there was a short message from the agent and he had attached some prospective properties for my perusal. At the end of the mail he had signed off, "Your friend, Ton", so now I knew the agent's name and things were not so formal between us.

I spent the next hour lying in my warm bed looking at the wind and rain battering at my window and feasting up pictures of my potential new home. The Bangkok districts of Silom and Sathorn are perhaps the most salubrious in the city, they are where the Banking, Retail and Entertainment centres are based and property prices reflect that. But still the cost of large, luxurious apartments did not seem too prohibitive and I began to mark off a couple that seemed to fit the bill.

My list of requirements went in a particular order; firstly, was cost that was apparent, secondly was location as ideally I wanted to be as close to Silom Road as possible. Thirdly was size and amenities, I wanted a one bed roomed well appointed apartment with access to a swimming pool and ideally a gym. Other than those requirements, I could not care about anything else.

Over the following few weeks I exchanged emails with Ton nearly every other day. Sometimes it was to clarify details on a property I was interested in, but mostly we started to become pen pals via the internet; cyber chums. We exchanged personal and intimate information about our whole lives: family, friends, education, likes and dislikes etc.

Ton lived in Bangkok, but was born in the north east of Thailand, his parents now also lived on the outskirts of Bangkok and he had a sister. He was thirty five and had attended university, but had not finished his degree in order to start working, a familiar story! He had worked mostly in the tourist industry, everything from hotel work, tour guide, travel agent and also as a translator. I was getting to know my new acquaintance so well he was becoming a friend so I did not hold back any of my own history.

After a few weeks I had narrowed my selection of potential apartments down to three and generously Ton had offered to go and see them personally and vet them on my behalf. It was something that he did not have to do professionally, but as our friendship was growing and growing he was more than happy to help me out. His generosity did not surprise me as I was aware of the kind unselfish nature of the genuine Thais and I felt Ton was no exception.

Three days later Ton sent a message that he had one recommendation for me; The Shangarila Suite Apartments, Naradhiwas Rajanagarinda Road, Silom. I knew where it was, it was the large road that crossed over Silom Road near Patpong. The apartments were also directly opposite Chong Nonsi BTS Skytrain station, it was an ideal location. The apartment was classed as luxury superior; fully furnished with a large lounge with integral kitchen, separate double bed room and separate bathroom. The building also housed a small swimming pool on the roof but unfortunately no gym.

Ton recommended it highly, because the building was slightly dated and had no restaurant or laundry the prices were considerably lower than more modern condos. The actual room and the location more than made up for any shortfall in that area and the monthly rent was only seven hundred pounds. To me seven hundred quid was expensive and a lot of money, but if I wanted that location then that was the price I was going to have to pay. I realised that I would not be able to stay at the Shangarila long term, but I could afford it for a month.

Unbelievably, Ton confided in me that his agency did not act on behalf of the Shangarila Suite and subsequently did not handle the rental. He had found this apartment himself as a favour to me. Confirming to Ton I wanted to secure the apartment, I wired him the required deposit via Western Union and he agreed to look after everything on my behalf himself. I knew that when I arrived in Bangkok I would have to give Ton something for all his hard work but that could wait till later.

After the hassle of opening a Western Union account and eventually sending the required amount of money to Ton I booked my Emirates flights the same day. I was to leave England on the 28th of October and return on the 16th December ten days before Christmas. Contented that I had done a productive days' work and elated that I had now arranged my return trip, I treated myself to a well deserved glass or two of wine that evening.

The following morning I woke early, very happy and smug with myself. I knew I would have to break the news to my friends that weekend and wondered what sort of reception my announcement would receive this time. I looked at my clock and it was quarter to nine, my brain was slightly foggy from the previous night's wine, but I calculated it was a quarter to four in the afternoon in Thailand. I took a chance, but I wanted to speak to Ton to thank him and to see if he got the money okay.

I had made a note of his cell number from his emails and had already stored it in my phone. I dialled the number and waited, the familiar ring sound of an overseas call was in my ear and then the phone was answered.

"Sawdti Krab?" I was surprised but I instantly recognised Ton's voice. I was great to speak again to my new found friend; he sounded just as pleased to hear me and confirmed everything was in order. He had already been to collect the money and had also taken it to the Shangarila and had a receipt for me.

The remainder of the conversation was taken up with enquiries over our email communications. It was so easy to converse with Ton not just because his English was so good, but it was as though we had been friends for years. I was eager to renew our relationship when I was in Bangkok, it would be fantastic to have somebody who knew the city so well and could show me around. I mentioned about some sort of monetary reward for all his hard work, but he casually dismissed the offer as ludicrous and I felt embarrassed that I had mentioned anything.

My regular Sunday lunchtime rendezvous with Richie was quite interesting that weekend. I was so excited about my forthcoming trip as soon as I saw him I blurted out my news. Grouchily he enquired had I booked anything and I confirmed to him about the apartment and my flights.

"Stupid twat," he said over a gulp of Tetley's. I looked at him. "I was going to suggest to you a holiday over there," he replied as a translation of his previous obscenity. The next hour I spent pacifying my friend instead of as I had hoped eulogising over my new apartment.

Eventually he calmed to the idea and suggested that our proposed holiday could wait until the New Year. In fact Christmas was the busiest time of year in the butchers and he could probably not have taken the time off anyway. Why the fuck had he made such a big song and dance about it then? I inwardly smiled at the contradiction that was my friend; he was a contrary bastard that would argue black was white to the sodding Pope if he thought it would fuck up the Pontiff's nice day.

As other friends came and joined us for a libation their interest in my next trip sparked Richie to become more inquisitive. By the time I left the Bug in the early evening Richie was waxing lyrical that my next excursion was totally his idea and it was a fact finding mission for his upcoming holiday. The fact that he had not booked anything was a mere detail and something that he refrained from telling anybody.

The following weeks flew passed as I continued my music project and completed the necessary tasks such as getting a new three month visa from Boodle and Dunthorne's. I also worked hard on losing the weight that I had gained and was pleased to get back to under twelve stone. It was the level I wanted to maintain for the rest of my life and was six and a half stone loss from when I had my stroke.

Then on the twentieth, eight days before I was due to fly out to Thailand something quite devastating happened in my life. That morning my telephone rang whilst I was still in bed, it was around 7am. At first I thought it might be Ton as it was such an unusual hour, but realised he did not have my land line, then a sickening feeling filled my entire body; I knew it was bad news. Dread and apprehension slowed my hand reaching across the bed for the phone. I took a deep breath and picked up the receiver to my ear. "Hello, is that you Francis? It is your brother, Anthony."

My brother never phoned me, and the last time I had actually seen him was when I was in hospital. It confirmed that my earlier suspicions had been correct, something bad had happened.

"I had a phone call from the home last night, mum has passed away." I could not find the words to reply to my brother, I was stunned into silence. "Francis, are you there?" he pressed. I softly said, "Yes." It was all I could manage to get out. My brother must have sensed my distress and terminated the call, immediately saying he would call me back later in the evening.

I dropped the phone, lay back on the bed and wept like a child. It was a phone call I knew would come one day as my mother had been ill for years, but you cannot protect yourself in preparation for such awful news. I was devastated. Although I had agreed with my brother I would cease to visit as I could not face my mother's torment any longer, I had never stopped loving her.

My mother had received the best care that we could get her, but because of the nature of the disease the last few years of her life was a gradual stripping away of everything that had once been precious to het. Alzheimer's is a slow and undignified death that demeans the values and morals of its victims and takes away all memories, functions, intelligence and eventually wipes the brain clean. Dementia is something that as it progresses you are more unaware of and it then becomes in some respect worse for the relatives and loved ones as the person slowly declines.

On my last ever visit to see my mother she had no idea of who I was and didn't even know my name. After that visit I was physically sick and vowed I would never see her again: I wanted my memories of my mother to be of the mum she used to be not this thing she had become. I was not a strong enough person to face her gradual decline and since I had my stroke, a fact that she was blissfully unaware of, I was physically and mentally not able to.

That day became a haze for me. I could not focus on anything and I would often spontaneously burst into tears. I took to just sitting in my chair in silence and could not stomach anything to eat. God had not particularly been kind to the Abel family, I had already seen my father and brother buried and now it was the turn of my poor old mum. I had nearly died of a stroke and my mother's death was prolonged torture and not an easy one for her to endure; no! On reflection God had not been kind to us and apart from my estranged brother, I had no immediate family left. Perhaps I would get through the next few days and piss off for good.

Somehow I managed to phone Richie and shared my grim news, he assured me he would let people know and I was relieved I did not have to make any further phone announcements as just trying to speak was an ordeal for me. Later that evening my brother phoned back to see how I was; I was always the most emotional one of the family and it was obvious he was concerned about me even if he did not say it. He did not mention anything of note as that could wait; he just wanted to talk to his brother.

I went to bed early, but could not sleep as my distress was so severe, pictures and memories of my Mum flooded my mind and I wept selfishly at my loss. In the weeks ahead I would come to terms with the fact that my mother's death had come as a great relief to her, but that night that fact would come as no succour to me. I tossed and turned for hours, but finally found a little solace by possibly the only thing that could calm me, my music. The opening bars of *Too Shy To Say* by Stevie Wonder from his classic album *Fulfillingness' First Finale* broke the absolute silence of my bedroom.

The song's title was ironic; as I had grown older and my mother's condition had steadily deteriorated I had often berated myself for not telling my mum earlier of how much I had actually loved her. I had left it too late and Alzheimer's had robbed me of the last right every son should have to say to his parent before their death. A chance to confirm and declare their lifetime's love, affection and appreciation.

Morning came slowly through the dark despair of night and as the wind whistled around the trees outside and the rain battered at the panes of glass on my bedroom window the new day greeted me. I sat up in bed having had no sleep and even though the central heating was on I shivered with cold and nervous grief. The phone's loud ringing startled me into the awareness that I was not in some nightmarish dream and the fact that it was going to be another very, very shitty day.

My brother had waited a day before passing on the rudimentary facts of my mother's death. She had died in the night, but because she had been sleeping face down there was going to have to be an autopsy. Anthony was going to handle all the legal aspect of her death down in Oxfordshire, but suggested the funeral should be back in Liverpool and that she should be buried in the same place as my dad and my other brother Sam. I agreed wholeheartedly as all my mother's friends and her life had been here and it was fitting she should be put to rest with her adoring husband and beloved son. He asked me if I could contact the undertakers, church and find somewhere to hold a reception. The problem was we had no idea of a date when the body would be released or when we could hold a funeral.

The fact that I now had actual jobs and tangible things to occupy myself with brought a sort of morbid automatic response from me. I could now be of use and help my mother in this one last way, to help organise her last goodbye. The funeral home was of great help and was going to liaise with my brother when the body was going to be available and to transport it home. They could then organise with Sefton Council a date for the cremation and try and find a church for the service. My mother was a devout Catholic and she would have wanted a proper mass for her funeral. But because of the demise of entrants into the priesthood there was going to be a big problem finding somebody to hold the service.

A thought suddenly occurred to me, I was due to fly to Thailand on the twenty eighth only one week away. I had paid for my apartment and flights, but could not change or cancel anything as I still did not know what dates to alter anything to. There was only one thing I could do and that was to continue with the preparations of the funeral and throw all my attention and effort into that. I knew the worst problem was going to be to find a priest and that was the primary concern for me at that time. I did send off an email to Ton explaining that there was a family crisis and the dates of my arrival may change.

I contacted Emirates who were more than helpful and confirmed I could change the details of my outbound flight once I knew the new dates. They would also waive any fees if I faxed them a copy of the death certificate. My apartment was confirmed and so a delay of arriving would simply mean a loss of rent, no big deal considering the reason why. I was relieved that the trip could be reorganised and knew that after my mum's funeral it would be exactly what I would need. A place to go and reflect upon what would be my next bit out of life. If I remained in Liverpool then I could very possibly regress into a dark malaise.

The next few days were quite frantic in a hunt for a priest. My friend Sharon in Kuala Lumpur, also a very religious person, had heard of my loss and contacted me to pass on her condolences. I told her of my priest problem and she told me that she would explore some avenues for me, but I did not expect too much help with her being eight thousand miles away. I alerted my network of friends to pass the word of my plight and just about dismissed an idea I had of putting an advertisement in the Liverpool Echo: "Wanted urgently, Priest or something similar! Trainees or retired Clergymen equally accepted."

Donna, another stalwart of help during my rehab days, became one again invaluable to me. She constantly gave me her time to assist my quest, ferrying me around funeral parlours, hotels, and churches ensuring that I actually occasionally ate. My appetite had deserted me since my news and with all the worry over the organising I was losing weight rapidly that now I could not afford. My concern over the time issue was not my trip as Thailand would wait for me, but my abhorrence after all that my mum had gone through she was laying on a shelf in a sterile morgue somewhere and I could not put her to rest.

On the morning of the 26th my brother phoned and informed me the authorities would release the body satisfied with the autopsy there had been no foul play. He had organised the undertakers to collect the body and they were trying to get a date at the crematorium. I had to go to the funeral parlour to sign some documentation for them that day and to discuss some of the funeral's details.

The visit to the funeral parlour was frustrating in the extreme as everything was in abeyance until we could find a priest. They had left the whole funeral hanging in the air and had not started to finalise anything. We needed a date to inform relatives and attendees so I knew I had to give more direction and pulled a reasonable date out of my mind to concentrate their efforts. I told them to work for the twenty eighth and arrange everything for then, I would somehow find a priest. I was not going to let my mother wait for yet another weekend it just seemed so unfair and so cruel. Had I not taken so direct intervention we would still be trying to put my mum to rest even now?

I then went the Royal Hotel in Waterloo and booked one of their reception rooms for the Wake under the proviso that I would inform them the first thing in the morning if the event was postponed in order that they would not prepare the food. Finally, I contacted Emirates and rescheduled my flights to Thailand for Saturday the 30th, two days after the funeral.

The rest of the day was manic, with Donna's help we contacted just about everybody we knew was a Catholic in the hope that somebody, somewhere knew of a priest available. I was totally unaware of the severe shortage the Catholic Church was now suffering in respect to their ordained Priests. I was a lapsed Catholic and had only attended Mass in order to attend Funerals or Weddings. My decision originally came about with apathy and not some great conflict of faith, but as the years passed I really blamed religion for the cause of many of the world's great conflicts. Great cruelty and oppression had been suffered by many in the name of religion. I had decided to follow my old schools motto, 'Fidem Vita Fateri', and to show my faith by the way I lived.

After a succession of negative phone calls and SMS messages my hope was waning fast of achieving what I was hoping for when miraculously a strange voice was on the other end of my telephone line.

"Hello, is that Francis?" I answered my name nervously. "We have a mutual friend living in Kuala Lumpur, I am Father Joe." I nearly dropped the phone; it was Sharon from Malaysia who was our mutual friend. She had come to my aid from thousands of miles away, I did believe at that moment that God behaves in strange ways. Father Joe confirmed his availability to conduct the service and would visit me later on that evening to run through some things.

I do not know if it was the correct emotion to be pleased to be able to finally arrange my mum's funeral, it was more of a relief I suppose, but I certainly felt happy. I sent an email to Ton confirming my new dates and asked him to notify the Shangarila that I would be arriving late by a few days. Although I had paid a deposit, I did not want them giving my apartment away.

Donna asked me what was I going to wear for the service and it dawned on me that I had given all my formal clothes away during my rehab. I had completely forgotten about myself, I had been concentrating all the time upon my mother and the funeral. She suggested making a trip into town to buy a suit, but I declined wanting to be at home in case there were any visitors or phone calls. Surely I could borrow something from one of my mates, but I had no idea what size I was these days.

Father Joe arrived early and I was quite surprised as he knew quite a bit about me already from Sharon. He was a young priest and apparently had visited the Bug once with Sharon; he immediately went up in my estimation when I heard that snippet. Apparently, Richie had tried to involve him in a heavy drinking session when he saw him there, but he luckily escaped from the clutches of the playful but dangerous Butcher. Father Joe was very sincere, calming and overall exactly what I needed at that moment in time. He helped me to take a breath and calm down after my recent activities and to focus more now on how to celebrate what my mother had given to me during my life.

After around an hour he left and just as I was closing the door an old friend Spud was opening my gate and walking up my path. Mark or Spudrick as we affectionately called him was one of my oldest and closest friends and he had gone through the same troubles as me losing his father and mother. There is an understanding and unwritten bond between friends who have suffered family loss, often words do not have to be spoken just contact or closeness is sufficient to give immense support. Over a glass of wine and Mr Wonder in the background we talked in great openness of our parents and both of our losses.

Spud offered to loan me some of his clothes for the occasion, but he was such a skinny git I doubted any of them would fit me. Spud had always been skin and bone ever since I had known him, from a scrawny kid to an adult who smoked 30 tabs a day keeping him thin. I have always been jealous of his capacity to regularly drink copious amounts of Tetley Bitter and remain so thin, I just had to look at a pint and I would gain two pounds.

He had come straight from work so I tried his suit jacket on; to my amazement it fitted me. Christ, had I lost too much weight? Did I also look puny now? I knew I had hardly eaten for days, but it was ridiculous that I was as thin as Spud Murphy. I had been so proud of my weight loss regime and my constant efforts, but perhaps recent events had taken it a tad too far. But it had sorted a problem out for me, I could borrow the clothes I needed from Spud and that was one less problem to solve.

The morning of the funeral Nick and H called to drive me to the church. Nick had to help me fasten my top button of my shirt and to fix my tie. My right hand had permanently lost its fine motor controls and I was unable to perform even this simple task. I had not worn a tie since my stroke and it felt very strange to once again have one around my neck; strange, uncomfortable and something I did not want to do again in a hurry.

I think part of the reason I no longer wear a shirt and tie is the same reason I never wear a watch anymore, they are symbols of an old life that I have left behind. Symbols of materialism, conformity, ambition and in some way greed; things that almost drove me to my grave. But secondly, less heroic, but more pertinent is that I find putting on a watch, tie or even fastening the top button of a shirt extremely difficult. So, as in all my rehab, I have learned to adapt and the easiest way was simply not to wear such items.

The funeral was as expected; harrowing, formidable and an arduous test of my stamina and emotional thresholds. The church was full of relatives and friends a fact later I was to gratefully appreciate but at the time most daunting. Standing before the Altar I could feel dozens of pairs of eyes on the back of my neck studying my movements and I found it impossible to raise my eyes from my fixed glare on the floor. The uncomfortable feeling of being the target for all the scrutinised attention was enhanced during certain parts of the service when I sat instead of kneeled. I cannot kneel as my right leg will buckle under me, but did people think I was being disrespectful?

For the main I held up pretty well, but on occasions my stupid, highly emotional nature broke through my barrier and I was glad that I had remembered a handkerchief. Once the crematorium was over with and my mum was finally put to rest I felt more stoic and I knew my true grieving could wait until I was by myself in Thailand. Never before had the desire to return to my beloved Thailand been so strong. This time it was for pure selfish reasons; I could have time to reflect on my mother and her passing away without having to put a brave front on for anybody.

Back at the Royal Hotel, only really close friends and relatives attended, and it was a fairly upbeat reception as many of the people there had not met for such a long time. It only lasted a couple of hours as many of the attendees had travelled far to come to the funeral and would have a long journey home. But then the day was rocked by some news a close cousin confided in me.

My cousin Mike was about the same age as my brother Anthony and had always been a favourite cousin of mine since I was little. He was my confirmation sponsor and I had taken his name to add to my own. I had greeted him at the church and noticed the genial man had looked very sombre and tearful. I thought it was because of his grief for my mother, Auntie Mo, but what he told me was devastating. Recently, he had been diagnosed with some form of cancer. I could not really understand what he was saying to me but it was terminal and he had only been given a few months to live.

The bombshell was devastating, I did not know what to do or say to him. My emotions were fragile enough and just to keep standing was a major success. His wife Glenda came to join us as Mike and I just looked at each other both unable to speak or communicate. She apologised for Mike breaking the news on that day, but hoped I understood that they did not know how much time they had and wanted to tell me personally. I grabbed my cousin's arm and all he could say was "I know, I know, I know." He raised his arms up to chest high with palms facing upwards in a gesture of "What can you do, there is nothing you can do?" not to me, but for himself.

They were the last ones to leave the wake and as Nick waited outside to take me to the Bug I retired to the lavatory, bolted myself in a cubicle and howled like a banshee in total despair and unabashed sorrow. It was a double whammy as the sports commentators say, and the 28th of October was a date that was burnt into my memory as the blackest of days. That was the last time I saw my cousin as six months later he died, but I was glad, even though the circumstances, that I had the opportunity of seeing him that one last time.

The hours after the reception the wake continued in the Bug and unashamedly I got rotten drunk. I think part of the Irish Catholic heritage is that the drunker a bereaved person gets on the passing of a loved one then the greater the homage is paid. If that is so then I certainly gave my mum a good send off.

The following day I rose late with a bad hangover, after fixing some strong coffee, I reflected upon the day of the funeral, but did not dwell for too long as I did not want to open fresh scars yet, not while I had things to do. There would be plenty of time for that in the days and weeks ahead. It was a coward's way out, this I knew, but by going away I would not have the love of close friends breaking down the self preservation emotional barriers I had formed.

The rest of the day I spent ensuring I had everything I needed for my trip ahead and thankfully my mind was fully occupied. That night I went to the Bug to give Spud his clothes back and to say my goodbyes yet again. I did not drink too much as I was up early for my taxi and did not want to undertake such a long journey dehydrated and hung over. My farewell this time was a more sombre affair than previously, both because of recent events and my perception that something inside me was close to making a big decision.

Sitting in one of Manchester Airport's bars waiting for my flight I ordered a pint of Stella and toasted my mother. I noticed my jeans and T-shirt were quite baggy on me, but I was not elated as normal by my weight loss: I had shed pounds by grief, not diet and exercise. I looked pale, thin and emaciated and was glad I was getting out to the sunshine and some relaxation. Going home had proved to be a disaster with the catastrophic events that had happened and Liverpool was proving to be far closer to reality than I could take or really wanted.

Chapter Fifteen

A NEW FRIENDSHIP

After clearing the insufferable Bangkok immigration and collecting my luggage, I walked into the Arrivals Hall to meet Ton. We had exchanged emails and he had insisted on meeting me at the airport a gesture that I was highly impressed with. I had my doubts if I would recognise him out of his normal habitat and was wary that such an incident could be highly embarrassing.

We had arranged to meet at Hertz's car hire desk and luckily for me I saw him almost immediately standing by the side of the desk waiting for me. After such a long pen pal relationship I felt Ton was my friend and unusually for Thai's Ton gave me a huge hug as a welcome. I felt a little embarrassed by the embrace not for sentimental reasons, but because I knew I must have smelled a little ripe after the long journey.

We were not going to actually hire a car, but it was a good place we could meet and Ton asked me how I would like to get to Bangkok. I suggested a taxi as I was too lazy to take my luggage on a train after the flight, Ton smiled at my suggestion and we went down the escalator to the first floor to the taxi rank.

Sitting in the green and yellow cab speeding along the expressway to the city Ton and I babbled away in the back seat. His English was good when speaking, but hesitant in understanding me when I spoke. He remarked upon how thin I looked and I was surprised how well he had remembered me, he also passed on sincere condolences for my loss, but we did not dwell on that subject. Most of our conversation was based around my new apartment and he seemed almost as excited as me about my new home.

Ton guided the cabbie with directions once we came off the expressway and soon we turned right off Silom Road onto Naradhiwas Rajanagarinda Road and pulled up outside a Chinese restaurant. The pavement was busy as many people were making their way to and from the Chong Nonsi BTS station just a few feet ahead and the huge Sky Trains' overhead railway stanchions blocked the sunlight from the street.

Just to the right of the Chinese restaurant were some steps leading to two glass doors. Ton led the way up the steps carrying my suitcase and a security guard opened the doors to gain us access into Shangarila Apartments. The reception area was fairly small and by no imagination was it opulent. There was a couple of staff behind the reception desk and I proceeded with completing all the formalities and received my room key and an electronic tag for the glass doors.

Within minutes a desk clerk, Ton and I were all crammed into the tiny lift and exited at the eighth floor. The landing housed about five doors and we went to my one; apartment 803. Fiddling with the key the receptionist eventually opened the door and led me into what was going to be my new home for at least one month. Ton had already vetted the apartment so was not as interested in the tour I was receiving and instead was busy testing some of the appliances such as air conditioners and TVs.

The door opened right into the main living area that was considerable in size. Ton had already told me that this was one of the largest apartments in the building at 75 square metres. The lounge area featured a two seater sofa and two armchairs set around a coffee table, then to the left under one of the two windows in the room was a dining table with four chairs and a flat screened TV on the wall. To the right was a fully fitted kitchen with a door leading to the bathroom and in the centre of the room was another door that led to the bedroom that housed a huge King sized bed and another flat screened TV.

There were two narrow full length glass patio doors that opened for access to a small ledge big enough to stand or to house one chair. The ledge looked down on a side street to the side of the building and on the ground underneath were several tables belonging to the restaurant opposite. Back inside the bedroom there was a cupboard complex covering an entire wall and in the centre was another door leading to the bathroom. The bathroom had a fairly tired suite, but was functional and would suffice, there was also a small window facing the same direction as in the bedroom.

Going back into the lounge area the room seemed fairly dark even though it had two windows, perhaps because of the excessive use of dark wood on the floors and kitchen and I could see what Ton had meant when he said the apartments were a little dated. I tipped the desk clerk and Ton and I were left by ourselves to further explore the apartment and discover all its workings.

After unpacking whilst Ton read the buildings' resident's regulations I showered and changed into shorts and T-shirt. I had purchased a few small gifts for my helper and he was most gracious in his acceptance of the tokens of gratitude. In one of his mails to me he had told of his passion for playing volleyball, so I had bought him a genuine shirt and a pair of shorts from an American on line store knowing nobody would have such kit in Bangkok. He was so thrilled he went into the bedroom and changed so he could wear the clothes immediately.

So, the pair of us donned in our summer attire went to explore the rest of the apartment block. The building had a tiny roof top swimming pool that had four sun loungers, two of which were crocked, but the area was open to the sun on all sides. The views of the city from there were spectacular and the pool was not really overlooked. The swimming pool was about the only amenity the building really offered, there were no shops, restaurants or lounges it was exactly as I had been told by Ton. The main attraction of the

Shangarila was its location and its size; it only housed forty to fifty apartments so it was quiet and private.

After the quick exploration of the Shangarila we strolled about the vicinity and again Ton was vindicated by his choice of my location. The BTS station was seconds away from my door and I had availability of the whole of Bangkok just a few flights of stairs away. Locally; there were many small, traditional Thai restaurants that serviced local workers or commuters. A few convenience stores and Seven Elevens were dotted around handy for essentials and the best thing of all there were hardly any farangs.

Ton expressed his hunger and we agreed that a late lunch was just the ticket. We found the restaurant that I could partially see from my bedroom and bathroom windows on the side of the Shangarila building. The kitchen of the restaurant was on the main road to attract passersby, and it had one air conditioned dining room. The rest of the restaurant comprised of open air tables pushed against a wall of a small Soi, it was this part I could see from my apartment.

The menu was only in Thai so Ton ordered on our behalf and the food arrived promptly, was delicious and very inexpensive. Although frequenting the place numerous times I never did find out the restaurants name, sometimes I would just sit in the open air having a cold beer in the alley trying to cool down from the oppressive heat of the city.

It was getting to be the hottest time of the year in Thailand and in the centre of Bangkok with the heat being generated from the buildings and traffic it was occasionally unbearable. Only idiots walked about in the middle of the day, most locals and expats preferring to stay in the cool or shade to reappear later.

After our late lunch Ton said he had a few things to attend to, but would come to my apartment around 7pm so we could both go out for the evening. I left him walking down the road in the opposite direction of Silom, looking resplendent in his new USA volley ball kit. I went back to my room for a rest as I had not had any sleep on my two plane journeys and the lure of my new comfortable looking bed was to hard to resist; I noticed Ton's discarded clothes in the corner and was glad he felt comfortable leaving his possessions with me.

I woke to a strange sound some hours later and realised it was my own door bell. I quickly pulled a pair of shorts on and dashed through the living room to open the door. Ton was standing there smiling and let me know he had been waiting for about ten minutes. I embarrassingly ushered him immediately into the apartment apologising constantly as I did so feeling that I had been very rude indeed to my new friend who had done so much for me.

Whilst I showered Ton watched TV and within fifteen minutes we were walking down Silom Road heading towards Lumphini Park. Ton had told me he did not drink very often but I insisted taking him to a few of my old haunts. Firstly, we turned right down Soi Convent and had a beer in Molly Malones then a Margarita in Coyote Bar, retracing our steps back on to Silom Road we then went to Patty's Fiesta Bar for more Margarita's. Ton was surprised how well I was known in these places, but did not seem that impressed and simply said that I must drink a lot.

Then finally we went to the Duke of Wellington for our last aperitif, I was slowly getting to know my new friend as we spoke of many things that previously we had not communicated to each other by email. Ton was a fairly serious young man and he did not look anywhere near his age of thirty five. He shared an apartment with an old friend about twenty minutes walk from the Shangarila and had worked in the travel/hotel industry most of his life.

Although he smoked too much he kept fit by playing volleyball about five times a week. I could tell that Ton was not rich and was just an average Bangkok citizen just getting by. As nearly all Thai's he had close ties with his family and saw them often every week and although he did not say anything I knew he would have to help them financially as well. Ton's English was beginning to falter from the amount of aperitifs we had consumed, so we decided to drink up and dine.

Ton said he knew a place very close and as we exited the Pub we turned right and immediately stumbled upon a tiny alley, it was even not quite a Soi. At the entrance was a large static food cart and down the narrow alley were a row of plastic tables and chairs. The smell of frying garlic and chilli bought tears to my eyes and we both started coughing as the pungent concoction hit the back of our throats. Ton pushed further down the alley and it opened up into a large concrete square reminiscent of a car park. There were some small shops more like stalls on one side and some vehicles parked at the rear, but in the centre were an array of dining tables.

Against the wall opposite the stalls was a covered kitchen with tanks full of fish in front. We took a seat at one of the tables and Ton said, "I hope you like fish?" I nodded and looked around, we were sitting in the open air and the large buildings around us dwarfed the little courtyard. Although I knew this part of Bangkok well, I never knew of this place and it was far off the tourist trail. However, my guide did and that was all that mattered. It was somewhere the Bangkok workers and local residents could afford to eat and it was tucked away from the prying eyes of farangs.

The courtyard was fairly quiet as we had missed the after work dinner trade and only a few stragglers were left consuming the last of their booze. A teenage girl rushed to our table, produced a fork and spoon for us both together with a menu. I opened the menu, as I suspected it was all in Thai, but there were pictures so I could gather what some of the dishes were. There was all manner of shellfish; lobster, prawns, mussels, crab, clams, all prepared in differing ways, then a variety of river and sea fish most unknown to me, but some familiar such as bass and eel.

Ton constructed a piscatorial feast for us, but was shot down on some of his selections as his choices had already run out. It seemed that the place served fresh fish from the tanks and when it was gone then there was no frozen backup available. It did not matter, what arrived at our table was sumptuous. We had Blue Crab in Yellow Curry Sauce, Deep Fried Fish in Sweet and Sour sauce, Mussels with Garlic and Chilli and my favourite a whole fish presented in its steamer in a Lime, Chilli and Garlic Soup. All with the ubiquitous steamed rice accompaniment and washed down with Leo beer resting in an ice bucket.

Had this meal been in a more fashionable restaurant with tablecloths and fine cutlery I couldn't have possibly enjoyed it any more than I did. Sitting in a dim, outdoor sort of car park in my shorts and T-shirt made no difference to the taste of the exquisite banquet and there was something quite bohemian about the experience.

Eating fish back in the UK is always portrayed as a luxurious, expensive treat and the restaurants for some unknown reason charge the Earth. Suspiciously, the last time I checked the UK is an island and is surrounded by water, and I remember my school lessons that fish live in water. Here in Asia eating fish is a common everyday experience for the whole population and not just the wealthy and elite. I cannot remember the exact cost of dinner, but I knew it was very reasonable indeed and I would return often to the hidden gem.

Over dinner Ton teased me about keeping him waiting at my apartment and suggested that I purchased a new phone with a Thai SIM card so that we could keep contact with each other easily and cheaply. I agreed and we arranged to meet at Chong Nonsi BTS station the following evening after he had finished work to go shopping. Then Ton took his leave and pottered off into the crowded streets of Silom to make his way home.

I decided to walk down to Patti's Fiesta bar for a night cap, but wavered just before I reached it and looked down Soi Patpong at the Night Market and all the neon signs outside the many bars. I turned left and entered the twilight world of Patpong it was a very different place at night time compared to that of the day, a completely different species of life now patrolled the pavements and alleyways.

Patpong at this time of evening is a real dichotomy. In the centre that runs down the whole road is the Night Market which attracts tourists and late night shoppers all vying for a spot of retail therapy. It is flanked on both sides by sleazy sex joints offering everything from Beer Bars and Strip Clubs to Ladyboy Entertainment Venues. Both crowds mingle together with very unalike intentions of how they want to spend their holiday savings.

The market caters more for clothing than anything else with many alleged cheap brand name jeans, trainers, T-shirts and questionable mementoes. But I was not looking for a new pair of shoes I wanted a drink and to experience some of Bangkok's soft underbelly. I had been through Patpong many times, but had never stopped to be entertained in one of the shady establishments.

Attracting a great deal of attention as I peered through different doorways to select somewhere to go I felt a tweak on my bum as somebody had pinched my arse. I turned to see a very pretty girl dressed in a school uniform. Her hair was in pigtails and she was wearing a white blouse tied around her waist so her naval was in full view with a blue tie loosely tied around her neck. She had a very short, blue plaid skirt and a pair of fishnet hold ups. I estimated the girl was around eighteen or nineteen and was far too old to be coming back from school.

She beamed an enticing cheeky smile towards me and beckoned me to enter her bar. A second girl similarly attired joined her and took my arm trying to drag me inside. I resisted laughing as I wanted to walk around and see what other mischief was occurring and declined their invitation with a promise I would return. The girls turned around rather miffed and searched for another target to lure into their dubious club.

Looking up I saw the bar was named Obsession and I could see the sort of clientele it was trying to attract. The next door down was a bar called Ambiguous and a group of girls stood outside almost exactly attired as they were at Obsession. They too were dressed as wayward St. Trinian's schoolgirls with white school blouses, short plaid skirts, stockings and midriffs on display. The only difference I could see was the colour of their shirts and ties being red.

I stood slightly aback and noticed that these girls were louder and more aggressive trying to lure potential clientele from the street. I pondered how many late night shoppers had disappeared from their wives snatched by these mischievous and disorderly students. How many bags of shopping had been lost in the bowls of Obsession and Ambiguous? I had seen girls like the ones outside Ambiguous before; their racket gave them away as katoeys.

On further investigation, as it was not obvious, I noticed that the buildings housing the two bars were attached. It was actually the same place, but with two entrances offering two quite different experiences. I was intrigued and had to delve into this little poser more, so I walked into Ambiguous simply because it was the nearest door.

The club was big, and the techno music was painfully loud. The strobe lighting inside made it very difficult to actually see things clearly, but I could see that the bar was fairly full of punters. There was a snaking runway that wound its way around the whole establishment and numerous poles were dotted along its length. Many girls were on the raised platform or dangling from poles gyrating to the pulsating rhythm.

Their school uniforms were in different stages of undress, and I could imagine Sister Monica, the Headmistress of Seafield Academy for Young Ladies, being particularly annoyed and distressed at how the standards of wearing the uniform were being flagrantly disregarded by the girls.

An errant student with a red skirt led me to a small table and I ordered a beer as she snuggled up to me asking for a drink. This is customary in any Beer Bar, for the price of a drink you enlisted their company for as long as the drink or drinks lasted. At this stage no impropriety is suggested and may never be. Although in a lot of cases the hostesses are prostitutes and negotiations may begin, then if you wish more intimate services you have to pay a fine to the bar to take the member of staff off.

Many such establishments have rooms available and for areas around such sex locations as Patpong there are many seedy hotels nearby that cater for the demand of the areas patrons and will rent rooms by the hour. It is a very lucrative industry, but mostly controlled by the Thai Mafia and gangsters operate a lot of the boarding houses or small sex hotels together with their clubs.

The girl at my table was laughing at some of the antics going on inside the club and was squeezing my knee as she did so. She had a badge pinned to her blouse with a number two advertised on it and told me her name was Song. Actually her English was fairly good and she began to tell me more about the two bars. It was one big club with the girls from Ambiguous all being ladyboys and they wore red skirts. The blue skirts designated the girls were from Obsession and they were totally female. I looked down at Song's skirt and rather disconcertingly I noticed it was red.

"We have a lot of fun fooling stupid customers" Song mischievously confessed to me as her hand moved disquietingly further up my thigh. I was rather flattered by the attention Song was showing me all be it disturbingly so. I thought I had better qualify my intentions and I informed Song I was just there to have a drink and to chat. Song was initially disappointed as there would be no off with me, but then she relaxed, I supposed relieved she did not have to perform any deviant sexual acts with me. Her hand nevertheless remained high up on my leg only for me to push it down occasionally when it got too near its intended target.

Greenstreet and Back

There are many old wives tales about recognising ladyboys. The first thing, and probably most importantly, is that ladyboys, as with women, are all different. More so in the case of a katoey as their transgender can vary from simply wearing drag to a full blown transsexual and every permutation in between. The fallacy about protruding Adam's apples and various other tell tale signs are simply not true as there are medical procedures for just about anything in Thailand.

In my experience it is simple things like height, size of feet or hands and definitely the sound of the voice are the biggest ways of telling. A quick grope in the groin area will sort the matter out faster and unequivocally, but even that will not tell you that there was something there originally. It is normally a combination of all of the above that gives the game away. However, a group of katoeys is another matter, it is unmistakeable due to din and racket produced by battery of them assembled together. You can hear a conglomeration of ladyboys four blocks away as they howl and screech at each other just in general conversation, it is a most disturbing cacophony that I can not do justice trying to describe.

Song had ordered two more drinks and asked could her friend join us. I had never spent so much time in the company of a katoey and was surprisingly enjoying it immensely as I had not laughed as much for ages. It was going to cost me a few quid in buying the drinks, but it was worth it for the free entertainment and gossip I was receiving. Number twenty seven joined us and I was introduced to Mam also perturbingly wearing a red skirt. It was like having a night out with a takeaway menu and on reflection I was!

Mam was quite stunning and I was quite contented to have her nestle up on my other side knowing that this was as far than anything would get. If any of my friends would have walked in at that moment I would have had some embarrassing explaining to do. The two girls chatted away together and then went into fits of hysterics. Song explained to me that Mam and her cousin had a scam going on and it was at the expense of a rather drunken American serviceman.

The whole place was designed to confuse the ignorant and often drunk tourist. Predominately the girls from Obsession danced and plied their trade on the right hand side of the club where the punters had entered and had expected ladies. The same was for the girls from Ambiguous who mostly gyrated and postured on the left hand side where their customers preferred ladyboys. But occasionally they swapped over and confusingly duped their patrons who in some cases where blissfully unaware any sham was going on.

Mam's cousin, number twenty five, joined our merry crew; a side order from the takeaway menu had arrived. She was actually wearing a blue dress and looked a doppelganger of her cousin Mam. The resemblance was quite striking and whatever subterfuge the two pixies had cooked up I considered they had an excellent chance of pulling it off. Number twenty five pointed over to the back of the club where I noticed for the first time was a small swimming pool full of soap suds. A handful of scantily clad people were thrashing around in it with foam flying everywhere. Mam nodded with a Machiavellian grin on her pretty face, the cousins swapped ties and hand in hand they walked off into the rest rooms.

Song then explained to me that an American sailor had been in the club for the last two nights and Mam really fancied him. However, he was straight and always kept to the Obsession side of the club. The two cousins had hatched a plan where number twenty five would lure him into the play pool and then they would swap over.

That is what was occurring in the rest room at that very moment. Song and I monitored the situation closely to see what was to transpire. The sailor had already ditched his jeans and climbed into the pool wearing only his shorts. At that moment, the rest room door opened and a lithesome creature wearing school blouse and bikini bottoms sashayed towards the pool. I had not noticed, but number twenty five had rejoined our table.

The figure flaunting her assets toward the pool was actually Mam. Her breasts protruded from the cotton blouse and the garment accentuated her sublime curvature as she had tied it just under her ample bosom. Number twenty five and Song were holding hands tittering in nervous expectation. Mam gently lowered herself into the pool whilst the strong hands of the sailor gripped her around the waist and pulled her into the foam.

Legs, arms and shrieks shot up in the air as bubbles and foam flew around the club as the amorous couple writhed about in the water. The sailor hungrily sought Mam's lips as he pressed his head close to hers whilst his roving hands ripped off her blouse to reveal two perfect and slightly upturned breasts. Song and number twenty five were euphoric how events were progressing and were clapping their hands rapidly together like penguins seeking food.

Then the inevitable happened and if you will pardon the expression, but everything went tits up. The sailor had obviously gone for gold and put his hand down Mam's bikini bottoms only to find a seven inch and rather excited cock. "Whoa! Whoa! What the fuck!" The sailor lurched out of the pool as fast as a dog getting its summer bath. He too was excited, as a huge erect penis was quivering in front of him as it protruded from the fly in his shorts. The whole club fell into hysterics and any ideas of violent repercussions the sailor had were instantly dispelled. How could he start a pub brawl in his current condition? He was more likely to have accidental sex, he was that hard.

Two girls ran over to the creature from the soap suds lagoon with towels to cover his embarrassment. I looked at Mam and she was just staring with mouth agape in awe of the sailor's manhood wishing "If Only" I could not take any more of this madness and requested my bill. Song, number twenty five and a soaking wet

Mam all crowded around me at my departure fixing many goodbye kisses on my lips and cheeks.

I strolled home with a fixed grin on my face like Jack Nicholson in Batman as I recalled the evening I had just experienced. I had never quite had a night out like it before, but for Patpong it was just a normal day at the office. It would be strange to go back to the normality of shopping with Ton the next day, if indeed anything is normal in this crazy city.

Bangkok has many Shopping Malls and some are more famous for selling certain items than others. For instance Central World is very good for Fashion whilst MBK is famous for Street Ware and Mobile Phone. Perhaps the biggest is Siam Paragon that has just about everything including a Cinema and Restaurants. I made sure I was on time the following day to meet Ton and we took the BTS to the Siam station and walked to the MBK mall.

Ton led me directly to the Mobile Communications floor and within minutes I was the owner of a brand new Nokia 1280 and connected to the True Communications Network. I was aware the 1280 was probably one of the most basic phones on the market, but I only needed to phone and SMS and did not need a more expensive Smart Phone. I was staggered at how cheap it all was, the handset was just over fifteen pounds, but the SIM card and connection to the network was for buttons. I have mentioned earlier exactly how cheap making overseas calls was compared to the UK Networks, but calling inside Thailand was literally a few pence a minute. It was one of the best purchases I have ever made.

The following days I saw Ton almost daily, normally after 8pm when he had finished playing volleyball after work. Normally we would just have dinner together and Ton took me to some amazing eateries tucked away in the depths of hidden Bangkok. Occasionally we would arrange something special and I was introduced to his friends one by one either in a nightclub or at local concert.

I would spend my mornings relaxing at the roof top pool which was always permanently deserted and then later in the afternoon I would explore the area around my hotel or even do a spot of sightseeing. I had now found my way around the small Sois by the Shangarila and had developed shortcuts to most of my regular haunts. For instance if I wanted to go to Molly Malones I could just nip up Narathiwat Ratchakharin Road to St Joseph's School on Convent Road and turn left. If I wanted a Margarita in Patty's I could wind myself along Soi 5 avoiding the crowded Silom main road full of tourists and commuters.

The little stalls, street restaurants and local Thai bars became familiar friends to me as I became more and more familiar with my environment. I was even asked for directions to places in Sathorn and Silom by some of Ton's friends who where not from the area, a fact that he found most amusing.

Then one evening we planned to go to see the Harry Potter film the Deathly Hallows at Siam Paragon Cinema and Ton wanted me to see where he lived and to also meet his room mate Khun Aun. He came to my apartment then we took two motorbike taxis to where his apartment block was. The journey took under ten minutes, left down Sathorn Road and before we hit Rama Four Road turned right and I then started to get lost. Ton's apartment block was more akin to our high rise concrete monstrosities of the late sixties not as tall, but not exactly auspicious and definitely not in a very salubrious area.

We took a battered lift up a couple of floors and I could sense Ton was extremely nervous. It was a great honour to be taken to his home and it was an indication of how close he now considered our friendship. The lift opened and we faced a maze of small walkways open to the elements on one side, on the other were identical doorways which were the entrances to the flats.

Stopping at one of the doors Ton turned and looked at me with an uncertain expression on his face. He then opened the door into a small room with two wooden chairs; sitting in one was his friend Khun Aun. We both kicked off our shoes and entered Ton's home, Khum Aun bowed and I responded. We both shook hands and Khun said to me in faltering English, "Pleased to meet you at last." He was most softly spoken and had an air of calm about him. Ton gave me the very quick tour of his flat, the living room in which we were in had a small TV on a shelf against the wall and adjacent was a double ring table top gas cooker. There was a sink with one tap next to the petite cooker. The two chairs were the only real furniture apart from a small coffee table.

Through a sliding door was the other room of the apartment which was the bedroom, it had one single bed squashed against the wall and Ton must have seen my quizzical glance as he reached under the bed and pulled out a sliding camp bed: "I sleep here," he explained. Because of the lack of space everything in the apartment was functional; there were plastic boxes with lids for storage that doubled as extra stools, rails against walls that acted as cupboards. One thing I did notice that the flat was spotless. Ton told me later he had cleaned it especially for my visit; I was a little embarrassed that he had done so.

Khun Aun was a few years older than Ton who considered him more of an older brother than a friend. I was to become aware in the future that Khun was a controlling, sensible influence on Ton who had quite a tempestuous youth. I never knew exactly how they met, Khun was gay and a very private person that I never really got to know that well, but I did know it was good for him to be around Ton.

Ton was proud of his small home and I think it was because it was his first place after leaving the family home. His parents still lived in the outskirts of Bangkok and Ton would normally go to see them over the weekend. Khun came with us to the cinema and we ate street food after for a late dinner which I was pleased to pay for, all in all it was a very pleasant evening and I was doing exactly what the rest of the Bangkok residents did and loved it.

The days passed amazingly quickly as there is so much to explore in Bangkok and with Ton acting as my guide things were never dull. I was fully aware of the delicate balance of our friendship, a relatively rich farang and a financially struggling working class Thai. Ton was just about fiscally surviving and I had to be careful not to be seen to be frivolous with my money. It was hard at some times as we would forgo relatively cheap activities because they were an extravagance he could not afford. It would have been easy for me to fund everything, but that would have been totally the wrong thing to do. Our friendship was based on two equal parts and that way Ton kept his dignity.

This policy had its benefits as I experienced true Bangkok life the way the Thais live it. I ate street food, drank Thai whisky in small dens, travelled by public transport and saw areas and places a tourist would never be shown. Occasionally I would go sightseeing by myself and one such time I went to visit the Grand Palace. It is probably the one must see thing in Bangkok as the site also houses other wonderful attractions: The Temple of the Emerald Buddha and behind that Wat Pho which is the Temple of the Reclining Buddha. The Buddha is spectacular and huge over forty five metres long, covered completely in Gold Leaf. It is extravagant, glitzy and quite fantastic, even its feet are three metres long.

I was coming to the end of my month's rental of my apartment and still had nearly three weeks left before I returned to the UK. I had already come to a decision to return to Thailand as soon as I could after Christmas. I was not certain how I was going to fund it; I would work on that when I got home. There was nothing left for me now back in Liverpool apart from the upcoming savage winter. Yes, my friends still remained, but I had constant contact with them and they were the only thing stopping me completely emigrating.

Even though I adored Bangkok I missed the sea so Ton came up with the idea that after my rental period expired I should go to one of the islands. Then on one of my last nights in Bangkok I met Ton the same time as usual and he seemed very excited which was unusual for him. He had been asked to go to Phuket by his company to vet a couple of hotels they advertised to tourists. He suggested I go with him and as I had never been to Phuket I readily agreed.

Ton arranged the flights and the accommodation and a couple of days later we were on a Nok Air flight to Phuket. He had suggested that we stayed out of the major tourist areas and had booked a small beach chalet in a place called Bang Tao. He could get a really good rate and so it made perfect sense. Ton would work during the day whilst I sat in the sun, an occupation he and few other Thais enjoy then in the evenings he would show me around the island.

Phuket is Thailand's largest island and is on the west coast of the country facing the Andaman Sea. The island is actually connected to the mainland by two road bridges and it is possible to drive all the way there, but the flight was so cheap it did not make any monetary or time sense to do so. The main two towns are Phuket Town which is the capital and is on the south east of the island; and Patong which is the main beach resort on the west coast. Where I was staying in Bang Tao was about thirty kilometres north of Patong. Similar to Koh Samui; the centre of the island is mostly jungle and plantations but is quite beautiful.

Our resort consisted of around thirty wooden chalets dotted around sporadically under a canopy of trees; it faced its own stretch of the quite secluded Bang Tao beach. There was a hut that acted as the reception and a nice sized swimming pool, apart from that there were no other amenities. There was a restaurant on the site called Mario's that catered for residents for the resort as well as outside clientele and sufficed for lunch or drinks.

The chalet was ideal, it was fairly large and had two Queen sized beds and a third single one. There was a TV, A/C, fridge and an outside wooden deck, complete with a Bamboo table and two chairs. The whole resort was fairly run down with some chalets actually demolished, apparently there was a land dispute and rumours of the resort's imminent closure. I had never before shared a room with Ton, but I now considered him a friend and was not in the least embarrassed. I was relieved I had stopped snoring with all my weight loss as previously I had a bad reputation as being a bit of a grunter in my sleep and that would have been most embarrassing.

Bang Tao is one of the more affluent areas of Phuket. International five star hotels are to be found there alongside golf courses and expensive restaurants. Our little resort was off the beaten track, there was a small road that acted as an access road through the forest and it had a few little shops, bars and restaurants. It was ideal, and after maelstrom that is Bangkok it was a perfect place to chill and relax.

Ton's work was not demanding and he only had to spend a few hours the whole of our stay devoted to it so we had plenty of time together. On our second day we both agreed that we should fill the fridge up with food and drink and Ton suggested a trip to Patong to visit the beach and shop in one of the town's supermarkets.

I did not like Patong one little bit. I had read that Phuket is rapidly becoming Thailand's version of Ibiza and if that is so then Patong is San Antonio. The beach was absolutely crammed with sun loungers and packed out with tourists. It did not resemble any Thailand I knew, it could have been any cheap package tour resort and attracted the sort of clientele such a place would. The streets were thronged with scantily clad youths swigging beer from bottles and the bars were doing a very brisk trade even though it was barely midday.

The stalls and shops on the main beach road were selling cheap tat and crappy seaside mementos only drunken people would buy, and the predominant language to be heard was Russian. Over the months and years I have been visiting Thailand there has been a large increase of Russian holidaymakers and for the most part they are hated by the Thais. In some ways it reminded me of the Brit's invasion of the Costas in the Seventies.

I do not know what part of Russia these package holidaymakers are from, but I certainly do not want to go there. They are extremely rude, very impatient and for the most part permanently drunk. Most of the bar brawls and street trouble involves the younger louts and I avoid them or places that cater for them like the plague. The older ones disrupt orderly queues at lifts or in shops and barge their way to the front with ignorant arrogance. Interestingly though it is only certain places that are affected, any thinking man's destination such as Bangkok or Chiang Mai they do not frequent. But because of the recent turbulent times for Thailand's tourist trade I am afraid the Russian Rouble is gladly accepted.

During our shopping an ugly incident appeared in the supermarket with some Russians. Ton amazed me and a side of him appeared that I had never seen before from the quiet, polite character I had got to know. He actually squared up to three Russians who tried to jump the queue, they seemed like a family and the mother barged her trolley right to the front where we were waiting.

Under his breath, Ton growled, "Fucking Russians, I hate them," and smashed our trolley into theirs forcing them out of the queue. The other Thais around us closed ranks in solidarity and the interlopers were shut out.

Amazingly the Russian woman did not seem the slightest bit perturbed or embarrassed and walked off pushing her trolley to jump some other queue. I thought if that was accepted behaviour in Russian supermarkets then I would never be doing my big shop in Vladivostok, not without Ton at any rate. We had not spoken since the incident and outside whilst waiting for a taxi I said something flippant to Ton, he turned quickly to face me and for a minute I thought I had offended him. Then a big grin came upon his face. Laughing, he said, "Fucking Russians!"

The rest of our holiday in Phuket was fine and we visited a few of Ton's friends around the island even returning to Patong one night to see somebody who worked in a Cabaret Show. But my time in Thailand was rapidly running out and Ton's work was finished, so we flew back to Bangkok and I checked in at the Holiday Inn for my last couple of days.

My last night I met Ton at Patty's Bar then we arranged to eat at the fish restaurant in the Car Park for our final meal together. Again, I was gutted to be leaving Bangkok and more so this time as I was also leaving behind a true friend. Luckily for me, Ton is not an emotional type of person so the evening was very upbeat. We took a table at the restaurant and it was far busier than I had ever seen it. We discussed where I should go to on my return in January and Ton said he would come up with some ideas for me and we could communicate by email in the coming days and weeks to decide.

Half way through dining an argument sprang up between two tables in the Car Park. One table had a group of eight men all wearing the same type of shirt and I presumed they were a work party. At the other table were two men and a woman, all the people were Thai and judging by the glasses and bottles strewn around I estimated both groups were fairly drunk.

Ton saw me staring at the disturbance and bade me to immediately look away whispering, "Mafia." But I could not, the argument was getting extremely heated and the voices had turned from shouting to almost hysterical screaming. I looked around and noticed that there was no staff to be seen, they knew the same thing as Ton and knew these were dangerous people.

But it was not the larger group that were the gangsters, one of the men sitting with the woman stood up and drew a pistol pointing it at the other table. His colleague also stood with a large commando style knife in his hand. I had never been in such a situation and did not know what to do. Ton seemed nervous but quite calm; how did he know the people were Mafia? Then the woman also rose pointing at a man in the larger group screaming at him. I had seen this sort of thing before, a drunken woman convinced she had someway been dishonoured and causing a shit storm between her man and the alleged perpetrator.

The larger group then backed down realising the mistake they had made, not initially knowing that their opponents were Thai Mafia. They were almost fawning in their acquiescence and were bowing low to their adversaries in a gesture of defeat and submission. I could see that they were very afraid of the other men and their evening had just turned into a nightmare. The woman ran over and viciously slapped the man she had been pointing at numerous times across the face. I suppose she would have been described by Mickey Spillane as a gangster's moll. Sensibly the man kept his head down and did not look up; if he had caught the gaze of one of the other men then he would have been shot or stabbed.

The incident seemed to be at a stalemate, her honour had been restored and the large group did not pose any threat. The man with the gun sat down and the woman went back to his table. The other man with the knife brandished it in the air with hint of arrogant gusto of a victor but thankfully also sat. The large group gathered their things quickly, left some money on the table and exited sharply bowing in reverence as they did so to their superiors.

It seemed that the gangsters were staying, so in order that we were not going to be the next innocent targets for the moll, we hastily beat our own retreat. Ton walked with me back to the Holiday Inn and we had our final drink together in the lobby bar. I quizzed Ton how he knew who the men were and he just shrugged his shoulders, but I knew he was hiding something from me. It was easy to forget just how dangerous Bangkok or for that matter

Thailand can be. Ton was always telling me to be careful, but until now I had not really heeded his warnings.

He only stayed for one drink and we said our goodbyes outside on the street in front of the hotel. I grabbed Ton and we briefly hugged knowing it would not be too long before we saw each other again. I owed him so much for all he had done for me, Ton was an enigma and I had just scratched the surface of this complex character from a completely different culture. I had learned so much from him but to my defence I had also imparted knowledge of a different kind to him. I was glad that our relationship was not based on money and I had not just flashed my cash in an attempt to impress as that would have been shallow and Ton would have never been a true friend to me.

Sitting on my Emirates flight home the following day I thought deeply about my recent visit. My mother still occupied my thoughts heavily every day but whilst I was learning new things in Thailand the ache of her passing was kept at bay. But I was fully aware I was returning to winter and more misery and one thing kept on nagging at me; how was I going to afford to come back?

Chapter Sixteen

A REFRESHING SURPRISE

I arrived home on the 16th December and whilst I had been away, had agreed by email with Hendo that I would help with a Christmas Soul Night on Saturday the 18th. Hendo had booked Waterloo Rugby Club for the venue and we were going to use all my equipment so apart from ticket distribution there was nothing to organise.

The event was already a sell out by the time I returned home so the next few days I spent getting my music together. I␣was a relief to have my energies devoted to a project so that I did not have to time think about my bereavement. It was fucking cold in Liverpool and the night before the gig it snowed heavily. The whole evening was in jeopardy, but Hendo, Sandy and I all agreed that we would press ahead with the event regardless of the weather. It was too late to call it off and we could not contact anybody to do so.

I felt like a proper twat having a deep sun tan walking around on the snowy streets of Liverpool. But there was nothing I could do about it apart from wearing a sodding balaclava all the time. That is acceptable, if slightly spooky, when outdoors, but I could not possibly continue to wear it indoors. In Liverpool it is rather common for some of the ladies to have an all year round tan: I have not a clue where they achieve this false colour from, but it certainly does not resemble anything that you might glean from the sun. It is a sort of fluorescent orange colour like they have been nuked or something. I suppose it must come in handy in dark nightclubs to spot their mates coming back from the bar or a snog.

By the time Saturday came, the snow had stopped falling and had settled. However, we were all concerned how it would affect the attendance of the Soul Night. Getting the equipment to the venue was a miracle in itself as our van was sliding on the icy roads, but eventually we did and set up was complete by the appointed time. Although the venue was only half full the night was a roaring success as the punters that had braved the conditions were determined to make the most of it and they seemed to appreciate the fact we had continued ahead with the evening.

An added bonus to the whole evening was a particular guest that attended. An old friend I had previously played football with called Eddie McMahon came. On my return to England I had been given the news that he had some sort of inoperable cancer and was very sick, so it was thrilling to see my old friend that I had not seen for years enjoying the night with a contented smirk all evening on his face. It was a privilege to shake hands with him at the end of the evening and I would have organised the whole thing just for him if it enabled him to forget his troubles for just one night.

The days after the Soul Night leading up to Christmas Day I took stock of my finances again. My recent trip had not quite cleaned me out of savings and my current account was healthy with just the same amount of money going out as there was coming in. Then on Christmas Eve I received an article in the post that had me hopping with joy (as I am unable to jump!).

It was a Christmas card from my brother that included a cheque for two and a half thousand pounds. It was nothing to do with my mother's estate as she had left no will and the legal wranglings were in their infancy being handled by my brother's solicitor. I did not expect to receive much in respect of an inheritance as the vast majority of her estate would go to pay debts we owed the nursing home. But reading the note that accompanied the card it explained that an old friend of my mother had passed away and left five grand between my brother and me. I know it was wrong to be so happy at the recent demise of Little Dot, but I had only met the poor woman on a couple of occasions and for once I had been given a piece of good fortune.

My funding for my next trip was complete; I could now go ahead with all guns blazing and start organising things with Ton. Christmas Day, I was invited for Dinner at Richie's parents house, it had become a generous and welcome invitation that I had received regularly since my mother had become ill. That night Richie and I discussed the date for our trip to Thailand and settled on the 12th January, a damn fine way to start 2011 and the New Year.

We agreed that we would spend a couple of days in Bangkok and then have a two week holiday together in Koh Samui. After that Richie would return home and I would stay in Thailand for an extra month. I contacted Ton on Boxing Day and let him know my dates and enquired if he had any thoughts of where I should stay and should I return to the Shangarila.

His response by email surprised me totally; he suggested that I did not return for a long stay in Bangkok. He had another idea, as he knew I liked the sea and he had just had a new job offer; would I consider Pattaya. I was quite taken aback that Ton would suggest Pattaya as the reputation the city has in Thailand is legendary. It is renowned for being possibly the bawdiest place in the world and is a sex tourist's haven. I knew Ton had worked and lived there before and he also knew my hatred of such places, he had seen that in Patong.

The news was so staggering I phoned Ton immediately to try and understand his thinking behind the suggestion. We had a long and expensive telephone conversation and Ton explained that he had been offered a job as a Tourist Guide from a company that was in Pattaya. He was adamant that the sex industry was only a part of the large city and there was much more to the place than just that. Of course, I did not have to follow Ton I could go anywhere I wanted, but his insistence that I should try Pattaya was most convincing.

Reluctantly I agreed to try Pattaya for a month and once again left Ton to find accommodation for me. He knew my requirements and I gave him a budget matching that of the Shangarila. The following weekend Ton travelled down to Pattaya and personally searched on my behalf for a suitable place. I had sent him five thousand Baht around one hundred pounds to use as a deposit on anywhere he thought suitable and I stressed how grateful I was for all his efforts. I knew that Ton felt flattered by my complete trust in him, not with just the money but my acceptance of his decisions.

A week before my flight back to Bangkok I received an email from Ton confirming that he had found somewhere on my behalf and attached a web site address of my future home. View Talay 5 was a condominium complex in Jomtien which is a couple of miles from Pattaya City. He had chosen a large apartment with two bedrooms on one of the top floors of View Talay 5D. The apartment looked fantastic and Ton had been correct when he advised me that I would get a lot more for my money down on the coast compared to Bangkok.

My holiday with Rich in Koh Samui was excellent although it was a bit disappointing to see that the Russian Invasion had spread as far as Koh Samui. Even Din had replaced Eddie and employed a Russian girl as the restaurant's meeter and greeter, emphasising the increase of the pesky interlopers. Richie was quite lyrical when stating that he hoped that Thailand would not cow tie completely to the Russians; it would change the country's identity if it did so, and not change it for the better.

It was strange checking out of the Centara and leaving Richie behind, but his flight home was much later in the day. Normally we always travelled together, but times had changed and entirely down to me. I had an early morning flight to Bangkok where I had arranged to meet Ton at the airport so we could both travel to Pattaya together.

Arriving at Suvarnabhumi, I had a short wait for my luggage and I did not have to suffer the normal delays at Immigration because I was on an internal flight. I used my new Thai phone and phoned Ton who was already waiting at the taxi rank on the first floor. A couple of minutes later I was reunited with my new friend who was waiting together with two large bags, I had forgotten he was moving home.

He greeted me with his familiar smile and we shook hands warmly as we immediately started babbling together. We went to the desk and informed the officer of our destination, Ton got a copy of the receipt and the fare was to be one thousand five hundred Baht. I thought that was excellent, thirty quid for a Taxi all the way to Pattaya. Ton said that going in the other direction the fare for some inexplicable reason was only eight hundred Baht.

Speeding along Highway Number Seven in the taxi, I asked Ton how long the journey would take. The road from Suvarnabhumi Airport to Pattaya is all motorway and normally it takes an hour and a half, being about one hundred miles. Because the airport is on the south side of Bangkok and the journey is predominately south, there is no snarl up with the city's traffic.

It was a Saturday and Ton did not start his new job until Monday, so he said it gave him time to find somewhere to live. I rejected his idea out of hand and insisted that he stayed with me until he could find somewhere that would give him at least a month. I pressed him to accept by embarrassing him that it was his idea that I had come to Pattaya and he could bloody well show me around. I genuinely thought that Ton had not expected my offer of accommodation as I had offered him loans in the past which he had never accepted. However, on this occasion he did, and for the second time we were going to be room mates.

Exiting from the motorway we hit Sukhumvit Road on the north side of Pattaya and driving on the outskirts of the city I was surprised how big the place actually was. I had always considered Pattaya to be nothing more than a long strip of beach with bars and strip joints in abundance. But here we were driving through dense traffic in an urban hinterland. Sukhumvit Road is one of the main thoroughfares that skirts the city to the north and progresses on towards Rayong. It is the longest road in Thailand and is officially known as highway three. Starting in Bangkok and taking a coastal route, it passes through Pattaya, Rayong and eventually ends in Trat.

I suppose it is a bit like the A1 starting in London and ending all the way to Edinburgh. Although in some ways you could compare London and Bangkok there is no way imaginable you could liken Edinburgh with Trat. I would surmise that the Firth of Forth is a tad chillier than the Gulf of Thailand, and sharing a border with stiff old England does not sound quite as exciting as sharing your border with exotic, tropical Cambodia.

Ton knew Pattaya well and was directing our driver past two huge supermarkets. One such chain was called Big C, not a very welcoming logo to inspire your weekly shopping! We turned right, down a long wide road named Thepprasit, it was packed either side with shops selling diverse goods from motor bikes, furniture, ceramics and all manner of household items. At one stage on our left was a huge outdoor market and Ton pointed to it, saying, "It's the night market, open at the weekend."

At the end of Thepprasit, we stopped at a junction and I could see the Gulf of Thailand ahead of us. There were also several large buildings reaching into the sky, they were Jomtiens' condominiums and there seemed to be many of them. Ton pointed to one and smiled, I gleaned from his gesture that was our new home. The driver also slowed down and questioned my friend; "View Talay?" Ton started to speak Thai to the driver and confirmed the condo on the other side of the road was our destination.

Thailand has a curious system on its highways. Seldom will you find any roundabouts they prefer to have a gap in the central reservation and the traffic is directed to U-turn. Not by lights or markings on the road surface just by the very fact there is a gap to do so. It sounds chaotic and it often bloody well is, as nobody seems to have the right of way. Or if there is a right of way nobody pays much attention to it and many accidents occur on a regular basis.

It is widely accepted that perhaps the Thais are the worst drivers in the world and it is a fact widely accepted by Thais themselves. Certainly to navigate the roads safely is at the very least hazardous and at worst fatal. I am not bringing into the equation the many drug or alcohol related incidents or even in some cases the actual poor quality of the roads. I am simply stating a fact that the Thai nation is not adept in the skills of handling a motor vehicle be it two, four or fifty wheeled varieties.

There are many contributing facts to my theory and I have taken the opportunity of listing some; firstly, indicators are frequently ignored either by the driver or by other vehicles they seem to have no purpose whatsoever and are something that has been activated mostly by mistake. They are however; a terrific way of confusing the fuck out of hesitating pedestrians as nobody is quite certain if the blinking warning light is for real or not.

Parking is another big problem as the Thais feel it is acceptable to just stop their vehicles and abandon them wherever they came to a halt. This can be at junctions, traffic lights, pedestrian crossings of if the whim arose in the middle of a road. It does not seem to matter where the location is and normally the more bizarre the position then the more popular the obstruction is.

Finally, is road consideration and etiquette; it just does not exist. It is acceptable to overtake or undertake, stay in lane or weave about like a drunken Tug Boat captain. All at varying speeds designed to confuse other road users. For instance speeding up when approaching a junction or especially if a pedestrian is crossing is favoured by most drivers only to jam on the brakes at the last minute to avoid a collision. The Thai's seem to have no grasp on the fundamentals of road safety and have no idea whatsoever of when to join or how to exit a stream of traffic, they are simply menaces behind the wheel.

I do not know who on Earth teaches the Thai people how to drive, but it must be a blind quivering alcoholic with a propensity for sudden erratic behaviour; come to think of it, it sounds like my first instructor! Perhaps their BSM stands for the Blind School of Maniacs.

We navigated our U-turn quite successfully with only a couple of scooters having to swerve to avoid us and one car screeching to a halt. Our driver had an expression on his face almost saying, "I think that one went quite well." The other vehicles did not beep their horns or stop to remonstrate; this was daily driving in Thailand and a common occurrence.

Turning left we, pulled into a huge condominium, it must have been over twenty stories high and over five hundred meters long. Painted brilliant white it gleamed in the afternoon sun, and the whole length of the building was interfaced with balconies of the individual apartments. The building pointed towards the sea so most of the balconies were facing either Jomtien to one side or Pattaya on the other. The taxi finally came to a halt under a canopy where a security guard monitored our activity.

Ton bade me wait and returned with a trolley which we loaded our bags onto and he pushed it up a ramp into the lobby. The ground floor reception was cavernous and the large open entrance we had entered was matched by an identical one opposite allowing a refreshing breeze through the building. There were no doors or windows at either entrance as there was twenty four hour security and everybody was monitored accessing the lifts.

To our right was the building's reception for administration and to our left was a large glass contained office advertising property for rent or sale. Ton opened the door to the office and I met a lady who was handling our rental. Completing the paperwork and handing over my forty thousand Baht cash payment I received my rental agreement. The cost was a little less than the Shangarila, but I intended to check out Pattaya and if I liked it look for something cheaper.

The lady took us to the seventeenth floor we walked to the end of the building nearest the sea. The last door we came to we halted and the lady fiddled with the two locks barring our entrance and eventually managed to open the door. With my propensity of fucking up any lock the trouble she had did not bode well for the future. The door opened into a huge, bright and very airy room and I fell in love with it instantly.

The apartment was one of the few corner units in the Condo and the living room was completely surrounded by glass on two sides. The conservatory type doors were from ceiling to floor and could be opened completely on to the massive wrap around balcony that encompassed the whole apartment. Where the Shangarila had been dark and fairly dated with the abundance of wood, View Talay was ultra modern and chic with white ceramic tiles and plenty of glass.

In front of me was the ocean and looking down I saw the Condo's large swimming pool, to my right were marvellous views of Pattaya City in the distance. The apartment was one hundred and ten square meters about a third bigger than in Bangkok, but this was enhanced even more by the massive balcony. We were given a guided tour by a very proud agent, I presumed this must have been one of her top apartments and that is why it was expensive by Pattaya standards.

There was a fully fitted open kitchen to the left of the entrance door, it was not large, but had everything including cooker, large fridge, microwave and washing machine. The cabinets were a futuristic bright white matching the floor tiles and blended in perfectly to the modern design. In the main living room was a huge white leather corner suite facing a flat screen, surround sound entertainment system. There was a small glass dining table and two chairs and that completed the massive room's furniture. I did not know if it was minimalist design to make the already large space look even larger or the owner had run out of his decorating budget.

Three doors led off from the living room, one led to a bathroom big enough to contain a glass screened shower, toilet and basin. Another led to a double bedroom, it had no windows and was fairly snug, but had storage and a small TV on the wall. The third led to the en suite master bedroom. It was a large room with the same big windows covering one entire wall that could also be opened onto the balcony. The furniture was of light teak that blended with the white tiles and the King sized bed did not dwarf the ample sized room. Facing the bed was a large flat screened TV sitting on a long teak bureau. Opposite the windows was a massive teak storage system integrated into the wall. It had matching recesses which housed mirrors and acted as dressing tables, a chair was in front of each. The system also incorporated cupboards and drawers that had a quality feel to the handles and fittings.

A thought occurred to me that this room was meant to be en suite. There was only one place a door could be and that was part of the storage system. I looked at the centre of the teak furniture and knew one of the handles must open a door and not just a closet. After tugging at two false representations I found one that yielded and a teak door swung open to reveal a stupendous bathroom. I walked through the wardrobe and into the en suite.

Everything was of the highest, modern quality and the room was entirely covered in black and white tiling. The shower enclosure was the length of the bathroom and encompassed a large overhead rain shower as well as a multi headed system fixed to a wall. Four large floor to ceiling glass curtains separated the enclosure from the remainder of the bathroom and bright ceiling spot lights illuminated the whole space. It was like stepping into a photograph in one of the glossy House and Home magazines, and apart from one or two swanky hotels I had stayed in, I was not used to such luxury.

The whole apartment was magnificent and I think Ton was as pleased with my reaction than I was myself. Once again my trust in him had been completely justified and I knew I would be happy living in such surroundings for a month. I could not wait until the estate agent left and we could both start unpacking and start to make the apartment a home.

We explored the apartment from top to bottom getting to know how everything worked and where things were. The inventory encompassed just about everything needed that you would find in a hotel and had much more on top. Ton had not really paid much attention to the second bedroom on his previous visit as he had not expected my offer of hospitality, but seemed to be elated unpacking his belongings in the luxurious bedroom. It was a far cry from a pull out bed in Bangkok and I could sense his happiness and I was glad that I had managed to repay a little of his kindness. Besides; having Ton staying with me did not cost me any extra; I was paying rent for the whole apartment if he lived there or not.

I was glad that Ton had not let pride stop him accepting my offer as I knew I would get more out of the deal than he would. In retrospect it must have been a hard decision for him to make and that he did not perceive it as any sort of charity on my behalf. It would have been disastrous for our relationship had he thought so and I was fully aware to be most politically correct with all my suggestions concerning Ton.

After we unpacked and showered we decided to go and look around the rest of the Condo then find somewhere on the beach to have dinner. The facilities View Talay offered were ideal. The two lifts were in the centre of the building and there was a long corridor leading from one end of the building to the other. Turning left there was not much to see, but turning right heading towards the pool was a different matter. The corridor was flanked by small businesses for the benefit of the residents; there were four laundries, one convenience store and a couple of massage places.

The best thing was the number of little cafés and restaurants offering a few tables for patrons or takeaway facilities for In-Room dining. They all offered Thai cuisine cooked by Thai chefs, but had some western dishes on offer for homesick residents. The corridor ended opening out on to a large swimming pool flanked by two pool side restaurants for the use of View Talay patrons exclusively.

It was magnificent and everything about the Condo impressed me. There was an army of security guards around the place and a team of cleaners constantly working on the building. There seemed to be a mix of nationalities around, some European and some Thai. Ton told me that some of the apartments were owned by rich Thai's that come down from Bangkok at the weekend. The others are owned by expats who either permanently live there, or like in our case, rent them out.

There was a duplicate building to View Talay 5D in front built by the same developers; it was View Talay 5C. To my knowledge an "A" or "B" did not exist or if they had, were very well hidden. View Talay means Ocean View in Thai and was not deceiving as the sea was plainly visible from both buildings. Alongside the condos ran a private access road that led from the main Thappraya Highway that we had earlier taken the U-turn on, down to the beach. It stopped at a locked gate that residents had an electronic fob to open and two security guards permanently were situated.

The gate gave us access to the beach road or more accurately where we where it was the beach path that was closed to traffic during the day. The beach only fifty meters away was obscured slightly from view by a plethora of trees adding another element to the picturesque vista. Ton informed me that the beach directly ahead of us was Dongtan Beach and was probably Thailand's biggest gay beach then continuing down the coast it became Jomtien Beach, perhaps the longest in Pattaya.

Along the path were several small restaurants and a couple of bars and the area was very bohemian and atmospheric. At the end of the path was Jomtien Beach Road that runs six kilometres along the length of the beach. Here there are many condominium developments along the stretch of the coast dwarfing the low beach facing buildings. Jomtien is an affluent area of Pattaya and many farangs have settled and live permanently in this part of Thailand, affluent Thais mostly from Bangkok also own a second or holiday home in Jomtien and at weekends the area is bustling with activity.

This part of Pattaya surprised me as it was nothing I had imagined it would have been like. I knew that the centre part of the city would hold other attractions, but for now I had been proved wrong and I would reserve my judgement until I experienced it myself. Strolling around with Ton in the early evening was enjoyable pleasure; there were many expensive restaurants that were interspersed with little Thai gems that I was keen to experience. Down the small Sois off Beach Road were dozens of Beer Bars; these also were quiet and quite reserved, nothing like Soi Green Mango in Samui. Here there were also many small Thai restaurants serving the local community.

All this was on my doorstep a few minutes down the private road from my condo. It could not have been better and I thought that I would get to like Jomtien very much indeed. We ate at an inexpensive Thai fish restaurant facing the sea and although not quite up to the standard of the Bangkok Car Park, it was very good. Both of us were a little tired from quite a hectic day so after dinner we went back to crash.

The following few days were spent settling in to Jomtien, Ton went to start his new job which was based in central Pattaya and I hung about the pool and the beach. He worked six days a week from 8am till 7pm, but it could be later if clients wanted a guide to work late. For that effort he was paid the princely sum of seven thousand Baht a month, around one hundred and forty pounds.

Normally he would take a Songthaew or Baht Bus which from Jomtien to Central Pattaya which only cost twenty Baht. These buses are licensed by the council and are an excellent form of public transport. They are normally converted Japanese pick up trucks such as Toyota Hilux, Mitsubishi Triton or Isuzu D-Max and have two bench seats in the rear and a lowered metal platform at the back, so it gives easy access to the bus - or people can stand on it if the bus is busy.

They stop literally anywhere and usually travel in straight lines. There are no markings of destination and if a bus suddenly starts to go in the wrong direction then you have to quickly press the buzzer and get off rapidly and wait for the next one. There are many Baht buses all over the city so the wait is not normally more than a minute or so. After a while you become familiar with the routes and if your destination is a little difficult, i.e. not in straight lines, then it's often easier to take a motorbike. These taxis again are licensed and the drivers wear bright coloured vests indicating they are official; helmets must be worn at all times.

On an advisory note, wearing a helmet is essential and especially at night. Thais, especially younger ones, will drive their motorbikes on an evening's revelry. In Pattaya that can be till 7am and drinking and driving whilst inebriated is a daily occurrence. The police occasionally have road blocks, but the fact is there are too many people on too many bikes to enforce the law. Daily accidents, injuries and deaths are a shameful, but a common feature of Pattaya's sometimes lethal roads.

Ton had many friends dotted around Pattaya from previously living there and slowly I was getting to know them. My first initiation was coming back to the room after a spot of shopping to be greeted by a rather rotund Thai man coming out of the bathroom wearing a towel. Ton was nowhere to be seen and the man smiled at me, not in the least bit bothered and went out onto the balcony to sit down. I was a little bemused, was this the owner of the apartment? Was I in the correct apartment? Opening the door to check the number I confirmed to myself I indeed was correct. It is strange that in this situation that it was me feeling awkward not the intruder.

I checked both bedrooms and there was still no sign of Ton. I walked back into the living room and the rotund man was helping himself to a drink from the fridge. Still, not a word had been spoken between us and the man did not seem to be particularly arsed to start up a conversation with me anyway. At that moment, the front door opened and Ton entered nodding to me as a gesture of greeting. He had in his hand two new packets of L & M cigarettes that I presumed he had just gone to buy.

Ton then went out onto the balcony to join the man who was obviously an acquaintance as both of them lit a new cigarette from one of the recently acquired packets. He waved at me through the window and I went out to join the pair.

"This is Taam," my friend introduced the stranger. His name was actually pronounced Damn. "He needed a shower so he used our bathroom." It was never explained to me why Taam needed to bathe and at that particular time, but it was obviously a matter of some urgency. Did all Thai friends pop around to a mate's for a shower? Or was it something particular to Taam? I had a mate back in Liverpool called Shawry whose penchant was to christen peoples lavatories. Perhaps Taam was the Thai Shower version?

Taam hardly spoke any English, explaining his previous reluctance to engage in conversation. However, once introduced, he became most loquacious to me in a very animated way. I could not understand what the Hell the chain smoking man was saying, but it seemed very amusing as Ton was laughing heartedly at nearly everything Taam said.

This was another side of Ton I had not seen before: I had never seen him laughing like this and it suited him. Ton explained to me all about Taam, he was a Mammasan at one of Pattaya's strip clubs.

It was his job to look after the girls and ensure they were good to their clients but also that no harm came to them. He was openly gay, posing no threat to the girls or clients and the jovial man kept the bar ticking. He admitted to drinking around two bottles of Tequila a night as he would ensure the clients bought shots for all the girls not just the one he had paid to be with.

Looking at Taam and hearing about his lifestyle, I did not think he was going to be long for this world, but if that was the case he was certainly enjoying every second of it. After about half an hour the whirlwind ceased as Taam had to go to work and took his leave of us. The apartment seemed suddenly quiet and Ton rose and said he was going to get his things together for volleyball. He suggested I went with him as tonight he was playing fairly locally and thought I might like some air. I had now hired a motorbike as it was so cheap being one pound fifty a day, and was an excellent way for us both to get about. I never drove the vehicle, but often I would be with Ton or he could take me somewhere and it made economical and convenient sense.

The leisure complex staggered me; it was only about ten minutes away but right off the beaten path. We traversed small roads, Sois and lanes right out into the thick bush of the countryside. Then out of absolutely nowhere a vast entrance appeared to open into the long, wide drive of the leisure centre. I had no idea where Ton had been playing volleyball, previously thinking perhaps it had been on the beach or some waste ground. I berated myself for the presumed assumption that because Ton and his friends were poor they would not have access to decent leisure facilities.

We slowly drove along the wide road and to our left was a full sized football pitch. Behind that was a large building Ton told me was an indoor court for many games but was quite expensive to hire. Unlike the vegetation outside, there were luscious, well maintained areas of lawn and the road continued winding around with each corner a new vista. A second building housed changing rooms and more indoor facilities, but Ton said it was seldom used. We stopped outside and parked the bike with dozens of others; how the Hell the owners ever found their own bike again was a mystery?

There were four or five volleyball courts all floodlit and every one being used. Past those were several slightly smaller courts hosting a game I had never seen before. Most of Ton's friends were hanging about the nearest volleyball court waiting their allotted time and he went over to chat to his mates whilst I informed him I was going to go for a walk.

I went to investigate the game I had spied and wandered over to where the court was. It was a similar size to that of badminton court with a net about one and a half meters high in the centre. There were three players on each side playing, for all that I could see, keepy-uppy with a small Rattan woven ball. Sepak Takraw, as I later found out: its name is played to similar rules as volleyball. The three players of one team can have three touches before the ball has to be returned back over the net, the players can use their feet, heads and knees but anything else is a foul.

The speed and dexterity of the players was amazing and I was transfixed on watching the play. One of the most common ways of producing a 'smash' was to acrobatically leap into the air and 'scissor' kick the ball downwards from a great height over the net. Once executed, the player would then crash very painfully back down onto the concrete floor. It was fascinating stuff and I considered the skill needed to control the small ball that the players must be good at football.

This observation was to be proved totally wrong when later I sat and watched a game of football. Most of the players were determined to dribble the ball up their own arses and did not give a fuck about passing it to any of their team mates. A thought occurred to me: *Did they need a coach?*

After watching the engaging game of Sepak Takraw for some time, I decided to see what else was occurring. Two large expanses of land housed some form of musical keep fit and dozens of participants male and female exercised after work. I passed one volleyball court that was constructed from deep sand and there was quite a crowd gathered. There was a lot of noise being made by the competitors, a great deal more than anywhere else and I was intrigued why.

I stood next to a tree and studied the game and it seemed at first it was a ladies match of beach volleyball. The players and spectators changed places regularly and it became apparent I was the only one not participating. One substitute came to stand close to me and I realised she was a katoey. Without make up and a full coiffure ladyboys are a little easier to recognise. I studied the players more earnestly and realised everybody there was a katoey but me.

Only in Thailand would you see such a thing, nobody else in the whole leisure centre was the slightest bit perturbed or interested at the event which would have made the headlines of the Sun newspaper back home: "Sick Trannies Perform Publically" would probably have been the caption under a photo showing a close up of a bulge in a katoeys shorts. The scene in a way sort of summed up the dichotomy of Thailand, on one hand a very traditional, religious nation and on the other a modern, tolerant and often extremely permissive society.

Getting very confused by the rotating substitutions and not having a clue what score it was I moved on, leaving behind me the screams and yells of the very energetic players interspersed with howls of laughter. Whatever the score was, the katoeys were certainly enjoying their evening's sport and exercise. Ton's game was altogether different being very serious and fast and I wondered who was having the best time? I was quite impressed by my friend's skill and saw that he was one of the better players in a fiercely contested game.

It was now getting dark and all the matches were being played under artificial light. The later the time got the more new competitors arrived as it was more popular to play late due to the cooler temperature. Ton's game finished and he asked if I wanted to go out that evening as a couple of friends were meeting up for a drink. I readily agreed, never having to be coerced to have a beer. We drove home first so Ton could shower and I also changed my rather grimy attire, I did not know how I got so dirty as I had not done anything, but dirty I was nevertheless. Perhaps I was suffering from the same mysterious dirt bug that had affected Taam.

We drove to the centre of Pattaya to the beach road. Pattaya beach is four kilometres long and almost along its entire length are hotels, bars and more bars. This was more akin to Patong and what I had expected of Pattaya by its reputation. At one end of the beach road is 'Walking Street' which is probably the most debauched stretch of road in the world. Here mostly tourists frequent sometimes for the numerous beer bars, but mostly for the sleazy sex shows.

We parked the bike down a small Soi and walked along the beach road towards Walking Street. At night, Pattaya Beach is not for the faint-hearted and can be extremely dangerous especially if you are drunk. There are numerous katoey prostitutes, some of which are illegal immigrants, who are renowned for robbing stupid sex tourists looking for paid company. Drugs are also a major problem in Pattaya and on the beach often pushers will offer 'ice' which is slang for Crystal Meths or Yaba, a form of Methamphetamine. The latter is produced predominately in Myanmar and is a very popular drug with the Thais. The Thai authorities are extremely strict on drug trading and use and often severe prison sentences are meted out to law breakers, be they Thai nationals or tourists.

Walking Street was a Zoo of a place; the road was pedestrianized hence its name, but ironically, it was difficult to walk down due to the massive throng of party goers drunkenly jostling from one side to the other. I instantly did not like it, not because I am a prude of what was on offer, but because it was gathering place for the farang Idiot Brigade to congregate. There are a few places that are quite acceptable down Walking Street, but getting to and from them is a nightmare. We were there to just to say hello to Taam, and found him in his pole dancing bar that was up a flight of stairs in a Soi off Walking Street.

I didn't recognise Taam at first as the bar was fairly smoky, but he rushed over to greet us wearing a full length silver dress and high heels. He had a long black wig and full make up but in no way resembled a katoey. He was just in drag and enjoying his night at work. There was a stage in the centre of the room and about twenty girls in different stages of undress were writhing about to the deafening techno music. A lot of the girls to me did not look over fifteen, but seemed to be creating the desired effect to the packed room of men. Thai law states that the minimum age to work in such a place is eighteen, but sometimes the girls use false ID. As with drug offences, the Thai police will severely deal with sex offenders flagrantly disregarding the law.

Around Walking Street and the immediate area, there are scores of such places catering for every taste; girls, boys, katoeys, uniform, S & M, old, young... absolutely everything imaginable. It is a place you could lose your soul, your grip on reality and fade away into a world of debauchery. Taam was very busy so we had one quick beer: Taam had Tequila and we left to find Ton's friends.

We made our way back to the scooter and drove down a myriad of small Sois until we came to a small bar. It was a Karaoke Bar and was crammed with Thai crooners enjoying their evening. Again, I was somewhere that I was the only farang, but much preferred it to where I had just been. Ton's friends were already there sitting around a long table enjoying the Thai favourite tipple: whisky!

The cheapest and most popular way for a Thai group of friends to enjoy an evening is by sharing a bottle or two of whisky. If they are short of cash it will be Thai whisky, some of which is almost like rum; Sang Som, Mekhong, Sang Tip, Hong Thong, Blend 285 are amongst the more popular. Mekhong has added glycerine to boost the alcohol content, but sometimes had the added affect of acting as a hallucinogenic. If budget allows then Red Label, 100 Pipers or Chivas Regal are much preferred. It is not expensive to buy a bottle of Whisky in a bar or nightclub and allows the average Thai worker to enjoy an evening out. The cost of a litre bottle of Johnnie Walker's Red Label in a club is about twenty five quid, and there will be no entrance fee. Coke or Soda are the preferred mixers and they are extra, but still it is extraordinary cheap for a night out clubbing.

Normally accompanying the bottle of whisky will be a designated waiter whose job it is to keep topping the glasses up with ice and mixer. That way the establishment sells more soft drinks and balances out the discounted alcohol. But it is quite decadent having your own personal waiter for the evening even if he is there to try and quicken up the pace of your consumption. A bit like Mike from the Bug sending Richie over with your tray of drinks, the only difference being Richie would drink them for you.

Not every night was a party night and Pattaya has plenty of options for a permanent resident. There are swanky shopping malls, cinemas, a plethora of all manner of restaurants. Food markets, clothing markets, day markets and night markets: everything is available. The city has a population of around two hundred thousand people, but during the height of season, that number can be doubled by tourists.

Around the city were many attractions from idyllic islands and other coastal towns to the mountains, where the air is cooler and they actually produce wine. Many temples, zoos and wildlife sanctuaries were close by and occasionally on Ton's day off we would visit one.

Jomtien was different than Pattaya City and I liked it very much. There was a large Gay community that were mostly expats mixed together with affluent Thai residents and the normal Thai workers. The mix was a very harmonious blend and gave the area a very tolerant and engaging atmosphere, the Greenwich Village of Pattaya. Jomtien also has some of the best massage places in Pattaya and is famous for its really authentic treatments and well trained Thai masseurs.

It was also home to four very important things in my life. The first was Jomtien Language School as I had enrolled in Thai speech classes. The second was Tony's Gym; my one year subscription cost eighty pounds and was open 24hrs every day. The third was the Siam Commercial Bank; I had opened my own Thai bank account due to NatWest overseas charges. Lastly was Shenanigans; my local Pub, here I could watch Everton and keep abreast of the news.

The month in Pattaya flew by and I had made my mind up to return, but this time for one year. During the last week I searched for some cheaper accommodation, but in View Talay it all seemed so expensive. The large apartment I was renting was nine hundred per month and was far too much for my budget, most of the other apartments in View Talay were Studios, about the size of a large hotel room; they were cheaper around three hundred and fifty pounds per month. But they were too small to live permanently in and I started looking outside the Condo.

But one day I had some luck, I saw an advert on View Talay's Notice Board for a large apartment of 86sq metres. There were only a few of such apartments and they rarely come up for rental. I phoned the number and it was a private rental by a German man, he was a contractor and had to leave quickly to go to work in Dubai. We met and we struck a deal that suited us both, I would sign a twelve month agreement in return he would reduce the rental if I commenced my stay on the 1st April. The cost was four hundred and fifty pounds per month and that was also including his new motor bike as part of the deal. It would mean that Ton would have to find alternative accommodation, but we both knew that would happen anyway.

When I left Pattaya, Ton had already found a room: it was somewhere close to work and he was going to share with a friend. I had made my decision to stay in Pattaya and was excited about my move, everything was sorted and I was eager to return home to attend to all matters there. I had agreed with the German man that I could store all my clothes for my return in my new apartment and travelled home with only hand luggage.

My month back home was hectic, I had decided to rent my house out and so everything was going to have to be stored away and the place cleaned from top to bottom. My army of friends pitched in to help and most of my personal stuff I managed to store in the loft, but my music and films were a different matter. All my vinyl and its shelving went to Morgo, my CDs to Sandy and my films to Tony: it was like saying goodbye to my children and I had just fostered them out.

I went back to Boodles and this time secured a multi entry one year visa, it had a restriction that I must leave Thailand every three months and then re-enter. Most expats with the same type of visa do a day trip to Cambodia and this suffices for Thai immigration purposes, but I thought I would take the opportunity to explore more of South East Asia when the time came.

An agent visited my house and said they would be prepared to put the house up for market and would handle the rental whilst I was away. But fortunately I did not have to take that option as some friends heard about the opportunity and agreed to rent my house from the first of April. This would more than cover my rental in Thailand and I was solvent, I knew my insurance pay from work finished in September, but that was six months away and off my radar for now.

I was flying back to Thailand by Etihad this time as they were the cheapest. I had to change planes in Abu Dhabi, a small inconvenience for such a momentous step. The night before I left, I packed two bags of winter clothes and left them at some friends who kindly offered accommodation whenever I came home. Jo and Keith were old acquaintances and owned a fantastic house close to where I lived, their offer of hospitality was a godsend and it was the last obstacle to my leaving.

My arrival in Bangkok was greeted with the normal delays at passport control at Suvarnabhumi Airport, but again the wait was offset by my new luggage waiting for me at the carousel. I had purchased a new suitcase as I had crammed in many essentials for my lengthy stay. Two boxes of wine took most of the space along with coffee and plenty of DVDs.

Ton had arranged to meet me at the airport and take me back to Pattaya in one of his friends' car. But there was no sign of him when I came through customs so I phoned him. He was having lunch with his friend as he had got fed up waiting for me, I was not angry: on the contrary I was quite flattered. It was a sign how deep he considered our friendship to be, if I was a mere acquaintance then it would have been very rude and he would have been waiting for me.

I took the escalator up a floor to where all the restaurants are in the airport. I could not find Ton anywhere; I phoned repeatedly confirming his whereabouts but I still could not locate him. I stopped in my tracks as it dawned on me he was taking the piss and was somewhere watching me hauling my bags around the airport. I stood still for a minute being buffeted by the airport's manic crowd when I saw a familiar figure sitting outside Starbucks. It was Ton and he was looking directly at me laughing quite heartedly.

Walking up to the coffee shop I was shaking my head in mock disapproval at his prank. In fact I didn't find it funny at all after my long flight; I was a bit knackered and could have done without a game of hide and seek. But he seemed to have thoroughly enjoyed the ruse so I let him have his entertainment without complaint. He looked so different, he was much thinner although he was slim before and he had died his hair slightly red.

Ton hugged me, and laughingly he apologised for his behaviour. His excuse was that he was bored waiting and blamed me for Suvarnabhumi Airport's Immigration delays. He introduced Nan whom I had met before and she had taken the time to accompany Ton to collect me at the airport. The arrangement was that I would pay her petrol money and also stand dinner for the three of us that evening. It was her that had dyed Ton's hair and she was most proud of her handiwork perhaps later they would decide to paint my bald head.

Nan was a lunatic of a driver and I didn't feel safe at all, she was more interested chatting to Ton than paying any attention to the road. We were burning up the miles at a rapid pace; undertaking, overtaking, tailgating and occasionally slamming on the brakes. All manoeuvres performed without any indicators and to the accompaniment of blaring Thai Issan Music. It was a whirlwind of a trip and the passing countryside was a blur. The journey from Bangkok to Pattaya was quicker than my passing through the airport's processing procedures.

We shot up the entrance ramp to the View Talay Condominium and almost fired out the exit just as quick if it were not for dropping anchor by executing an emergency stop. I peeled my head off the rear headrest and pushed my cheeks back down from my eyebrows and unsteadily exited the car. It was like Harry Potter and Ron being ejected from the magical Ford Anglia. The security guard stared at us disapprovingly as Ton unloaded my luggage from the boot; he just about managed to close the tailgate before the car with wheels spinning sped down the ramp almost taking his fingers with it.

Ton came up with me to my new apartment helping with the luggage and also to have a look around. I had a set of keys given to me before I left and fished them out of my rucksack and opened the door. The room was exactly as I remembered it; it was designed like my previous apartment in a very modern fashion. The living space was long with large white ceramic tiles on the floor ending at four huge glass windows that opened up on to a large balcony with a table and four chairs.

To the right of the entrance was a fully fitted kitchen luxuriously finished in polished grey slate and separated from the main room by a glass partition. Then there was a long formal dining table with solid black dining chairs leading to the relaxing area. Its main feature was a white leather corner sofa big enough for six or seven people facing a Flat Screen TV and a long, low white cabinet housing Surround Sound DVD and accompanying speakers. Finally, in the corner was an office area with built in black desk and black leather chair. There was also a small bathroom opposite the kitchen area that would be ideal for visitors.

Another door led from the main room to the en suite double bedroom. It too had access to the balcony via its own glass doors and also had a TV fixed to the wall and a DVD player. A glass door opened to reveal a bathroom that was small but well appointed. The main feature was the shower housed in a glass cubicle and had an overhead rain fitment as well as a traditional wall one.

Perhaps one of the most endearing designs of the apartment was the lighting, use of false ceiling recesses and decorations enabled the housing of discreet blue illumination in different part of the main room and at night looked most impressive against the white walls and ceiling. A bank of switches by the sofa controlled all the lighting so in lazy fashion a person could operate the mood of the apartment from the comfort of being seated.

In a way I preferred my new apartment to the old one, it was smaller, but had more luxurious décor and because I had signed a contract for a year it immediately felt like a home and not a hotel room. The balcony had views of Jomtien as the apartment was on the other side of the building than previously, but I could still just about still see the sea.

I settled quickly into my new home and after two weeks was going to celebrate my second Songkran in Thailand. Pattaya is probably Thailand's biggest party town and it will let its hair down at any excuse, more than it usually does. Songkran is celebrated at slightly different times in different places throughout the country. There is normally one big official day of celebrations and perhaps another day added on but not so in Pattaya. Yes, it does have one special day, but celebrations go on for nearly a week before hand. These extended days allowed in some regions are called Wan Lai, which back home when I was a kid we would have called Barley.

It actually is a big pain in the arse if you work during this period or you are simply going about normal day to day activities. It is a common sight to enter a bank or shop to see the staff drenched from their journeys into work. On one such day I was trying to stealthily get to my language class and turned an innocuous looking corner to come face to face with a small boy toting a large water gun and behind him was his younger sister similarly tooled up. Another time and another place, the two children would have been quite cute, especially the little girl who had two pigtails sprouting out of her head like Shrek's ears. But there and then they were baby faced assassins and had I been armed I would have had at them.

Their faces lit up with glee at my sudden appearance and it became a classic Mexican standoff. It was straight out of *The Good, The Bad and The Ugly*. I do not know who was Clint, Lee Van Cleef or Eli Wallach, but the haunting music of Ennio Morricone was playing in my head as I faced my adversaries. The boy's steely glare followed my every movement while his partner in crime shadowed behind. I took one slow step to the left and was cut off by the little girl, so I moved carefully to my right only to be thwarted by the boy levelling his weapon at me.

There was only one thing that I could do; I put my thumbs in my ears and waved my fingers at my assailants whilst sticking my tongue out, I had made a similar infantile gesture quite recently with the same dire consequences. I then made a dash for it; in retrospect it was a stupid thing to do to rile my adversaries in such a manner as they walked behind me every step of the way to Jomtien Language School. I was squirted at every stride as my giggling miniature assassins followed me doggedly. My arrival at school was a damp one as I was soaking wet and as I hurriedly entered the building a torrent of water plastered the glass door behind me. I stared at my two attackers from behind the safety of my glass protection put my thumbs in my ears and waggled my fingers at them; I had survived to live another day.

My tutor was quite surprised at my squelching entrance into class, but it was upstaged by the dye covering most of her blouse. I froze in the classroom as the A/C was full on and did not pay much attention to the lesson due to my violent shivering and my oncoming bout of pneumonia. I had paid for private tuition so I could not rally any support of protection from classmates if the two bush whackers were lying in wait for me after school. I asked the teacher how to say, "Bugger off you little bastards" in Thai, but she refrained from telling me, so once I left the building I was vulnerable.

After my lesson I went downstairs and peered out of the school's windows to see the lay of the land. I could see no sign of the two tiny terrors and hoped their mum had called them for dinner. What I could see was an ugly scene in front of me on the road, featuring vast sways of water and many sodden people and vehicles. I studied a potential exit route and worked out if I sidled out right from the building I could take cover under some shops awnings. There I could wait for a lull in engagements and dash over to the sanctuary of shenanigans. Festivities normally finished around tea time every evening when the weary battle hardened troops returned back to base for dinner at home. I considered that if this is what is was like five days before Songkran then what the Hell would it be like on the official day?

The days got progressively worse and more manic, it was impossible even to do the most mundane tasks out of the confines of Fort View Talay without getting a proper drenching. Trips to the gym, shopping or school were major expeditions and planned with military precision, maps and schematics of the local area were studied and risk evaluation was taken on different route options. Eventually Pattaya's official Songkran day came around; Tuesday 19th March 2554, and it was a civic holiday for all in the Bang Lamung district. Ton had been in contact and had planned the whole day which disconcertingly started at my apartment at noon.

The Thai Solar calendar is the Siamese version of our Gregorian Lunar one and is based on year's of the Buddhist era which is five hundred and forty three years greater than the Christian one. To be in Thailand in the first quarter of the year is pretty exciting if you enjoy parting as the Thai's like to celebrate the traditional Western New Year followed later in January with the Chinese New Year and eventually in April with their own New Year or Songkran. I have never known a nation young and old that love to party so much, any excuse whatsoever and it is down tools for a spot of revelry.

The first part of the year is also peak time for tourists as the rainy season normally ends around November and the six months following is the hottest part of the year. So, numbers around Songkran are normally swelled by the influx of farangs, especially in the tourist regions of which Pattaya was probably the capital.

Ton arrived early the morning of Songkran and put some bottles of Leo in the freezer compartment of my fridge to chill. He asked for a water tight bag and I offered a beach wet bag that I had bought in Samui. It was like a small duffel bag made of PVC that became totally water tight if you rolled the top couple of inches down and fixed two plastic clips together. Then Taam arrived with three other people for the first drinks of the day. We stashed all our belongs for the day in the wet bag; plastic bags full of money, phones, cameras, keys, cigarettes, lighters and motor bike keys and Ton being the most sensible was designated the official guardian.

The new arrivals were already showing signs of battle with white dye smudged on their damp shirts. Whilst we toasted Songkran Ton and his friends filled their water guns and prepared themselves for the fray. I didn't bother with a gun as my right hand could not grip one and I would need my left for other things. One of Taam's friends had a fantastic Ghostbusters type back pack rifle. He had a magazine of water strapped to his back attached to a pump action gun by a plastic hose.

The plan was to drive to another friends' room closer to town, leave the scooters and then walk to Beach Road to spend the day. We left View Talay in a convoy of three motor bikes and it was a treacherous journey across town. Every main road, side road and small Soi was full of party goers soaking anybody or anything that passed. I was riding with Taam and the motor bike in front of us skidded and its rider was unceremoniously tossed to the floor, he had been ambushed by a reveller throwing a bucket of water at him whilst he was travelling at thirty miles per hour.

Pattaya's hospitals are inundated over the Songkran period with serious injuries normally arising from motorbike incidents and I could see why. This was not particularly fun, it was fucking dangerous. Taam slowed to a walking pace and we got drenched, but it was better that than ending up in hospital. Small groups seemed to have their own particular bases be it by the side of the road or mounted on Pick Up trucks. Their bases would include large plastic barrels of water for ammunition, sometimes iced! And a copious amount of alcohol to hand, beer and whisky being the norm. Then there was the method of delivering water; standard water pistols were essential and fancy shop bought guns and rifles were common but it was the improvised weapons that were the most deadly. Buckets, hoses, even powerful air compressed fire pumps were used.

We arrived somewhat dishevelled at Ton's friend's room and parked the bikes. Poi came down to meet us and it was the first time I had met her, she was attractive and had quite a fantastic, fit looking, slim body. This was accentuated by her attire which was a two piece "leather look" swim suit with a sarong tied at her waist for a touch of modesty. She had a friend with her who was similarly attired, but who was a great deal more buxom and the bra part of her swimsuit barely contained her ample breasts.

Ton asked me for some cash as we needed some beer for our walk, so furnished with my money he and one of the others walked over to a little shop to buy the cans. Ton came back almost immediately with a flustered look on his face; he passed my money to Taam who went over to join his friend in the shop. Ton had explained that there had been a large group of katoeys outside the shop and they had almost stripped him naked. Apparently, he was very popular with ladyboys and gays as he was so tall and handsome and incidents like that happened to him quite frequently.

I looked over to see if I could catch a glimpse of the roving katoey sex pests and was greeted with a hullabaloo from outside the shop. Taam was in the centre of the gang and he was actually stripping and showing that he too was wearing a Bra under his baggy shirt. The ladyboys did not seem so attracted by the rather overweight, flamboyant and extrovert gay as they were to Ton. The fracas ended with a great deal of water being thrown about and a chuckling Taam returning with our beers.

Walking to Beach Road took ages as we were continuously engaged in water fights along the way. Along with water at Songkran it is traditional that a type of dye is smeared over a person also. The white powder is sold in a sort of dried cake form and is then diluted in water to produce a chalky liquid that sticks to flesh or clothing and dries like thick white mud.

I noticed during the motor bike journey over and on the walk that the Thai's loved to target farangs. It as if they get extra points for dousing and plastering a farang than one of their own countrymen. After a few vicious attacks I did not even bother to try and wipe the sticky goo off my face and arms, if I left it on long enough sooner or later I would take a bucket in the Mush and that normally did the trick and swilled the dye off. But if the horrid stuff got into your eyes it was quite painful so I brought some cheap kid's sunglasses for protection. They did the job protecting my eyes, but big pink Dame Edna copies made me look a daft twat.

We eventually got to the beach and it was rocking. The road was completely blocked off, about three miles of it. The crowds of people were reminiscent to a football crowd after the final whistle. I was quite surprised how organised everything was compared to the free for all I had just previously experienced. Hotels and bars had outdoor stages and platforms sponsored by local companies where bands played live or dancers strutted their stuff. Along the length of the road PA systems battled against each other for supremacy in a cacophony of conflicting loud music. And each venue had its own water themed public attack system.

Some of the water dispensers along the road were quite unbelievable and could soak dozens of people at once. At one stage I saw a fire truck blasting a powerful jet of water hosing a crowd of over fifty people. And at another manic stage there were two Water Cannons so forceful they were blasting small children off their feet. Every few yards there were entrepreneurs with make shift stands selling beer, snacks or dye. Also, there were water top up stations supplied by beach businesses, free for the partygoers.

There was only one word that could describe the scene: carnage! As the day progressed the throng became more and more inebriated and totally dishevelled. It was reminiscent of a zombie movie as people were walking glossy eyed and faces white in a sort of drunken trance. As the sun went down my wet clothing was making me cold as we walked and I saw that some of my friends were also shivering, my arm and leg started to contract as the cold penetrated my system and I was now limping quite severely. Then we hit another party zone where my body heat shot up due to the dancing and other manic activities of the throng. I was certain that after the day I would definitely come down with a bad cold or the flu.

Going to the loo was quite simple for the men as the ocean was an excellent lavatory, Pattaya Bay was an odd sight as it was littered with people standing up to their waists in the water taking a pee. But it did mean that you were continuously getting soaked from your shorts down regardless if you had been in a water fight or not. I realised I was getting drunk, but I noticed Ton was even worse, I had only seen him drunk once before and he got really surly and his character had completely changed.

I kept my eye on him, but truthfully I was having enough trouble looking after myself with all that was going on around me. A few scuffles were breaking out as the day progressed and the drunker people became a troop of army reserves were on standby. Songkran was notorious for trouble later in the evening and the army were placed in strategic places along the road. Officers seemed to be high up on walls and stages observing potential flash points and sending hit teams in to diffuse situations.

At one stop for beer I noticed our gang had become fairly depleted and we had lost Taam and a few others along the way. Ton was close by buying more beer and I heard a smash and saw Ton looking bemused at the broken glass all around him. He had dropped two of the bottles and they had broken cutting his leg as they did so. I knew I had to get him home and soon before my own capacity for alcohol ran out.

Ton walked across the road onto the sand towards the sea. I needed a pee also so followed him to ensure he would be okay, and then the soft bastard dived straight into the water. As he was splashing about I noticed he still had the wet bag, but it was open, he had not closed it after buying the last beers. I raced into the water, but Ton's capacity for speaking English had deserted him and he could not understand why I was so frenetic. I clutched at the bag and his face dropped as he realised what had happened.

Pulling him to the shore we tipped the bag up on the sand. It was half empty; phones, watches and cameras were missing. Luckily for me my keys were still there but I had lost my money. My little plastic money bag was somewhere in the sea never to be seen again. I was not overly worried about the money as it was not that much anyway and I had been lucky. Ton was just staring at the little pile of valuables hoping it would grow larger and that some of the lost items would swim out of the sea to join us. I thought he was going to burst into tears and he was getting morose over losing his friends possessions.

I decided to take control of the situation and get him home; we could sort out about the wet bag in the morning. Ton was deathly quiet and we went back to the others to say goodbye. We did not mention about the incident with the bag and nobody seemed to need anything from it before we left. Poi was determined to make Ton stay and she was even suggesting going to a nightclub. But Ton was a mess, he was getting shirty as he thought the nightclub was a good idea and wanted to stay. I glared at Poi in an effort to make her understand Ton's condition but she too was pissed.

Grabbing his arm I guided him away despite his remonstrations. I noticed there were some taxi's at the corner of a Soi and haggled with one to take the two of us. Occasionally motorbike taxis will take two passengers depending on the driver, it was not allowed by law but sometimes I would see whole families together with their pets on an old Yamaha. Ton and I had no money and I could not risk him getting into trouble with the taxi driver so I thought it prudent to take him back to View Talay.

Convincing the driver I would be back with some money I left Ton as security and nipped up to my room to get some cash. Ton was nearly asleep when I returned so I paid the driver and bundled Ton into the lift. Propping my drunken friend by the door I hurriedly threw some towels on the floor, in minutes the room was soaked from the pair of us in our dripping clothing.

I quickly went and took a shower whilst Ton sat out on the balcony, then refreshed and changed I threw a towel at him and bade him to do the same. He was staggering all over the place so I helped him take his shirt off and he pottered off in his shorts. It took him some time to shower and change into some shorts and T-shirt I had left for him on the bed. He came to join me to sit on the balcony as I watched and listened to the last throws of revilement coming up from the streets below.

For some reason I was stupid to have poured two beers for us both and Ton gulped his down with the gusto of an alcoholic. His speech was very slurred, but I could just about understand what he was saying. Ton's mood was getting very dark as he was reminiscing about his youth in Bangkok, he was starting to unveil facts about himself that we had never discussed before.

When he was about eighteen and before he had a chance to go to college he had joined a Bangkok Street gang and had been involved in selling and taking drugs. That explained his knowledge of the gangsters in the restaurant back in November. He had come to Pattaya to get away from his troubles but had returned one day to see his family and got into serious trouble.

Whilst walking to his parents' home he was recognised by another gang on their turf and they presumed he was selling drugs without their permission. The leader of the gang came at Ton with a knife and Ton defended himself by punching him in the eye with his thumb. Ton morosely said he felt the eyeball squish and later found out the man had permanently been blinded in that eye by Ton's violent actions.

I looked at Ton in shock and stared at his face for his reaction to his narration, I was surprised to see a blank expression. He did not seem to show any remorse and I knew that my friend was capable of extreme violence and retribution. He had always seemed to me to be a fairly serious, but fun loving man, but if what he was telling me was true there was certainly a Dr Jekyll to Ton. I persuaded Ton to sleep on my couch that night; I did not want to risk him going out again in the mood he was in.

The following morning I woke around eleven and was relieved to see my friend was still there lying on the couch asleep. Sleeping is a national pastime for Thais, I don't know if it is because they are always partying so much and are exhausted or they just like kip. They can literally sleep on a washing line and at one point I was so surprised where I unearthed a slumbering body that I decided to keep a book to write down unusual Thai sleeping places. Another oddity of their sleeping habits is that they are not particularly bothered who or how many share their sleeping space and do not get the least bit embarrassed if it is a relative stranger.

I pulled back the blinds and opened the windows to the balcony to air the room. Ton looked up from his duvet and smiled at me seeming to have no recollection of the later part of the day before. He was aghast when I told him about the broken bottles and incident with the wet bag and was planning to phone all his friends to see what they were missing; Ton had been one of the lucky ones and had not lost his mobile. I considered his proposed activity and suggested to him he might have to speak to a lot of fish that day as all his friend's mobiles were submerged. Ton found this highly amusing and I was refreshed as my friend seemed back to normal. We never spoke again of what he had told me and I do not even know if he remembers telling me.

About six weeks later after Songkran Ton came to see me and told me that his job required him to move back to Bangkok. I was sorry to see him depart, but was glad for him as it was a sort of promotion and he would get more money. We kept in touch often at first and even saw each other a couple of times, but it was getting more infrequent as the days went by.

It is a friendship that will always remain and I would like to think it was a friendship that both of us contributed to and got something out of. My life will always be richer for knowing my quiet, sometimes solemn friend and I am thankful in the extreme that I was fortunate to have met him.

Chapter Seventeen

KIK

At the end of May there was a Royal visit to Thailand by the Laird of Crosby. Riche was going to go on holiday to Koh Samui and was spending two nights in Bangkok so I readily agreed to meet him in the capital and spend some time with my friend. The taxi from Pattaya cost eight hundred Baht and when I arrived I knew where I would find my friend.

Taking the lift eight floors up to the Holiday Inn's swimming pool I instantly saw Richie lying face down, spread eagled on a lounger. He had just arrived and I knew he would be knackered as Rich never sleeps on planes. The pool bought back fond memories as I spent so much time up there in the past and I inwardly smiled as I recollected the incident with the Red Shirt activist.

I made my way across to where my friend was dozing it was quite amusing as my friend was lightly snoring. Not quite etiquette for sunbathers at the Holiday Inn Silom, his body was white as he had not been away for some time; I took his big toe in my hand and yanked. The soft git squealed like an eight year old kid and everybody looked over. Rich turned around and a large grin lit up his face, the amicable oaf rose and we embraced glad to see each other.

I had travelled in shorts so I just sat on the lounger next to my friend listening to some Frankie Beverley whilst he continued his nap. I have always found Maze's music ideal for a spot of relaxation; it is at the ideal tempo. Not too fast and not too slow, apart from the occasional ballad, and it just hits the spot required for a lazy day in the sun.

Mid afternoon Richie seemed quite refreshed by his sleep and was ready to go out on the town. I dumped my bag in his room as

I would be sharing it for two nights and we both cleaned up and changed. I revisited all my old haunts around the Shangarila and was warmly received back; Richie wanted to know what the Hell had I got up to whilst living in Bangkok and over the course of the evening I regaled some of my stories. Unwittingly we had drifted near Patpong and as we came out of Patti's Fiesta Bar charged with the invigorating alcohol of Tequila a man accosted us.

He was a strange looking man reminiscent of a pirate from a Johnny Depp film. He had a deep scar on his left cheek and an eye patch over his left eye. I could scarcely believe the authorities would let this man roam the streets as he scared the crap out of most of the people he bumped into. He lent close and whispered "Ping Pong Show," and looked at us enquiringly. He repeated his statement which was more a question: "Ping Pong Show?"

I had heard of these bawdy performances before in Patpong but had never been to one. I think the Margarita's had kicked in and we both agreed to follow the man and have a laugh. For the continuation of this story and to continue my narrative in a correct manner I will refer to the female genitalia as a Mary. It is a term I was introduced to by a close female friend whose family used it when they had to discuss delicate matters.

We were led into the throng of Patpong Night Market and our guide scampered around like a sewer rat. Weaving in and out of the crowd, between stalls and past bars, but all the time ensuring we still followed him. We eventually came to a doorway with a tawdry neon sign outside and were led down a dingy corridor then up a narrow flight of stairs. I was aware of the situation we might be getting ourselves into and was ready to flee at a moments notice. Ton had told me that the sex part of Patpong was mostly controlled by the Bangkok Mafia, and was a dangerous place indeed, perhaps a fact that unsuspecting sex tourists do not quite grasp.

The stairs opened out into a large room and it was where the Pirate guide left us, the place was noisy in the extreme with loud music blaring and the accompanying high pitched shrieks of performing women. It was fairly dimly lit, but in the centre of the room I could make out a round stage raised about two feet from the floor and it was surrounded by a horseshoe of banked seating against the walls. We were shown to a vacant space on the continuous, tatty, upholstered couch where we took a seat. A waitress took our drinks order and as is customary in such places or beer bars added her own drink to the order.

The room's patrons were a mixed bunch but predominately tourists of varying nationalities. I was a little surprised to see so many women, but like the majority of the punters they were there more out of curiosity than anything else. I suppose the odd deviant would take sexual gratification from some of the acts, but for the most part Rich and I viewed with an almost disbelieving wonder interspersed with howls of laughter that were not really appreciated by staff or performers.

Each new performer took to the stage announced by a loud trumpet fanfare. The noise came from a toy bugle that a rather overweight, scantily clad hostess had inserted into her Mary. The first act was a slim lady who once stripped turned her attention to several balloons tacked to the ceiling. She lay on her back face upwards and took what looked like a bicycle pump from a silver tray on the floor beside her. It was in fact a narrow, hollow tube which she proceeded to gently push partly in her Mary.

Appendage properly inserted she then reached over and grasped a small paper dart from the tray. This she dropped into the tube then angled her body and thrust her hips up to face the first balloon. The Mary fart was silent to the gobsmacked audience, but a small white object flew out of the tube and in a nanosecond the balloon burst with a loud popping noise. It was incredulous how she could be so accurate and it was amazing to think exactly how powerful a Mary fart could be.

One by one every balloon was destroyed by the flying paper darts, not a single missile missed its intended target. Surely this lady was some sort of Olympian? Or had relatives that came from dart blowing descendants in the Amazonian jungle?

Taking her tray of accessories the dart lady left the stage to rapturous applause. I took the opportunity to signal for two more beers before the next act as Rich and I discussed our amazement of what we had both witnessed.

The bugle blared again and the music stopped for the next act. This time the performer was a very large lady and it did not suit her one jot to be wearing a two piece bikini. She stood on the stage just standing and waiting for what I presumed were her props to arrive. Two more ladies then ascended the platform with a huge birthday cake, it was obviously fake, but it was around five feet high and at the base probably four feet wide. The cake was illuminated with numerous candles all lit and glowing in the dark club with little wisps of smoke emanating from each small flame.

The fat lady then dropped the lower half of her underwear and bent over arse facing the cake. The first candle was almost destroyed by a good old fashioned anal broadside of a fart, the second and third soon followed the little flames extinguished by fierce bottom blasts. The lady then sat astride a chair, legs akimbo and Mary farted one of the upper tiers candles. What on Earth had she been eating? It must have been very embarrassing for her husband or partner when they ate out at a restaurant! One by one all the candles were extinguished, she was not as accurate as the Dart Lady as a lot of forced air missed its intended target. I suppose candle extinguishing by Mary or Bottom fart is not an exact science and I had to allow her some margin for error.

She left the stage to a more muted ripple of applause as the interim dance music started up again. We decided we would watch one more act then go and get some dinner; just as Richie ordered two more beers the squeaking shrill sound of the toy bugle announced the next performer and the star of the show. Onto the stage walked a tall rather lithesome figure dressed in a see through white satin gown. It was plain to see that the attractive lady was completely naked under her garment and that she had a fantastic figure. She was clutching a purple felt bag in her hand down by her side, was she going to draw the FA Cup ties? Or was some sort of creature enclosed in the confines of the cloth bag? I hoped it was not a snake, I hated snakes.

With a few preliminary poses and tantalising glimpses of bare flesh the woman untied the cord at her neck and the gown drifted to the floor revealing the young lady in her full nakedness. More prancing and posing ensued, titillating the expectant crowd until she finally reclined on to the floor of the stage. She took a similar pose to that of the Dart Lady, groin forced upwards and legs wide apart whilst laying flat on her back. However, her trajectory was flatter and she was disconcertedly aligned more to the audience than the ceiling.

Rummaging around in the purple bag, reminiscent of Bert Millichip, she produced a Ping Pong ball and plopped it into her Mary. After a few seconds and taking her aim the young lady fired the plastic ball right at a group of Japanese Tourists. It was almost if Enola Gay had just released her payload, Japanese tourists scattered in all directions knocking drinks over and standing on perverts who were prostrate on the floor trying to get a glimpse of the young lady's cannon.

Another broadside was released and hit its intended target square on. The leering man was unfortunate to be bending towards the stage at the time when the ball hit him in the glasses making a dull "thwack" as plastic hit glass and the ball cracked. The performer was getting into her stride and the missiles were firing from the stage in rapid succession producing alarm in the crowd. One ball flew straight past Richie's left ear, hit the wall and bounced back into his glass of beer. "Bugger!" my erudite chum exclaimed, disconcerted that his drink was now untouchable.

The ferocity of the blitz ceased just as quickly as it commenced and the room began to form a little order. All in all it was a humorous if not somewhat slightly degrading experience, I probably won't rush back again but it was fun to see. Paying the bill was different; it had been quite a rip off as the club charges you per act and you are timed at your entrance. Each act is exactly twenty minutes therefore we were charged for three acts. Five hundred Baht each act per person. So, the entertainment had cost us three thousand Baht and another one thousand Baht for our drinks, a grand total of around eighty quid for an hour of fun.

None of this is explained to you on entering the club and we presumed that the high tariff for drinks gave you free entertainment. Another tourist was complaining vehemently and things got very ugly. He was loud and quite drunk, but foolishly was protecting his honour in front of his friends brashly and rudely. Men arrived from all corners of the room in a flash and were not waiters, they looked as though they had been brought up from the same neighbourhood as the pirate and I did not want to get involved in any mass altercation. We paid our exorbitant bill and left poorer than we entered, but probably a little wiser and most importantly undamaged.

I went to sleep weary that night after the day's exertions and wondered if any stray Japanese tourists were still hiding under sofas not to remerge until the all clear was sounded a few years later by the shrill toot of a plastic bugle.

Our second night together was a far gentler affair, I took Rich to a famous restaurant in Bangkok called the Mango Tree, it is just off Soi 6, Silom Road. The restaurant is renowned for having traditional Thai classical live music for its patrons and it is situated in an old colonial house. Richie was fairly pissed and was arguing across a table with some American blurt about football, sometimes

I despair when I make the effort to take him somewhere a little more formal. I do not know of the two of them who actually knew more and spoke the most sense about soccer, but regardless it was a conversation only to be enjoyed by drunken squirrels.

The following morning it was my turn to wave goodbye to my friend as I was going to stay one more night in Bangkok to meet up with Ton. I went to the foyer with Rich and we said our goodbyes, but he was cheerful as he still had his holiday to look forward to. I was glad we had the chance to meet up and I had been able to see him again, he could be the most infuriating of friends at times, but I did miss the Oaf when he left.

As time was ticking on and it was getting close to my first visa trip out of the country, I had been surfing budget sites and Air Asia had a fantastic deal for cheap flights to Vietnam. Although I had already visited Ho Chi Minh City I had been ill and not seen much of the city and I could not turn down the opportunity to return for less than forty quid return. I booked a flight for the 22nd of June and was also fortunate enough to get a good deal at the Hotel Continental Saigon for two nights. It was coming into the rainy season in South East Asia and was low season so good deals were to be had.

Ton had only been gone a couple of weeks but strangely I bumped into somebody that gradually filled his place as a companion. I regularly took coffee at a little shop after my daily Gym session at Tony's where I would sit sipping my Americano whilst reading the free daily copy of the Bangkok Post or the local Pattaya People paper.

Recently, a bubbly little chap had started working there and was always asking customers questions on any topical points on the TV or in the newspaper. His English was not quite up to Ton's standard, but still it was good and my conversations with Kik were getting lengthier and more frequent. He made me laugh as he was always in trouble for being late or other small misdemeanours and nothing seemed to bother him at all.

He was loud, effervescent, and full of life constantly surrounded by friends. Bit by bit we got to know each other and started enjoying each others company. He was actually a dance teacher, but had to supplement his often sporadic income with regular work and would regularly sachet around the tables in some new dance move or something quite often to customer's disturbance.

Kik was the antithesis of Ton; he did not seem to think before he spontaneously burst into some loud activity and the coffee shop became a dance studio for a minute or two. Ton was more serious and polite whereas Kik was a steamroller of fun and it was highly entertaining to be in his company. He was only twenty seven and his favourite pastime was going out partying at nightclubs with his friends hence his frequent tardiness at work.

I was introduced to his friends over the weeks and they were quite an eclectic bunch of mates who had one thing in common; they all liked to party. Ton Nam was tall and worked at a wine importers, Wi Wi sold real estate and was the quiet one of the group, Daang Mao was a mystery, but whose pastime was getting drunk, Rista was the livewire of the Party Mafia, as they called themselves, and lastly was Pookie a stunning agency model who lived in Bangkok, but often hung around Pattaya at weekends.

Occasionally I would go to a club with them for a couple of hours or normally a late night bar. Bur mostly I would meet up with Kik and one or two of the others at a cheap restaurant where I or Pookie would more often than not pick up the bill, it was never over twenty pounds and we could afford it but they certainly could not. But as time went by I was starting to get invited to more private party's and functions and hanging out with the fun loving bunch was a great laugh and really enjoyable, Pookie had a car and sporadically we would all go on a trip together.

Kik found out about my impending trip to Vietnam and since he had never been out of Thailand in his life desperately wanted to go with me. Pookie secretly suggested a deal to me, if I paid for Kik's flight she would pay for his hotel, but we would have to tread carefully approaching Kik with the proposal as not to offend him. She knew him far better than me so I agreed with the proviso she broach the subject with Kik.

He agreed far easier that either of us expected so I amended the accommodation to a twin room for Kik and I and a single for Pookie. I took a hit of forty quid to treat my new friend to a holiday of a lifetime. The day before the trip Pookie had to pull out as she was offered a lucrative contract to work at a car show in Bangkok so it was going to be just the two of us going.

I arranged a taxi to take us to the airport and typically Kik was late arriving at my Condo. Once heading up to Bangkok he said the reason he was delayed was that he could not find his passport, but then remembered he had given it to Pookie. I was surprised he even had a passport as he had never been out of the country, but he explained he had gotten it a few years ago just in case. So, we had to make a detour to Pookie's apartment in Bangkok to pick up his passport before we eventually arrived fashionably late at check-in.

This was the way Kik lived his life, in a constant confusion and rush. I was exhausted and had only been with him for two hours. We separated at Immigration as I joined the foreigners queue and unusually passed through fairly quickly. I waited for the small bundle of havoc to join me at the baggage X-ray machine, but after a few minutes there was no sign of Kik. I made my way back to immigration, something that is frowned upon, and saw Kik in animated discussion with a female officer at the control point.

On seeing my face Kik shouted for me to join them as there was a serious problem with his passport. I stared at his documentation and it looked as though a dog had eaten half of it, I shook my head in disbelief. Who on Earth would expect to travel using that passport? The answer was for all to see, the forlorn figure standing in front of the immigration counter! I had only known Kik for a few weeks and I had to personally guarantee his return back into Thailand, my passport was linked to his electronically. Shouldn't this work the other way? Surely the Thai National would be vouching for a foreigner, but not as I was to learn when Kik is part of the equation.

The flight went smoothly and I had my second horrid time with delays at Ho Chi Minh's visa processing. Eventually we both exited the airport and took a taxi to the city centre. I was impressed with Hotel Continental Saigon, it was perfectly situated opposite the Opera House and the building was fashioned in the old French Colonial style. I was not as impressed as my companion who continued to constantly take photo's using his phone of every aspect of the hotel.

Our room was dated, but was large; it had high ceilings and a balcony facing the Opera House. Louvered doors gave access to a balcony and the evening's bright lights of Saigon lit up the buildings in a neon wash. Kik was transfixed staring in awe at the alien vista stretched out in front of him and at that moment I realised I had just spent the best forty quid of my life.

The two days passed quickly and it was like a whirlwind trying to do everything Kik wanted to. I did my utmost as a tour guide and was impressed how the little Thai conducted himself in the strange environment. He did not for one second behave as uninitiated, uneducated green tourist; he adapted to Saigon perfectly and blended in like a seasoned traveller. After the abortion at the airport I had my doubts how he was going to handle everything, but Kik came through with flying colours.

Arriving in Thailand, Kik immediately phoned Pookie raving about the trip, but to my surprise back in Pattaya he did not brag about his experience to his other friends. I admired him for that, for all I knew none of them had been abroad either and it was not

Kik's place to seem superior to them. In many parts of Thai culture it is often the case that a pecking order is quickly established within a group and it is one of the few facets about the Thai social structure that I do not like. But within the relationships I had experienced with Ton and his friends and now Kik's group there was certainly no Alpha King within either party and I was glad that was the case. I had been accepted by Ton and now by Kik as a friend and an equal and had behaved correspondingly.

I loved my new apartment and also the condominium had endeared itself to me greatly. The swimming pool was always empty and it was never a problem seeking a place in the sun. I had bought my own deck chair a few weeks back with Ton's help at the Big C on Sukhumvit Road. It was a little anal taking my personal lounger down in the lift everyday, but it saved me fifty Baht hire cost. The condo's little restaurants offered really authentic Thai food and a very low cost. My regular one was called simply NT and although I would rarely sit in to dine I often took takeaway food to my room. A Thai Green Chicken Curry with steamed rice would cost in the region of one pound twenty five and was as authentic as any that I had eaten.

My laundry was also called NT and was opposite the restaurant in the corridor. Sod was the owner of the two establishments and we struck a discounted deal for my washing, he was the person who also arranged for any cheap taxi's I needed to take me to Bangkok. Sod was definitely the Arthur Daley of View Talay and would turn his hand to anything if a few Baht was in it for him.

My daily routine, if I was not meeting up with anybody, was not scheduled and depended entirely on the sun. But it would include a period of sunbathing, a trip to Tony's Gym, a visit to the coffee shop and normally an early evening trip to Shenanigans.

Everything was in walking distance and local to Jomtien; the pub was about five minutes walk either along the beach or through the Jomtien Complex, but took a little longer on the way back. The

Jomtien Complex is the area's Gay Quarter and has many Beer Bars and massage places, but mixed with some really good but slightly expensive restaurants. Walking back through the maze of activity was sometimes a little risky and normally quite funny with cat calls being levelled towards me.

Shenanigans is billed as an Irish pub, but is run by an Aussie from Melbourne who was very dedicated to his job and staffed entirely by Thais. He was always in attendance and every night the pub offered some different attraction. Mostly it was the expat residents of Jomtien who frequented the place so there were many regulars. It served cold draught beer and importantly was not too expensive as it had a Happy Hour every day until 7pm. The staff were all Thai and by local standards were well paid, good at their jobs but were always good fun.

My favourite night was Wednesday's "Toss the Boss" night; from 7pm until 8.30pm you had the right to challenge Stuart the manager for the price of your drink. Once you had ordered a drink one of the barmen called the boss over and he tossed a large coin in the air, if you called right then it was free. Occasionally I have left the pub with the same amount of money I entered with having consumed a fair amount of free alcohol.

I was adapting to my new life well and loved Pattaya, I rarely went into the madness of Walking Street as I had no need to; all that I needed was on my doorstep. Occasionally I would go further afield with Kik and his mates but that was normally somewhere tucked away and far removed from the tacky tourist haunts that the arseholes frequented.

The weeks and months flew past as I was enjoying myself so much, but I was aware I had to take a trip out of Thailand in September to get my Visa Stamp. I could scarcely believe that it had been nearly three months since my visit to Vietnam. I was discussing my options over coffee with Kik one day and he came up with an idea. He had to make a visit home to see his parents and suggested that I accompany him and then I could go to Laos for my Visa requirements.

His parents live near Sakon Nakon which is situated in the North East of Thailand, the nearest airport was Udon Thani and we could get there by Nok Air from Bangkok. Nok Air are Thailand's domestic carrier and are extremely cheap. They operate out of Bangkok's old airport Don Muang and were offering flights to Udon Thani at a snip. Kik usually travelled by Nok Air preferring it to a ten hour bus ride from Bangkok, but only went home sporadically due to the cost.

I felt in a generous mood and offered to pay for Kik's flight and in return he was to be my tour guide. I think that was what he was hoping for as he immediately thanked me and took me up on his offer. I went on line to check for travel restrictions to Laos and was pleased that there did not seem to be any, it was possible to get a VOA, a visa on arrival at the border.

Kik had arranged for us to be collected at the airport by his sister Ohm, she was married and lived in Iceland, but was on a two month visit home. That was one of the reasons why Kik had chosen that time to visit his parents; he could also meet up with his estranged sister. The other fortunate thing about Ohm was that she had a hire car for the duration of her stay and Kik had taken that fact fully into consideration in his own plans.

Ohm was late arriving to collect us, a trait that seemed to run in the family, so we sat outside the small airport terminal and Kik had a cigarette. Eventually a silver Toyota Yaris car came tootling up and with no particular hurry pulled into the No Parking bay. Then the two siblings met for the first time in a year and an argument ensued. Ohm was Kik's older sister and although I did not ask her age I estimated it to be around thirty. She was definitely from the same mould as Kik, approximately the same height and a bubbly personality, but if anything and amazingly so, she was actually louder than her younger brother.

I was introduced and Ohm greeted me as though she had known me for years, she spoke excellent English as that was the common language her and her Icelandic husband used together. The argument had finished and was replaced by an animated conversation between the estranged brother and sister, it was completely in Thai and I did not understand a word so contented myself looking out of the window. The noise in the small car was almost unbearable as it seemed the only way either of them could communicate with each other was by yelling.

We drove through the outskirts of Udon Thani which looked the same as many large towns' suburbs. Udon Thani is a large city of about one million people, but was not at all what you would consider as a pretty city. It is however, surrounded by countryside and the main economy of the region is agriculture. We took the main highway east from the city which is Highway 22, and were heading towards Sakon Nakon about a two hour drive away.

The scenery was engaging; luscious green Paddy fields were occasionally interspersed with thick jungle vegetation and every now and then orderly rows of Rubber trees. As the landscape moved further north the flat fields changed to slowly rise into bluey grey distant hills. The road changed dramatically once we left the hinterland of Udon and what was once a two lane, tarmac surfaced, modern road became little more than a single red clay thoroughfare.

Our progress was slow, I had gathered that Ohm was not a particularly confident driver and she was hesitant in overtaking obstacles in our way. All manner of slow agricultural vehicles obstructed our progress and coupled with many heavy goods wagons using the road made it impossible to travel at any speed. However, our biggest obstruction was the road itself. The monsoon rains and the heavy trucks had caused widespread destruction to the road surface; vast stretches of Highway 22 were almost impassable. Some of the stretches of the road resembled a lunar landscape with huge pot holes and crevices waiting patiently to snap a back axle or explode a tyre.

Making things worse was the gradual waning of daylight, it was getting darker by the minute and there was no lighting along the road. We were driving into deep, rural Thailand surrounded by jungle. The only illumination came from oncoming vehicles or occasional hamlets that we passed. I did not care a jot, as I was not in a hurry to get any ware. I did not even know where I was so how could I be impatient to go some place else?

After around an hour and a half, Kik pointed out to the blackness on the left hand side and told me that was where his parents lived. Were they nomadic? Did they live in the whole blackness or just some of it? Anyway we did not stop or turn we just kept on going. I was used to being in a state of confusion when I was with all my Thai friends; they never fully explained what was happening or going to happen, they just made things up as they went along. "Always expect the unexpected in Thailand." Was that Plato or Aussie Eddie who had said that?

Another twenty minutes passed and we came to a small town called Phang Khon that seemed to have been built on the crossroads of two highways. I wondered what came first; the crossroads or the town? There was some life here a few little restaurants and convenience stores. We stopped outside a Seven Eleven and Kik turned to me and said, "Should we buy some drink?" I did not have a clue what the drink was for; were we going to sit in the car and get pissed?

Anyway I was glad to stretch my legs and stiffly got out of the rear door of the Toyota to stand on the pavement. There was a group of people hanging around the shop and my arrival was if I had just been beamed up from another world. I suppose not many farangs go shopping at the Seven Eleven in Phang Khon and if they did they were not accompanied by two Thais. Ohm helped me select some beer, whisky and coke whilst Kik purchased some cigarettes, he was always such a help! I could not help thinking that it was a lot of hooch for three people.

Once back in the car Ohm drove down a little Soi and after two or three minutes we were almost back in the countryside. At one of the last houses out of the town she stopped, got out of the car and entered the dwelling. A short time later she came out of the house with an older woman and a tall young man. Kik suddenly became very animated and started shouting, "Dome, Dome!" out of the window towards the young man. The stranger instantly recognised Kik and rushed to the car to greet his pal.

Dome, pronounced Dom, was Kik's oldest friend and they had known each other since school. In fact. the two families were very close and we had stopped to collect a Suckling Pig that Dome's mother had specially cooked for our dinner with Kik's parents. Dome's mother had a small catering business and apparently she was quite famous in the area for her cooking. She was also quite famous for holding impromptu drinking soirées a fact that I was later to find out that her son had richly embraced.

After the pig was loaded into the boot and Dome climbed into the car with us we set off to Kik's parents' house. If I had thought I had been in the outback before then it was suburbia compared what was to come. We returned back the way we had come for about ten minutes and then took a tiny road into the wilderness. The road narrowed and eventually became little more than a jungle path with all manner of wildlife crawling, flying, hopping and running all around the car.

I was not certain if I wanted to ever get out from the safety of the vehicle, but the rest of the occupants were blasé about the habitat, they were used to it. One by one small wooden houses started to appear and the road widened again, larger brick built buildings were now appearing and we had reached the village. It was illuminated by lights and I was impressed with the technology taken to bring power to such a remote area. Small children stopped their playing whilst the car slowly passed greatly interested in the interlopers to their world. Dogs roamed freely between the houses with other domestic wildlife scattered around.

We came to a clearing and in front of us was a large two storey house with a small balcony upstairs. The noise of the vehicle had brought two people out of the house and they were standing on the raised porch in front of a wooden door. It was Kik's parents and he could hardly contain himself trying to exit the car as quickly as possible. It was an honour to be introduced to Mr and Mrs Puttisa and they were very gracious in their welcome and their extension of hospitality to me. After all I was just some Farang who happened to have met their son in Pattaya.

The village and its inhabitants were not affluent, there were few cars or material trappings to be seen, but it was obvious there was a bond, a trust, and a community spirit that galvanised these people. The car was unloaded and I was warmly greeted into the family home, kicking off my shoes I entered into a large room that seemed to constitute most of the downstairs of the property. To the left was a door and I could just about make out that it was a rustic kitchen area.

Dome and Kik's dad hauled the suckling pig into the room on some plastic sheeting and rested the carcass on some rush matting on the floor. Then the parents both started to prepare the pig for eating. Whilst kneeling on the floor on the matting they proceeded to cut the pig and carve small slices from the flesh. Kik's mother was softly singing in her work happy to have her family around her once again. Dome was outside busy with the largest pestle and mortar I have ever seen, I decided to investigate as Kik and Ohm had disappeared into the kitchen.

He was making a traditional dressing or dip to accompany the pig and I was quite taken aback by the pungent concoction he was assembling. Handfuls of raw garlic and red bird's eye chillies where thrown into the stone Mortar and bashed vigorously with the large

Pestle. Perhaps the juice of a dozen limes and some sugar was then added to the mixture and it began to loosen its consistency. Then large splashes of Naam Plah or fish sauce were stirred in and potent aroma of the Naam Plah bought tears to my eyes.

Dome constantly tasted his work and more chilli and garlic were added, finally fresh herbs were ripped into the sticky sauce and it was done, it was time for him to reward his work with a cigarette. Ohm bustled into the room carrying bowls, spoons and forks followed by her father with a large woven basket lined with banana leaves full of his speciality; Sticky Rice. Everything was placed on the floor by the pig and the family started to take their places at the feast and kneel or sit by the food.

I was ushered to take my place, but found it difficult to get down on the floor so I requested Kik to explain to his father about my disability so as not to cause any offence. I was cordially invited to sit at the large table and Kik and Dome were given dispensation to join me. Dome seemed like one of the family and it was he who went into the kitchen and furnished everybody with some Leo Beer.

The meal was fabulous it was simple, rustic, but delicious and was washed down by several bottles of beer. The pungent dip that Dome had concocted nearly took the back of my throat out, but I loved it, the food in this region is notoriously spicy and Issan cuisine is one of my favourites of Thailand's varied and wide selection. I felt right at home and was so glad that I had been so readily accepted into this families' way of life. The beer was followed by some whisky and I got to know Ohm and Dome better as we got a little drunk.

As with infrequent family get-togethers all over the world the meal was an opportunity for old family tales to be regaled. The family were all Catholics and there was actually a small church in the village. Ohm recounted that every Christmas time at the schools nativity play she was chosen to play an Angel whilst her younger brother was elected year after year to be one of the sheep. Kik countered this accusation by saying if the shepherd happened to be herding pigs then Ohm would have made a super porker as she was so fat and ugly.

It was like listening to two seven year old children as they bickered and argued, but nonetheless some of the tales were hilarious as Ohm proved that she was a most capable raconteur. Kik was the butt of all of her narrations as she depicted her haphazard younger brother as hapless and his calamitous and untoward behaviour led to many catastrophic and riotous events.

Ohm translated all the tales for me into English simultaneously to enable me to laugh alongside the whole family. For an evening I was one of them an honoured guest let into their private world. It was much harder to communicate with Kik's parents as they spoke no English whatsoever, but they did seemed impressed when I tried to make an effort speaking Pigeon Thai, ignoring Kik's constant barracking of me. As the whisky flowed something that I was totally unaware of was that a plan was hatching within the family.

Later we drove back to drop Dome home and Kik, Ohm and I checked into a little lodge for the night. The room was perfectly acceptable was clean, had its own bathroom and was less than ten pounds. Kik was also staying there with me to keep me company and Ohm checked in as she did not want to drive home in the dark by herself.

It was as I was settling down for sleep Kik told me of the plan that had been agreed upon after dinner. Kik had craftily persuaded Ohm and importantly her car to come to Laos with us. She was reluctant at first as she did not want to drive that far and she had banned Kik from ever driving again; apparently in the past he had taken an old car of hers without permission and went out partying, he had crashed it and written it off. It was a typical tale about my new friend and I would hear dozens more about the ill fated little

Thai as I got to know him better. Perhaps Frank Spencer had an Asian doppelganger that no one ever knew about.

However, Dome solved the impasse by offering his services as chauffer and he was to come too. The phrase 'head working' could have been written about the whole scam, but I admired their voracity at the sniff of a potential party. But that was not all; Ohm wanted to treat her mum and dad to a little holiday and had persuaded her parents to join the Francis Abel Visa Stamp pilgrimage.

The trip was planned to take place in two days and in the interim I was to be shown around the area. I went to visit Sakon Nakon about half an hours drive from Phang Khon. It was a large university town and I quite liked it as a lot was going on and it had the exuberant feel of a young persons place. For some reason there was a plethora of gold shops in the town; most Thai cities and towns will have a few of such establishments catering for the Thai's love of jewellery and they are instantly recognisable from the gaudy red shop fronts and bling window displays. Sakon Nakon however seemed to have devoted a whole district to the Gold Shops. The reasoning for it was unfathomable to me as it did not seem an overly opulent town.

After visiting Sakon Nakon we drove to visit a close college friend of Kik's who had recently just opened a small internet café and Kik wanted to see what it was like. I was introduced to another Daang, but unlike the quiet often frequently drunk Daang Mao in Pattaya, this Daang was a livewire and as mad as a box of frogs. I could not help liking Daang instantly he had an engaging personality that sucked the life out of you. His little business catered mainly for the local youths who visited to play games and it was the only place for them to hang around in the small town. Daang was almost like a father figure to them and in his own madcap way took care of the kids.

A party was arranged for my honour and numerous phone calls and text messages sent to gather a correct forum. Everything stops in Thailand at the very mention of a party and it was a serious business getting the organisation right for the event. No other activity can possibly be considered when party organising is taking place it consumes almost as much effort as the party itself.

There was an open air Fair in a nearby field that the party was to start followed by a visit to a nightclub. Where there was a nightclub around Phang Khon I didn't have a clue, but I would leave that to the experts. We drove back to the little hotel and on the way had some food, then we relaxed for a couple of hours before getting ready for the evening.

I was not quite prepared for any of the events that happened that night and they are a little difficult to narrate for me to give them the proper justice they deserve. But in one way or another I thoroughly enjoyed my bizarre evening, but nothing quite like it has ever happened again.

The Fair was huge and seemed to have attracted people from all over the district to attend. In one part of the field there was a massive outdoor screen similar to the old American Drive Inn's and hundred's of people were sitting on the grass enjoying some old Thai movie. The cheers, boo's and laughter could be heard for miles as the crowd followed the movies plot unravelling in twists and turns. It was reminiscent of the Saturday Cinema Club I went to with my brother as kids in Crosby.

Every Saturday Lunchtime the Regent Cinema was turned into a large crèche where parents could deposit their children and for a nominal sum some poor bloke had to entertain two hundred screaming kids in between episodes of Flash Gordon and the Lone Ranger. Hendo even remembers the official song that the kids used to sing-a-long to at the start of proceedings, his capacity for retaining such trivia amazes me as I had long deleted it from my own memory bank.

The compare was called uncle Charlie and used to wear a large, check baggy suit, straw hat and bow tie and whatever he was paid it was not nearly enough. The kids used to make his life pure, undiluted Hell and the only rest bite he had was when there was a film showing on the screen. The same children every week took the stage for Birthday Roll Call, but uncle Charlie never cottoned on to the weekly gag. One week there were more Birthday Boys and Girls on the stage than there were kids in the audience.

Thankfully we were a little late for the movie so we strolled through many small little booths offering challenging games with the sole purpose of relieving the competitor with as many Baht's as possible. Ohm and I stopped at a darts game to try our skill; the object of the game was to burst as many balloons with your ten blunt darts as possible. To my delight Ohm was hopeless at the game; even using my left arm, as it would have been far too dangerous to attempt the game with my right, I beat her easily and obnoxiously celebrated the triumph in front of her. I think I forgot my age a little for a brief moment and ten minutes later I was a trifle embarrassed at my exuberance.

Past the booths were the obligatory Fete food stalls, but in Thailand the offerings are far more exotic than Candy Floss and Toffee Apples. The aromas were intoxicating and alluring even though some things on offer were completely alien to me. I could not imagine children back in the UK clamouring to buy bags of dried fish or slices of bitter, green mango with chilli dip.

As we battled through the excited throng many people stopped and performed a double take on me. Unlike my paranoid thinkings during my period of rehabilitation, this was a genuine pause and ogle. Clayton Moore had demounted from Silver and stepped out from the screen, and I was now the Lone Ranger. Obviously farangs did occasionally visit the area, but tonight I was riding solo and it was a little unnerving.

Greenstreet and Back

Away from the booths and stalls was a stage area with rows of long tables laid out in front. There was a make shift bar selling beer and whisky and already it was obvious many people had consumed a great deal of both. Kik spotted Daang in a group of around ten people and we went to join them. Daang and his friends had a couple of cases of Leo and three bottles of Blend Whisky, they had bought the alcohol with them and that seemed acceptable enough if we purchased the mixers from the bar.

We took our seats on the rough wooden benches and I was introduced to every one of the group individually. Even in such casual surrounding certain proprieties are retained and I played my part in responding correctly. There was blaring Issan music emanating from the large speakers on the stage and the ubiquitous troop of dancers performing the required synchronised movements. Issan Music is one of Thailand's more traditional types of Country Music and should never be confused with Dolly Parton or Willie Nelson. It is usually performed as a type of review with many different singers and dancers performing a non stop extravaganza for many hours. Such troops of Issan touring companies regularly travel all over Thailand to perform their specialised art in open air spectaculars.

Another integral partner of the music, dance and costumes is alcohol. Normally a major brewer like Chang sponsors the event which allows such lavish performances to take place. Large beer towers containing over two and a half litres of larger were dotted around the tables with groups of happy festival goers decanting their own refreshments at will. Immediately our group opened the bottles of whisky and the evening's entertainment started in earnest.

I took a sip from my whisky and surveyed my habitat; at one or two of the tables already heads were lowered and resting drunkenly on the comfort of the planks. Several punters would sporadically attempt to climb the stage to join the performers encouraged by cheers of jubilation at rare successes. They would unceremoniously be pushed off by security guards and land on the floor heavily and painfully.

Looking at one group of dancers on the stage it became apparent that the main attraction was a six foot tall, well built ladyboy. The other dancers seemed to treat her very reverently and with great respect. I could not fathom this as to me she was an Amazonian of a creature and quite the ugliest 'Belle of the Ball'. Her movements were more akin to Bernard Bresslaw than Wayne Sleep and I found the whole performance highly amusing. I had to refrain from laughing out loud as my fellow party goer's also seemed to pay homage to the katoey's bewildering talents.

As the night progressed I saw more and more of the katoey as she was definitely the star of the show. I was bemused where she could have got such an elegant costume to fit her, but I was rather taken aback that she had not deemed it necessary to shave her armpits before wearing her sequined dress. Who on Earth sold size twelve High Heeled shoes in Phang Khon?

The party was getting more and more out of hand as the whisky took its inevitable effect and the stage became a free for all. The Amazonian katoey gave up trying to perform professionally and took to dancing on tables to be rewarded by Baht tips thrust into her bodice by drunken farmers grabbing the ample flesh on show as they did.

To my horror the Amazonian katoey suddenly spotted me, I do not know if she had mistaken me as Simon Cowell and hoped that I would pluck her away from obscurity, but she charged over a couple of tables in my direction. A couple of drunken farmers lying prostrate on the wooden planking were unceremoniously trampled on as Miss Bresslaw made her clumsy way towards me, bottles tumbled off the tables and glasses were smashed. Then lurching to an unsteady halt she stood elevated on the table in front of me. My companions were most delighted at this turn of events at such a celebratory taking such an interest in their new friend.

They encouraged Miss Bresslaw to perform numerous dances for me by stuffing 20 Baht notes into various parts of her clothing and giving her numerous shots of whisky that she mostly swigged straight from the bottle. The katoey was almost catatonic and I must admit I was a trifle scared and concerned where all this was leading.

Was I going to be taken away to be her sex slave? Was I ever going to see Pattaya or humankind again? Miss Bresslaw's dancing was far from the sensuous intention that the katoey was trying to achieve and at one point I thought I was going to suffocate as my face was being gripped to her gyrating groin region so hard. It was at this point I came to realise Miss Bresslaw was actually a pre operative ladyboy as the large bulge in her panties was pressed firmly against my forehead and disturbingly twitching. I do not know if Miss Bresslaw was aware of her wayward manhood causing me the discomfort it was or it was just her way of being erotic.

I now feared for my life and was gulping for air, but was acutely aware not to open my mouth. The music suddenly ceased and thankfully the ladyboys paid personal attention had come to an end. I hoped encores were not common in this part of Thailand and that my ordeal was over.

But I was mistaken as Miss Bresslaw got down on all fours on the table grabbed my ears then fervently kissed me full on the lips trying to force her tongue into my mouth. Whilst doing so I felt one of her hands leave my face and it was thrust down between my legs to roughly grope my penis which luckily was as flaccid as it ever had been in my life. A loud cheer from my table went up as indeed I had been most fortunate to receive such attention from the extremely popular Miss Bresslaw.

For my own part I had to tip Miss Bresslaw handsomely as was expected, but I felt kind of strange having to pay for probably one of the most uncomfortable experiences I have ever endured. Ohm touched me on the shoulder and was smiling she was offering me a tissue. What was left of Miss Bresslaw's bright red lipstick was now smudged all over my face. I looked around the faces peering at me and unbelievably I could definitely sense a certain mood of jealousy within the gathered throng.

Thankfully all of a sudden our whole party stood up and it was apparent that it was our time to leave. It is a trait I am always completely surprised by when go out in Thai company, just when you think everybody is settled and having a good time with no warning whatsoever the party breaks up.

We were now to visit Bao Dang the only nightclub for miles around. Ohm was driving and I had a lift, but everybody else was to follow on their motorbikes. I knew Ohm had taken it easy with the alcohol, but some of the others should definitely not have been driving and I was glad I was not on the back of one of the scooters.

Bao Dang was a place that can only be described as a nightclub not of its time. What time and what place it did belong to I really cannot say. A large, dark car park crammed with vehicles was situated just off the main road and just beyond that was the Club. Ohm took her time to park what seemed to her was a juggernaut to Kik's constant annoying chiding of her driving ability. Eventually when Ohm managed to moor the Ark Royal we walked across the grass to Bao Dang.

At first the outside of Bao Dang reminded me of the double deuce in the *Roadhouse* movie because of its desolate location. But on entering the Double Deuce seemed like Buckingham Palace in comparison. Rather ashamedly space was made for us by clearing a couple of parties of locals away from their tables. This was due to the Abel effect, the perception that the strange farang would be far more affluent than the usual incumbents.

Nothing in the Bao Dang matched. Tables, chairs, floors, glasses, flooring and most importantly people. You could not have got a more eclectic group of people under one roof if you had deliberately set out to do so. There were hillbillies, farmers, katoeys, goths, gays, straights and people off all ages; the only thing they had in common was that they were all Thai. The room was a barn of a place and possibly originally it had been; the floor was treacherous and made of roughly nailed wooden planking and for no logical reason was on varying different levels. People were constantly tripping and crashing into unsuspecting tables to the complete indifference of others sitting there.

A loud Issan band played on the stage and the whole room seemed to vibrate with the combination of the volume and the shaky wooden interior. Two bottles of whisky arrived together with our attendant waiter and soon ice was clinking and glasses were charged again. A loud cheer went up from our group at the arrival of a rather glamorous lady in a full length, figure hugging, blue dress. I did not recognise Dome at first, but then it dawned on me who the rather elegant figure was.

Kik leaned over and whispered to me that Dome had the occasional penchant for cross dressing, but I was staggered by his transformation. He was wearing a long black wig with full make up and carried a matching silver handbag to accompany his silver slippers. I suppose the flooring made it impossible to wear heels in Bao Dang. I had not noticed he hadn't been at the Fete, but it was obvious he was preparing for his grand entrance. My only comparison to his arrival in Bao Dang that night would be Marilyn Monroe appearing suddenly in the middle of the Gwladys Street End at Everton wearing a bikini.

I could not go anywhere in the Club that night without being stopped and heartedly welcomed. Frequently I refused invitations to join tables and even though drunk the inquisitive nature of the Thais still shone through impressively. I have always considered my fellow Scousers as a nosey bunch and their gregarious nature is one of the reasons Liverpool is generally such a friendly place. Perhaps that is why I like the occupants of Thailand so much.

The night was raucous in the extreme with Dome leading most of the entertainment seemingly determined to show the whole nightclub how beautiful he was in his costume. The Blend 285 Thai Whisky was taking its toll and was certainly a powerful and incredibly astringent brew; the previous other two hundred and eighty four attempts to produce the whisky must have been disgustingly bad if this was the finished article!

One of the plumper male members of our party had decided to treat me to a fantastical display of Pogo dancing that I had deemed had long ago disappeared from memory. The problem was he was jumping up and down on a loose plank whose other end was under Ohm's chair. Every time the energetic youngster landed Ohm was catapulted twelve inches into the air spilling her drink on every occasion. Ohm was getting extremely mad with his antics and doing so encouraged Kik to spur his tubby friend to continue at an even more vigorous pace.

We left the club close to 5am and headed back to the little hotel, a little worse for wear, but nothing more than a hangover to deal with in the morning. I cannot remember actually getting into bed and I slept deeply, fuelled with the alcohol running around inside my body. I was told once that the unconscious sleep achieved after drinking does not revitalise and refresh the body, in other words it is not good sleep. But reflecting that, it was Richie that had told me the snippet. I rejected it off handily as pure bollocks, sleep is sleep.

Chapter Eighteen

LAOS

It had not occurred to me previously, but the fact became apparent that six people were going to travel to Laos in the tiny Toyota Yaris rental car. Dome was driving and Ohm bagged the passenger seat as she was paying the hire cost. That left Kik, his parents and I to all squeeze in the back. It was fortunate Kik took his small stature from his families' genes as both his parents were very petite and under five and a half feet tall. Still, it was a tight fit in the rear of the car and frequently everybody had to get out and walk whilst Dome steered over the dirt road that lead from Kik's parent's house.

The noise of the junior passengers was soon tempered by Kik's mother. When she spoke everybody was silent and she was obviously the Matriarch. Her voice was addictive to listen to; I couldn't understand one word she uttered, but Kik's mother spoke in such melodic soft tones that undulated with every word and sentence. It was hypnotic and soothing to listen to and I regret not being able to empathise with the old family tales she was regaling her husband and offspring with.

This trip was a rare treat for the couple and they had the added bonus of being accompanied by their cherished young whom they only saw sporadically. It was quite humbling as an outsider sharing this most coveted of family times and it is a period of my life that I will never forget. As soon as we had traversed the dirt road we followed Highway 22 travelling west towards Udon Thani.

Dome seemed a confident and proficient driver and even with the car heavily loaded he made better and faster progress than Ohm had a couple of days back. I was glad Dome had changed out of his evening wear as I do not think there would have been room for his hat box in the boot of the car.

We did not have to go into Udon Thani as we could skirt the city by one of its bypasses and then take the short trip north on Highway 2 to Nong Khai on the border. We had been travelling for over two and a half hours and my right limbs were aching being pressed against the door. I could not really move to alleviate the discomfort and I wish I had taken more Baclofen before we set off on our journey.

Although my seating position was bad I was amazed at the discipline of posture that Kik's mum maintained the whole time. She was perched almost cross legged on the edge of the rear seat supported by the backs of the seats in front. It was some sort of Yoga position that even when I was fit I couldn't have maintained for more than two minutes on a cushioned floor; certainly not for two and a half hours in a bumpy motor car.

The occupants of the car started to become more attentive as Dome announced we had arrived in Nong Khai and an expectant air permeated the vehicle. We were heading for one of the numerous processing agencies that ensured Thai immigrants had the correct identification to cross the border. Thais do not need a passport to cross into Laos, their identification card is sufficient as long as it is accompanied with some proof of residency. The agencies check the details for a nominal fee then it is a very quick and simple process at the border.

Once everything was complete we parked the car at the agency and Dome negotiated with a Taxi driver of a minibus to take us across the border. The large vehicle was luxurious compared to the Yaris and it was a blessing to relieve the pressure on my leg and arm. As the bus made the short journey to the border a huge bridge came into view and across the Mekong River on the other side was my first glimpse of Laos. It seemed exactly like north Thailand, but I do not know what I had been expecting, Tyneside?

The bus halted at the Thai border control and we all alighted to pass through Immigration. Our little group drew quite some attention as it looked as though I had been captured by some Machiavellian Thai family that intended to trade me to the Laos Underworld. Kik's mum was transformed into Ma Baker leading her wayward family in a rampant spree of murder and robbery and general bad behaviour. I was glad Boney M were not in attendance to sing the theme song; or even worse, Mr Seng with his dodgy Cambodian rip off version.

My processing took a little longer than the others so they all passed through before me and waited in the bus for me to join them. Then driving across the mighty Mekong over the Friendship Bridge we arrived in Laos to everybody's excitement and expectancy. We collected our luggage from the bus and joined the small queue at Laos Immigration. Again, my fellow travellers passed through passport control quickly whilst my visa took about ten minutes to complete. We were reunited on the other side of the border and cleared customs by simply walking through.

Dome once again sprang into action as the official tour guide and busily went to get a deal for some transport for our stay. He came back sitting in the front of a rather posh looking minibus. It was ideal for the six of us and the driver had agreed to be our chauffeur for our entire stay, we were to pay him seventy five dollars and he was at our beck and call for three days and two nights. If we decided to go on a trip then we would have to pay extra but that was fair enough. The currency of Lao is the Kip, but like its neighbours Cambodia and Vietnam the US Dollar is widely accepted.

Laos is a totally landlocked country and has borders with Burma, China, Vietnam, Cambodia and Thailand. Although in population at fewer than seven million people it is a relatively small country, Laos is really the hub of South East Asia and is really accessible to come and go into. Its main commercial activity is rice production, but about every one in ten Laotians are involved in the tourist industry. Laos is a fairly safe country to visit and it is rapidly becoming a popular destination for the more adventurous traveller.

It is an ancient civilisation and is steeped in culture; the treasures of Laos are varied and diverse from Tiger spotting in Namet to the Backpackers havens of Muang Ngoi and Neuatvang Vieng. There are dozens of noteworthy wats, temples and religious sites and deep, treacherous caves to explore around Thakhek. In the north of the country are remote hill tribes seldom seen by the eyes of a farang.

We were on the short trip to Vientiane which is the Capital of Laos and I had booked three rooms at the Inter City Boutique Hotel situated on the banks of the Mekong River and right in the centre of Vientiane. Driving through the streets of Vientiane I was reminded of the French Colonial influences that formed part of the city and was impressed by unique architecture. There are no sky scrapers or any really tall buildings in the capital and there is a sense of order and law on the roads that is highly unusual for South East Asia.

Everything is at a slow pace in Laos, similar in a way to its cousin Cambodia. Advertising and commercialism is in its infancy and you would be hard put to find a fast food chain or shopping mall within Vientiane. Everywhere you looked there were many residents in traditional dress and it added to the authenticity and atmosphere of the whole place; somewhere, thankfully that had not yet been tainted by the stain of capitalism. The Laotians were courteous and very friendly; they would stop and take time to give their assistance in any way they could.

Inter City Boutique Hotel was enchanting; small, unique and very traditional. I had found it on line and it was right on the river's edge. The whole interior was decorated in dark wood from the walls to the flooring and traditional art was displayed generously around the foyer. I had booked three deluxe rooms, the best the hotel had to offer and they were less than twenty pounds per night. I was sharing with Kik whilst Dome and Ohm were to share the other twin leaving a large double for Kik's parents.

My room was large and in fitting with the rest of the hotel was mostly furnished in strong, sturdy dark wood. The room's décor was a little tired and the bathroom slightly antiquated, but I looked past all that as it invoked strong atmospheric feelings of the country I was in. This was no large hotel chain box to sleep in, that was the same as all the other boxes around the world. The room was unique and not even similar to any other in the same hotel.

We had all agreed to meet in the foyer in thirty minutes and it was Kik's parents that were the last to arrive. Kik's mum was laughing and immediately told the party what was amusing her. Kik's father was so impressed with the luxury of the room he had explored every nook and cranny and tried every appliance. He had been playing with the remote controls of the TV and it had stuck on full volume; a member of staff had to be summoned to come up to the room to assist him. Kik's father was standing behind his wife acting like a naughty schoolboy when the porter arrived and would not say a word as he was too embarrassed to speak.

I looked at Kik's dad and he was still highly embarrassed especially as his wife had spilled the beans of his juvenile misbehaviour. He was looking down at his feet as the family and friends laughed heartily at his expense. I felt a little sorry for the quiet man as it was obvious that he had not spent a lot of time in hotels.

We strolled along the Mekong as the city's early evening activities were drawn to the river. Stalls and vendors were setting up and small groups of exercising dancers blew the cobwebs away from another day's work. Later that evening Dome took us to Moon the Night, a restaurant overlooking the Mekong, that was very popular amongst Vientiane locals. It was my first taste of Beerlao and I really liked the refreshing brew as it was similar to a good lager with a strong flavour.

During the meal Kik nudged me and tilted his head towards his parents sitting opposite. They were holding hands and smiling contently at one another.

"It is a long time since I have seen my mum so happy," Kik confided in me. "Thank you." I looked at my friend and saw moisture in his eyes and felt guilty. The shared cost of the financing of the trip had been so cheap for me I would hardly notice the expense, but the gesture had meant so much to these genuine people. I was glad that I could share my comparative wealth in such a rewarding way.

After dinner, Kik's parents went back to spend some time in the hotel whilst the rest of us sampled Vientiane's nightlife and returned in the early hours. The following day was spent sightseeing around the city, all be it with a few hangovers from the younger members of the party. We had an addition to our group with a young Laotian accompanying Dome, apparently Ohm had to sleep in the bathroom during the night as Dome had met the young man in a nightclub and had taken him home.

No one, not even Kik's parents seemed to bat an eyelid at the new member of the tourist party and nobody seemed remotely surprised by Dome's behaviour. The young man's name was M and for the most part was very quiet and seemingly very polite. The strange fellowship was now seven in number not quite the Magnificent Seven, but more like the Eclectic non Eight.

That day was crammed visiting Pha That Luang a stunning Buddhist Stupa followed by the Wat Si Muang Temple. The sun was high in the sky so Dom and M visited a small stall and hired seven of the most tired looking umbrellas I have ever seen. I was glad it was not raining because the sorry looking articles would definitely have not lived up to their former glory and held any water off. So, now the Eclectic non Eight were resplendent tourists from another land causing havoc as our brollies bashed into peoples heads as we ambled along on our sightseeing adventure.

Perhaps the most central attraction is Patuxai the Memorial Monument based on the Arc du Triomph. It was constructed to celebrate the liberation from France in the 1950's and is actually made from the concrete originally intended for an airfield in the Vietnam War. From afar it is a most impressive structure, but up close it is easy to see that it is not well engineered with steel beams protruding from rough cement.

Our final night we ate together at a more modern restaurant and the party was a little subdued as we were to travel home in the morning and the small fellowship would part. The restaurant was chosen by Dome as it was fashionable, but everybody preferred the previous night's location. Once again we separated after dinner and Kik's parents went home whilst the rest of us went to a rather bizarre and odd nightclub on the outskirts of the city.

Rather late in the morning everybody surfaced including Dome's new companion and we made our way to the border. Kik's mum was showing some gifts she had bought for friends back home to Ohm whilst Dome was very loud entertaining everybody and impressing his new beau. Our taxi driver together with Dome's romantic interlude bade us goodbye at Friendship Bridge and we made our way back to the car.

The journey home was more or less in silence, I was going to spend one more night in Phang Khon and return home alone as Kik was going to stay and teach students for a month. As we neared Kik's parents village the weather turned and the road became almost impassable due to the torrential rain and the fast rising floods. We left the main highway and turned into the small road leading to the isolated hamlet. The road had become almost a stream and in the headlights of the car we could spot the local wildlife coming out to play.

Fish were actually swimming in the road and then a large snake appeared slithering after a bouncing frog. The creatures on the ground were terrifying enough, but the air borne things flying chaotically about the Yaris windows were straight out of a Hitchcock Movie. I had no intention whatsoever of getting out of the car's confines until we got back to civilisation and out of the wild, deep blackness of the jungle.

The following day I was driven to Udon Thani by Ohm and also accompanied by Kik's parents as they wanted to formally say goodbye to me. Kik had stayed behind to start work, but I knew I would see him back in Pattaya in a month or so anyway. I was honoured to say goodbye to the Puttisa family after my recent acceptance as a temporary guest. I had been given all the courtesy and welcome that they could afford and that hospitality had been heartfelt, warm and genuine.

One week later I was surprised to be on a Nok Air flight back to Udon Thani. In my absence some news had reached Ohm of a business opportunity she wanted to invest in. I was met at the airport by Ohm and Kik and she explained to me what the opportunity was. It was a chance to buy some land near the Lao border that was ready for Rubber Cultivation. Such land rarely came up for sale as it normally got handed down through immediate family and it was a case of a friend of a friend had passed the news on to her mother. I had mentioned to Ohm during my last trip that I needed to find some sort of revenue stream as my limited finances would soon dry up, but I did not ever think she would have acted so quickly.

Her parents were already up looking at the site and we were due to follow them directly from the airport. At this time I did not know or understand what my involvement was to be in this, but I was thrilled of the adventure I was now undertaking. As we drove north the countryside became more beautiful, away from the flat paddy fields of the plains the terrain was more varied and undulating. The distant hills and mountains of Lao could be plainly seen to the north and west and I knew somewhere ahead was the Mekong River.

The surroundings changed to that of plots of orderly rows of trees with little vegetation between them. They were the little rubber plantations in various forms of development. Most of the latex in northern Thailand is harvested by small individually owned farms, or in some cases Co-Operatives. The raw material is then sold on locally to refineries who then sell it to large treatment processing plants mostly for the Japanese and Chinese Automotive Industries.

A plot of land is measured in Rais and each Rai is approximately the equivalent of half an acre. Then the value of the plot is measured on how many Rubber Trees it has, the condition of the land and at what stage the trees are at. That is to say if they are ready for cutting and harvesting or still growing.

Ohm had a chance of purchasing a plot of eleven Rai about two hundred trees ready to be harvested. Once cut a tree will continue to produce latex for about thirty years if correctly maintained, after that it can be sold for lumber. A by product is harvesting the gas produced by the trees in large canopies this also can be sold to be used as alternative fuel mostly to Japan.

We left the main highway after much discussion and argument between Ohm and Kik and turned into a small path leading directly into the jungle. The path lead us to a small village of no more than a dozen simple dwellings and Ohm stopped to ask directions. The local children pressed their grubby noses to the windows of the car to glimpse the strangers who had just entered into their world. A little girl stared at me with an open mouth curious of my intent leaving a small patch of steam on the window with her breath. I smiled back at her and she blushed, turned and ran away to find her mother.

With fresh directions Ohm drove slowly straight ahead looking for a turning. After some minutes a dirt track appeared on our right which was our intended route. Progress now was slow due to the thick vegetation and the condition of the track we were travelling on, a little wonder all the vehicles I had seen were 4 x 4 pick up trucks. The trail started to rise and widened into a small road, the vegetation changed from wilderness to orderly semi-cultivated plantation land and then we spotted Kik's dad sitting by the side of the road smoking a cigarette.

He had come to guide us and must have been waiting for an agreed time to be where he was. Mr Puttisa walked in front of the car directing Ohm slowly over the treacherous terrain of rocks, pot holes and trees. I considered what the inhabitants of this natural habitat could be, but tried to force my fear of snakes from my mind. Kik's dad guided Ohm around a corner then told her to stop; apparently we had reached our destination.

Leaving the car blocking the road we were instructed to follow Mr Puttisa into the shallow undergrowth. I was wearing only sandals and was acutely aware of the nakedness of my feet as I trudged along behind Ohm. It was difficult for me to walk on the undulating jungle floor and I was slowing the party down, Kik must have told his dad and Ohm of my condition as they were most attentive to assist me whenever I tripped or stumbled.

Thankfully it was only a short hike and we came to the plantation. There was a small stream we crossed with the aid of a fallen tree and finally we came to stand on the rubber tree plot. The first thing that struck me was how beautiful everything was, I could see the hills in the distance seemingly all around us and the lush green canopy's of all the small plantations marking the landscape in their respective squares and rectangles.

It was so quiet; the trees seemed to form an eerie silence as they shaded us from the sun. There were three other people already on the plantation one was Kik's mother and the other two were cousins, the only noise for miles around was emanating from their activity. Thai's often refer to good friends as their brothers, sisters or cousins and it can be most confusing at first. I have learnt since to clarify their validity as a blood relation compared to often of a simple acquaintance from the Post Office or supermarket.

Kik's mum was busy over a fire cooking food for us all and she smiled and waved to me by way of a welcome. Ohm gave me a guided tour of the plantation, I had no real idea how big eleven Rai of land is and was quite surprised how large the area was and how many trees there seemed to be. One boundary was against a neighbouring plantation that was already producing latex. Little black plastic buckets were hung by wire on the silver bark of the trees just under a diagonal cut into the wood. There was a viscous, milky white substance collected in the small pails and that I was informed was the raw latex.

A small lake constituted another boundary with the other two sides fading into the jungle. The tree line ended well before it reached the lake and a small hut was located just away from the waters edge. A hermit fisherman lived there, a man who had simply opted out of life to live in the tranquil wilderness; he existed by the fish he could catch to eat or sell to local villages. The current owner of the land let him reside there free as a sort of piscatorial security guard. Who on Earth would have the tenacity to steal anything from such a remote place? Whoever it was they deserved to keep their booty in my book!

Ohm continuously chatted to me as we traipsed around in a sort of sales pitch and I knew the real reason for my invitation was due to become apparent very soon. Ohm already owned Rubber Tree land and knew her stuff, she was raving on about how good the soil, drainage and condition of the trees was. The plantation was almost ready to have its first harvest as the trees had grown to the correct age and size and would produce latex almost immediately.

Kik shouted over to us from the camp fire and informed us that lunch was ready. A couple of plastic sheets had been placed on the floor and a make shift seat for my benefit was provided by way of a dead tree stump. Already there were plates and spoons waiting and Kik's mum was ladling some hot food out to the party. She had made Laab especially for me as Kik had told her it was my favourite; it is a spicy salad which in this case had minced pork. In the boiling pan was Kaeng Ka Ri Kai a chicken curry with eggplants and coconut milk and it was served together with Mr Puttisa's famous sticky rice. There were other accompanying dishes that had been pre cooked at home and were still tepid to the palate even hours later due to the ambient heat.

I can never really overstate the Thais attention to the importance of food to galvanise friendship and togetherness; the care and attention of the preparation is as important as the communal consumption. Even the most simple of fares is treated with respect as somebody; somewhere had taken the time to prepare it. I could not imagine an English picnic in such a remote location being so lavish, usually a picnic is constituted by shop bought pies and plastic wrapped sandwiches, the convenience being more important that the end result. But the truth of it is that the result is considerably more expensive and nowhere as near as delicious.

As I was devouring my second plate of Laab I saw a movement in the grass by my foot, I looked down to study what had caused the disturbance and to my horror I saw a three foot long orange coloured snake. I nearly deposited my lunch there and then in my trousers I was so shit scared. One of the cousins also saw the snake and nonchalantly shooed it away with a branch. Nobody knew what type of snake it was called in English, but admitted to my discomfort that it was quite poisonous. I immediately lost my appetite and spent the rest of lunch on a David Attenborough Wildlife watch.

After our safari, we made our long way back to Phang Khon; it was to take over three hours and it was already after 4pm so I knew the later part of the drive would be at Mak Ohm, which is slightly faster than a tandem. On the way Ohm started her gambit;

she wanted somebody to come in with her on the deal as she did not have the whole twenty thousand pounds to buy the land. She had already been calculating the extra cost needed to make the whole business viable. There needed to be an access road built and a concrete drainage tunnel underneath so the road would not wash away. Next a tree house had to be built for the workers to protect them from the wildlife plus all the tangible things needed for production. Buckets, wire, compost, manure, tools; the list was quite extensive and I was impressed with her knowledge of the business.

The whole cost was near thirty thousand, but the good news was the land could be paid for in staged amounts over twelve months. If her calculations were correct then nearly eight thousand pounds profit could be harvested from the land to help the final payment. Ohm then had calculated a possible return on investment of four years if an average yield was taken from the trees. It was a feasible business opportunity and I had to start getting some money in soon or my savings would disappear. I had known I would have to take a calculated risk sometime and this idea seemed as good as any I had so far come up with.

Purchasing land in Thailand for a foreigner is not easy, it is not impossible, but it is complicated. A business with foreign investors can own land but it is imperative a top legal man handles the affair together with an honest accountant. Many people have advised me that neither are easy to find in Thailand and there are many law suits awaiting trial of disputes between such parties. In other words setting up a small business is a minefield and open up to corruption and dishonesty from officials, legal representation and robbing bastards of accountants.

My own risk was limited to a short lived friendship as Ohm would be legally the owner of the land and business. A private agreement could be drawn up between Ohm and me, but in a Thai court that would be as valid as putting salt and pepper on a curry. It all boiled down to whether I trusted Ohm; both with her calculations and to be honest in a business relationship.

The following day when travelling to Udon Thani Airport I had an honest discussion with Ohm as we were alone in the car. She alleviated some of my concerns by telling me that her mum and dad were going to live and work on the land. I was surprised by the hardship the two rather mature parents were prepared to undergo, but Ohm said they both needed the money. It would be good for them, but also for the business as they would be attentive in their duties and not cheat on production or costs. It all made sense, but I needed time to do some research into Rubber Tree production and to go over her figures. She agreed to give me a couple of weeks, but neither of us could afford to delay more than that.

Back in Pattaya, I considered my options and tried to decide if the risk was worth losing my money and just importantly potentially destroying a friendship. My mother's estate had been finalised and after all the debts and legal deductions my inheritance was fairly small, but still it was a few of thousand pounds. It something that I had not budgeted in receiving as I thought the nursing home debt would swallow the entire proceeds from the sale of the family home, but thankfully there was a little extra to be divided between my brother and me. But what was I to do with it?

I was due to go to Malaysia on the 19th of September to visit my old friend Sharon who lived there. The actual purpose of my trip was twofold as I also had to buy more of my stroke medicine. Some of the medicine sold in Thailand is not genuine and I could not afford to take any risks whatsoever with my health. I made my mind up to give my decision to Ohm before I left, I was only going away for four days, but it would concentrate my mind to do sufficient homework on the proposal and give me a time frame to work to.

It actually only took me about three days surfing the internet and debating in my mind. I could go over figures as much as I wanted, but the major deciding factor was based on whether I was going to risk a punt on it and be prepared and afford to lose my investment. I phoned Ohm and agreed to join her as a partner with a third interest in the business. She was elated and would get the deal rolling in my absence and I would fly back up north when I returned from Malaysia. I couldn't quite believe what I had done; I was now a landowner of a small plot of land in North East Thailand. I would have to buy the required Panama hat and Safari suit of a Plantation Owner!

Chapter Nineteen

MALAYSIA AND OTHER LANDS

The Air Asia flight into Kuala Lumpur was fairly smooth and short. Looking down out of the plane window at the Jungle City below me I was taken aback how isolated the Metropolitan and Modern City actually was, for miles around and as far as the eye could see was the lush countryside of Palm Trees. Palm Oil is one of Malaysia's biggest exports and it was obvious why. However, after a few minutes I became almost blasé about the tropical landscape as it was never ending and uninterrupted by anything else.

Air Asia has its main hub and operating base in Kuala Lumpur and is almost the only occupant of the City's second airport. There were rumours that the airline was to move to K.L.I.A the countries largest international airport in the future, but for now the plane touched down at a rather modest Sultan Abdul Aziz Shah International Airport whose name is bigger than the Terminal.

There is no Visa requirement for UK citizens and passing through Immigration took a matter of minutes. I was quite impressed with the finger print security procedure at Immigration Control, but having never been there before I wondered with what the machine was comparing my smudges to?

Not having to wait for my bag as I was travelling as I normally did with hand luggage only I was out of the airport in about fifteen minutes. Sharon was waiting for me and we greeted each other warmly, I have not forgotten the help she was to me with my mum's funeral and I don't think I ever will. Sharon lives in KL with her husband and two children and has been an expat for some time moving with Brendan's job.

Greenstreet and Back

The first thing that you notice about Sharon that it is difficult to get a word in edgeways into her continuous and always animated conversation. Every time you meet her it is like somebody had just removed a gag from her mouth seconds before the encounter. And this persistent tirade switches topic and theme frantically as new ideas pop into her head. The one sided conversation is fast, furious and frantic and leaves the other party gasping for breath themselves. But her company is warm, sincere, genuine and never ever dull.

I had been to Malaysia twice before, but never visited KL. I had travelled to Penang on holiday with the oaf and had loved the country. So, I was most keen to explore, especially with my knowledgeable guide by my side. I was introduced to Sharon by Richie; they had been old school friends together back in Crosby, but had never really got to know her very well until my stroke. Up to then it was always a rather drunken meet up in the Bug on one of her visits home. But Sharon and her sister Noreen had been very kind to me in my recuperation.

We took a taxi from the airport with the very long name to her house in the centre of the city. Sharon is quite a private person behind the external glamour and does not readily reveal her personal life to many people perhaps that is why I had never got to know her well in the past. Therefore, I had no idea what to expect when arriving at her home. The house was magnificent with plenty of natural wood used in the construction giving a modern but traditional feeling to the property. Inside the large dwelling the use of light coloured wood continued the theme from the polished flooring to the décor.

Before moving to KL, Sharon had lived in Dubai and the Arabian influences of furniture and soft furnishings were everywhere to see, but seem to complement the Asian feel to the house. There was plenty of natural light flooding into the building from large windows and that gave an airy and fresh feeling to everything. But more importantly the house was a home and it became evident during my stay that it was a happy home. My room was actually a small lodge in the garden with its own entrance, bathroom and double bed. Sharon had actually put an exercise bike in it for me so I could continue with my daily routine. Either that or she thought of me as a fat bastard who needed to lose some weight!

Sharon took the whole time I was there off work to show me around and I was glad of her company. KL is a city of two million people and unlike the rest of Malaysia is very modern and High Tech. It is an international city in every respect and has some of the tallest buildings in the world in the magnificent Petronas Twin Towers and the Putra World Trade Centre. Walking around the city part of KL, you are dwarfed by the ultra modern office skyscrapers and fancy hotels, but it still retains its own identity. It is not as sterile as say Singapore or as dirty as Bangkok and because it is a relatively small city in comparison to some large metropolises it does not feel fragmented and an urban wilderness.

The feeling of being close and part of the city is accentuated by many of the old colonial type buildings remaining to stand side by side with their modern counterparts. The old town is very much in the heart of the centre and Little India adds a noisy confusing counterbalance to the more formal business district. It is, however, a Jungle City and all around you are reminded of that fact with exotic trees and birds.

It is as if KL was just plonked in the middle of tropical wilderness as nobody knew where to put it. I could imagine two Navvies on a Friday night five minutes before they finished their work for the week. Somebody had just given Paddy Kuala Lumpur and he had asked Kelly what to do with it.

"Oh, just throw it over there, I want to go to the pub" was his friend's reply, and it had remained there ever since. Actually, Kuala Lumpur means Muddy River, so I assume the growth of KL was due to some fact related to that and not as I aforementioned named by two thirsty Irishmen.

Unlike the rest of my Asian trip so far, Malaysia is not a Buddhist country and Islam is the official religion. There were many cultural differences evident whilst walking the streets and I was duly respectful that I was in a Muslim country. It was rather strange that things could be so different here compared to Thailand and it had only been an hour long flight.

On my last night Sharon took me to an area called Bangsar where we met Brendon for a drink and a meal. Bangsar is packed with trendy bars, restaurants and nightclubs and the choice is many and varied. However, in the middle of all the plush, expensive eateries was a little street crammed with street food vendors and small ethnic restaurants.

It was one of the things I had noticed about Malaysia before and loved the diversity of the street food. Malay, Thai, Indian, Chinese, Japanese and Korean cuisines all were available side by side to choose from. In Penang they were sometimes corralled together in open air food courts with communal tables to sit and eat inexpensively.

My stay in KL was four days, but it passed so quickly that it seemed like it was an overnight stop over. During the whole time, I kept in constant contact with Ohm over the progress of the Rubber Plantation and things were moving at a pace. Sharon could not have possibly been a better guide and hostess to me and my stay was luxurious but quite hectic. Her two children were perhaps the politest siblings I have ever met and it reflected how hard Sharon and Brendon had worked to make it that way. I was glad that I got an insight into her life as brief passing greetings not always tell the whole story.

I decided to have a rest for a week back in Pattaya before I took a trip up North again as I needed some gym time and also just some moments relaxing in the sun. Standing on my balcony one night I began to reflect upon the current part of my life, I looked down at the twinkling lights of Jomtien below and imagined what was occurring in the bars and streets. In the distance I could see the Khoa Khiao Mountains dark, menacing and black against the fading light of the sky. I was truly happy, I loved where I was and what I was doing and I was contented. But I knew if I wanted my life to continue in the current mode it was, I needed more finances in my coffers.

The coffee shop was quiet due to Kik's absence and over the following few days I caught up with all the local happenings in Pattaya News newspaper. The first headline to grab me was "Four Men Arrested in Shooting". There had been a partial solar eclipse recently and four men had been arrested for their celebrations of the event. A large amount Sang Thip whisky had been consumed and the men were quite drunk and hallucinating, during the eclipse. For some reasons the men thought that shooting their firearms into the sky gave homage to the celestial event. Unfortunately, a totally innocent man lying rather inebriated on the floor nearby experiencing the eclipse was struck in the leg by an errant shell returning back to Earth.

The headline was delivered in a manner to describe the actions as part of normal life and almost to insinuate the guy should not have been where he was and he was at fault. The incident was bizarre and was not common at all, but did highlight the recognised fact that firearms are a part of normal Thai life. The paper was also full of stories of other shootings and gang related violence around Pattaya. Most was drug orientated and concerned quite young antagonists, but the police seemed to be fighting a tough battle to uphold order.

Pattaya Police have their hands full trying to keep a lid on the city, but endeavour to strain their resources in doing so. The protection of visitors is high on the agenda with tourism being such a major contributing factor to the city's economy. Because of the lewd reputation the city has gleaned over the last few decades

Greenstreet and Back

it tends to attract a potential explosive mix of people. On one side, there are determined tourists eager to spend every last Baht in the pursuit of self gratification and on the other side an eclectic group of prostitutes, drug dealers, thieves and vagabonds determined to take everything they can.

Around the Sois and beach of Walking Street is a very popular area for the two parties to get acquainted and is a notorious trouble spot. Many prostitute katoeys patrol this region and if they do not succeed in luring their prey with the promise of sexual services, then they will illicit their cash by other crooked means. There is a weekly game of "Cops and Ladyboy Robbers" where the Pattaya City Police periodically round up a few score potential miscreants and take them to the Nick. Documents are checked and the whole bunch are released a couple of hours later with a two hundred Baht fine and no charges being made.

I have always wondered what the noise would be like in the police station on such an evening. Imagine some unfortunate granny reporting the disappearance of her cat that night and being caught up in the bawdy scene. I am sure there is some old Pattaya saying to describe a group of corralled ladyboys, perhaps a "Chaotic Clamour of Katoeys" or a "Loud, Lavish, Lorry Load of Ladyboys", but whatever it is, it could never be accurate enough.

My trip up to visit Ohm was fruitful, we drove up to the plantation from Udon Thani and on the way Ohm excitedly related what progress had been made. Already the little access road over the stream had been built and a drainage channel of concrete pipes had been laid. Work on the tree house had started as now wood could be brought onto the site. When we arrived the place was a hive of activity, Ohm's parents were there along with relatives, friends, children and dogs all contributing something worthwhile to the land. Perhaps the dogs most of all as they were acting as excellent alarms for any predatory snakes on the prowl.

A couple of the men where starting the construction of the Tree House whilst the women and children were busy clearing forest debris from the floor and laying compost in the soil. I breathed in deeply and the luscious fresh green smell of foliage permeated the air, it was cooler standing under the canopy of the trees and I felt at peace in the tropical wilderness. I was wary of the snakes so had dressed in jeans and wore training shoes, apart from my arms and face no bare flesh was visible and I felt a little better protected. I could hardly believe, no matter how small, I owned a part of this land. Legally it was not the case as my name was not on any official documentation, but Ohm had insisted that we had drawn up a private agreement.

I stayed another couple of nights in Phang Khon and grew to know the rural area better. It was very different to the commercial Thailand that I knew so well and I was not ready to settle down somewhere so remote, but perhaps I should be residing somewhere nearer the business? The day of my flight I asked Ohm to take me to Udon Thani early so that I could look around perhaps for a place to live.

The rains in late October were persistent, even though the Monsoon Season had officially finished. That year there had been an unusual amount of rainfall and there was widespread flooding across the country. Getting into Udon Thani was a nightmare as many of the roads were completely flooded, but slowly we made it and I was glad that I had made the journey early so that I was near the airport.

After lunch Ohm drove me around Udon. It is a large conurbation with over one million inhabitants, but the city centre itself is quite compact. I did not like Udon at all, there seemed to be no alluring features to enamour a person to it. The choices of Town House accommodation seemed limited and the properties seemed dishevelled and ramshackle. It was not a pretty town and the run down areas reminded me of parts of my own city; I had not come halfway across the world to live in bloody Bootle!

My flight home was shocking as I could see the devastation of the flooding for miles around from the eagle eye view of the plane window. Of the seventy seven provinces in Thailand sixty five of them were declared Flood Disaster Zones, only a few in the mountainous north and the distant south were spared the horrific tragedy of nature's uncaring ferocity.

The World Bank estimated that the Thai economy suffered losses of around eighty billion pounds and that over thirteen million people were directly affected. Most of the financial losses were in the manufacturing industry as factories were lost in many of the industrial estates around Bangkok. Around sixty thousand square miles around the Cho Phraya River basin drains towards Bangkok and then out into the Gulf Of Thailand; Bangkok was devastated. A thousand people lost their lives and many more their homes and their treasured possessions. The event warranted brief news coverage in the UK as there was more pressing and world stopping news of Louis in X Factor to report on.

I had considered a trip home to spend Christmas and to also act as a visa run, but with things busy with the plantation I decided to have my first ever Christmas away from Liverpool. No matter where I was I had always come home to spend Christmas Day with my family or more recently due to my mother's prolonged illness at Richie's parents' house. I therefore needed to go out of the country in late December for my visa stamp.

So, on the 12th of December I booked an Air Asia flight to Yangon in Myanmar formerly Rangoon of Burma. Trying to get a visa to visit Burma was not easy and it should have given me an indication of troubles to come from the military state. It seemed that a visit to the Burmese Consulate in Bangkok was required until I noticed that certain travel companies authorised by the Burmese Government could help assist in visa procurement. I contacted one of them by their web site and sent the necessary photographs and document copies to them. It all seemed very woolly and I had to bring cash in pristine American Dollar bills to pay for their service when I was met at the airport.

My flight to Yangon was in the early evening and as the flight officer announced we were soon to be landing I stared out of the plane window trying to get a glimpse of the city. I could see nothing but blackness down below and considered that the airport might be some way out of the city. Even so, the urban surroundings of a five million strong conurbation should be illuminated enough to see even from two thousand feet up. It was baffling; I could not make out any buildings, roads, rivers or traffic it was bizarre. It was not until the planes wheels almost touched the runway that the airport's own powerful lights lit up the sky.

Walking through the terminal was quite strange as normally airports are loud busy places, but Yangon International Airport seemed strangely quiet and ominous. There seemed to be multiples of officials and Army Security and it was the most least welcoming airport I have ever arrived at. Trying to clear passport control was difficult as the man who had my visa appeared to be standing behind a glass screen holding a placard with my name on. Most of the few tourists seemed to be getting processed as part of official groups and the authorities were definitely suspicious of lone travellers.

Burma has been under military rule since the Coup D'état in 1962 and has been a military dictatorship ever since. The airport advertised that fact quite succinctly by the officious offhand manner of the officials and there was no warm welcome waiting to greet weary visitors. Eventually it was my turn to get grilled and the very rude Immigration Officer brusquely demanded my visa. I had a simple letter from my contact and at one point they were going to boot me out of the country as fast as I had arrived. The man with the placard banged on the window at the officer and they communicated something that was not said verbally.

The officer then checked a list of four names on a sheet in front of him and luckily my name was on it. A few minutes passed and he fucked around to make himself look important, then issued me with a visa and I was admitted into the oppressed country of Myanmar. My contact was there to greet me wanting his seventy five dollars in payment, unlike the rest of South East Asia there was no formal greeting of hands placed together in front of the chest just a grubby outstretched hand.

I gave him the dollar bills I had got from the bank in Pattaya, he took two but refused the $50 bill. I could see nothing wrong with the note, but he was adamant he was not going to take it. Producing my wallet I showed him the other three $50 bills I had and asked him to select his favourite. He did not seem very enamoured by any of my choice of offerings, but ended up taking one of them when I convinced him that was all that I had. I had never had such hassle after getting off a flight in my life before and was glad to leave the airport.

Hailing down a cab outside the terminal was easy and the next available beat up old mini bus pulled up. I negotiated a fare of twenty dollars to the Park Royal Hotel in Downtown Yangon. The cabbie was very friendly compared to the rest of his countrymen I so far had encountered; he was young and spoke excellent English. As we drove down the road I realised why I had not been able to see the ground from the plane, everything was a weird twilight world. The street lighting seemed to be operating at quarter power and there was very little illumination emanating from the buildings that we passed. It was eerie in the extreme and I wondered, *did Burmese people have trouble with their eyes - did they have to be kept in semi darkness like albinos?*

I remarked to my driver that I had not yet managed to procure any Kyats and could he stop at an ATM on our way to the hotel.

I was stunned at the young man's reply that there were no ATM machines in Yangon and that few banks would change my money. However, he knew somewhere that could help me out. We drove fifteen minutes until a few more buildings started to appear and we were on the outskirts of the city. My driver stopped the cab on the side of the road outside a few wooden buildings and bade me to follow him. I took my worldly possessions that were in my rucksack and followed him.

On reflection it was a stupid thing to have done - I had only known this man twenty minutes and I was a complete stranger in a very foreign place. In my rucksack there was my passport, credit cards and what cash I had in my wallet and it was on my back as I followed the man down a small side passage between two houses. Dogs barked fiercely at our passing and strange eyes peered from dark shaded doorways. We entered a small courtyard formed by low, squat wooden houses and then we stopped. I looked for an escape route should the occasion demand and could see none; we were enclosed on all sides the only way out being the way we had come in.

The driver oblivious of my nervous disposition rapped his knuckles on one of the wooden doors. The door slowly creaked open and crimson light fell into the courtyard from within. An old lady stood in front of us barring our entrance to the room behind her. She was silhouetted by the red glow behind her, but I could see that she was poorly dressed and did not look like a Bureau De Change or her house a Western Union office.

She knew the driver and stood back to let us into the room. It was tiny with a sort of wooden bench being the only furniture in the room. Several small emaciated kittens played on the wooden floor and I wondered when was the last time they had some of their mother's milk. The woman gestured for me to sit on the bench and I was immediately attacked by the thin feline tigers. Whilst I was being scratched, bitten and becoming a sanctuary for their fleas, my driver negotiated a favourable exchange rate.

He requested I paid him then for his services as he too wanted to change that money with the woman as her rates were very good. I could not believe that this old lady was an illegal moneychanger, but knew that somewhere lingering in the dark would be her protection. What if the police came now, would I be deported? I handed my three remaining $50 notes to the woman, but she too rejected one of them. I do not know if Burma is inundated with forgeries, but with no exception would anybody take a bill if it was in the slightest way discoloured, torn or crumpled.

The woman disappeared behind a curtain and returned with two large bundles of Kyats. I had no idea what the exchange rate was between US Dollars and Myanmar Kyats was, but went through the pretence I did by dutifully counting every one. To be honest I was glad that I received anything from the transaction; I just wanted to get the Hell out of the place as fast as I could with my remaining valuables and my life. The woman roughly picked up one of the kittens by the scruff of the neck and held it out to me. It was today's bank deal, change one hundred American dollars and receive one starving kitten. I looked at the small creature in her pincer grip and stared at its little frightened, screwed up face and pitiful blue eyes then declined the day's free offer.

I was a bit perturbed putting myself in that sort of needless danger, but events transpired rapidly from a simple request to stop by at an ATM machine. The legacy left me by my stroke means that I could not punch my way out of a wet paper bag should such need arise and I could definitely not scarper away from any altercation. I had been stripped of all my natural defences from fighting to escaping and therefore left very vulnerable.

Driving to the hotel all seemed very quiet and asked my driver was this usual. He told me it was not normally that quiet and perhaps news of a curfew had been announced. The authorities of

Yangon regularly called curfews if there were rumours of potential civil unrest or they want to keep something away from foreign eyes. In 2001, the Myanmar Tourist Promotion Board passed an order to "Protect Tourists and to Limit Unnecessary Contact". The full details of this order are rather prolonged, but suffice to say the government are still intent in keeping Myanmar domestic policies away from prying foreigner's attention. Most of the country is still off limits to tourists as there are still stringent controls on interaction.

We arrived at the Park Royal Hotel and my driver was impressed as he said the location was excellent right in Downtown Yangon. He continued to inform me all the restaurants, bars and shops were a short walk if I turned right outside my hotel. I tipped my driver with my new Kyats and thanked him for all his help and walked into the hotel.

A large Christmas tree decorated the foyer and it was the first reminder of the festive season that I had yet seen in Asia, I had almost forgotten about it. Burma is almost totally Buddhist with other religions banned from public celebration. Rangoon however is a melting pot of ethnic peoples with Indian being the most dominant. The land mass of Burma make it the largest country in South East Asia and borders Bangladesh and India in the North and West and Laos and Thailand in the South East. But its population of sixty million people is behind that of Thailand and Vietnam.

Not a largely well publicised fact by the world's media is that thousands of refugees still live in atrocious conditions along the Thai / Burma border. There are rumoured to be over two hundred thousand displaced people who have fled the cruel regime of Myanmar for the safety and freedom of Thailand. The Thai authorities do their utmost to provide shelter, medicine and protection for these wretched people, but they can only aid those who successfully manage to escape from Burma, which apparently is not a particularly easy thing to do.

Greenstreet and Back

The hotel was modern and even housed one of the city's few nightclubs; it had an outdoor swimming pool and a gym. However, the charge of one hundred dollars for the pleasure of a night's stay made it very expensive for my tastes. I was not to know at the time but after my four days stop in Yangon I was most glad that I had afforded the expense. My room was not as modern as the rest of the hotel but had all the amenities you would expect from a Myanmar Four Star Hotel. To be honest whilst trying to find a decent place to stay in Yangon I had struggled with the lack of choice and also the expense.

I did not spend long in cleaning up as I wanted to explore the streets for myself and to get something to eat as I was starving. I left the hotel and turned right as previously instructed by my driver. It was dark, not just because it was night but because of the inadequate street lighting. The pavement was a joke and walking was difficult on the uneven floor. Whole stone slabs were jutting from the pavement surface and in some places the pavement just disappeared. It was treacherous in the half light and I had already tripped twice and not even had a drink. In instances like this when I am not certain of my footing I get nervous very quickly and that nervousness turns into a muscle constrictant and I start to limp. The fear is valid as I cannot cushion a fall with my weak arm and have had bad injuries to emphasise that fact.

After five long minutes I crossed over a road bridge and underneath I saw an antiquated train trundle noisily past below. There were beggars sitting cross legged on the bridge holding outstretched hands as I limped passed. They called out to me, but did not run after me or pester me in any other way and I passed unharmed.

From the bridge I was walking past an old decrepit wall that seemed to enclose a large decaying, crumbling building and just at that moment a figure jumped from the top of the crooked structure to land in front of me. The energetic wall vaulter turned out to be a young man, fairly shabbily dressed and about eighteen or nineteen years old. He must have spotted me from his high vantage point and saw an opportunity to make some cash.

"Mr, you want massage?" he said in very faltering English. I was not certain if he knew somebody to perform the treatment or rather suspected he intended to offer his own dubious personal services in the decrepit building, either way I was not interested and walked past staring at the floor.

As I was about a hundred yards past the man a loud yell was directed towards me; "Mr, come back, come back!" I then heard footsteps racing behind me. A hand grabbed my arm to halt me and it was the teenager. "I love you, I love you," he repeatedly shouted out. I looked around in deep embarrassment to see if there were any bystanders to witness this declaration. I then looked at the forlorn figure gripping my arm to see if he was having a big joke at my discomfort, but could not see any devilment in his face.

I then estimated that not too many eligible western bachelors pass his old neglected and tumbledown estate and what I had in my pockets would probably feed him for a month. I was a symbol of freedom and wealth and I was not even wearing my best jeans. "I love you, I love you," he continued to shriek and I was only two feet away from the delusional love struck Romeo.

I had to make my getaway before somebody misconstrued the situation and I thought that I was trying to solicit the young Burmese man for sexual favours. God knows what the punishment was for solicitation in Myanmar, but I knew it would not be pleasant. I shrugged off his arm and started to walk as quickly as I could ignoring my young suitor. When I try to walk fast, I start to limp and the faster I attempt to move the more pronounced the limp becomes. Eventually it defeats the object of what I am trying to achieve.

So, I made my escape at a jaunty stroll which my intended misinterpreted as a "Come on!"

"Mr, Mr, I love you," the amorous parrot continued doggedly. My evening was not panning out as I had planned, but I was at a loss of what to do, evasive manoeuvres were not one of my strong points as I have never had to study the art of being a Casanova before.

I then reached a junction where a major road crossed the one I was traversing and a stream of unending traffic blocked my progress. Things were brighter here and I could see shops and stalls in front of me and many people milling around. To my right was a dilapidated cinema with posters on its walls advertising movies, the cinema looked as though it had seen better days and almost that it was not modern enough to show the current blockbusters.

My beau continued to follow me reiterating his undying devotion, but he was now also graphically describing how he would like our love to be consummated. The queue outside the cinema turned to see what the commotion was on the street and I hoped that none of them had the rudimentary grasp of English that my pursuer owned. It was all highly mortifying and very unsettling.

By the side of the cinema was a small shop that I thought that I may find some sanctuary in. It worked as I was not followed into the store by my amorous admirer and I had time to catch my breath. I could see through the windows of the shop that my love struck chaperone was waiting outside smoking a cigarette. Had the young Burmese man mistakenly taken a love tonic? I had never had such a public declaration of unrequited devotion before. I am not what you would call overly handsome, but in the correct lighting I could be considered averagely attractive.

What would Philip Marlowe do now in such a predicament? I mused for a few seconds then an idea came to me I would buy a disguise. I looked around the tatty general store and I ferreted out a large black, floppy sun hat that was obviously meant for ladies, it also had a matching silk scarf. Then in the same section I rummaged around in an old cardboard box and dredged up the biggest pair of plastic sunglasses that I had ever seen. I paid the Indian gentleman for my wares and left his shop looking like Sofia Loren.

My intention was not to fool my loud, persistent, amorous suitor, but to deceive any witnesses of my identity. It transpired it had the reverse effect as even more people were interested why the confused love struck Burmese man was chasing after the strange white guy in drag looking suspiciously like an aged Italian movie star.

The whole farce came to an abrupt end when on a particularly loud exclamation of undying love, two policemen crossed the road to investigate. The young admirer seeing a potential incarceration for his fraternisation with a foreigner jumped over the nearest wall and disappeared just as he had arrived. Was he a besotted Burmese love entranced gay Spiderman? The two policemen slowed when they reached me and stared curiously at the creature strolling past with scarf billowing behind. It was at that moment I slightly tripped which ruined the whole affect of my graceful retreat.

Turning right at the junction, I ditched my disguise in the first bin I came to. I looked about me and it was like I had just entered Bombay or another exotic Indian city. Nearly all the small restaurants were offering curry of some description and the aromas were mouth watering. They were more like cafés than restaurants and were decked out in plastic furniture, plastic cutlery and plastic crockery. I was so hungry I had to try one and picked a brightly coloured establishment advertising Biryani as its signature dish.

There were four huge pans at the front of the restaurant labelled fish, chicken, meat and vegetable, and that was your only choice. I ordered a meat Biryani and took a seat next to two Indian gentlemen devouring their dinner with gusto. My plate of food arrived and then a selection of chutneys, pickles and chillies were placed before me to add as required. I was surprised how mild the food was, but it was simply delicious and with the addition of fiery chillies and tart lime pickle, it was fantastic. Possibly the best Indian food I have eaten and definitely the cheapest as the bill came to under two quid.

The restaurant was dry and I needed a beer to wash my dinner down and cool me from my walk. I walked the whole length of the busy, bustling street but could not find a bar anywhere. I crossed the road and tried the street opposite but it was exactly the same; full of small eateries and tatty shops selling fake goods. I stopped outside what looked like a newspaper stall and asked a Hindu guy to direct me to a more lively area with bars and proper restaurants. I was informed by the helpful chap and his band of nosy customers that I was already in Downtown Yangon, he seemed a little bemused at my request as to him it was plainly obvious.

I could not believe that this was as good as it got in Yangon and surely there must have been something lost in translation. So, for thirty minutes or so I traipsed around the streets of Rangoon like some demented alcoholic in search of a beer eventually to be defeated and to return back to the hotel. I sat in the Lobby Bar of the Park Royal and quenched my thirst with two very expensive beers then retired early to bed.

Waking early, I wandered off in search of the gym and was pleasantly surprised to see a fully equipped modern Gymnasium. I did my normal daily hour and fifteen minute routine and was constantly attended to by polite and friendly staff. Feeling a little knackered by my excursions I considered a little lay down by the pool would be in order. Down a short corridor and up some steps was the roof top pool; it was ideal as it was quiet, secluded and nobody else was there. I put on my iPod and decided that some James Brown was in order to liven me up. The hypnotic guitar and saxophone rhythm of *On the Good Foot* blared out of the headphones and a brand new day had started.

My stroll around Yangon had surprised me the day before; I had always pictured Rangoon as a romantic, tropical place full of elegant colonial buildings straight out of a Kipling novel. I suppose at one time it had been like that, but now the old colonial architecture was decaying and the city was littered with decrepit reminders of its former more affluent days. Unlike most modern cities, Yangon has not built on the past and these derelict sites are left untouched and not restored or replaced. There are no skyscrapers or tall buildings in Yangon which is no bad thing, but there is nothing to replace the old grandeur of bygone days.

However, there is a grace and happiness about the inhabitants that disguises their poverty and strict oppressive rule. The national dress of Burma, the 'Longyis' which is an elegant sarong and is widely worn everywhere by women and men, even by the cute looking schoolchildren. The women also favour the use of wearing a pale yellow powder on their faces, but for what purpose I do not know. But the general feel of the country is that it is more closely related to its western neighbours than its eastern ones and its ancient cultural fabric comes from India, Tibet and Persia.

It is the political situation that dominates the very air in Burma and it is impossible to get away from. Soldiers and military police are everywhere and their authority is not to be questioned. After years of oppressive domination it is sad to see ordinary Burmese people bow their heads and almost cower in the presence of this authority. Whilst I was there a movement was taking shape that would allow Aung San Suu Kyi to be allowed to stand in upcoming government elections and there was a small flicker of a flame of optimism that there might be change coming.

My second night was just as frustrating as my first as I never seemed to find the centre of Rangoon or what made it tick. I did literally stumble across a couple of bars one of which was called Lion World that was upstairs in a concrete monstrosity of a building overlooking a road bridge. After sampling a Lion beer, which is Myanmar's famous brew, I took my leave of the rather depressing place and once again returned home early. I was not surprised there were no ATM machines as there was nothing to spend your money on. Walking home I came a cropper and fell quite heavily tripping on a concrete slab. I cut my hands and knees and to my dismay nobody came to my aid: I suppose that would be considered fraternisation and unnecessary contact with a tourist.

Once again, I was reduced to sitting in the Lobby Bar isolated from the world outside. I struck up a conversation with a man at the bar who was American and was living and working in Yangon. He was in the electronics industry and actually lived in the hotel. He told me that all the bars and restaurants are housed in the larger hotels like Park Royal or Traders and there was little to offer for entertainment out on the street.

This made perfect sense as the average resident was so poor they could not afford fancy dining or drinking establishments and there were so few tourists such places would not survive. The government did not seem intent to open its doors to foreign travellers and so I could not see the situation changing for many years. Although Burma is reputed to be a beautiful country with stunning countryside and ancient traditional cultures it is difficult to access that part of the country to see for yourself and is criminal that it is hidden away.

Despite the rigid rule of law Myanmar does lead the world in one particular export and that is the illicit drug trafficking trade. In the North East region of the country near the Thai border known as the Golden Triangle. Myanmar is the world's second largest Opium producer. Only Afghanistan produces more Heroin and Methamphetamines, and the whole region is collectively named the Golden Crescent.

Its exports to Thailand are proving to be a major headache for the Thai authorities as drug use and addiction is on the rise. Yaba tablets are a favourite and relatively cheap drug for the Thais to buy, and there are an estimated 1.2 million addicts in Thailand. The drugs are freely available everywhere and the police have taken to random batch drug testing on the streets in a desperate attempt to clamp down. For such a strict regime such as Myanmar, it is surprising the military does not know who the culprits are.

Arriving home was, to be honest, a relief, as I could not have endured much more of the ever present oppressiveness of Burma and the nagging feeling that you were always doing something wrong and being watched. Even getting out of the country was almost as hard as entering and it was as though the officials were instructed to be as rude and as unhelpful as they possibly could. I would not have been the least surprised if there had of been a large sign in the departure lounge saying, "I hope you have not enjoyed your stay in Myanmar, now fuck off and don't come back!"

Chapter Twenty

CHRISTMAS IN THAILAND

After Myanmar it took me a couple of days of permanently wearing sunglasses to become accustomed once again to proper lighting. I looked like a blind tourist as I kept my shades on everywhere I went or for everything I did. At one point a man was going to assist me across Jomtien Beach road until I told him to bugger off and snarled at him.

Pattaya was like Las Vegas compared to Rangoon and I considered the merits of two very different worlds. Pattaya was dirty, lewd, brash, noisy and regularly dangerous, but one thing it had that was precious; freedom. Its citizens had civil rights and access to education, health care and to practise whatever religion they wanted to. Liberty is like health, something you take for granted until it is taken away from you, but unlike health some people have never experienced liberty.

There was no need to travel to visit the plantation until after New Year as all work had stopped for Christmas. Although the birth of Christ is not widely celebrated in Thailand, Kik's family were Catholics and everybody had left the plantation land to go home to be with their loved ones.

I had decided to cook Christmas dinner at my apartment and to have a small gathering to celebrate the season of goodwill. I even went and bought a small Christmas tree and decorated View Talay. In a way it was refreshing how the commercialism of western culture does not taint the event in Thailand and it is more of a civilised and refined period.

However, there was one big event especially held to bring the celebrations to life; and that was one of the world's largest firework competitions. The mayor of Pattaya is a young dynamic person and is constantly driving the Pattaya Tourist Office to hold events and performances that will attract global attention. America, Canada and China where among the countries competing over two days.

As always on large festive occasions the whole of Pattaya Beach Road was closed for the duration of the event and many thousands of people from miles around flooded into the City. It was a festive and party atmosphere for all to enjoy the free show and many poor families could sit on the beach, shoulder to shoulder with rich tourists and see the amazing spectacle. And that is the only word that can truly describe the event, it was spectacular! The coast and night sky were lit up the whole of its four kilometre length as different nationalities competed with their amazing pyrotechnic displays. I watched the first night's show down on the beach then on the second night took a few beers to Pratamnak Hill with Kik and Dang Mao to get a more aerial view.

It was staggering the effects of the pyrotechnics being so close; the bangs were explosions and the fizzes were lightening bolts crackling in the air. The colours of the fireworks were bright, almost neon. And the night sky changed from black to vivid green or blood red before a golden hail burst and showered down shimmering to the ground. We drank a fair amount of Leo that night, shouted and whooped as loud as anybody else enjoying the show. Getting home on the scooters was a bit tricky after the alcohol, but we took it easy chatting all they way excited as small schoolchildren.

The decision to cook a Turkey dinner was scrapped as I did not know how my oven worked and did not want to completely ruin the poor bird. So I decided that I would treat my Asian friends to Tapas, not particularly traditional, but something that I could do using the grill and hobs. I had to go to a Deli in Central Festival Mall to source all the authentic and expensive ingredients, but I decided if I was going to host Christmas Day, then I would do it correctly.

Greenstreet and Back

My menu was authentic; Patatas Bravas, Chorizo Stew, Chilli Prawns and a plethora of Cured Meats and Sausages. I had also stumbled on a small bakery and had some real Italian olive bread. I was happy with what I was going to serve, I was missing something, but I did not know what. I had the food, Christmas tree, decorations... Then it came to me in a flash; music. So, I spent the whole of Christmas Eve trawling through the iTunes file on my PC and collated three special CDs that the like of my guests would never of heard before.

Christmas morning was very relaxing as most of the food preparation had been done. I spent the first few hours sunning myself down by the pool and gave myself a day off from the gym. I had invited four friends to dinner; Kik, Daang Mao, Ton Nam and Rista, so including myself I would be catering for five. It was a normal day for all of them so they all had work and would arrive sometime after 7pm. I must admit I found it difficult to refrain from the occasional tipple as I prepared everything. I had bought a cocktail shaker with me from the UK and had topped up my booze cupboard to include tequila, triple sec, gin, vodka, whisky and all the mixers to add to a fridge packed with beer.

My guests all arrived promptly and at the same time, it seemed they had arranged to come together, but for what reason I have no idea. Perhaps they thought that there was some weird English ritual that is practised on Christmas Day and none of them wanted to risk being alone with me. On entering immediately Daang and Rista fought for control of the alcohol, Rista eventually won nominating himself Cocktail Waiter for the evening. Daang Mao just shrugged and contented himself with consuming any concoction Rista served up. It was an explosive pairing; a madman making potentially lethal cocktails and a drunkard quite happy to sup every one of them.

I have noticed that once you have invited a Thai into your home as a friend then everything in it, especially the fridge is also free for them to indulge themselves with. At first I thought it was an endearing trait as they were simply making themselves at home and were showing they were comfortable with your hospitality. But after several raids on my food and drinks on previous visits I was aware that opening your door can be an expensive action. I was comforted by the knowledge that this is normal behaviour and they frequently did it to one another if somebody happened to be lucky enough to have some booze hanging around.

When these random visitations happened to me I enjoyed them immensely. There was never any prior warning of the incoming plague of locusts just a knock on the door a kicking off of shoes then uncontrolled mayhem. It made sense that my apartment was a popular venue as it was large and many of my guests either shared rooms or could only afford a studio bedsit. I did not mind having these fun loving people call on me one iota I actually encouraged it as I loved the fun and the company.

Kik was very intrigued with what I was making and hovered about in the kitchen with me whilst quiet Ton Nam just turned the TV on and sat on the couch. Rista had managed to find my Tetley Bitter tankard that Richie had bought with him from the Bug on his last visit. It held one litre and Rista was intent on filling the whole tankard with every different type of alcohol that I had. Once topping the insane Rista Special with a dash of soda, he then inserted a long straw made of cobbling six standard ones together. Putting one end of the long tube in his newly created concoction he then pushed the other end in between Daang's lips who was sitting the other side of the table.

Daang did not blanch and began earnestly sucking the muddy coloured poison out of the tankard over the table and into his mouth. Kik gasped in disbelief as he was not a big drinker by any stretch of the imagination whilst Ton just shook his head. Rista was like a demented scientist shouting how good his new creation was, but he could not remember how he had made it. I was concerned for poor Daang, the small guy could die if he drank a whole litre of the crazy brew and was relieved when Rista wanted to share his own cocktail.

Dinner was fun, my guests were typically most honest in their opinions and if they did not like something they had no hesitation in telling me. I was gratified that most of the food had been digested and everybody seemed to be having a good time on their first English / Thai / Spanish traditional Christmas dinner. During the meal I played my music; Slade, Wizzard, Jona Lewie, The Pogues, Band Aid. All were received with mixed reviews, but one track everybody seemed to love was Santa Baby by Marilyn Monroe. Kik was enchanted by it and played it over and over again trying to teach Rista and Ton Nam the words. Meanwhile, Daang Mao was sitting stationary with a glazed look in his eyes, the Rista Special had taken affect and he was tripping out.

Then an impromptu session of spontaneous physical activity took place. Rista took centre stage as he is somewhat of a gymnast; the drunken antics of the manic barman were hilarious but also dangerous. At one stage he was doing a one armed handstand perched on a chair, even Daang managed to open one of his eyes in appreciation. Kik was not to be outdone and did a complete split with his legs outstretched flat on the tiled floor. His dancing physique allowed him fantastic flexibility and I was amazed at some of the things his body could actually do.

It was just after midnight when bodies were tiring and brains very muddled that Ton announced he had work in the morning. Everybody else, including Daang who had done an impersonation of a dormouse all evening, said the same. One last playing of Santa Baby was requested by Kik then they all were to leave. The evening had been a tad loud, but not excessive and the hour was not too late so I was a little surprised when there was a loud rap on the door.

Opening it, I gestured for Kik to turn the music down a little. My fat German neighbour was standing in the corridor wearing only very tight briefs. He was red faced and shouted at me to turn the music down otherwise he was going to call security. Kik unfortunately thought the irate Bavarian was a party crasher and waltzed up to the door. He tickled the furious fat man under the chin and continued to sing Santa Baby to him imitating Miss Monroe as he did. The man became even more infuriated and mistakenly stepped across my threshold. Rista and the others saw the ridiculous looking individual with paunch hanging heavily over his small briefs and burst into spontaneous rather drunken laughter pointing at him.

My neighbour turned ashen faced and marched down the corridor to the lifts obviously to inform security of what was going on. *Mein Herr nein amused,* I thought to myself, and ushered my guests out of my apartment to wait for the visit by security. I hoped that they would not add to their misdemeanours if they bumped into my neighbour in the lobby, but I knew if they did they would. Five minutes later a rather embarrassed security guy knocked on my door with the German sumo menacingly loitering behind him. I felt sorry for the security guy as he too knew it was Christmas and there were celebrations all over the condominium that night. Somebody should have told that fat twat of a neighbour that it was Christmas too!

It had been my first Christmas in Thailand and although no presents had been exchanged or a consumption of traditional fare I had enjoyed it immensely. The end of the evening had put quite a dampener on proceedings, but it had come at the end when my guests were leaving. I had missed my old friends, but had not dwelt on that fact for long as I knew I could not afford to. My new acquaintances had stood up to their billing more than adequately and would have been a great addition to any party back home.

Relations with my neighbour deteriorated quite significantly from that night on to the point of completely blanking each other if we met. It seemed his capacity for tolerance was minute and I did not understand why on Earth he chose to live in a noisy condominium in the first place and especially in Pattaya! Surely a Tibetan Monastery on a remote mountain in Nepal would have been better suited to him. Perhaps Jomtien Estate Agents did not have any on their books when the fat old Frankfurter came looking for a home.

It was just my luck to have him of all people as my neighbour. I have been to Germany many times and have grown to know them as a nation to love revelry and to thoroughly enjoy a good party. A bit slap stick and oomph pah pah, but nevertheless Germany was a party going country who had no problems letting their hair down. However, the one I had living across the corridor from me in Thailand was a rotten egg in a basket of one.

New Year was just as spectacular as Christmas with free events, concerts and firework displays all over the city. The Thai Authorities realise the poverty most of their citizens live under and try to enhance their quality of life by providing as many free things as they can whenever an appropriate occasion arises.

Due to my feud with my neighbour I decided against having a party at home and arranged to meet Kik's Party Mafia in a nightclub to celebrate the start of 2012. It was as to be expected a crazy night of celebrations similar to anywhere else in the world. I am not really one for clubbing, even though I am quite happy to DJ an event, but after my illness I tire really quickly if I do not sit and cannot stand being jostled as I often fall over. The evening was enjoyable but not memorable; give me a party any day over a nightclub.

The New Year bought with it many things, but one unwelcome one was the complete halt in activity on the plantation. Something was wrong, but with Ohm who was now back in Iceland, I could not get any answers when I questioned Kik. He simply referred me back to Ohm and told me to communicate directly with her by email. After several attempts I received a brief message from Ohm stating there were complications and she was trying to sort things out. I was not over duly worried as it was just as much in her own interest that she fathomed what the problems were.

Late January I had a phone call from Rich stating he was coming out to see me on holiday. This time he was going to have a couple of days in Bangkok and then was to spend the remainder of his trip in Pattaya with a few days tagged on to Samui at the very end. I was gob smacked as he had previously believed all the hype from the experts in the Bug who decried Pattaya as a shit hole.

I did not join my friend on his arrival in Bangkok, but decided to keep my powder dry for his visit to Pattaya. Expecting a visit from Richard was always ominous and double edged. On one hand, I was really looking to seeing my old friend again, but on the other, I was not looking forward to ten days of hangovers.

His arrival bought immediate confusion as I received umpteen frantic phone calls from his taxi driver not knowing where she was. The driver was a friend of Apple that Richie had met up with again whilst in Bangkok. However, she was a Bangkok driver and did not know her away around Pattaya at all and the oaf in the back of her car was obviously not helping.

Eventually the poor demented woman found her way to View Talay and I greeted my friend outside the Condo to the crashing of his personal belongings as he dropped them absent-mindedly to give me a hug. I had secured an apartment for him on the floor above mine from my friend in the laundry. Knowing that he was in holiday mode, I thought it wise that Richie had his own place that way I was secure for at least some peace.

I was glad he liked the Condo and he seemed very happy with his room even though I knew it would be a bombshell in two days. That night I thought I would break my friend in gently and just stay local in Jomtien, central Pattaya might have proved a little too full on for his first night. I walked him down the private road from View Talay to Dongtan Beach, but had already forewarned him that the area was very gay so he would be prepared. After a couple of pointings and chuckles he got used to the ambience and did what everybody else normally did, just got on with whatever they were doing.

Our first port of call was my local Shenanigans; I knew it was a bit of a risk taking Richie there as he would either love it or hate it and he has a reputation for making his feelings very obvious if he does not like something. I on the other hand frequented the place often and had many friends, staff and customers inside. As usual the door was opened for us by the normal welcoming committee of the floor manager Nancy and her team. I had pre warned all the staff that Richie was incoming and they were all waiting with expectant anticipation to meet him.

Richie lapped up the warm welcome as I introduced him to Ning, Nang and Noi who were standing by the door. I saw the confused look on his face as I pronounced their names and knew immediately there was the first disaster waiting to happen. We took two seats at the bar and Peter the head barman rushed over to meet us together with Benz the very amusing barman.

Tonight was Toss the Boss night and it was an excellent way for Rich to be sucked into the Shenanigans love of gambling and sport. Peter served two beers which were paid for by him as I had a bet the previous weekend that Everton would beat Fulham in the FA Cup which they did comfortably with a 2-1 win at Goodison Park. Richie was quiet taking his environment in whilst Peter and I looked at the weekend's fixtures looking for a good bet.

Then Benz rang the bell and Toss the Boss was started bang on 7pm. Actually, it was more like ten past seven as the clock Benz always used was ten minutes fast, but it didn't really matter as it would finish at twenty to nine and not half past eight as scheduled. Rich asked what did we have to do and Peter chipped in.

"Just ask for a drink!" Two beers were ordered and Stewart the boss was signalled to come over. I introduced Rich and the big Aussie genially shook his hand then took his special coin out and flipped it in the air. I called heads and dutifully the coin obliged and our drinks were for free. Stewart is a bad loser and muttered under his breath at having been beaten then walked off to the next contestant.

"How long does this last?" Richie asked. "Until half eight," I responded, and Richie's face lit up, he was thoroughly enjoying this caper. The next two rounds we won one and lost one, but Richie seemed more delighted in beating Stewart than getting the free beer. He was making it into a personal battle between the two of them and Stewart was playing up to it cheering when he won or grumbling when he lost. Richie was ordering drinks thick and fast, sometimes before we had even finished the previous ones. I was getting drunk fast and knew I would be in bed early that night once again destroyed by my pest of a friend.

I could hardly wait for twenty to nine and Benz to ring the bell and stop this frenetic behaviour of my lunatic friend. Normally I consume two beers and a couple of glasses of wine at the very most during a whole evening, but I had consumed more than double that in ninety minutes. While Richie was busy ordering himself another celebratory Singha, I had a coffee, then another and then another. I was afraid to get off my stool as I was quite inebriated and couldn't really focus on what anybody was saying to me.

Rich had worked out that half our frantic consumption of Singha beer had been totally free and was keen to introduce the game to Pat, the landlady of the Bug, as soon as he got home. I just thought of it as unnecessary and quick way to get pissed and would rather have paid the correct amount and lasted longer into the evening to enjoy myself.

Greenstreet and Back

Thirty minutes later I took a motorbike taxi home and was in bed for just after 10pm and cursing the fact Rich had come to visit. The oaf did not surface till well after noon the following day and when he did finally come down to the pool he looked a shed. Apparently, he had stayed in the pub until 4am playing pool with Peter and taking all the poor man's money. He had also been responsible for introducing the whole staff of Shenanigans to the Bug's new fashionable drink, the Jager Bomb. It is a smaller shooter glass of Jagermeister Liquor dropped into a tumbler containing Red Bull. This concoction is then downed in one. Jagermeister was originally developed as a cough remedy mixture and has a distinct taste like one.

My plans for showing my friend some more of Pattaya were dismissed as he declared his preference to stay around Jomtien and return to Shenanigans for Safe Cracker Night. Stewart was a good attentive landlord and had different promotions on every night to attract custom. He was always in attendance in the Pub keeping an eye on things and ensuring the smooth running of the place including the regular weekly Premier League Forecasting competition.

Richie agreed that we would dine first as the previous night I was too drunk to handle a knife and fork and had nothing to eat. So, we explored a little more of Jomtien and I took him to Mr Moos, a great, cheap Thai restaurant that is more about authentic food than décor and finesse. Close by Mr Moos is a large estate of over twenty Beer Bars and we washed our dinner down with a couple of bottles of Leo whilst Richie played pool with the loud hostesses. The hostesses can be fun once you decline their sexual advances in the correct manner and are to be dismissed at your peril over a game of pool for money.

I no longer play pool as my cueing arm cannot go back in the required controlled manner and length. I would probably end up destroying the table's cloth or screwing the ball off the table and smashing somebody's glasses or something. I missed the pool contests we often had especially when we were away together. Richie was probably the better player of the two, but it was always close and I took my fair share of games. Like in life, Richie's pool playing was full of bluster and bravado and sometimes my guile would overcome his brasher playing.

When we walked in to Shenanigans, Richie was greeted as though he had been drinking there for years. And he was also presented with the tab he had run up after his money ran out the previous evening. I looked at it and there was twenty two Jager Bombs along with an assortment of other drinks. The bill was nearly two thousand Baht and he was questioning Peter about its validity and arguing vehemently that two of the bombs were not his. I know Richie did not have a clue what he had consumed or what on Earth he had bought for others; in fact, he didn't even remember running up a tab, that was his way and over the next ten days they would arduously find out for themselves.

Benz sidled up to me and told me of the previous night's activities. I liked Benz; he was always very kind and friendly to me and was learning English fast. His favourite catchphrase was, "Have you had a nice day tomorrow?" At first it was a mistake but as it always produced laughter he would often still say it. The first time he said it to Richie, I thought the oaf was going to explode with laughter as he spat his mouth full of beer back out.

Benz told me that Richie had beaten Peter in nearly every game of pool and that at one point he had discovered Peter on his knees in the toilet praying for his luck to change. Peter now declared his hatred for Richie every time he spoke to him and demanded to have a chance to get his money back later. I shook my head that Richie's standard arrogant pretence was already grating on everybody's nerves, it normally took a little longer than one day.

Safe Cracker is another free game that the pub offers to its patrons. Every Thursday until 8pm with every purchase you receive a raffle ticket. At 8pm a ticket is drawn for a chance to win ten thousand Baht if you guess the right combination out of ten choices to open the safe. This night our ticket was drawn and three of the ten combinations had already been eliminated. I had a one in seven chance to win two hundred quid, it was pure luck and people were shouting out numbers at me in quick succession. One of those persons happened to know the right numbers, but I could not hear her properly. Anyway suffice to say I opted for the wrong combination much to Richie's disgust so we paid the bill and left. Richie's parting words were ,"I will be back later" and pointed to Peter mouthing the word, "Loser."

I had opted for a nightcap and then I was going to retire for the evening as last night's alcohol was still taking its toll. I suggested a visit to the Pink Cocktail Car which is on the way back through Jomtien Complex to View Talay. The Jomtien Complex is a very gay area full of boy Beer Bars and massage places, but it does also have some very good restaurants and excellent coffee shops. The Pink Car is parked on the edge of the complex by the main road once you have walked through the small streets and all the action and entertainment.

It is actually an old VW Camper Van with an assortment of tables and chairs outside. It offers genuine cocktails for the princely sum of seventy Baht, just over a quid and is one of my regular stop off ports of call on my way home. The Camper Van houses all the Liquor and it is where Baz the barman stands and mixes the drinks visible to all by means of a drop down side of the vehicle. The van is painted vivid Pink all over to celebrate the area's identity and plays decent music over an outdoor PA. I find it quite relaxing to break my arduous ten minute walk home by sitting outside tapping my foot to some track and sipping an excellent Margarita. Not a bad way to spend one pound twenty of my hard earned cash.

The Pink Car is not unique it has sisters and brothers dotted around all over the city of Pattaya. I do not know why a Volkswagen

Camper Van was deemed as the most appropriate vehicle to be turned into a Cocktail Car, but all these impromptu establishments are focused on the old Caravanette. I suppose the export manager of some old second hand Camper Van Garage in Berlin is bemused at the excellent sales of its Caravanettes in Thailand and has no idea what they are being used for.

The following few nights I took Richie to Walking Street and other areas of Pattaya, but to my surprise he preferred Jomtien. I was glad he had said that as I was a little concerned he would find it a little quiet. Of course it is all relative, it is not quiet compared to Crosby, but to Walking Street it is like a back water.

Richie was by now renown in Shenanigans and was both loved and hated depending on who you spoke to. He had taken to referring to Ning, Nang, Noon, and Ni as the Goons and regularly to their confused amazement would burst out into a Peter Sellers voice and sing the Ying Tong song. The staff had no idea whatsoever what he was babbling on about and thought he was quite mad, something that I encouraged. Actually I thought Benz was a little scared of him and he always was very wary when Richie was around, sometimes I just could not translate well enough to explain my friend's unique transgressions and behaviour.

His visit as always was painful but also passed so quickly and unfortunately I had something planned that I would not be able to see him on his last day. I was due to go to the Silverlake Music Festival with the Party Mafia, even Daang from Sakon Nakon was making the trip down and he and Pookie were to stay at my apartment.

I said my goodbyes to Rich on the Friday night and we had a bit of a party around Jomtien ending the night in Shenanigans. I asked had he enjoyed his stay and was the apartment comfortable enough for him. He confided in me that on his very first night he had a complaint from his neighbour and had two more during his stay. Lord knows what he had got up to, but I knew it would have involved beer and loud music. It had taken me over six months to have gotten my first complaint, but Richie had achieved his in one day. I left my friend in the pub about 1am and knew he would be staying for hours after that and annoying as many people as he possibly could.

The following morning, Pookie arrived in her car at my condo already with Kik, Ton Nam and Daang Mao on board and we headed for some breakfast and to wait for the other Daang. My head was a little groggy from the previous night and I was glad to have some strong coffee. Silverlake is a vineyard up towards the Khao Khiao Mountains about an hours drive north from Pattaya. It is owned by one of Thailand's most famous actresses and is one of the few parts of the country that produces grapes.

I had been there once before with Ohm and Kik for a day excursion stopping off at Pattaya Floating Market on the way. It is a beautiful part of the country, the air is cooler as you climb up on the windy road that ascends to it and the landscape becomes more verdant and luscious. At one stage there is a huge sixty foot golden Buddha drawn on a cliff face that is simply stunning and can be seen for miles around. There are also temples and monasteries frequented by pilgrims hidden away in the elevated country that are worth a visit alone on their own merits.

But today the whole area around Silverlake was one big outdoor concert arena with two massive stages. It was Thailand's version of Glastonbury, but only for a day, some of the most popular bands in the country were playing with Incubus who were headlining. My favourite Thai band called Singular was there and that is how I was persuaded to go. They are a sort of an acoustic jazz duo that I love and play a lot of in my apartment, but they are relatively new and do not have much material to buy.

After a late breakfast Daang appeared at the Outlet Village that we were in on Sukhumvit Road and the Mafia were reunited, only Rista and Dome were missing. For some reason they had all decided to dress up rather Camp for the day and Pookie had been the clothing advisor for the group. Thankfully my only adornment was a rather daring green hat that looked just the ticket tilted at a jaunty angle on my head. Daang had a long white vest that reached his ankles with black leggings and boots whilst Kik wore a very loud red outfit. Daang Mao and Ton Nam were a lot more discreet and sombre in their choice of attire, but Pookie stole the show in a figure hugging bodice that highlighted her more than shapely figure.

Everybody wore extravagant, flamboyant hats and the party had begun without a drink being consumed as all six of us piled into Pookie's little Honda Jazz car. The music was cranked up and the expedition started with much noise and plenty of laughter. As we neared the mountains ominous black clouds were gathering behind them and it looked very much as though bad weather was on its way. The mountains often protect Pattaya from inclement weather elsewhere and that is why it is often one of the sunniest places in Thailand.

As we were noisily making our way my phone rang and I saw it was Richie. He had just surfaced after a very late night in Shenanigans and gone to meet the taxi I had arranged for him but it had not turned up. He was afraid he was going to miss his flight to Samui. It was typical Richie leaving everything till the last minute and trying to sort things out with a bad hangover.

I was not particularly worried as there were many daily flights to Samui and what did he expect me to do from where I was anyway? I told him to go to the laundry in View Talay and ask for Sod; he was my friend who had arranged the taxi for him and he had never let me down before, I wondered had the oaf been late and missed the damn thing.

We parked the car and took little buggies laid on by the organisers to the Festival Site entrance which was located in a remote field near the vineyards. It was a perfect spot for such an event and very atmospheric with the mountains on one side and the vineyards stretching far away to the right. We were fairly early as there was little in the way of a queue and the bands had not started playing. We had made the right decision because just as we passed through security the heavens opened and we could take shelter from the torrential rain in one of the refreshment tents near the entrance.

The downpour lasted nearly an hour and the temperature dropped significantly, Daang and Kik were intent on enjoying themselves and often braved the lashing rain to dash about outside for some trivial excuse of some sort. The Party Mafia amazed me as the close group of friends were all nearing thirty and still they behaved like teenagers. Unlike many such groups back home they did not rely on booze or drugs to have a good time in fact none of them took drugs and Kik, Pookie and Ton Nam rarely drank alcohol. To be all together was enough for them to have fun and I admired them greatly for their capacity to forget their daily struggle to exist.

Eventually the rain ceased and the first band of the day could be heard on the main stage. The ground was quite muddy and slippery in places, but already the organisers had teams of workers spreading fresh straw on the worst affected places. Inside the promoters had not cow tied to commercialism and although the event was sponsored by Chang most of the small food outlets were independent Thai concerns selling noodles, rice dishes and typical Thai cuisine at a very reasonable price. There was even a Silverlake Wine stall selling the local vintage by bottle or per glass.

The two stages were close together so it only took a few minutes to walk from one to the other through the food service area. The six of us were all traipsing over to the second stage to see Singular perform when a TV crew spotted us and made a bee line towards us. I suppose there were not many farangs there and there was certainly nobody dressed like our crew. It was national Thai TV and they were covering the whole event live on one of the major channels. There was a break in between performances so they took the opportunity to focus on the crowd.

Kik and Daang decided to put a dance show on for the camera whilst I was interviewed. They asked where I came from and what I was doing there, luckily for me I knew the name of a Thai Band and said I was an avid Singular fan. The interview lasted for some minutes whilst the dancing got more frenetic and Daang Mao and Ton Nam joined the others. Then just as the interview came to a close with Pookie and me trying to stay serious for the camera a rather merry Daang Mao went flying in the mud and took his other three dance companions skidding to the mucky ground with him. They landed in a heap, hats in disarray and clothes a soggy brown mess; then as one they collapsed in laughter rolling around the floor attacking each other with fistfuls of mud.

It had been my first ever interview on Television in any country and it ended in a debacle thanks to the four dancing stooges. They picked themselves up off the floor and Pookie and I howled with laughter at their condition. We had only been at the Festival for two hours and it looked as though they had been fighting at the battle of the Somme. We arrived somewhat dishevelled at the second venue just as Singular took to the stage amid constant chuckles from other festival goers that we passed.

The concert was really good although only about forty minutes and I asked Pookie to watch out for them playing in Bangkok and I would go and see them with her there. The sun was now shining brightly and the ground and the four stooges were drying out rapidly. The boys had all washed their hands and faces in the temporary lavatories, but their clothing was beginning to smell and they looked a sight. We spent another three enjoyable hours just sitting on the grass listening to the music and consuming the occasional beer or wine; it was a perfect day out.

Then Kik suggested we go back to Pattaya so they could change and clean up before returning to Silverlake to boogie the night away. It was an ideal scenario for me as I knew I could not stand up for the whole night at the festival. At around 6pm, Pookie drove us back and I requested she drop me at Shenanigans on the way. I gave her my spare set of keys to the apartment so Daang and her could use the shower and don their evening wear also they could let themselves in later.

Entering Shenanigans, I was greeted like a movie star as most of the bar had seen my interview on the screens in the pub. They were all laughing about the antics of the others and were adamant the clip would be shown again and again as it had been so funny. But I was not laughing long when I took a bar stool and Benz produced a three and a half thousand Baht bill that Richie had run up on his last night.

Peter said to me "It was good your friend came to visit, but it is better that he is gone." He had a sort of wry smile on his face and I knew some of the sentiments he said were for my amusement, but I also knew in some ways he meant what he said. I think Richie had fleeced Peter out of quite a bit of money in their drunken "after hours" pool games. Just then my phone bleeped and I received an SMS message: "Arrived in Samui, all OK." I sent one immediately back to him, "Just arrived in Shenanigans, everything not all OK." He phoned me shortly after I sent the SMS and could not remember racking up the bill and was convinced that he had paid if he had of done so.

It was typical Richie; he didn't remember a thing so to him it had not happened, I could not be bothered arguing so passed my phone over to Peter. "Yes you paid one bill, but ran out of money." Peter laughed incredulously at Richie's adamant denial of debt. So he read out some of the items on the list: "Thirty One Jager Bombs, Twenty Seven Bottles of Singha Beer, Five Whisky and Coke!" The list went on and on and it was almost a duplication of his previous night's tariff. The bill could not be possibly anybody else's. Richie finally conceded and told me he would settle up with me the next time we met. I just shook my head and smiled and wished my friend a good holiday and pitied the staff of Zico's as they did not know who was just about to arrive.

Sometimes Richie is like a nagging cold, you just can't shake it loose and when you do it just keeps coming back. My friend's intentions are never to harm or upset people with his constant barrage of Mickey taking and supercilious tomfoolery, but sometimes people just do not know how they should take him and get upset. One time in the Bug an exasperated H had once called Richie 'thrush', as explanation she said: "An irritating Mary that won't go away!"

About two days after the weekend I was flicking through the many channels on my television set when I recognised Silverlake. I remember the band that was playing on stage as the lead singer had a weird white outfit on and large white glasses. It was the band that was performing just before the interview. I wondered if it was just highlights or would they also show us as well. I was glued to the TV in anticipation of seeing myself and the four stooges.

The group finished the set and the stage camera cut to a mobile unit bearing down on a really odd bunch of characters; it was us! I sat forward on the couch nervous but enthralled. There I was; resplendent in a Green Titfer and sounding just like John Lennon. I have never heard myself on TV before and although my accent has faded over the years there was a definite nasal Scouse pronunciation of my words very similar to Lennon.

I was transfixed listening to myself when suddenly Benny Hill and his mates Henry McGee, Bobb Todd and Jon Jon Keefe appeared behind me and proceeded in their Keystone Kops slapstick performance. I must admit although they spoiled my interview it was hilarious and all that was missing was the *Yakety Sax* theme tune to accompany the whole farce. It was great TV, and at one point the frame of the picture went very shaky as the camera man started to laugh. Apparently, it is frequently shown on Cable TV advertising tourism in and around Pattaya. But to date I have not received any royalty cheques!

Things were a little quiet after Richie's departure and Silverlake and I managed to dry out for a couple of weeks and repair my damaged liver. I had booked a trip home in early March to renew my visa and to catch up with events on my house; it would also be a great opportunity to see all my old friends again. I had also been contacted by old employers who mysteriously wanted to meet up with me, even though I had not received any money from them since September, I was still officially on their books.

Two days before my departure, I received a terrible phone call from Nick back in Liverpool. His mother had passed away and she had lost her long battle with cancer. Lydia was almost like a surrogate mum to me as I had known her for so long and she was closer to me than any relative save intimate family. She had always referred to me as her fifth son, an honour I have never taken lightly and Nick was devastated. His mum had been a true matriarch and had been the glue that had stuck the family together through all their troubles over the years, she would be irreplaceable.

It was fortunate that I was due to go home, but I would have tried to make a special trip anyway just to be with my mate at a really shitty time. I have been there so many times myself and I know the value to have a good friend beside you, not particularly to do anything but just to be there. I had left some formal clothes back in Liverpool just for an occasion like this should ever happen, but I did not expect to be wearing them on my first bloody trip home.

Just as my plane was about to land in Manchester I was in a sombre and reflective mood. It seemed like every time I went back home it was for something really grim and I was beginning to hate the place for its association with unhappiness. I was not really even going home as my house was rented out and I was staying with friends so the allurement of Liverpool was cooling for me.

Richie collected me from the plane and we went straight to the Bug as I thought I might catch Nick in there and have a drink with him. Joe and Keith my friends who were putting me up for nearly three weeks were there so at least I was secure for a bed for the night. Later Nick and H came and I was able to have a brief chat with my old friend and pass on my condolences there would be plenty of time in the following few days to reminisce.

The funeral of Nick's mum was a traumatic day for everybody, especially the four sons. But as these things are a part of life somehow the family muddled through the day and came out the other side, all be it bruised and battered. The next few days I had the pleasure of having Nick's company quite a lot and I was so relieved that I was there. We had grown slightly apart since I left to go to Samui, but petty grievances pale into insignificance at such momentous times.

My stay with Joe and Keith was luxurious as their house is magnificent and I was given the run of the place. Nearly every night I was out trying to catch up with as many friends as I could and I consumed more alcohol than I normally allowed myself. During the day I did all my required tasks I had drawn up when I left Pattaya and only had the meeting with work to contend with before I could comfortably return back to Thailand for another year.

I had discussed my situation with my old employers with all my friends. Some said that they were responsible for my stroke; others said that if my employers were not responsible it still happened whilst I was working for them. I myself knew that work was definitely a contributing factor to what happened to me, but also was my physical condition and lifestyle. My employers had been fair to me in every respect and although I live in a world of law suits and that legal proceedings are common I wanted to be reasonable also.

My decision never to work under such stress again and to put my health at any sort of work related risk had been made. My employers did not know this and they might even consider offering me some sort of employment. But what work was I fit for? I could not drive, to all intentions my right arm was useless, my attention span sometimes is very short and I get fatigued very easily. No! I did not intend to return to work and especially in England, my body now was accustomed to warmer conditions and climates. I would therefore accept a pay off and haggle the sum to be agreed.

It was to be a game of chess; both sides would keep their true intentions hidden, but the opposition parties both knew what the general outcome would be. On my employers side they would be quite happy elongating the whole process asking for various conditions such as medical examinations and offering me dubious positions in inaccessible places. On my side I was not prepared to wait in England and haggle, the cold was already making me hitch when I went outside.

The day arrived that my old boss and human resource officer were to visit me at Jo and Keith's house. I knew things did not look good on my side, I was tanned, thin and residing in a mansion; I didn't quite look as though I was on my uppers. The meeting was very polite and my visitors very courteous and they seemed genuinely concerned about my present life. They proceeded to enlighten me with the options that were open to me, including a severance pay off and wanted me to take my time, get my own legal advice and notify them of my decision when I was ready. They could not have been fairer to me and behaved as they had done all along; honourably.

As they left the human resource officer said she would email me the exact figures and details of what the pay off sum was to be and we all shook hands for the last time. I knew what figure I wanted and would hold out until they reached that. I wanted enough to last in Thailand for one year at least and knew how much that would cost; it was fair to both parties.

My doctor's visit did not go as smoothly and she refused to issue me with a prescription unless I had some blood tests done. She wanted to know how I had been receiving my medication and who had been requesting my prescriptions. When I told her Linzi had been posting pre signed letters through her door and Richie had been posting the tablets to Thailand she went ballistic. Perhaps I should not have told her the whole truth, I should have taken a leaf out of Richie's book and just bare faced lied to her. It took me ten minutes trying to explain to her I did not have time for any blood tests as I was flying back to Thailand in less than two days. Eventually she gave way and gave me enough medication for two months; I would have to sort something else out when I got back.

I was glad to get back to View Talay after an arduous and stressful trip home and spent a full week just chilling out and relaxing. Going back to Liverpool had taken its toll on me both mentally and physically, I had forgotten how frenetic England is and how life is at such a dictated and fast pace. It was good just to amble down on the beach with nothing more to plan than what to eat for dinner.

After a week I contacted Ohm to get news on the plantation and things were not looking good, she had omitted to tell me that we had only bought half the land. Her excuse was that she had to act quickly to buy the land and her plan was to try and finance the second tranche of money herself but her husband had stopped her. No more work could be done on the land until the impasse was sorted out one way or another. Therefore, I was in limbo with my investment and was glad that I was sorting something out with my employers.

April was always a busy month with the Songkran celebrations and my birthday to cope with and this year, my third Songkran in

Thailand, was to be one of the most enjoyable. I had discovered a route that I could take from View Talay to Shenanigans that had almost no exposure to the water fights. If I took the private road down to Dongtan Beach then along the closed off to traffic part of the beach road, I could cut up a small Soi then only had about two hundred yards to walk to the sanctuary of the Irish Pub. Coupling this with the ruse to go to the Gym early enough before the start of festivities I remained fairly dry the week leading up to Pattaya's big Songkran day.

Kik had invited me to join the Party Mafia for their Songkran celebrations and I was pleased that I was invited as it was always fun in their mad company. Unlike the previous year we took a bus straight to Pattaya Beach Road and immediately joined in the mayhem outside Hard Rock Café. It was not such a manic drinking day as it had been with Ton and his crowd, but it was definitely just as chaotic and frantic. After getting thoroughly wet and covered in dye we joined a special party outside Central Festival.

It was surreal it was like being in an outdoor rave club at 5pm in the afternoon. But with one main difference it was water themed. Kik and his mates danced their legs off with hundreds of other ravers as gallons of water were poured over them from above. I had secured a space by a wall and was enjoying the *Tiswas* antics with Pookie and her friend from Bangkok and keeping relatively dry, apart from one annoying Japanese twat that kept on spraying me with a water pistol full of ice cold water. Eventually I was so fed up with the persistent perpetrator I threw my empty can of Leo at him. Not politically correct, but he was Japanese anyway and what did he know of Thai Songkran etiquette!

I survived Songkran and left the Mafia behind me to continue their bedlam into the early hours of the next day. I had to shower thoroughly before I climbed wearily into my bed and drifted off to sleep to the noises of the last squeals and shouts from Jomtien below.

My birthday party was quite extravagant and I decided to have it in a local restaurant followed by a nightclub. I was honoured that Pookie came down from Bangkok and that Dome and Daang travelled all the way from Phang Khon to be there. Kik had not told me that his friend had decided to move down to Pattaya to come and live. I knew that there would be crazy times ahead now that the pair was reunited.

Later that month I finally settled on a figure with my employers as severance pay and termination of my contract. It was almost double to that of the first figure I had been offered and I was happy with the settlement. I approached my brother for details of the solicitor's who handled my mother's estate as they had been very efficient. I had a long discussion with one of them who painstakingly went through the whole contract and thought that it was a fair to both sides. So, once again I had just taken the next bite out of my future life.

Chapter Twenty One

AN UNEXPLODED BOMB

I had booked a trip to Hong Kong on 19th June as I needed to get my visa stamp and I had never visited the iconic place. Kik had been saving hard as he wanted to come also and it would be his third trip outside Thailand. I had suggested if he funded his own flight then I would pay for the room, it is often no more expensive for two people sharing than single occupancy in most hotels these days.

A week before I was due to make my trip a spot on my back became very painful if I caught it with my nail showering or something. The zit had formed on one of my moles and was uncomfortable. I had waited a couple of weeks to see, like most zits do, if it would burst on its own accord. It would fade, but then come back again and was becoming a bit of a bore.

I went to Pattaya Memorial Hospital, a place I had already enrolled with for previous minor body infringements. I first went there with Ton when I had some eczema on my cheek and he suggested the hospital as a medium class facility. Medical care in Thailand is not free and there are different levels and qualities of care depending on how much you could afford. There is a basic level of treatment that you will be given if say you have an accident or something, they will not let you die in the gutter if you are knocked over.

The Memorial Hospital was ten minutes away on a scooter so it was fairly handy from my apartment to get to. Also, it was more or less opposite Central Festival Mall and not out in the wilderness somewhere. Within five minutes of arriving at the hospital and with no prior appointment I had my blood pressure taken, was weighed and was waiting to see a doctor. If this was medium treatment, what was first class like?

A few minutes later, my name was called and I was ushered into a small consulting room with a doctor sitting in attendance. I lifted up my shirt and he examined my back, I think he was Thai or Malaysian and spoke fairly good English. After a few seconds I was told to replace my shirt and the doctor told me quite mater of fatly that it was a cyst. I asked him what he suggested that I did with my cyst. He replied that they could remove it for me and it would only take a few minutes. The cost would be around two thousand five hundred Baht or fifty quid. I asked when this could be done as I was going to Hong Kong in five days. "Today," was his answer, "right now." I did not have time to get worked up about the small operation so agreed.

After consultation with a nurse I was taken to A & E and told to sit outside and wait. I was used to hospitals with the amount of time I had spent in them, but I still felt uncomfortable being in one. I think it is because they are forever fluctuating, that is to say the people within them are constantly changing. There is always somebody new knocking around in more pain with an even worse scar or injury than the last person you saw there. Also, I was waiting for an operation and there was always the consideration of the unknown pain about to be inflicted. My blood pressure was taken and it had rocketed, that was usual for me. A nurse had once told me that there is a name for the anxiety and the ensuing rising of blood pressure and it was called white coat syndrome.

The nurse taking my blood pressure dutifully noted the readings and jotted them down on my records. A little while longer a doctor came to sit by me and told me he was going to be doing the procedure but was going to wait twenty minutes or so as my blood pressure was too high. I was a little taken aback, the previous doctor had hinted that the procedure was a quick five minute job; this sounded a little more serious and I started to sweat a little, my nerves joining my blood pressure and rising. The doctor did not speak much English and it was difficult to communicate with him, but unlike the UK at least he was letting me know what was happening.

After half an hour of watching patients troop in and out of A & E, it was my turn to go in. The room was fairly small and only had four beds, actually they were gurneys. or as the British National Health Service like to call them, trolleys. Separating them were just plain green curtains hanging from a rail that could completely enclose a trolley if pulled around. I was surprised by the din in the place as together with medical staff there was a plethora of other people, mostly relatives or in one case a motor bike taxi driver waiting for his payment from a prostrate fare.

It did not seem as hygienic and as medically strict as similar such places I was familiar with. I sat up on a vacant trolley and my blood pressure was taken again. The man opposite me seemed to be in considerable pain, the curtains were not drawn around him and I could plainly see what was happening to him. He was wearing an oxygen mask and was groaning constantly as two nurses attended to a vicious wound on his chest. It looked as if he had been slashed by a knife and there was a lot of bleeding coming from the wound. I felt a little inconsequential sitting there with a zit on my back and turned my attention to a sign on the wall to avert my gaze from the man.

The sign was a Triage notice and had a list of ailments; next to them was a colour coded scheme of priority. Red was highly urgent whilst Green was an indication that the nurse had time for a cup of tea before attending to the patient. I gulped when I looked at the bottom of the list and under Dark Green was DOA. I could see the logic as a dead person did not need attending to, but my problem was; who had pronounced the person DOA before they got to hospital?

My doctor came over to me and he had changed from his previous outdoor clothes into a blue romper suit made of paper. He was still not happy about my blood pressure, but with the aid of a nurse I told him about my condition and the medication that I was on. A little uncertain of the names of some of my medicine he was happy that they would not interfere with the anaesthetic he was going to administer to me.

The nurse helped me take my shirt off and I was told to lie face down on the trolley. I could not believe that they were going to do the operation in A & E but if it was only minor surgery then it probably would only take a few minutes. But if that was the case why didn't the doctor just put a pair of latex gloves on? This fellow looked like an extra from M.A.S.H and I expected Radar O'Reilly to pop his head around the curtain and shout: "Incoming helicopters, Hawkeye!"

A second doctor joined the party of two nurses, attendant surgeon and patient and it was all getting a little too claustrophobic in the enclosed green tent for my liking. Another nurse wheeled in an overhead lighting arrangement, but thankfully left as there was little room for him to stay once he had deposited the floodlights. I was now re living a scene from my favourite movie of all time; *A Night at the Opera* by the Marx Brothers. It was the scene on the boat where a crowd of people were crammed into the Stowaway's cabin only to tumble out like an explosion when a cabin boy opened the door.

Back in A & E, things were getting a little more serious. A small, but tall trolley with an assortment of lethal looking torture implements was pushed through a gap in the curtains. "This might hurt a little," the doctor warned me as he pushed a long needle into my back. I could feel the anaesthetic being forced painfully into my body and he repeated injecting me another three times. Fuck! It was bloody painful, but was nothing compared what was to come.

To be honest I did not feel the scalpel make the first incision and for the first ten minutes or so there was moderate pain as he removed the cyst from my back. There was plenty of blood as Hot Lips Hoolihan was very busy swabbing my bleeding back. She deposited the swabs in a metal dish on the trolley and I was aghast how much blood there actually was; my face was squashed that way on the trolley so I could see every implement and cotton bud being used.

Once the cyst had been removed came the very painful part of the whole operation. The second doctor told me what they were doing step by step and it was the one time in a hospital that I would rather not of known what was going on. They were now intent of scraping away all the tissue that constituted the rather large mole and the skin around it. I felt every scrape of the scalpel and tug of the forceps. It was agony and the pain was so severe I felt as though I was going to vomit at any second. My body kept alternating from profusely sweating to almost shivering, thinking back it was all the signs of severe shock.

Every time there was a slight lull in proceedings I prayed it was the last time I was going to get touched. But only to be thwarted by another bloody piece of my back being deposited in a second metal dish alongside the used swab repository. The male nurse saw my severe discomfort as my right leg was spasming quite violently in response to the pain; my condition was letting me know that it was not very happy at what was happening to me. The nurse touched my hand and calmly spoke, "Just a few minutes more," and I almost cried with relief. The stitches being inserted did not hurt so much as my back was almost numb with the pain. The operation took nearly three quarters of an hour and it was a lot more intense than I had been expecting.

I had to sit for a few minutes on the trolley whilst I recovered from my ordeal and adapted to the horrible feeling in my back. The stitches were tight in my wound and every time I moved I suffered a sharp pang of pain. I left the hospital with a bag full of painkillers and some antibiotics and told to return daily to have the wound cleaned and the dressing changed. That night it was impossible to sleep the pain was quite unbearable and I had been told I could not lie on my back.

The following morning I phoned Kik to let him know what had happened to me and to ask him to take me to get my dressing changed. Just getting on the bike without tearing the stitches was hard, but when we set off the journey was agony. Every bump, increase or decrease of speed was agony and when I arrived at Pattaya Memorial Hospital I was a considerable mess. The journey would normally take ten or fifteen minutes depending on traffic, but that morning with my howls of pain from the back of the bike it took over twenty.

Sitting in the waiting room my body recovered from its battering, but my posture was very strange as I could not put any pressure whatsoever on my back. The wound was cleaned and re dressed, I paid my fiver for the treatment and was out of the hospital in half an hour. The return journey with Kik was just as painful as the earlier one and that day I spent a miserable time laying face down on the sofa trying not to move a muscle.

The following two days were a repetition of the same exercise, but the stitches were loosening and the pain was regressing somewhat. I told the nurses of my imminent trip to Hong Kong and they were fine about it as there seemed to be no infection of the wound. I had to promise them that I would go straight to hospital on my return to check the dressing.

I was glad the flight to Hong Kong was relatively short at two and a half hours from Bangkok. Kik was like an expectant schoolboy on the Air Asia flight as he looked out of the window nearly the whole duration of the flight. We had a similar experience with his passport as the Vietnam trip, so much so that Hong Kong Immigration were refusing his entry at one point not convinced he was ever going to go home. Once again I had to persuade the authorities that Kik was travelling with me and show them evidence of our short two night stay in Hong Kong. After several nail biting minutes, Kik was eventually given entrance after copies were taken of our hotel details.

Travelling with Kik sort of summed my little companion up; it was uncertain, always hectic and never ever dull. I could never live my life the way he does, everything is so last minute and on a high wire. From the minute he wakes, which could easily be 2pm, the rest of the day and every day is a roller-coaster ride. If you spent too much time in his company you ended up exhausted and with a severe headache but it was always, always fun.

Our taxi took us to the Grand Harbour Hotel Kowloon; on arrival they had made a mistake and did not have a Twin Superior room available, only Doubles. Without hesitation we were upgraded to a suite which was nothing short of fantastic. The room had an en suite sitting area with a fully stocked bar and cable TV, the bedroom was colossal and faced the river with incredible views of the skyscrapers of Hong Kong island. The full length windows had electronic curtains operated from the bedside, its en suite bathroom was luxurious and there was an entertainment system in the centre of the room. For the first time since we had met Kik was stunned into silence, he had never seen luxury like it before or anything like Hong Kong.

It was quite late so we tried to find a restaurant that was still open local to the hotel. The only place we could find was a Pizzeria and the bill came to a stunning fifty quid for just the two of us. I had two glasses of wine; Kik only drank water so I was amazed how expensive the food was. Hong Kong is a very affluent place, but unfortunately that means it is also very expensive to dine out or entertain oneself. However, you are compensated by walking around a film set with iconic vistas around every corner.

The next day Kik wanted to visit a mall as he is fashion crazy and I went along as I wanted a few new trendy T-shirts also. It was mostly window shopping as the names included Armani, Gucci and a plethora of other luxury brands, but it was quite an education of high fashion. In one Japanese designer sunglasses shop, a set of Gigs could set you back five hundred pounds. I deferred as I would rather squint and look a twat than pay such exorbitant prices. At lunch time we sampled a Dim Sum; all the tourist guides that I had read recommend that when visiting Hong Kong a Dim Sum meal was an essential part of your visit.

On entering the restaurant the first noticeable thing was the noise; Kik had told me that even the Thais consider the Chinese to be loud and unbelievably he was actually correct. The service was a little surly, but the atmosphere was electric and although I am not a big fan of Chinese cuisine the food was really very good. Some of the dishes were extremely strange, but I had to try them and in fact I was more adventurous than Kik. Back home in Pattaya when I go out for a meal with Kik and his friends my food is by far the most spicy and when ordering a selection for the table, which is common; an extra spicy dish is normally ordered for me.

After the cacophony of the restaurant we took our shopping back to the hotel and took a taxi to the harbour to take a ferry to Hong Kong Island. The ferry was exceptionally cheap and is a deffo thing to do in Hong Kong: the journey is probably only ten minutes long, but the sights are to die for. Once in Hong Kong trying to cross a road is treacherous with the volume of speeding traffic, but it does have rules and regulations that residents adhere to, unlike Thailand a fact I pointed out to a complaining Kik.

It started to rain which made sightseeing a tad uncomfortable, but we made our way to an area called Lan Kwai Fong which is quite a bohemian neighbourhood and stacked with little bars and restaurants. I dragged Kik around a few pubs and he was complaining again as he was not a big drinker and was hungry.

We stumbled upon Wooloomooloo's, an Australian restaurant come bar. It is a business chain with a few outlets across Asia and is famous for its steaks. Kik instantly liked the place as it was glitzy and noisy and right up his street, we had a couple of cocktails as aperitifs and ordered two huge steaks.

After dinner, we returned back to Kowloon to our hotel and sat outside by the river, I had a coffee and a brandy whilst Kik had water and a cigarette. It had been a short stopover in Hong Kong, but had been worth every expensive minute and it was good that in some small way I was helping Kik experience the world outside Thailand.

Returning home I went directly back to the hospital as I had promised. They were pleased about the wound and said it was nearly healed; I was not required to come the following day as two days later I had an appointment to see the doctor to remove the stitches. Saturday came and I was a little apprehensive of going to the hospital, perhaps I was expecting more pain from the removal out of the stitches. I took a motorbike taxi to the hospital in good time for my 1pm appointment and was actually called into A & E five minutes early.

I recognised the surgeon who had done the procedure and he asked me to sit on the trolley. As usual many people were milling around the small room, some officially and some straying in to find friends of relatives. Then he said something to me that made time stand still and then shatter my world.

"We have had the test results back from pathology," I was staggered as I didn't even know pathology was doing any tests on my behalf. Then with no emotion and in a noisy crowded Emergency Department he continued.

"You have a malignant melanoma," I was stunned and I was not accepting what he was saying to me, so he reiterated: "You have cancer."

Panic filled every part of me and a dread fear entered my very core. How does one react to such news? How should one react to such news? I couldn't even speak, I was temporarily struck dumb. I had never expected this turn of events I had rocked up expecting a little pain from the removal of some stitches, but not this, not this!

The doctor's expression did not change or waiver as he waited for me to absorb the catastrophic information he had just delivered. Then on auto pilot I spoke and in a trembling, shaky voice said: "Can it be cured?"

Slowly, the doctor spoke, and in faltering English said that I needed an operation immediately and he should be able to remove the cancer. "Will I then be okay?"

He nodded, adding the proviso that it depended how far the cancer had spread, but he would know better after some X-Rays and once he had opened me up. I asked when could the operation be done and unbelievably he said he could do it that day. I was in serious shock, but I knew this nightmare had started and I wanted to get rid of it one way or the other as fast as I could. I then gave my permission for him to take any appropriate action immediately.

He asked me to return to the waiting room and after a short time a lady came to see me from the Hospital's Administration Department. She explained the operation and all the medical fees including a room overnight was going to cost in the region of fifty thousand Baht, my brain was slow in calculating, but it was in the region of a thousand pounds. Before the hospital started any proceedings, she would need a deposit of thirty thousand Baht. By pure fluke, I had taken my credit card with me as I had planned to do a spot of shopping at Central Festival in celebration of the removal of my stitches. I agreed and five minutes later I had signed all the necessary legal wavers and paid my money.

I then perhaps made the most emotional phone call I have ever made in my life and to a most unusual recipient. Kik knew of my troubles and it was too early UK time to phone anybody and what could anybody in the UK do anyway? I phoned my new friend and told him my news. My English was garbled and he could not fully understand, but he could tell I was distraught and bewildered. I blurted out again: "I have cancer, I have to have an operation." There followed a silence from both ends as both parties came to terms with the devastating bulletin.

The conversation continued, but was brief as I made my friend understand what had happened and what was going to happen later that day. I turned the phone off as I started to weep in self-pity and did not want my friend to suffer my babblings. I was very much alone and once again had to go through terrible torment by myself.

Re-entering the hospital everything was prepared, I was once again taken to A & E and placed on a trolley. Blood pressure and other similar small tests were taken, I was asked when I last ate and luckily I had not had any food. A lady came and took all my valuables and I signed for them to be placed in the hospital's safe. Then without delay, I was wheeled down to X-Ray and from there taken up in a lift to my room. A private room was prepared for me that was quite nice: it had a TV and a small settee plus a bathroom.

I was decanted from the trolley to a bed and stripped of my clothes. I was given a type of smock to wear in bed and the covers were pulled up. My heart was racing, but I really did not have time to get morose or dwell upon my situation. My hospital room was like a train station with many people coming in and out in quick succession. I despaired at not being able to understand them and was ignorant of what the Hell was happening to me. A drip was inserted into the back of my hand and I was given some pills and then everything went quiet.

Surprisingly I was fairly placid and just lay on the bed waiting for my next visitor. A senior looking nurse entered and took my blood pressure, I asked what time was my operation and was informed it was to be at half past four a little over an hour away.

Soon after my doctor came to see me and he had with him my X-Rays, he tried to explain to me the procedure he was going to do; but I really couldn't understand, but I was thankful he had made the effort.

Close to the allotted time my room began to fill again, a different doctor replaced the drip with some other white fluid and I was given a preliminary injection of anaesthetic before being loaded back onto a trolley. The lift was too small for me to lie fully stretched out and I had to bend my knees to fit in the blasted thing. It was obviously built for small Thai people, not for taller farangs. Not for the first time in my life I was pushed through a hospital on a trolley and we progressed to barge through some swing doors with 'Theatre' written on them.

I was parked in an ante-room and waited for my next journey, more blood pressure and temperature tests were taken and then two nurses fully kitted out in green suits collected me and I was taken to the operating theatre. I don't know what I had been expecting, but it was quite a dreary room and had the overpowering smell of antiseptic. I nearly balked. One thing that was clearly evident to me was that I was wide awake. I hoped the doctors had noticed that trait about me and were not going to start the operation until they had done something about my condition.

I thought that if I kept my eyes wide open for as long as I could it might indicate to someone that I indeed was not out. More injections to my arm ensued and then I don't remember anything more about the Operating Room. I woke in the ante-room which was post op feeling like I had been run over by truck. My whole body ached and my throat was sore from a tube they had inserted down me. I had a terrible thirst and the pain was relentless; it suddenly occurred to me that I was groaning out loud.

The groaning turned into more of a wailing and a nurse rushed in and gave me an injection of Morphine. I calmed down a little as the pain eased somewhat and reigned myself in. I have not got a clue how long I was under observation, but I was thankful for the Morphine. I was taken to my room some time later and screamed in agony as they tried to fit me in the lift. I then was reunited with my bed and a fresh drip was attached, after complaining vehemently of the pain a second bag was connected to my drip which I presumed was Morphine based solution and things eased a little.

I noticed the clock on the wall and it was a quarter to eight. Fucking Hell, it had been a long fucking operation. Feeling battered and bruised, I nodded off and when I awoke, two concerned faces were peering down at me. It was Kik and Dome and I was so glad to see someone I knew. I had no energy to move any part of my body to greet them; all I could do was rasp a hoarse "hi", and even that hurt. I knew Kik hated hospitals; he had a fear of them and whenever he had given me a lift he would never come in with me, but would prefer to sit outside and wait, so I was surprised that he had plucked up the courage to come.

Dome took control and wanted to know what he could go and buy for me, without waiting for a reply he recanted a list of drinks and various other essentials that he considered he might need after an operation. Kik was staying as far away from the bed as possible as he could see all the tubes attached to me and it was frightening to him. The pair had decided they would do some shopping and have something to eat; then Kik would return and as he was the smallest he would sleep the night on the little settee. They were concerned that even though I had a panic button by the bed the nurses would not be able to understand me. I was touched by my friend's attention and I had seldom been let down by any of my acquaintances in Thailand, occasionally maddened but never let down.

I was so full of drugs and was so tired I actually slept right through the night with the confidence Kik was riding shotgun over me. I woke early about 6am and was greeted by the onslaught of considerable pain, I looked over as Kik who was fast asleep on the couch and tried to call him. It was no use, I could not stir Kik from his slumbers so I pressed the panic button. A nurse came in almost immediately and I made her aware of my discomfort. She left and came back with some pills then pushing a pillow under my head she raised me up enough for me to swallow the tablets, I swilled them down with a carton of juice by the bedside. Kik still did not move a muscle from his sleep and I wondered had he cured his fear of hospitals.

Around 9am, a delegation arrived in the room and as they entered I threw my half empty carton of juice at Kik in an attempt to rouse him but to no avail. My examination by the doctor and my change and cleansing of the dressing by the nurse was all undertaken whilst Kik remained asleep. Fine shotgun protector he had been! I was informed I could leave in a couple of hours and my demeanour brightened at this news. Still, in my heart I knew that the sword of Damocles would be dangling over my head until the results of the operation came in two weeks.

Eventually Kik stirred when a nurse arrived with my belongings. He was amazed when I told him what had already happened that morning and looked a trifle dejected as if he had let me down. I could not dream of thinking of taking a motor bike home so paid the hospital for an ambulance to take me. Kik followed the ambulance and helped me settle in my apartment, I gave him a spare set of keys so Dome or he could let themselves in whenever they wanted and that was enough business I could attend to.

My mood blackened when Kik left and I was distraught having to face up to the possibility that the operation might not have been successful. The next couple of days, either Kik or Dome would take me to the hospital and the journey was pure agony. It was bad after the first op, but this time the wound was three times as large and had many stitches keeping it closed. The daily visits to the hospital took my mind away from the nagging torture of thinking about the cancer, but it was short lived as when I returned home I could not keep from thinking the darkest of thoughts.

It was probably the lowest I have ever been in my life and I was reduced to a pathetic scared wretch. I couldn't function and I was permanently in a half trance of despair and apathy. The pain of my back was a constant reminder of my plight and I had no respite from the eternal doubts of my mortality. During all this time I did not phone any of my friends back home, there was little point until I had something more definite to tell them and why should I put them through all my torments?

Four days after the operation I had been to the hospital in the morning and later that evening Dome was cooking a meal for a gang of my well-wishers at my apartment. I was sitting in the tall leather chair by my desk and actually was treating myself to a couple of beers. The door bell sounded and it was the View Talay's building guard, somebody had complained that there was too much noise coming from the apartment. The guard said it was my German neighbour from across the hallway. He was a shit -previously complaining on Christmas night! My friends were trying to cheer me up and to try and get me out of my malaise.

I rose from the chair quite rapidly to remonstrate with the guard, but Dome had already closed the door. I felt embarrassed by the intrusion and was glad that there was laughter once again in the apartment; I had actually forgotten for a brief couple of hours my terrible plight. As I returned to the chair Kik noticed a large stain on my shirt. I touched the back of the cloth and my hand returned with blood on it, I could feel a warm damp sensation on my back, but the wound actually felt quite okay.

Dome rushed me into the bathroom followed by Kik, my shirt was lifted and Kik blurted out "Oh my God!" He then proceeded to rush out of the room and I could hear him throwing up in my bedroom. I turned to inspect my back in the mirror and as I did I saw Dome's face ashen and very white. The stitches had ruptured and my wound was a bloody mess, it was like a large sword slash revealing the inside tissue of my body. The others came to see what was going on and they also were equally disgusted and sickened by the sight and did not linger long in the bathroom.

Not knowing really what to do, one thing was obvious: I had to get to hospital. Dome helped me tie a towel around my body and I replaced my shirt as there was no point ruining another. I was then rushed to hospital on the back of a speeding motorbike, but did not really feel any pain as my back was relaxed without the restrictive stitches.

A & E at Pattaya Memorial Hospital was like any other Accident and Emergency Department across the world on a Saturday night. Even though it was a medium quality establishment it was still jam packed with drunks with battle injuries. As I was a member of the club and they had all my records I was seen almost immediately and was soon lying on a trolley in the small emergency room. The curtains were drawn around me which was normally a sign of how severe the problem was. I wondered what colour I had been designated on the chart? By the speed I had been attended to I assumed it was a bright red.

Nurses attended to my wound and were busy cleaning it when a rather stern looking doctor arrived. He looked tired and pissed off and had probably been on duty all night treating self-inflicted or needless injuries. After reading my records his face lightened a little as he realised that it was not an injury caused by a bar room brawl. However, I noticed a look of judgemental distain when he smelled the beer on my breath. Once the wound was cleansed I once again received painful anaesthetic injections and the doctor roughly removed the remains of the stitches. It hurt in the extreme and was more painful than when he administered the new ones.

He must have been determined to sew me up tight to prevent a repetition of the occurrence as the skin on my back felt as though it stretched over a drum. The stitches were so tight the only way

I could relieve the pressure; and thus the pain, was to thrust my shoulders back. This action allowed the skin to sag a little within the gap of my shoulder blades and gave me a rest bite from my agony. The problem was that it changed my gait and I was walking like John Wayne swaggering into a saloon.

Once having paid for the pleasure of my treatment I could not face returning home on a scooter so a taxi was called for; and on its arrival I was gently eased into the cab by Kik who had been waiting outside the hospital the whole time. Considering his vehement aversion to medical establishments the fact that he was prepared to visit them on a regular basis with me spoke volumes for his character and our friendship.

The next day I did not have to go for my regular dressing change as I had been told to wait a day for the wound to settle. The day after I went back and the wound had become infected, the doctor was concerned by this turn of events and I was given a course of antibiotics and given instructions to return daily for inspection. It was a miserable time of my life, I was at an all-time low even more so than when I had my stroke. The severe pain and the gruesome uncertainty hanging over my life bought me to the very brink of my fortitude, I did not know if I could summon up enough inner strength to fight this one.

Days drifted into days and I was uncertain of time, day, and month as I had retreated inside myself to battle this thing out. I did not care about my dress, pleasantries to visitors or anything; only one thing mattered, survival. Then bit by bit as the stitches relaxed a little and the pain eased somewhat my thoughts became more rational, my operation was the first attempt at removing the cancer. If that had been unsuccessful then there would be other options offered to me. I grasped at this lifeline and pulled myself up out of the deep crevasse of self-pity.

July 7th 2012 is a date that will remain etched in my mind for all time, it was the day I was to return to the hospital for my appointment with Dr Anuvet Wongmekiat, the surgeon who had performed the operation; and it was the day I was going to get the pathology report. I had to agonisingly wait until 2pm in the afternoon for my appointment and was driven to the hospital by Kik with trepidation shaking my whole body. Kik could not bear to come inside with me so he waited in the shade at the back of the hospital.

I recognised Dr Wongmekiat instantly as I was sitting waiting outside A & E, my blood pressure and temperature had already been taken where I had sat and it helped to keep my mind occupied away from the real purpose of my visit. The doctor took the seat next to me and had all my hospital records on his knee. In silence, he scanned through the documents checking that he was going to deliver the correct verdict to the accused. "There is no lymphoma," he smiled at me. Was that a good thing? Well, he was smiling, it must be I suppose.

In faltering words that I could barely utter I asked "Does that mean the operation has been a success, there is no more cancer?" Dr Wongmekiat nodded and smiled, "Yes!" was his short affirmation. I could not believe the news; my heart was racing with unrestrictive elation and I have never been so happy in my life. I wanted to immediately rush into the open air and scream all my pent woes away into the sky, to eradicate every last bit of evil from my battered soul.

The doctor saw my desperate relief and I hoped inside he felt rewarded for his life saving skill. I will forever be in debt to Dr Wongmekiat, I did not even know how to pronounce my saviours name, but he had done something for me so precious that there will always be a place in my heart for him.

After pronouncing my all clear, I was still not out of the woods as I had to go into A & E to get my stitches removed. It was not a long procedure and Dr Wongmekiat surprisingly did it himself, the infection was gone and the stitches were painfully removed. When it was all finished I could not stop thanking the doctor and the nurses, eventually he left A & E before I did. I then paid twenty quid at the office for my treatment and was happy to do so; it was the best twenty quid I have ever spent in my life.

Stepping out of the hospital into the sunlight I was elated, a large weight had been lifted from me and I was sporting the largest grin that I have ever had in my whole life. Kik saw me and looked at the triumph in my face, he rushed up to me and we hugged briefly. I looked down at my true friend and saw moisture in his eyes, I had not realised just how much he had been living my agony also and he looked as exhausted and relieved as me.

Kik immediately phoned Dome who was at work to tell him the news. Kik was back to normal and bouncing around all over the hospital's car park excitedly phoning people. Pookie, Tang, Wi Wi and Ton Naam were all loudly contacted and a Celebration party was arranged without delay. With no stitches my back felt great and I had no more discomfort or pain, I was ready for a party and I deserved one.

We went to Central Festival first for some lunch and still Kik was busy contacting people. We had hardly spoken to each other since my declaration outside the hospital, but I didn't need to talk as I was coming to terms with the news I had received. Whilst waiting to be served in the restaurant I felt a familiar warm feeling on my back, I touched my scar and the sickening sight of blood returned on my hand.

My short lived elation collapsed. "Will this nightmare ever stop?" I cut Kik short from his conversation and stood showing him my blood stained shirt. He was just as shocked as me and just as despondent. I returned to A & E and the nurses instantly recognised me at the hospital and Dr Wongmekiat was phoned, luckily he was still at work and was available to come and see me. While waiting on a trolley a nurse told me I had very thin blood and that was the reason the wound was not healing. It was my stroke medicine; it was fighting against the coagulation of the blood within the wound.

Dr Wongmekiat strode into the room and looked concerned for me; he examined my wound closely and gently sewed me back up. It was nowhere as painful as last time and I resented the other doctor for putting me in so much agony previously. But the awful fact was that I had to endure another two weeks of repair and discomfort.

The party was cancelled and instead Dome suggested he cooked a meal at my apartment for about four of us. Dome is a really good Thai chef; his mother had taught him how to cook and to cater for large numbers of people. He cooked Issan food from the north of Thailand which is spicy and very tasty; a lot of the dishes I had never seen before but they were absolutely delicious. One dish was called Ong which was minced pork in a thick spicy, orange coloured sauce; I enjoyed it so much that I requested Dome to make me some so I could freeze it.

My temporary despair had lifted again as I no longer had my dread fear dragging me down and the new stitches in my back only gave me moderate pain. I was thoroughly enjoying the small dinner party when it was interrupted once again by a complaint from the German bastard neighbour I had. I was determined nothing was going to spoil the small celebration and ignored the complaint totally. But I knew I could not stand for the intolerant, interference much longer; there was not much noise and it was not too late in the evening.

When leaving the hospital, a nurse had told me that I could get my wound cleaned and dressing changed locally. I was not forced to come to Pattaya Memorial. So, the day after the dinner party I walked to a small clinic in Jomtien that I knew; I had been there a long time ago to get some skin tags removed from under my armpits. Kik came with me and explained my situation, I was lead into a small room with a bed and examined. They agreed to treat me daily and I was reassured to see an old doctor was also in attendance at the clinic.

My daily walks were a good way of getting some air and the clinic was friendly and convenient. Although, I never had to wait too long in the hospital that was in comparison to the UK. There was never a delay at the clinic and I was seen immediately every time I went, it was also slightly cheaper. I only had to pay two Baht for my daily treatment and redressing, and there was no taxi fare to get there.

Although I had not been to a pub in nearly a month I had put on a stone of weight due to my inactivity. I was not over duly concerned as my main priority was to get better, Tony's gym could wait. I had also taken a risky decision to stop my stroke medication to try and help the blood clot in the wound and form a scar. I was self-medicating and something I had promised myself never to do, but it was only going to be for a fortnight and I was prepared to take the risk as the lesser of two evils.

The rehabilitation went quite smoothly as my frame of mind was far more stable and I am a great believer that positive thinking aids recovery of even physical problems. It was something that helped me immensely during my stroke troubles and I reapplied the doctrine to my current condition. Two weeks passed quickly apart from one more altercation with my neighbour: he had convinced himself that I was a noise pest, but to be honest I think that he had lost the plot a little. However, the security people were getting pissed off with this ongoing feud and I was concerned that they might do something rash.

On the 21st July, I returned for the last time to the hospital and my appointment with Dr Wongmekiat was at 1pm. The stitches were taken out and I did not feel a thing as they were removed. I did not know if it was because the wound had healed and it was no longer as tender or Dr Wongmekiat's skill was superior to that of his colleague. My nightmare was over and all that was left was to pay my bill and I could leave.

Whilst standing at the cashier's desk waiting to pay, Dr Wongmekiat came out of the Emergency Room and saw me. He made his way over and we shook hands and said goodbye to each other, then as a parting aside he told me to return in six months to check that there is no spread of lymphoma to the lungs. And with that choice tit bit he turned and walked away. I considered his last comment and mused that our meeting at the Cashier's Desk had been by chance, his last rather chilling words to me would never have been spoken had we not bumped into each other. I therefore have stored them deep to lie untouched for six months until I go for a check-up.

The progress after my last visit to the hospital was slow due to the fear of opening the wound again and it took a further two weeks before I made my first tentative steps to Tony's gym. But, eventually a scar formed and my exercise regime started to slowly build. My strength has returned, not of the physical kind, but the psychological mental strength that left me during my recent troubles.

Due to the ongoing trouble with my neighbour, I made the decision I had to leave View Talay, but not Jomtien and definitely not Thailand. My severance pay from my employer will fund my new place and assure my survival out in Asia for another twelve months. One year is an extraordinary long time for me to plan ahead and I felt like I could justify taking a bigger bite out of life.

My life for now is secured, my health has been restored to me and my new friends remain with me. I still own my house back in Liverpool and all my old friends are still there, when I return or if I ever will return is something for the future to decide for me. Looking back over the last five years it has been an incredible journey not geographically, but in terms of learning about myself.

I now know that I am not as fragile as an egg, but to be realistic of my expectations what my body can and cannot do, but nevertheless to try. I have encountered many dangers and unexpected problems, but have found that nothing is insurmountable if you really want to achieve your goal.

I have survived such deep despairs and terrible anguishes that no man should have to endure, but along the way I have received incredible kindnesses and found love and compassion in the most unexpected of places. My strength came both from some internal belief of myself coupled with the amazing support given to me by others; and that strength gave me life. To fail is acceptable; to not attempt, unforgivable.

Recently, on a visit by Kik to my apartment we were viewing the photos of Hong Kong when I stumbled upon an old file on my PC. I remembered I had collated many photographs together of my past when I was preparing for my very first trip to Koh Samui, just in case I got home sick and needed some cheering up. Kik could not believe some of them were actually me and especially one taken when I was eighteen and a half stone. I was on holiday in Barbados and was wearing a large white almost colonial style jacket and I thought back to a comment Rich had said at the time that I looked like Sydney Greenstreet in the film Casablanca. I stared at the old photograph and thought for a brief moment, I could just about see a slight resemblance.

THE END